Romanian Crucible

The Trial of Corneliu Zelea Codreanu

Gheorghe Buzatu and Kurt W. Treptow

Romanian Crucible
The Trial of Corneliu Zelea Codreanu

Translated by Diana Livesay

The Center for Romanian Studies

Las Vegas ◊ Chicago ◊ Palm Beach

Published in the United States of America by
Histria Books
7181 N. Hualapai Way, Ste. 130-86
Las Vegas, NV 89166 USA
HistriaBooks.com

The Center for Romanian Studies is an independent academic and cultural institute with the mission to promote knowledge of the history, literature, and culture of Romania in the world. The publishing program of the Center is affiliated with Histria Books. Contributions from scholars from around the world are welcome. To support the work of the Center for Romanian Studies, contact us at info@centerforromanianstudies.com

All rights reserved. No part of this book may be reprinted or reproduced, or utilized in any form or by any electronic, mechanical, or other means, now known or hereafter invented, including photocopying and recording, or in any information storage or retrieval system, without the permission in writing from the Publisher.

Library of Congress Control Number: 2022932509

ISBN 978-1-59211-129-9 (hardcover)
ISBN 978-1-59211-448-1 (softbound)
ISBN 978-1-59211-261-6 (eBook)

Copyright © 2024 by Histria Books

Contents

INTRODUCTION 9

THE TRIAL OF CORNELIU ZELEA CODREANU MAY, 1938 63

FINAL ORDINANCE for the Arraignment of Corneliu Zelea Codreanu
for Treason, Conspiracy Against the Social Order, and Rebellion........... 65

Day One — Monday, 23 May 1938.. 87

Day Two — Tuesday, 24 May 1938 135

The Testimony of Iosif Frollo.. 149

The Testimony of General Dr. Constantinescu 153

The Testimony of Colonel Gheorghe Polihroniade..................... 154

The Testimony of Prof. Eugen Chirnoaga............................... 155

The Testimony of Priest Ion Moța.. 156

The Testimony of Dr. Ranețescu-Câmpina 157

The Testimony of Professor Traian Brăileanu......................... 157

The Testimony of Prof. Mihail Manoilescu 159

The Testimony of Prof. Nichifor Crainic 160

The Testimony of General Constantin Petrovicescu 162

The Testimony of General Ion Antonescu............................... 165

The Testimony of Professor Emanoil Antonescu..................... 167

The Testimony of the Counselor at the High Court of Cassation
Eugen Petit 168

The Testimony of General Mihail Racoviță............................. 169

The Testimony of General Constandache................................. 169

Romanian Crucible

The Testimony of General Dona 170

The Testimony of Engineer Stelian Ionescu 170

The Testimony of Sabin Morar 171

The Testimony of Alexandru Hodoș 171

The Testimony of Sextil Pușcariu 172

The Testimony of General Iacob Constantin 172

The Testimony of Gheorghe Pantazi 173

The Testimony of Mr. Nicolae Pop 173

The Testimony of Lawyer Dimitrie Popa 173

The Testimony of Traian Herseni 174

Day Three — Wednesday, 25 May 1938 175

The Testimony of Iuliu Maniu 176

The Testimony of Constantin Iarca 179

The Testimony of General Virgil Bădulescu 179

The Testimony of Sever Dan (former Minister) 180

The Testimony of Professor Carol Beker 181

The Testimony of Henri Ghica 181

The Testimony of Doctor I. Cantacuzino 181

Day Four — Thursday, 26 May 1938 183

The Indictment 183

The Afternoon Hearing 204

The Verdict 249

The Sentence 254

Communicating the Sentence of Corneliu Zelea Codreanu 254

The Appeal 254

The Trial of Corneliu Zelea Codreanu 7

TRIAL NOTES.. 271

ANNEXES.. 299

Annex I — The Letter of Corneliu Zelea Codreanu to Nicolae Iorga 299

Annex II — Corneliu Zelea Codreanu — Notes from Jilava
regarding the Trial, May 1938 303

Annex III — Notes from the "Journal" of Carol II Regarding the Trial
of Corneliu Zelea Codreanu... 321

Annex IV — The Testimony of Mr. Iuliu Maniu at the Trial of Mr. Corneliu
Zelea Codreanu. Final text submitted in Bucharest
on 24 September 1938 323

Annex V — A letter written by Corneliu Zelea Codreanu, from the prison at
Doftana, to his father, Professor Ion Zelea Codreanu, at Miercurea-Ciuc,
30 July 1938... 329

Introduction

The history of the Legionary Movement is not only one of the most interesting chapters in Romanian history during the twentieth century but also an area of scholarly research that deserves extensive future investigations in libraries and archives. These efforts must take an objective and bold approach to obtain a maximum level of understanding when analyzing the topic and its many layers to correctly integrate it into a broader understanding of twentieth century Romanian and East European history. The impact of the collapse of the Communist regimes all over Europe still must be felt in historiography, as future research needs to discard the clichés that were causally used to describe the Legionary Movement, among the most persistent, those related to Corneliu Zelea Codreanu and his party members being regarded as members of a gang or an organized crime syndicate. In this context, we will observe how strange these accusations were, considering that the Romanian Communist leaders (and not only them) escaped certain charges despite historical facts to the contrary. Objectively, the founders of the Communist Party of Romania and their followers did not appreciate any comparison to the Legionaries when it came to anti-national politics. The role of the Fifth Column was to defend the Kremlin's interests in Bucharest, and take responsibility for establishing a new political regime that aligned, at least in the first decades, with terror and unjustifiable mutilation of national integrity, sacrificing suzerainty and national independence. Future historical research will better define the role of the Legionary Movement in the country and in Europe that after 1918 was torn apart by conflicts and conflagrations, by economic and social crises, and by the chaos of collectivist thought. Later on, the dispute between the three *–isms* of the twentieth century, capitalism, fascism, and communism, could no longer be ignored.

We must acknowledge that the current stage of archival documentation and general research gives us every reason to reject the dogmas of Communist propaganda. As an example, we'll quote from the "renowned" textbook called *Istoria Romîniei [The History of Romania]*, published in multiple editions under the direction of

Romanian Crucible

Mihail Roller (a member of the Communist Academy of Sciences), during the period when the foundation of the Communist regime in Bucharest[1] was taking place. The passages from this textbook were used to indoctrinate a generation of students and pupils for at least a decade:

In Romania, fascism was created and developed by the leaders of the monopolistic capitalism and by the most conservative circles of landowners in the first years after the war (after World War I, 1914-1918), in the form of a [student movement] with a nationalist character. Support of this movement by reactionary politicians, on one hand, sought to suppress the students' struggle for certain objectives, while on the other hand, they wanted to create certain organizations to mobilize them at events intended to achieve certain political and financial maneuvers.

In 1927, some elements of the Christian League of National Defense walked away from A.C. Cuza and founded The Legion of Archangel Michael. In 1929 the Legion was restructured and changed its name to the Iron Guard.

The Iron Guard was a fascist party from a pragmatic and an organizational point of view. On the inside, The Iron Guard was asking to create a fascist state by destroying parliamentary government, and abolishing all civilian rights and freedoms. Through its external politics, it was asking for immediate alliance with fascist Italy and especially Hitler's Germany.

The restructuring of the Legion was done with the support of the National Peasant government (under Vaida), that used it as an instrument of police diversion, meant to fight against democratic movements, and especially those of the Communist Party of Romania.

In 1933, after Hitler came to power, the two fascist groups that represented the Fifth Column in Romania, the National-Christian Party, and especially the Iron Guard, intensified their activities with funding they received from Hitler. They became an instrument for political maneuvers by groups or bourgeoise property owners inside the country and by imperialists from abroad.

The Iron Guard enjoyed the support of the government formed by bourgeoise property owners, of Carol II, and of the great industrialists and landowners, who

---

[1]See Ministerul Învăţământului Public, *Istoria R.P.R.* under the editorship of acad. Mihail Roller, Bucureşti, Ed. de Stat Didactică şi Pedagogică, 1952, pp. 639-641 (ed. I, 1947; ed. II, 1948).

The Trial of Corneliu Zelea Codreanu

used its resources to destroy the Romanian Communist Party. Regular subventions from German sources empowered the fascist organizations, especially the Iron Guard. It was also supported by the peasant and liberal governments that alternated in the country's leadership and gave it the opportunity for propaganda, disruptions, and immunity against crimes and legal violations.

Between 1930 and 1937, the Legionary movement had the freedom to do as it pleased in the country. The Law of State Defense, which aimed to fight against the Guard, was not applied to the Legionaries. Between 1936 and 1937, there was no parliamentary election in which the government didn't support the Iron Guard.

The Iron Guard also received dedicated support from the National Peasant Party and from Iuliu Maniu personally, through favorable testimony given in the trial of Duca's assassins, and in 1938 at the trial of the Guard's leader, and especially through the "electoral pact."

Iuliu Maniu also supported them in 1939, following the assassination of Armand Călinescu.

In September 1940, the Iron Guard was brought to power alongside Antonescu, following the wishes of Hitler, who considered it as his agent in Romania.

Beginning with its establishment, until after the Legionary government's liquidation in 1941, the path of the Iron Guard was dotted with crimes and thefts, starting with the assassination of the prefect Manciu, and to the massacres before and during the time of the rebellion.

During the mass assassinations committed by Legionaries on the night of 21 and 22 January, a group of Legionaries, protected by the police, took the Communist activist Constantin David, dragged him in the Pantelimon forest, and riddled him with bullets.

When the Legionaries formed part of the government, incomplete statistics done only in the provinces showed that the goods they stole had a real and total value of 1,018,911 lei. To this were added numerous counts of mistreatment, sequestrations, home break-ins, goods taken through forced sales, requisitions, forceful occupation of buildings, and general devastation.

When it comes to the access they had to public money, the findings showed that by placing the patrimony of the old "Country Defense" in the administration and use of the Legionary movement, its leaders gained access to a fortune of around one billion lei.

Romanian Crucible

Inside the ruling fascist groups, a power struggle began between Antonescu's party members and the old leaders of the Iron Guard.

Both parties hoped for Hitler's support to ensure their control over Romania.

In January 1941, the rebellion of the Iron Guard against Antonescu began. The rebellion extended from the 22nd to the 24th of January and was suppressed by Antonescu's troops, supported by Hitler, who needed the Romanian army to attack the Soviet Union. A few leaders of the Iron Guard escaped to Germany where Hitler used them to blackmail Antonescu. The group led by Antonescu remained to accomplish Hitler's objectives in Romania, absorbing a series of Legionary elements.

During the rebellion, theft took on gigantic proportions. After the rebellion, no less than 174 trucks with goods taken illegally were gathered in front of the headquarters and homes of the Legionary leaders in Bucharest. They contained merchandise, home goods, clothing, and food.

The sums plundered during the rebellion from institutions and individuals, is said to have exceeded 100 million lei. To this, we must add the horrible mass assassinations committed on this occasion.

This quoted text, which is actually a bad summary of Communist documents that contain opinions about the fascist movement of the 1930s and is full of serious errors when it comes to the facts[2] presented, represents just one example of the

---

[2] We highlight some of these issues: 1. The phrase that said fascism was the doing of the leaders of monopolistic capitalism and of the "most conservative circles of landowners" is taken from documents of the 3rd International, which, in the 4th decade, applied it to explain *mutatis mutandis* the situation of various European countries or the general situation on the continent. 2. *The Legion of Archangel Michael* didn't turn into the *Iron Guard* in 1929, but evolved as a movement, and to gain political representation it successively established multiple political parties — the *Iron Guard* (1930-1933), *The Group of Corneliu Zelea Codreanu* (1931-1932, while the *Iron Guard* was temporarily suspended at the order of the Minister of Internal Affairs, Ion Mihalache and Iorga-Argetoianu's government), and the *All for the Country Party* (1934/1935-1938). 3. The fact that the *Iron Guard* apparently received *financial support* from Hitler is yet to be proven, especially because recent studies (the excellent monograph of the German historian Armin Heinen, *Die Legion "Erzengel Michael" in Rumanien. Soziale Bewegung und politische Organisation. Ein Beitrag zum Problem des internationalen Faschismus*. Munchen, R. Oldenbourg Verlag, 1986, passim) do not allow for mere accusations based on supposition, at least when it comes to the situation before 1938. 4. The statement implying the *Iron Guard* had leadership of the country between 1930 and 1937 does not correspond with reality. 5. The matter of Corneliu Zelea Codreanu's "electoral pact" with Iuliu Maniu in 1937 (and with the National Liberal Party — Gh. Brătianu, and the Jewish Party) is falsely interpreted. Similarly, the Legionaries didn't receive support from the leader of National Peasant Party after the assassination of C.Z. Codreanu. 6. The

The Trial of Corneliu Zelea Codreanu

distorted history of the Legionary Movement. Similar examples can be found in subsequent historical works. Two decades after M. Roller, Valter Roman, the director of the Political Publishing House of those times, opened a scholarly session in Bucharest (4-5 March 1971) around the "critical analyses and exposing of fascism in Romania," thus found — and this remains true — that "the history of Romanian fascism has not yet been written."[3] At the same time, however, the Communist ideologue also imposed directives: "One of the most important problems that are imposed on scientific research is that regarding the ideology and the socio-political base of Romanian fascism. The ideology of the Legionary movement constituted, as is well known, a mixture of vague conceptions that contradicted each other, a horrifying mix of primitivism and obscurantism, of irrational, mystical, and religious ideas. In this electric arsenal, there was some residue of feudal ideology, atemporal and ahistorical nostalgia for a mystical archaic past. A central spot was held by the idea that this was a political, social, and ideological gospel of an exacerbated nationalism, of chauvinism, and racism. From a sociopolitical point of view, the Iron Guard blended eclecticism, vague concepts with the boldest form of demagogy, with spreading illusions about a social-economical uplift (which brought it support from certain social categories for a short time), practicing the same politics — the Bourgeoisie politics — in whose opponents the Legionary leaders hypocritically pretended to be. Being consistent at least when it came to its ultra-retrograde, archaic, and anachronistic ideas, the Legionary Movement was the declared enemy of modernization, urbanization, and industrialization of the country, and despite a rich and demagogic phraseology, it was the declared enemy of everything that meant not falling behind economically and socially and the country's advancement on the path of civilization and progress."[4]

To counterbalance the Legionary Movement, the speaker presented the activity of the Communists, about which he wanted to emphasize a few "ideas" such as:

The politics of the Communist Party permanently expressed (after its founding in 1921) even in the harshest circumstances, the unmoving devotion of Communists for the good of the nation through their high patriotism. The example

---

use of flamboyant phrases is to create a propaganda effect: "the theft took on gigantic proportions." "massive assassinations committed," etc.

[3] See *Împotriva fascismului*, București, Editura Politică. 1971, p. 11.

[4] *Ibidem*. p. 13.

Romanian Crucible

of the Romanian Communists, their heroic fight, confirms a great truth about their politics, its justice and power of influence, decisively conditioned by the unity between the party and the nation, by the measure in which the party's politics blends in with the needs and the wishes of the Romanian nation, and with the national interests of the country. As comrade Nicolae Ceaușescu highlighted, the Romanian Communist Party gained the unanimous recognition as a leader of our society, due to the loyalty, devotion, and sacrifice with which it relentlessly served, ever since its founding, the supreme interests of the working class, of those who work, and of the whole nation. Its politics, which were inspired by the burning needs of the Romanian society, by the vital interests of the whole nation, was built on Marxist-Leninist principles, and became the flag under which the working class, the peasants, the intellectuals, and the whole nation united in tight lines.[5]

Soon after this nonsense spewed by Valter Roman, the first edition (2nd ed., 1980) of a work that for two decades represented the official point of view appeared, the only one allowed in the textbooks, about the history and evolution of the Legionary Movement.[6] The volume contained various information (deformed by an inadequate interpretation), and became controversial in the country as well as abroad,[7] by offering a *sui generis* image over the Legionary Movement, but readers today can separate the truth from fiction without much trouble. The final conclusion of the last edition was a more than convincing sample of this point of view: "The anti-democratic and anti-nationalist activity of the Iron Guard, the sociopolitical concepts of the Legionaries, that were unnatural to our nation's spiritual patrimony and its old traditions, represented a cynical disregard, a brutal betrayal of the most burning aspirations of the Romanian nation that hoped for the country's progress and national independence. This is why it is important to reveal these realities, the dissociation and explanation through careful research of their strategies and their multiple implications in different plans, also firmly combating the leftover

---

[5]*Ibidem*, p. 15.

[6] See Mihai Fătu, Ion Spălățelu, *Garda de Fier — Organizație teroristă de tip fascist*, București, Editura Politică, 1971, 430 p.; ed. a II-a, revised and completed, București. Editura Politică, 1980, 388 p. + illustrations

[7] For example, Walter Laqueur, ed., *Fascism: A Reader's Guide. Analyses, Interpretations, Bibliography*, Harmondsworth, Penguin Books, 1979, pp. 222-223.

The Trial of Corneliu Zelea Codreanu

Legionary ideologies, in the form of bourgeoise nationalism, various forms of irrationalism, mysticism, and obscurantism. This is a primordial duty of our time. Years passed from the permanent downfall of the Iron Guard. For the young generation of today, these events are unknown or known only from history textbooks or from the word of mouth. It is said that time helps us forget. This is true indeed, but we also have to keep in mind that not everything must be forgotten. The dark bloody pages that the Legionaries wrote in the history of interwar Romania, cannot and must not be forgotten by the Romanian people."[8]

Surprisingly, after the collapse of Communism in Eastern Europe in 1989-1991, Romania kept bringing up and judging the Legionary Movement according to the rigors of the Marxist-Leninist ideology. This, despite the obvious realities and the latest information raised in scientific circles, and a rich memorialist literature that was published in recent years, which, even if it does not attempt to vindicate the Legionary Movement, from which many enemies of the Communist terror were recruited, at least it is cause for attention and reflection. So, despite all of this, *the attack of the left wing* continues when it comes to events of the recent past, including on the history of the *Legion of the Archangel Michael*. We don't want to rashly conclude that they're doing the same things, just reborn in a new spirit after 1989, or that the judgements are so harsh because the Legionary Movement imposed itself, in the backdrop of the objective realities of interwar Romania, through its actions against the Communist agenda and certain Jewish elements. Between the last two, a certain relation exists that can be missed only by those who do not want to see it. We must remember that misunderstanding the past or seeing it in the wrong light can be the same as pretending to cover up history. In this case, teaching the truth is not the goal, but the process of clarifying a past reality, through speeches and historiographical evidence. We must use certain contextual examples. Worth mentioning are the articles written by Mr. Constantin Petculescu, in the post-Communist publication called *Societate și Cultură. Noua Alternativă*, among them an article entitled "Garda de Fier — Prototipul fascismului în România.*"[9] The author claims to set the role and place of the Iron Guard[10] in the history of interwar Romania, in the typical colors of historiography from the 1950s with its Communist

---

[8] Mihai Fătu, Ion Spălățelu, op. cit., ed. a II-a, p. 385.

[9] See "Societate și Cultură. Noua Alternativă," București, nr. 1/1993, pp. 22-27.

[10] The author confused the *Iron Guard* with the *Legionary Movement*.

16   Romanian Crucible

origins: "...The Legionary Movement detached itself from the other political formations belonging to the extreme right, fascist or pro-fascist, that appeared in Romania in the third and fourth decade [as many of them as there were], and through extreme reactionism and criminal terrorism, it met all the main characteristics of a fascist political movement in its most aggressive form — Hitlerism."[11] Claiming repeatedly to have detached from the old patterns, Mr. C. Petculescu actually presented a new "image," proving beyond a doubt that everything has changed, but actually nothing has. He wrote:

> The extreme right-wing movement appeared precisely on the foundation of this profound economic, social-political, and cultural-spiritual crises in postwar Romania [after 1918], by articulating and exacerbating chauvinist, mystical, irrational ideas, ideologies that have been present starting with the end of the nineteenth century and the beginning of the twentieth century.[12] This picture makes even Germany seem inferior to Romania!

> ...And in Romania, the extreme right movement was fascist when it came to the way it presented itself — Legionarism and Nazism was the "last resort" to save the bourgeoisie from an acute social and political crisis, and it received all their support, or lost it in times of social or political tension."[13]

Clearly, the author, thinking about the death of Corneliu Zelea Codreanu, or about the result of the conflict between Ion Antonescu and Horia Sima, generously offers stories to the reader with a recurrent theme of "There's the wolf — there's no wolf."

> ...An impulsive and treacherous nature, with adventurous tendencies, and above all, with aspirations of becoming a political celebrity, that's how Corneliu Zelea Codreanu appeared to be...[14]

---

[11] C. Petculescu, cit. art., p. 23.

[12] *Ibidem*

[13] *Ibidem*

[14] *Ibidem*

The Trial of Corneliu Zelea Codreanu

Corneliu Zelea Codreanu created in 1927 "a special organization — The Legion of Archangel Michael (which became the Iron Guard in 1930[15])," an unnatural situation considering the Legion did not become the Guard, but it continued its existence, the Iron Guard being a new political group that represented it.

In complete opposition to a number of democratic personalities from the interwar era, Mr. C. Petculescu discredits a number of "highly intelligent intellectuals of those times, such as Nae Ionescu, Nichifor Crainic, Emil Cioran, Constantin Noica, Dragoș Protopopescu, Mihail Manoilescu, Mircea Eliade, Radu Gyr, Petre Țutea, etc., who were more or less involved in the ideological "foundation" of the Legionary Movement, even if later on, when history declared this movement to be infamous, some of them tried to pull away from Legionarism and renounce it. Some of them only assumed the role of spiritual mentors or "theorists," a role just as bad, to provide content and ideas, thus justifying violence; others didn't just join in theory, but practice as well, by enrolling the National-Christian Party or the Legion (O. Goga-A.C. Cuza) or oscillated between the two (Nichifor Crainic, Toma Vlădescu, etc.). Nobody could deny the fact that Nae Ionescu, Nichifor Crainic, or Emil Cioran, for example, tied their names forever — through their entire publishing careers — to the history of the Legionary movement..."[16] Putting the problem in the equation in such a way, is not just inconclusive, but completely false. Fortunately, multiple recent practices offer us too many cases of such ideological labeling in order to remove certain personalities from history, all this with agreement from the "victims" if possible. It is as if we would blame Winston Churchill for siding with the Conservatives, the same way if one tries to cancel Mihai Eminescu from literature for being a fascist! According to a discredited idea about the past, we could expect miracles identical to Croce or Malaperte in Italy, to Esenin and Maiakovski in Russia, to Heidegger in Germany, etc.

Unfortunately, C. Petculescu returns to that problem, presenting a list and justifying it.[17] From that specific list we should extract the intellectuals of profound influence at the time: Nae Ionescu, Nichifor Crainic, Mircea Eliade, Constantin Noica, Mihail Polihroniade, M. Manoilescu, Radu Gyr, Traian Brăileanu, Octav

---

[15] *Ibidem*

[16] *Ibidem*. P.25

[17] See C. Petculescu, *Intelectualitatea în mișcarea fascistă din România*, in "Societate și Cultură. Noua Alternativă", nr. 5/1993, pp. 19-26. Also see the "annex": *Extrase din presa vremii*, pp. 27-34.

Romanian Crucible

Onicescu, I. Găvănescul, Petre Țutea, Dragoș Protopopescu, N. Crevedia, N. Roșu, D. Gherota, P.P. Panaitescu, Emil Cioran, Mircea Vulcănescu, etc. Not all of them "benefit" from the author's attention, but — from those taken to account — we must mention that M. Manoilescu is wrongly accused,[18] and Emil Cioran and Constantin Noica are judged superficially.[19] At the center of his attention remains Nae Ionescu[20] and Mircea Eliade,[21] the latter having international support: the book by the American writer M.L. Ricketts,[22] a former student and assistant of Eliade. It all has insufficient grounds. Other suggested people are Leon Volovici[23] or Norman Manea.[24] In every case, he uses as proof texts published by Eliade in the press of the times, and for what concerns us, we must come back to Mr. Petculescu, who summarizes certain statements, proving himself one of the harshest exegetes of the illustrious philosopher, by condemning him in ways that could only generate compassion from the reader: "...The implication that Mircea Eliade had a totalitarian ideology is shown by a great part of his published work, that he used as a support for the Legionary movement. He was and remained a constant spiritual supporter of the Legionary phenomenon, in which he truly believed."[25]

A group of texts that were included in *Societate și Cultură*, have the role to support statements such the ones we focused on. The process is not unusual, however, the texts we are about to analyze don't have a fair commentary, and the authors do not have a precise setting in that time, but have the gift of persuading the

---

[18] *Ibidem*, p. 24.

[19] *Ibidem*, p. 22-23.

[20] *Ibidem*, pp. 19-21.

[21] *Ibidem*, p. 21-22.

[22] See Mac Linscott Ricketts, *Mircea Eliade: The Romanian Roots, 1907-1945*, I-II, New York, 1988.

[23] See Leon Volovici, *Nationalist Ideology and Antisemitism. The Case of Romanian Intellectuals in the 1930s*. Oxford-New York-Seoul-Tokyo, 1991.

[24] See *Culpa fericită. Mircea Eliade, fascismul și soarta nefericită a României*, In *22* (București), nos. 6-8/1992; Daniel Dubuisson, "Metafizica și politica. Ontologia antisemită la Mircea Eliade," in *Societate și Cultură. Noua Alternativă*, nos. 4-5/1993.

[25] C. Petculescu, op. cit..., p. 21.

The Trial of Corneliu Zelea Codreanu

reader to believe the signatory, but not the editorial.[26] Let's mention the ones in case:

Nae Ionescu, with articles "Amintirile unui prieten cu prilejul zilei numelui," (from *Buna Vestire*, 8 December 1940) and "Sub semnul Arhanghelului" (in *idem*, from 27 June 1937).

Mircea Eliade, with "De ce cred în biruința mișcării legionare*"* (in *Buna Vestire* from 17th of December 1937) and "Noua aristocrație legionară" (in *Vremea* from 23 January 1938). The belief expressed in the article of 17 December 1937 in truth shows Mircea Eliade as playing a part in the plan of action of the Legionary Movement, but no less, it shows a genius loyal to the great ideals of his nation: "I believe in the fate of our nation; I believe in the Christian revolution of the new man, I believe in freedom, in identity, and in love. That's why I believe in the victory of the Legionary Movement, in a proud and strong Romania, in a new way of life that will give the Romanian soul universal spiritual values."

Emil Cioran, with "Impresii din Munchen*"* (in *"Vremea"* from 15 July 1934) and "Profilul interior al Căpitanului" (in *Glasul strămoșesc* from 25 December 1940, after a conference at Radio Bucharest from 27 November 1940).

Constantin Noica, with "Apelul Axei" (in *Buna Vestire* from 29 September 1940) and "Limpeziri pentru o Românie legionară" (a conference at Radio Bucharest on 5 October 1940).

Zigu Ornea[27] also insisted at the same time on the texts written by Mircea Eliade and Emil Cioran. Even though we do not entirely share the opinions of the distinguished literary historian (Mircea Eliade's choice for the Legionary Movement is now a "notorious act," his references to the "Legionary madness" from 1934-1935, etc.), we can agree with the author when he talks about "the tragedy of a confused generation who must be understood not treated as a pamphlet."[28] We will observe, however, that the effort to understand as he advises, can't be seen in the *Breviarul*

---

[26] See *Societate și Cultură. Noua Alternativă*, nr. 5/1993, p. 27 and following. More recently, see Dionisie Petcu, "Naționalismul dreptei românești din perioada interbelică" (I), idem, nr. 2/1994, p. 16 and following.

[27] See *Lettre Internationale* (București), Romanian edition, spring 1993, pp. 82-85.

[28] *Ibidem*, p. 85.

Romanian Crucible

of the Legionary Movement's history by Zigu Ornea.[29] After all, *Breviarul* reconstructs a well-known story with a new melody. Shortly before that, Mr. Zigu Ornea confessed to being against the "nostalgic trend" that tried to remake the history of the Legionary Movement: "The Movement was against a multi-party system, was cultivating and was enrolling in its plans, terror, death cults, the right to punish others without a trial, etc. These are things that must not be forgotten, the same way that we shouldn't ignore the Legionaries' inclination towards dictatorship, their confessed ecstasy when it came to the fascist movement in Italy (which couldn't even be suspected of democracy), and to National-Socialism established in 1933 in Germany. The Legionary Movement was more than sympathetic to them, we could say it was the equivalent of Hitlerism in our country."[30] For Nicolae Ceaușescu, as mentioned before, the Legionary Movement, as a comparison, represented "Hitler's agency in Romania" (1966). The question is: what is the difference between the two?

We must highlight the fact that as far as we are concerned, we don't believe that "nostalgic madness" could be embraced when writing the true history of the Legionary Movement, but, at the same time, we don't believe we should set the Legionaries and their political and spiritual leaders outside the times in which they were active. We shouldn't be obsessed by the "danger" of the Legionary Movement's return, thus losing our motivation to discover its mysteries, while we all agree that Corneliu Zelea Codreanu and the movement founded and amplified by him are a chapter that has already been written and played out in the contemporary history of Romania. Also, overloading the Legionary Movement[31] with anti-Semitic characteristics, which were not particular to it, correlated to the objective situation of Romania, should not cloud the attempt to seek the truth.

---

[29] See Zigu Ornea, "Istoria Mișcării Legionare. Breviar," I-XV, in *Dilema* (București), nos. 40/1993-54/1994.

[30] Toma Roman, "Nostalgia legionară reprezintă un pericol (Interviu cu dl. Zigu Ornea)," I, in *Formula AS* (București), nr. 50/1992, p. 9.

[31] See for example, Dionisie Petcu, "Particularități ale antisemitismului din România în perioada interbelică," in *Societate și Cultură. Noua Alternativă*, nr. 1/1993, pp. 28-32; Radu Florian, "Reflecții introductive pe marginea resuscitării antisemitismului în țările est-europene," in *idem*, pp. 33-36; Alexandru Florian, "Populism legionar," in *idem*, nr. 2/1993, pp. 21-28. The way in which Alexandru Florian changes reality is ridiculous, especially when he suggests that in the times of communist dictatorship, the *Legionary Movement* apparently enjoyed sympathy when it came to its past: "...It should be highlighted, no matter how conflicting

The Trial of Corneliu Zelea Codreanu

Another anti-historical perception of a complex phenomenon like the Legionary Movement, is shown in the series of studies called "Trăsături ale fascismului românesc," written by Radu Ioanid.[32] We won't analyze this "contribution," considering our opinion after studying it is that such "evidence" puts historical science in a tangled Leninist labyrinth: *One step forward, two steps back!*

***

The establishment and the evolution of the Legionary Movement up to the beginning of World War II, found its reflection of events in the rich contemporary literature. The Legionary press, oriented towards Codreanu (*Pământul strămoșesc, Axa, Cuvântul, Buna Vestire, Sfarmă Piatră, Porunca Vremii, Vremea,* etc.), first of all, showcased the daily events, while the monographic and memorialist writings, the doctrinal ones, the collections of documents, etc., that were published in the second half of the 1930s,[33] were the first real contributions to this subject, despite the hagiographic and differential character of many of them. Among them, the ones that stand out most are the volumes of dual purpose, memorialist and doctrinal, penned by the indisputable leaders of the Legionary Movement, Corneliu

---

it might seem, that the totalitarian regime aggravated this state of mind (the lack of "democratic reaction" concerning fascism), by minimalizing the influence of the Legionary fascist movement in the 1930s, through hiding the crimes committed by the military-fascist dictatorship, preserving an ideal image of history, which contributed to erasing from the historical memory all the acts of chauvinism and antisemitism from the decades of the first half of the century. Now hearing about them (when actually the Romanian public have only been hearing about it for decades), for the first time, many people, young and old, have the wrong impression that the real history is being suppressed, when actually the truth is close to how it is presented" (*Societate și Cultură. Noua Alternativă*, nr. 1/1993, p. 35-36). We will come back later to the statements above to prove these statements are fraudulent, especially to demonstrate that the history of the twentieth century (Romanian or worldwide) is NOT entirely made up of chauvinist or antisemitic acts, and NOT all societal events unfolded or unfold based on predetermined criteria. Periods of time and personalities were presented untruthfully after their time, through certain elements of effect, under pretexts of antisemitism or chauvinism. If we were to believe such "scientific" attempts, we should just erase the twentieth century nationalists from history completely.

[32] Published in *Societate și Cultură. Noua Alternativă*, nos. 2-3-4/1991. See the monograph of the same author, containing apocalyptic descriptions about "fascist" Romania: *The Sword of the Archangel: Fascist Ideology in Romania,* Boulder/New York, 1990.

[33] Cf. "Momente din istoria presei legionare," in *Cuvântul* (București) from 9 November 1940.

Romanian Crucible

Zelea Codreanu (1899-1938) and Ion Moța (1902-1937): *Pentru Legionari* (volume I)[34] and *Cranii de lemn.*[35] As many noticed at the time,[36] the two works presented events which were later confirmed as true by the *Cronologia legionară* written in 1940, and that had a remarkable impact when it came to the Legionary Movement. They were considered to be a *catechism* of the Legionary youth, and not without a reason.[37] Corneliu Zelea Codreanu published multiple editions of the *Circulările Căpitanului,* 1934-1937[38] and *Cărticica șefului de cuib,*[39] as well as *Testamentul* by Ion Moța. The writings, considered doctrinal, were predominant: *Ce este și ce vrea Mișcarea Legionară* (Ion Banea, multiple editions); *Rânduri către generația noastră* (Ion Banea, 1940); *Stil legionar* (Ernest Bernea, multiple editions 1937-1940); *Românul de maine și cum suntem* (Alexandru Cantacuzino, multiple editions, 1935-1940); *Crez de generație* (Vasile Marin,[40] multiple editions); *Revoluția fascistă* (Doru Belimace, multiple editions.)[41] A series of works approached real facts about the Legionary Movement's activity: *România Legionară și Axa* (Horia M. Cosmovici, 1940); *Mișcarea Legionară și țărănimea* (Traian Herseni, 1940); *Biserica și Mișcarea Legionară* (Priest Ilie I. Imbrescu, 1940) or *Între lumea legionară și lumea comunistă* (Alexandru Cantacuzino, various editions). We believe the perfect example of hagiographic literature was written by Ion Banea, with his *Căpitanul,*[42] from which we extracted the following quote:

> The Captain! He's a border stone, a barrier. A sword between two worlds. One
> old world, which he manly defies, destroying it; a new world, which he creates,

---

[34] Ediție originală: Sibiu, Editura "Totul pentru Țară", 1936 (Tip. Vestemean).

[35] Ediție originală: Sibiu, Editura "Totul pentru Țară", 1936 (Tip. Vestemean).

[36] See "Cuvântul Studențesc" (București), nos. 1-4/1937, p. 18.

[37] Apud Al. V. Diță, Dan Zamfirescu, eds. *Istoria Mișcării legionare scrisă de un legionar*, București, Editura "Roza Vânturilor", 1993, pp. 15-38.

[38] București, 1937 (ed. I, 1933).

[39] Bucharest, 1933 (ed. a II-a. 1935; ed. a III-a. 1940).

[40] It should be known that Vasile Marin (1904-1937) was awarded a doctorate in law for his work called *Fascismul* (1932).

[41] After World War II, Horia Sima published the book that can be considered a *summum* for this subject, while in exile: *Doctrina Legionară* (Madrid, Editura Mișcării legionare, 1980, 225 p.).

[42] Sibiu, Editura "Totul pentru Țară, 1937 (ed. a II-a cenzurată).

The Trial of Corneliu Zelea Codreanu

giving it life, calling it in the light. His outline at the center of the national movement, from the war until now, appears as a line of fire, around which gravitate all the great events. He was the leader and the animator..."[43]

At the junction of the fourth and fifth decades, the general evolution of Europe, marked by the accomplishments of Germany and Italy, the fate of Corneliu Zelea Codreanu, the evolution of the Legionary Movement from 1938 to taking the government in 1940-1941, held the attention of a few large foreign groups. This explains the publication of a whole series of foreign works dedicated to Corneliu Zelea Codreanu or to Legionary history.[44] Some of the books, like the one written by the Italian Lorenzo Baracchi Tua, have been translated into Romanian.[45]

The literary works we mentioned from a list that is far from being exhausted, introduce the reader to the main events or features that remained at the basis of the origin and history of the Legionary Movement (1927-1938/1939). It should be noted that there is a lack of archival research (public or private) from renowned authors, which was natural for those times. Nevertheless, the value or importance of information cannot be denied when it comes to: the situation in Iaşi in 1919-1920 and the launch of Corneliu Zelea Codreanu in the nationalist, anti-Communist, and antisemitic movements;[46] the birth of the "League of National-Christian Defense;"[47] the detachment of Corneliu Zelea Codreanu and his partners from LANC and A.C. Cuza, who became the "corrupt parents" of the young Legionaries;[48] the emergence and affirmation of the "1922 generation;"[49] the assassination

---

[43] *Ibidem*, p. 3 (from "Cuvânt Înainte").

[44] See especially, L.B. Tua, *La Guardia di Ferro*, Firenze, 1938; Klaus Charle, *Die Eiserne Garde*, Berlin-Wien, 1939; A. Panini-Finotti, *La Guardia di Ferro*, Firenze, 1938; E. Saleo, *Mussolini e Codreanu*, Palermo, 1942; Jerome et Jean Tharaud, *L'envoye de l'Archange*, Paris, 1939; A. Panini-Finotti, *Da Codreanu a Antonescu. Romania di ieri e di oggi*, Verona, 1941; T. Escolar, J. Nieto, *Vida y doctrina de C.Z. Codreanu*, Madrid, 1941.

[45] See L.B. Tua, *Garda de Fier*, Bucureşti, Tip. "Bucovina", 1940. Both editions (Italian and Romanian) received a preface written by M. Manoilescu.

[46] Ion Banea, *Căpitanul*, pp. 11-26.

[47] L.B. Tua, op. cit., pp. 24-29.

[48] I. I. Moţa, *Cranii de lemn*, pp. 121-128

[49] *Ibidem*, pp. 213-217; C.Z. Codreanu, *Pentru Legionari*, I, p. 76-77.

Romanian Crucible

of Manciu, the police prefect;[50] the founding of the *Legion of the Archangel Michael;*[51] the expansion of the *Legion's activity during the years of the economic crises from 1929-1933;*[52] the creation of the political movement of the Legion — *The Iron Guard* (1930),[53] and then the Legionary Senate;[54] the professed primary objective of the Guard — organizing the fight against "Romanian Bolshevism;"[55] the first dissolution of the Guard (January 1931) by the minister of internal affairs, Ion Mihalache; the founding of "Corneliu Zelea Codreanu Group;" the participation, for the first time, in the parliamentary elections (June 1931), the failure, followed by the victories in August 1931 in Neamț (Corneliu Zelea Codreanu) and in April 1932 at Tutova (Ion Zelea Codreanu);[56] the second dissolution of the Iron Guard (April 1932, ordered by the Iorga-Argetoianu government), the participation in the parliamentary elections in June 1932 and the winning of more than 73,000 votes (five seats in the Chamber);[57] the relaunch of the Guard in 1932-1933, and the third and last dissolution in December 1933, through an act of the Ministerial Council presided over by I.G. Duca;[58] the assassination of I.G. Duca, the assassin's trial (1934) and the restoration of the Legionary Movement's political representation — the *All for Country Party* (1934-1935), under the leadership of General Cantacuzino-Grănicerul.[59]

The events that marked the end of the first phase of the Legionary Movement (the chemistry it had with the masses in 1934-1937, the pact with the National Peasant's Party, National Liberal Party of Gheorghe Brătianu, the Jewish Party,

---

[50] *Ibidem*, pp. 211-212.

[51] L.B. Tua, op. cit.., pp. 55-56.

[52] C.Z. Codreanu, *Pentru Legionari*, I, p. 340 and the next.

[53] Ion Banea, *op. cit.*, pp. 62-63

[54] *Cărticica șefului de cuib*, ed. A II-a, București, 1935, pp. 76-77.

[55] Ion Banea, *op. cit., p. 63.*

[56] *Cărticica șefului de cuib*, p. 77.

[57] *Ibidem*; Ion Banea, *op. cit.*, p. 75.

[58] See *Cronologie Legionară*, pp. 21-22 (from "Almanahul 1941" of *Cuvântul* newspaper).

[59] *Ibidem*, pp. 22-23. In exile, professor Virgil Mihăilescu, the founder and former director of the Romanian Library in Freiburg im Breisgau, wrote an extensive *Legionary Chronology (Cronologie Legionară)* (Salzburg, 1953).

The Trial of Corneliu Zelea Codreanu

and Constantin Argentoianu's group in November 1937, the success in the elections of 20 December 1937, the establishment of Carol II's dictatorship, the self-dissolution of the All for the Country Party, the arrest of Corneliu Zelea Codreanu, the first trial of the Captain for slandering Nicolae Iorga, the second trial in May 1938, the sentencing and imprisonment at Jilava-Râmnicu Sărat, the assassination of the Captain and his comrades on the 29/30th of November 1938, the disruptions affecting the Legionary Movement and the fight for power in 1938-1939, the self-promotion of Horia Sima at the helm of the Legionary Movement), and directly succeeding that, the ones in the second phase that coincided with the conflagration between 1939 and 1945 (the first wave of the Legionary exile to Germany in 1939-1940, the assassination of Prime Minister Armand Călinescu and the repressions from Gh. Argeşanul's general government of royal dictatorship, the start of reconciliation between Horia Sima and Carol II, the inclusion of the Legionaries in the first government of Ion Gigurtu in July 1940, the proclamation of the National-Legionary State on 14 September 1940, the Ion Antonescu-Horia Sima government that was constantly threatened by the conflict between them, the Legionary rebellion of January 1941, Ion Antonescu's repression and the second wave of Legionary exile to Germany in 1941-1945, Horia Sima's government in Vienna in 1944-1945), all these were widely spoken about only after the end of World War II in 1945 by the Legionaries who remained in exile in the West. The literature written by the exiled Legionaries from 1945 to 1989, used new sources correlated with direct impressions or retelling, and it continues to be uneven, but what predominates is the way the problem is approached and this directly depends on the position of each of the authors (memorialists, exegetes, ideologists, or editors) had: pro-Sima or anti-Sima. The first group imposed their point of view according to which Horia Sima continued to work towards the goals of the Captain, while the others portray Horia Sima as a traitor to the commandments left by Corneliu Zelea Codreanu, even more — his moral assassin and one guilty of every trouble of those times that had a direct and brutal effect on the long post-war exile of the Legionaries. We will reference a few of the books with critical analyses, that made possible — through corroboration with other sources, researching archives and studying specialized works on Romania's contemporary history — the first solid history of the Legionary Movement. The first one to undertake the study of the Legionary

Romanian Crucible

past was the priest Ştefan Palaghiţă (1950-1951)[60] with the work *Garda de Fier spre reînvierea României*, republished in Bucharest in 1993, edited by Al. V. Diţă and Dan Zamfirescu.[61] The author, who ended up dying in suspicious circumstances, offered a text filled with details that were never known before and exact information starting with the biography of Corneliu Zelea Codreanu and the explanation of the Legionary doctrine,[62] continuing with the moment in 1920-1923-1924-1930- 1932-1933 and after 1934, which reported to the teachings found in *Cărticica şefului de cuib,* was considered to belong to the period of "crossing of Mount of suffering"[63] by the Legionaries, who then entered the "forest of wild beasts," which coincided with 1938-1941. The three evil men who dominated this, according to the author, and who caused great hardship for the Legionary Movement[64] were: Carol II, Horia Sima, and the General Ion Antonescu.[65] Ştefan Palaghiţă was the first Legionary historiographer who wrote about the serious conflicts that broke out at the start of World War II, and got worse during the exile in Germany from 1941-1945, between Horia Sima and his party members on one hand, and on the other hand, between multiple Legionary leaders (Ilie Gârneaţă, C. Papanace, Mile Lefter, etc.).

For Ştefan Palaghiţă, the years of 1942-1945, that also corresponded with the exile to Germany and with the Sima Government in Vienna,[66] coincided with the

---

[60] Ştefan Palaghiţă's book was printed in Buenos Aires at "Editura Autorului", the printing finished on 30th of December 1950, but on the first page it was shown that the publishing year was 1951. It's worth to mention that Ştefan Palaghiţă had started his work in 1945, when Horia Sima assigned him (together with other two exiled Legionaries) to gather and organize "the whole documentary material which concerns the Legionary Movement" (Original edition, p. 15).

[61] See *Istoria Mişcării Legionare scrisă de un legionar,* Bucureşti, 1993 (cited edition, note 37), 366 p. The volume contains, aside from the work written by Ştefan Palaghiţă (pp. 39-338), *Cronologia legionară, 1919-1940* (taken from *Almanahul "Cuvântul" 1941)*) (pp. 15-38) and the series of the four excellent conferences held in 1938 by the renown Nae Ionescu, with the title *Fenomenul legionar* (pp. 350-361), first edited in Rome by C. Papanacc for the collection "Biblioteca Verde". Nr. 17, Editura "Armatolii."

[62] Ştefan Palaghiţă, *Garda de Fier spre reînvierea României,* Buenos Aires, 1951 (Original edition), pp. 17-70 and 349-370.

[63] *Ibidem,* pp. 71-82

[64] *Ibidem,* p. 83.

[65] *Ibidem, pp. 83-175*

[66] *Ibidem,* pp. 175-308 (cap. V-VIII).

The Trial of Corneliu Zelea Codreanu

proliferation of the Legionary Movement crises. Horia Sima and his party members are consistently considered to be "brigadiers". The year 1945 meant, in Palaghiță's point of view, who made use again of the text from *Căpitanul*, the sinking of Horia Sima and his "brigadiers" in the "swamp of desolation."[67] Overall, *Istoria* compiled by Ștefan Palaghiță has an antisemitic overview. Sima was considered from the start to be responsible for the direct assassination of Corneliu Zelea Codreanu, of the *Nicadorii*, and the *Decemvirii*, through his terrorist acts initiated in 1938[68]. The author explains: *"... Opposite to Carol's oppression [from 1938], the Captain settled on the spiritual side of the Movement [...] Horia Sima either didn't understand or he didn't want to understand the tactical and strategic plan of the Captain [...] He worked against the Captain's orders, against the line endorsed by the Commander [of the Legionary Movement], conducting individual actions that completely opposed the orders he received, against the reality and rejecting basic discipline of the Legionaries."[69]*

The works that were published after *Garda de Fier spre reînvierea României* continued the debates and, depending on if they were *pro* or *anti-Semitic,*[70] gave many opportunities for investigations in the history of the Legionary Movement, figuring out its secrets and setting its main periods:

I — 1927-1938/1939 (its founding and ascension)

II — 1939-1945 (its rise to power, governing from 1940-1945, the rebellion, the exile to Germany and Sima's power in office)

III — After 1945 (the exile of the Legionary leaders to the West, and in the country dealing with the Communist terror by Legionary members of every category, with overwhelming cases of bravery, dignity, and a spirit of extreme sacrifice).

---

[67] *Ibidem*, pp. 309-347.

[68] *Ibidem*, p.95.

[69] *Ibidem*, pp. 96-98. What cannot be omitted from our attention is that fact that, no matter how much Ștefan Palaghiță admired C.Z. Codreanu, the superlatives he used in writing are not appropriate. For the author, for example, Codreanu was equivalent to "Moses" or a "basileus," "Hesperus," or "the greatest genius," "the most notable man the nation ever had" or "a great prophet," the direct successor of our great princes Ștefan, Mircea, Mihai, and Brâncoveanu.

[70] See Horia Sima's remarks, obviously meant as excuses (*Pour la connaissance de la verité. Declaration du Mouvement Legionnaire 1990*, Paris, Editura Dacia, 1992, 37 p.).

Romanian Crucible

We must mention a few of the books that were published during the Legionary exile after 1945, especially the ones belonging to the well-known collections from Madrid, Salzburg (the Miami Beach), Buenos Aires, and Rome ("Omul nou," "Biblioteca Verde," "Dacia," "Cuget românesc," etc.):[71] *Pământul Strămoşesc* (Ilie Gârneaţă), Buenos Aires, 1952); *Corneliu Zelea Codreanu. 20 de ani de la moarte* (N. S. Govora, I. V. Emilian, Gr. Manoilescu etc., Madrid, 1958); *Texte alese. Extrase de doctrină legionară* (Salzburg, 1952); *Însemnări de la Jilava (1938)* (Corneliu Zelea Codreanu, Salzburg, 1951); *Cronologie legionară* (Virgil Mihăilescu, Salzburg, 1953); *Nicadorii* (Toader Ioraş, Salzburg, 1952); *Miti Dumitrescu* (Mihai Tănase, Salzburg, 1952); *Cazul Iorga-Madgearu[72]* (Horia Sima, Madrid, 1961, ed. a II-a); *Gând şi faptă legionară* (C. Henţescu and V. Iaşinchi, Madrid, 1962); *Evocări* (C. Papanace, Madrid, 1965); *Facing the Truth. Face a la verité* (V. Iaşinchi, Madrid, 1966); *România şi sfârşitul Europei. Amintiri din ţara pierdută[73]* (Mihail Sturdza, Madrid, 1966); *Histoire du Mouvement Legionnaire[74]* (Horia Sima, ed. cited); *Semicentenarul Mişcării Legionare. Legiunea în imagini (1927-1977)* (ed. De Centrul de Studii şi Documentare al Mişcării Legionare, Madrid, 1977)[75]; *Fără Căpitan. Conducerea în a doua prigoană (1938)* (C. Papanace,

---

[71] At one point, Horia Sima considered that the literary works mentioned constituted "an impressive bibliography" concerning the subject (cf. *Historie du Mouvement Legionnaire*, Rio de Janeiro, Editura Dacia, 1972, p. 11).

[72] To justify the assassination of N. Iorga, Horia Sima stated the Legionaries killed the *political man*, but *not the scientist!!!*

[73] An English version was also published (which is more popular): *The Suicide of Europe. Memoirs of Prince Mihail Sturdza, Former Foreign Minister of Romania*, Boston, Western Island, 1968. LXVI + 331 pp.

[74] We consider necessary the brief references to the theme of *History*: the origins of the Legionary Movements — Romania after World War I, *Garda Conştiinţei Naţionale* and C.Z. Codreanu, L.A.N.C., the terrorist police and the assassination of C. Manciu, the trial of C.Z. Codreanu; the founding of the *League of Archangel Michael* — the people, the Captain, the extension towards the masses, the birth of the Iron Guard and the parliament activity of the *C.Z. Codreanu Group;* the first wave of oppressions towards the Legionary Movement (1934-1937) sorted on years: the reorganization (1934-1935) by founding the *All for the Country Party* (pp. 173-229); the consolidation (1936) (pp. 230-298) and the Legionary Movement winning the county (1937) — the nonaggression electoral pact with certain parties from the opposition and the victory in the parliamentary elections from 20th of December 1937 (pp. 299-407). We should mention that from a chronological point of view, *Istoria* is succeeded by other books of a memorialist nature (Horia Sima, *Era Libertaţii. Statul Naţional-Legionar*, Madrid, 1982-1986 etc.).

[75] To be compared with *Mărturii despre Legiune. 40 de ani de la întemeierea Mişcării Legionare. 1927-1967*, Rio de Janeiro, 1967.

The Trial of Corneliu Zelea Codreanu

Roma, 1984); *Era Libertăţii* (Horia Sima, Madrid, 1977, ed. I; Miami Beach, 1990, ed. A II-a); *Guvernul naţional român de la Viena* (Horia Sima, Madrid, Editura Mişcării Legionare, 1993); *Guvernul de la Viena. Continuarea statului român naţional-legionar, 1944-1945* (Faust Bradesco, Madrid, Editura Carpaţi/ Traian Popescu, 1989); *A Grenoble sur le traces du Capitaine* (L. David, Ion Marii, Madrid, 1971); *Sub steagul lui Codreanu. Momente din trecutul Legiunii* (Nicu Iancu, Madrid, 1973); *Martiri legionari* (C. Papanace, Roma, 1952); *Din viaţa legionară* (N. Pătraşcu, Salzburg, 1952); *Romanian Nationalism. The Legionary Movement* (Alexander E. Ronnet, Chicago, 1974) or *La Garde de Fer et le terrorisme* (Faust Badesco, Madrid, 1979).[76]

For decades, *the European fascist phenomenon was addressed and explained using the Comintern model.* Also, for decades it was avoided *to set a connection between fascism and communism,* in a sense that the first one appeared as an offense move against the last one. After in 1943-1945, the fascist states collapsed as a result of World War II and the Communist system was introduced by Soviet tanks in various countries from East-Central Europe, with all the complications of "local" Communist factors, the victory and superiority of communism over fascism were considered as "logical," in a context in which the meaning of that word was changed completely. In Romania, the situation couldn't have been identical, the *Legionaries* or the *Guardists* being automatically mixed in with the *fascists.* Called guilty of every misfortune that humankind suffered during World War II, despite de facto evidence that proved the great massacre was a result of the Nazi-Communist conspiracy from the 23rd of August 1939, while the fascists, the Legionaries and the Guardists became victims of the official politics of systematic destruction. All this was used under the pretext of the country's recovery, of its salvation from every bad and criminal consequences (here the list of adjectives was infinite) of the "old regime" etc. etc. *The Iron Guard* was named a simple agency of Berlin, and

---

[76] For critical opinions on the well-known literature related to the evolution of the Legionary Movement, cf. Especially Walter Laqueur, *Rumanian Fascist Emigres. A Survey of their Literature,* in "The Wiener Library Bulletin", July 1964; idem, *Rumania during the War. A Survey of Literature,* in "The Wiener Library Bulletin", April, 1936 and, especially, idem, ed., *Fascism. A Reader's Guide. Analyses. Interpretations. Bibliography* (cited edition — see note 7), pp. 215-247 (cap. III/6: Bela Vago, *Fascism in Eastern Europe*) and pp. 325-408 (cap. IV/9: Zeev Sternhell, *Fascist Ideology*) or Armin Heinen, *Die Legion "Erzengel Michael" in Rumanien...,* cited edition (see note 2), pp 19-32 (cap. I/A), pp. 464-490 (cap. XI/A-B) and pp. 528-511 (Bibliografia).

Romanian Crucible

the politicians and historians (M. Roller and his successors) rushed to prove this relation. The crimes of war and the antisemitism became a recurring theme of an exaggerated propaganda, even though it was easy to see, as well as today, that during that specific period of the war in the East, the Legionaries were not allied with Antonescu anymore, or that among the ideologists from Moscow and Bucharest predominated, in the first decade after the war, many Jews who discovered (not based on reality) that antisemitism was a weapon that excused their striking promotion, their new endeavors against humanity, their thirst for power, and not least, their unmistakable weakness. Therefore, the history of the Legionary Movement in Romania was, from the start, distorted and compromised in Bucharest. Whether we choose to admit it or not, its chance to be studied correctly originated from the fact that, during exile, its investigation continued uninterrupted, even if there were serious problems with interpretation and subjectivism. The facts discovered in the free world, the general idea of fascism, as well as the multiple controversies related to Romanian Legionaries became the theme of systematic investigations by those with high moral and scientific qualifications. Secondly, its chance came from the collapse of the Communist system in 1989, when the history of the Legionary Movement stopped being interpreted from just one point of view in the country — the official Marxist-Leninist one. But we will develop this in the following pages.

Everywhere on the old continent, Communism was to blame for the birth of Fascism, especially in Germany. Stalin contributed to the promotion of Hitler for the chancellor position in a few economic, financial and local political circles.[77] Until 1933, the great conflicts within the capitalist system had *economic motives*, after which appeared the *ideological conflict* between fascism and communism, between Moscow and Berlin. Because we're talking about two great powers that had great influence in Europe and in the world, and because Germany's internal structure was capitalist, the capitalist system was caught in this dispute between fascism and communism in the 1930s. The conflicts between the greatest three political powers had a direct impact on the conflagration between 1939-1945, from which S.S.S.R. came victorious with the help of Anglo-Saxon powers. An essential mistake the leaders from the Kremlin did, was that before eliminating Hitler, and

---

[77] See especially I.L. Diakov, T.S. Buşueva, eds., *Faşistskii mec kovolsia v SSSR. Krasnaia Armiia I Reichswehr tainoe sotrudnicestvo 1922-1933. Neizvestnîie dokumentî,* Moskva. Sovetskaia Rossiia, 1992, *passim.kumentî,* Moskva. Sovetskaia Rossiia, 1992, *passim.e dokumentî,* Moskva. Sovetskaia Rossiia, 1992, *passim.e dokumentî,* Moskva. Sovetskaia Rossiia, 1992, *passim.*

The Trial of Corneliu Zelea Codreanu

even after that, they copied the Führer exactly: they faced him while planning the funeral of the West. The result was obvious, just like in Nazi Germany, it led to the downfall of Communist Russia. In whichever way we looked at it, the problem at the center of everything for a long period of time was the dispute between fascism and communism. To showcase its victory, Kremlin used all its weapons — crime, espionage, war, and why not, ideology. The result? Not only *the change of the course of history (that was forced either way* after 1944-1945 for East-Central Europe), but more than that, *forgery of history!*

So, what did Fascism represent in the eyes of Communist ideologues? For a long time, it was considered that the *classic definition* of fascism (which apparently was the only accepted one) had belonged to Gh. Dimitrov, in the report presented in 1935 at the 5th World Congress of the III International. The Bulgarian Communist leader, who was the second man in power in the Comintern after I.V. Stalin, reached a general idea that aimed to avoid causing problems for their successors. Keeping in mind the dilemmas of the politruks from the Kremlin after 1945, who admitted that Fascism can lurk anywhere except for Communist groups and their close entourage, Gh. Dimitrov first came to the conclusion that "through its cynical approaches and its methods, Fascism surpasses every other form of burghers reaction. It adapts its demagogy on the national individuality of every country, even more, even from inside a country it adapts to the individuality of every social class within."[78] In its essence, Fascism — in Dimitrov's opinion — was equivalent to "the most despicable exploitation of the population, but presented to it with clever anti-capitalistic demagogy, exploiting the deep hatred of the working class towards the greedy burghers, the banks, the trusts, and the financial magnates."[79] In turn, Walter Ulbricht, the renowned leader of the Communist group of Eastern Germany, was denouncing Fascism as "the terrorist domination open to the most reactive elements, the most Chauvinistic, and the most imperialist of the German financial

---

[78] Gh. Dimitrov, *Opere alese*, București, 1959, p. 229.

[79] *Ibidem*, p. 231-232. J. Jelev recently considered that Gh Dimitrov's formula is still valid, when it comes to picturing the social and class essence of fascism, but adds: "It would be incorrect... to assume that the Cominternist definition covers and exhausts all the essential features of fascism" (cf. Dr. Jeliu Jelev, *Fascismul*, București, 1992, p.42). From the Cominternist definition are missed: the specific political system of the fascist state, the real estimation of the dictatorship of financial capitalism, the mandatory totalitarian trait, etc. (*ibidem*, pp. 42-44). About the characteristics of the totalitarian fascist state in the opinion of J. Jelev, cf. *Ibidem*, pp. 282-310.

32 Romanian Crucible

capital" or "a form of domination of the German monopolistic capital in its time of corruption."[80] We don't know how many of these "classic" traits we can identify in the activity of the Legionary Movement, but it's concerning to notice similarities between these quotes and the "evidence" in Roller's unique textbook, which we referred to in the opening of this introduction. Coming back to Dimitrov and Ulbricht, we can note that in contrast with doctrines proposed by them, Henri Miche, the reputable French historian of World War II, who studied Fascism closely, opposed every formula that generalized it excessively and treated this phenomenon in a direct relation with reality of European society (and not only) and with the effects of multiple crises (economic, social, political, philosophical, etc.) that took place in the time between the two World Conflicts.[81]

In the established international historiography of fascism, this phenomenon is studied from multiple aspects (general, European, or South European), most often correlated with the evolution of the Legionary Movement. Another collection of syntheses, monographs, and studies contain the famous ones that talk *especially* about the situation in Romania.

On an international level, it can be considered that a key moment when it comes to the scientific investigation of the fascist phenomenon occurred around the year 1965, when in Germany, USA, England, France, and Italy a series of related works were published by reputable historians who were to become leading authorities on

---

[80] Walter Ulbricht, *Sur la nature du fascisme hitlerien*, in "Recherches internationales a la lumière du marxisme" (Paris), no. 1/1958, p. 93. Other Marxist opinions were showcased in the same edition of the cited magazine (special edition — *Les origines du fascisme*, 192 p.), from Delores Ibarruri, Paolo Alatri, Fritz Klein, S. M. Slobodskoi, Paulette Charbonnel and Jean Gacon. About the "classic" Marxist opinions expressed by A. Gramsci, P. Togliatti, Luigi Longo, Ernst Thalmann, Wilhelm Pieck and (we must add) Lucreţiu Pătrăşcanu, cf. J. Jelev, op. cit., *passim*. For Romania, see the "theories" of Lucreţiu Pătrăşcanu, *Sub trei dictaturi*, Bucureşti, *1945; idem, Probleme de bază ale României, ed. A III-a, Bucureşti, 1946.*

[81] See Henry Michel, "Introduction — Sur le fascisme," in *Revue d'histoire de la Deuxieme Guerre mondiale* (Paris), no. 66/1967, pp. 1-3; idem, *Les fascismes*, Paris, 1977, *passim*. The well-known French historian despised the *national fascism* and, at the same time, the *international fascism* (*ibidem*, p. 22). Generally, as a historical phenomenon, fascism meant a period of "20 years in the history of Europe. Is the third major event of the interwar era, next to the decline of liberal democracy and the Bolshevik revolution" (*ibidem*, p. 3). For the traits of this phenomenon, cf. cap. I of the work (*ibidem*, pp. 5-22).

The Trial of Corneliu Zelea Codreanu

the subject. Concretely, "the debate about Fascism" in universal contemporary historiography[82] was established through the works by Ernst Nolte — *Der Faschismus in seiner Epoche*[83] and by Eugen Weber — *Varieties of Fascism. Doctrines of Revolution in the Twentieth Century.*[84] Both books that became classics and benefited from multiple references[85] or a certain chapter about the Legionary Movement,[86] were immediately followed by a true wave, a situation in which the fundamental problems of fascism (origins, general and local evolution, doctrines, victories and defeats, the situation after World War II, and historiography) were studied to the core: *The European Right. A Historical Profile* (Hans Rogger and Eugen Weber, editors, Berkeley and Los Angeles, 1965);[87] *International Fascism, 1920-1945* (Walter Laqueur and George L. Mosse, editors, New York, 1966);[88] *Die Faschistischen Bewegungen* (Ernst Nolte, Berlin, 1966);[89] *European Fascism* (S. J. Woolf, London, 1968);[90] *The Rise of Fascism* (F. L. Carsten, Berkeley, Los Angeles, 1969);[91] *Native Fascism in the Successor States, 1918-1945* (Peter F. Sugar,

---

[82] Cf. Stanley G. Payne, *Fascism. Comparison and Definition*, Madison, University of Wisconsin Press, 1983, p. 215. Above all, we shouldn't leave aside the fundamental book written by Hanna Arendt, *The Origins of Totalitarianism*, New York, 1958.

[83] Munchen, R. Riper und Co. Verlag, 1963. The work was translated in 1965 in English, receiving multiple editions and greater access. When it comes to us, we relate to the edition by Ernst Nolte, *Three Faces of Fascism. Action Française. Italian Fascism. National Socialism*, New York, New American Library, 1979, XIII + 699 p.

[84] Princeton, Toronto, New York, London, D. Van Nostrand Co. Inc., 1964, 194 p.

[85] See Ernst Nolte, *op. cit.*, pp. 569-577 (the two annexes).

[86] See Eugen Weber, *op. cit.*, pp. 96-105 (cap. 9 — *Romania)* and the documented annex with multiple texts selected from C.Z. Codreanu (pp. 165-169).

[87] With a chapter about Romania belonging to Eugen Weber (pp. 501-574).

[88] It also appeared as a special edition in the prestigious "Journal of Contemporary History" (New York — London), I, nr. 1/1966. In the volume there was a special study on C.Z. Codreanu and the Legionary Movement — Eugen Weber, *The Men of the Archangel*, pp. 101-126.

[89] It was also published as a French translation (that was more well-known): *Les mouvements fascistes. L'Europe de 1919 à 1945*, Paris, Calmann-Levi, 1969, 363 p. (with a heavily argumentative special chapter about the Romanian fascism, pp. 235-251).

[90] Also, with a sharp chapter about Romania (pp. 146-166) that was owned by Zevedei Barbu.

[91] In this volume there's a special chapter: *Anti-Semitism and Anti-Communism: The Iron Guard* (pp. 181-193).

Romanian Crucible

editor, Santa Barbara, 1971);[92] *Fascismes et ideologies reactionnaires en Europe 1919-1945* (Pierre Milza, Paris, 1971); *The Place of Fascism in European History* (Gilbert Allardyce, editor, Eaglewood Cliffs, 1971); *Universal Fascism The Theory and Practice of the Fascist International, 1928-1936* (M.A. Leden, New York, 1972), followed, among others, by: *Les fascismes* (Henri Michel, 1977);[93] *Fascism, A reader's Guide...* (Walter Laqueur, editor, 1979);[94] *Fascism. Comparison and Definition* (Stanley G. Payne);[95] *Fascism and Prefascism in Europe, 1890-1945. A Bibliography of the Extreme Right* (Philip Rees, Sussex and New Jersey, 1984);[96] *Les Fascismes* (Pierre Mizla, Paris, 1985);[97] *Inside the League. The Shocking Expose of How Terrorists, Nazis, and Latin American Death Squads Have Infiltrated the World Anti-Communist League* (Scott Anderson and John Lee Anderson, New York, 1986),[98] and, finally, *The European Dictatorship, 1918-1945* (Stephen J. Lee, London and New York, 1987).[99] We can't neglect, of course, Jeliu Jelev,[100] from whom we must mention a few definitions of fascism, that were memorable through their originality and wisdom: "an act of violence against the capitalist class that was not sanctioned by law" (Luigi Longo); "the most reactive contra-revolution in history" (G. Poltzer); "the revolution of nihilism" (H. Rauschning); "the shadow, or better, the monstrous child of communism" (W. Churchill); "the epileptic fainting of the German nation," "a general schizophrenia of a nation" (R.

---

[92] With a special chapter (VI) about Romania: a) *The Background of Romanian Fascism,* by Emanuel Turczynski; b) *Fascism in Romania,* by Stephen Fischer-Galați (pp. 99-102).

[93] Cited edition (see note 81).

[94] Cited edition (see note 76).

[95] Cited edition (see note 82).

[96] Works referring to the Legionary Movement (pp. 146-153).

[97] With special references to the evolution of the Legionary Movement (pp. 321-326): "Still, the society that Codreanu is dreaming about, differs greatly from the one which Mussolini and Hitler have started to model in the image of the new man. His ideal [C.Z. Codreanu's] remains the same, a social Christianity based on a respectful peasantry towards traditional values and who's capable to rid the country of its corrupt traits — communism, democracy, Jews, etc." (p. 322).

[98] References to the activity of the Legionaries during exile in 1941-1945 (pp. 14-20 and 30-33).

[99] About Romania, pp. 284-287.

[100] See *Fascismul,* ed. cited (translation from Bulgarian) (Note 79).

The Trial of Corneliu Zelea Codreanu

Binyon); "a statement of the irrational structure of a man modeled by society" (Wilhelm Reich) and certainly, the most striking one that we owe to the Italian philosopher and sociologist Luigi Sturzo: "In truth, between Russian and Italy there is but one authentic difference — the fact that Bolshevism, or the Communist dictatorship, represents a left-wing fascism, while fascism, or the conservatory dictatorship, represents a right-wing Bolshevism."[101]

It was easy to see that the history of the Legionary Movement and the Legionary phenomenon were and are in the attention of foreign specialists, who are interested in international Fascism or the European one. Even more so, this is valid for a smaller group of researchers, especially the ones in the East European area. Keeping this in mind, we must look at the works of general history in this area,[102] putting the accent on the ones that talk about the local fascist movements, among which some of them excel: *The Shadow of the Swastika: The Rise of Fascism and Anti-Semitism in the Danube Basin, 1936-1939* (Bela Vago, London, 1979) *The Green Shirts and the Others. A History of Fascism in Hungary and Romania* (Nicholas M. Nagy-Talavera, Stanford, Hoover Institution Press, 1970; second edition Palm Beach: Center for Romanian Studies, 2021) or *I falsi Fascismi. Ungheria, Jugoslavia, Romania, 1919-1945* (Mariano Ambri, Rome, 1980). American Joseph Rothschild accurately portrays the process in which the Legionary movement expanded their influence, the reasons for their electoral success in December 1937 and the hit received in 1938; it can be observed that the Legionary Movement was not on the offensive from the start, but became a victim of violence committed towards it by the Gendarmes and the Police.[103] Nicholas M. Nagy-Talavera and Mariano Ambri agree on one aspect, which is that, in the interwar period, the only uncorrupted

---

[101] Apud Dr. Jeliu Jelev, *op. cit.,* pp. 37-39.

[102] Cf. C.A. Macartney, A.W. Palmer, *Independent Eastern Europe. A History.* London-New York, 1962; Joseph Rothschild, *East Central Europe between the Two World Wars,* Seattle-London, 1974 and 1977; Ezra Mendelsohn, *The Jews of East Central Europe between the World Wars,* Bloomington, 1983; Klaus P. Beer, *Zur Entwicklung des Parteien und Parlamentssystems in Rumanien 1928-1933,* I-II, Frankfurt-am-Maim, Bonn, 1983; Vincent e. McHale, Sharon Skowronski, eds., *Political Parties of Europe,* II, Westport-London, 1983, p. 801-802 (about *The Iron Guard* and *All for the Country Party*).

[103] Joseph Rothschild, *op. cit.,* p. 309.

36 Romanian Crucible

politicians in Romania were Iuliu Maniu, Corneliu Zelea Codreanu, and General Ion Antonescu.[104]

Of all the studies we mentioned on fascism in general, and when it comes to setting the Legionary Movement in the universal phenomenon or the European one, some of them constituted pioneering works, from multiple points of view: the level and depth of the research, the value and originality of their conclusions, the temerity in approaching the subject, and the bravery in communicating the results. In this regard, we mention Ernst Nolte, Eugen Weber, Z. Barbu, and Nicholas M. Nagy-Talavera. First, thanks to their research on the history of the Legionary Movement, it came out from the shadow of local studies, and became integrated or received a parallel comparison of the Legionaries with the European or universal fascist phenomenon, and they found well-defined traits and common points, but above all, they left behind the area of historiography or of Communist historiographical propaganda. Thus, they undoubtedly demonstrated the power of scientific investigation on this subject. The German philosopher and sociologist Ernst Nolte, in 1963, started the discussion, examining Corneliu Zelea Codreanu's activity and the role of the Legionary Movement in a European context.[105] In 1966, Nolte returns with a special chapter about *Fascismul român* (*Romanian Fascism*) in one of his most well-known syntheses about the European fascism.[106] Nolte correctly presents the ascension of the Legionary Movement in the context of interwar Romanian politics, adequately placing it among the fascist groups in the country[107] and among the foreign ones — a "unique" place in Europe.[108] *The League of Archangel Michael*,

---

[104] Nicholas M. Nagy-Talavera, *The Green Shirts and the Others. A History of Fascism in Hungary and Rumania,* Stanford, Hoover Institution Press, 1970 (second edition, Palm Beach: Center for Romanian Studies, 2021), p. 411; Mariano Ambri, *I falsi fascismi,* p. 268.

[105] Ernst Nolte, *Three Faces of Fascism...,* pp. 27-40 (cap. II — *Fascism in Europe, 1919-1945)*. In fact, Ernst Nolte was preceded by two of his countrymen, the renown Andreas Hillgruber and Martin Broszat, who, however, didn't talk about Legionaries in the strict setting of the European fascist phenomenon, but focused on the role and place of the *Iron Guard* in the evolution of Romanian-German relations: Andreas Hillgruber, *Hitler, Koning Carol und Marschall Antonescu. Die deutsch-rumanischen Beziehungen 1938-1944, Weisbaden,* editions 1954 and 1965; Martin Broszat, *Die Eiserne Garde und das Dritte Reich,* in "Politische Studien" (Munchen), nr. 9/1958, p. 628 and following.

[106] Idem, *Les mouvements fascistes,* pp. 235-251.

[107] *Ibidem,* p. 240.

[108] *Ibidem,* p. 243.

The Trial of Corneliu Zelea Codreanu

founded on the 24th of June 1927 under the leadership of Corneliu Zelea Codreanu,[109] didn't have a defined plan, according to Nolte, but was based on the four principles: the belief in God, the belief in its own mission, mutual trust, and song.[110] The birth of the *Iron Guard* as a political movement, marked the beginning of the national[111] expansion of the Legionary Movement, with immediate electoral victories in 1931-1932, M. Stelescu and I.I. Moța imposing themselves in the Parliament, Corneliu Zelea Codreanu being removed.[112] Even though the Iron Guard was dissolved in 1933, in the same year, oddly, the Legionary Movement gained power, its success being owed to its own efforts, not Hitler's.[113] In 1934/35 a Legionary party was reborn — *All for the Country,* and Nae Ionescu became the renowned theoretician of the Legionary Movement. The great victories belong to 1936-1937, after which the decline happens once the royal dictatorship is installed in 1938, the date after which the Legionary Movement is constantly attacked by Carol II and Armand Călinescu. These factors led to the arrest, trial, and sentencing of Corneliu Zelea Codreanu for social misconduct, for acquiring and giving away secret documents of the Romanian state, for possession of a firearm, and for receiving money from abroad.[114] It's possible that Hitler had an unwanted role in the assassination of Corneliu Zelea Codreanu, since he could have suggested to Carol II, in November 1938, that political power in Bucharest should be given the Captain.[115] The Legionary Movement remained "a force" even after the assassination of Codreanu, and Carol II tried to reconcile with it in 1940. When in power in 1940/1941, the Legionary Movement became guilty of terrorist acts (against its political opponents and Jews), which makes Nolte state that, actually, the movement was more anarchist than fascist.[116] However, there are a few elements that are

---

[109] *Ibidem*, pp. 240-242 (the short biography of C.Z. Codreanu).

[110] *Ibidem*, p. 243.

[111] *Ibidem*, p. 244-245.

[112] *Ibidem*, p. 244-245.

[113] *Ibidem*, p. 245.

[114] *Ibidem*, p.246.

[115] *Ibidem*.

[116] *Ibidem*, p. 246-247.

comparable to the European fascism: the opposition against corruption and the parliamentary and bourgeoise life; setting as one of their goals the commandment for a "moral renovation" of society; the principle about the leader's role and exaggeratedly establishing the life of the Captain as an example; the decision to destroy their adversaries; anti-Semitism; the unconcealed and unconditional friendship with Hitler and Mussolini.[117] In analyzing Ernst Nolte's text, we present the conclusions that are worthy of remembering: the Legionary Movement showed more similarities than differences with the other fascist movements in Europe; the last ones are explicable through social and national conditions specific to interwar Romania. In summary, the Legionary Movement "brings together pro-fascist traits, as well as radical fascist traits," a fact that made it "the most interesting and complex fascist movement."[118]

In 1964, Eugen Weber (who was born in Bucharest in 1925), investigating the *Faces of the European fascism*, studied the Legionary Movement and Corneliu Zelea Codreanu, while trying to discover the essence of Legionary doctrine. Weber briefly examined the biography of the Captain, the situation of Romania after World War I, the take-off of the nationalist and antisemitic current in Iaşi,[119] the assassination of Manciu, and the birth of the *League of Archangel Michael* (in the subchapter named *Murder as Method*).[120] It is useful to underline that the author, even though he doesn't agree, pictures the violence committed by the police prefect Manciu against the Iaşi students with Corneliu Zelea Codreanu at their helm, who decided to "make his own justice with the law in his hands."[121] The ascension of the Legionary Movement in the 1930s and the success of the *All for the Country Party*, grabbed the author's attention. The elections in 1937 — he claims — placed the party in 3rd place nationwide and, more than that, made it the political group that was "by far the most popular and dynamic one."[122] In disagreement with the Legionaries transgressions (I.G. Duca, Armand Călinescu, etc.), Weber also rejects

---

[117] *Ibidem*, p. 249-250.

[118] *Ibidem*, p. 250-251.

[119] See Eugen Weber, *Varieties of Fascism...*, p. 97-98.

[120] *Ibidem*. pp. 98-100.

[121] *Ibidem*, p. 99.

[122] *Ibidem*, p. 102.

The Trial of Corneliu Zelea Codreanu

the "wave of violence" caused by the authorities, because "blood asks for blood, death feeds on death." "It's true — we continue reading — that violence stained the activity of the Legion right from the beginning, but violence in a country where the law applies for the leading party and where political banditry is historically tied to the memory of patriot outlaws that held foreign occupants for ransom. Legionary assassinations were committed as a reply to the crimes that would have never been sent to trial..."[123] Codreanu's assassination and those of his comrades appears to Weber as *acts of martyrs,* but, no less, like an end of the Legionary Movement, a *Götterdämmerung;* "high ideals transformed into vile condemnation."[124] From a doctrinal point of view, Weber considers that Corneliu Zelea Codreanu's ideas are of a "completely different essence" than those of other social European movements, his being more *inclined towards Christianity,* simpler than the ideologies of the West, and yet, *more subtle* when taking into consideration *more issues* that were elsewhere ignored.[125]

Shortly after his contribution in 1964, Eugen Weber came back to the history of the Legionary Movement, in a collective volume that he co-edited,[126] this time giving it a full study, accompanied by a short fundamental bibliography.[127] This time, Weber insisted over the conditions that in Romania started manifesting nationalism and antisemitism, at the junction of the nineteenth and the twentieth centuries, the evolution of these two currents after World War I[128] being connected to the emergence of the Communist danger.[129] The activity of Corneliu Zelea Codreanu[130] in Iași in the first years post-war and after that in LANC, until establishing the *Legion of Archangel Michael,*[131] the problem of crimes and Legionary

---

[123] *Ibidem,* p. 103.

[124] *Ibidem,* p. 105.

[125] *Ibidem,* p. 96.

[126] See Hans Rogger, Eugen Weber, eds., *The European Right. A Historical Profile,* cited edition (1965).

[127] *Ibidem,* pp. 501-574.

[128] *Ibidem,* pp. 501-517.

[129] *Ibidem,* p. 518.

[130] *Ibidem,* pp. 518-527.

[131] *Ibidem,* pp. 527-532.

Romanian Crucible

violence related to the repressions from authorities from 1924 to 1941,[132] the League's ascension, especially in 1934-1937,[133] the events in 1938 that ended with the assassination of Corneliu Zelea Codreanu,[134] and the ones between 1939-1941,[135] all these are closely examined by Eugen Weber, who proves to have knowledge of this era, a fine analyst and an objective judge of events that history will definitely not give the right to appeal. The reputable specialist, based on his own investigations, reconfirms the German Harald Laeuen[136] in a sense that "Sima's Legion was not Codreanu's Legion. The last one ended up by being persecuted in 1938-1939 and in the bloodbath that followed. The new Legionary leadership — Weber observed — had risen from second class citizens. What was even worse, the new leadership was more independent, more heterogeneous, less dedicated, less disciplined, less educated."[137] When it comes to the conflict between Antonescu and Sima, Weber describes the General as a representative of the old world, Sima — "was something completely different."[138] Antonescu was victorious, but not without major support from Berlin, which "cared less about its ideological ally than an old regime that ensured internal peace and proved to be a trustworthy henchman who delivered oil, cereal, and workers it needed."[139] The Legion in power — concludes the British historian, meant more than a disillusion; it was

---

[132] According to the author, after incomplete calculations, between 1924 and 1939 resulted in the following report: 11 crimes or acts of violence committed by Legionaries compared to 501 Legionaries killed by the authorities (*ibidem*, p. 537). The results of the investigation done by a committee designated by general I. Antonescu, after the rebellion in January 1941, shows that 292 Legionaries have been killed without any trial between November 1938 and October 1939. After that, between September 1940 and January 1941, a few hundred Legionaries either died or were executed. "Crime and contra-crime — it's concluded — seemed to have been escalated until they exploded in a *Götterdämmerung* way in the glacial Bucharest of the rebellion from January [1941]" (*ibidem*, p. 537-538).

[133] *Ibidem*, pp. 547-553.

[134] *Ibidem*, p. 555-556.

[135] *Ibidem*, p. 557-566.

[136] See *Marshall Antonescu*, Essen, 1943.

[137] Eugen Weber, *op. cit.*, p. 560-561.

[138] *Ibidem*, p. 560.

[139] *Ibidem*, p. 563.

The Trial of Corneliu Zelea Codreanu

equivalent to a "despicable and bloody collapse."[140] According to the official documents that the author uses, the Legionary rebellion ended up in 370 deaths and 44 injured in Bucharest, and in the rest of the country, 46 deaths and 78 injured; the Legionary leaders fled to Germany, and in the months that followed around 8,000 people were imprisoned.[141] The Legionary "Rebellion" had become "its resistance to a hit given by its equal governmental partner to remove it from power."[142]

Next to Ernst Nolte and Eugen Weber.[143] there was Zevedei Barbu (born in Romania), and he imposed himself, in chronological order, as the third prestigious international researcher on the Legionary phenomenon. His study of reference, that was already mentioned, represents less an attempt to establish the steps that marked the history of the Legionary Movement, and more an effort to penetrate the social origins of the Legionary phenomenon, to explain its success and the reasons for the "cult of violence." He expresses with conviction that the essential traits of the Legionary Movement only partially derive from the conditions of belonging to a certain class or to the economic situation of its members, and in a more relevant measure it's founded on a "series of psychological factors, a state of mind, typical to the individuals and groups that were differently affected by a lack of social integration and its results." These aspects were elaborated in later works by the same specialist.[144]

Reaching the junction of the sixth and seventh decade, the specialized studies about the Legionary Movement, that were already published at a general level, are not rarities anymore. Dominated by Nicholas M. Nagy-Talavera's[145] book, the published studies by foreign specialists (some of them originating from Romania) focused their attention and discovered a few fundamental aspects of the history of the

---

[140] *Ibidem*, p. 572.

[141] Nicholas M. Nagy-Talavera refers to the 3,999 people who were arrested, among which 1,333 were released in two weeks at most (cf. *The Green Shirts...*, p. 456).

[142] Eugen Weber, *op. cit.*, p. 566.

[143] In 1966, Eugen Weber was presented with a new contribution (see Walter Laqueur, George L. Mosse, eds., *International fascism, 1920-1945*, cited edition, pp. 101-126 — *The Men of the Archangel*).

[144] See Z. Barbu, *Rumania*, in S. J. Woolf, ed. *European Fascism*, London, 1968, pp. 146-166; idem, *Psycho-Historical and Sociological Perspectives on the iron Guard*, in S. U. Larsen etc., eds., *Who were the Fascists? Social Roots of European fascism*, Bergen, 1980, pp. 379-394.

[145] Mentioned already (see note 104) and we'll return to it.

Romanian Crucible

Legionary Movement. We make a special mention of the contributions authored by the prestigious Stephen Fischer-Galați,[146] Emanuel Turczynski,[147] N. I. Lebedev,[148] Teodor I. Armon,[149] and F.L. Carsten.[150] And even so, we're far from exhausting the list. Some works covered the general history of contemporary Romania, and we recommend them to the reader, especially because we focus on the exceptional competency of the authors and the fundamental value of their contributions,[151] and we also cannot leave aside some smaller studies, even the occasional ones.[152]

---

[146] See *Romanian Nationalism,* in Peter F. Sugar, Ivo J Lederer, eds., *Nationalism in Eastern Europe,* Seattle-London, 1969, pp. 373-395; *Fascism in Rumania,* in Peter F. Sugar, ed., *Native fascism in the Successor States, 1918-1945,* cited edition (1971), pp. 112-122. From this last study we take these thoughts: "... The survivors of the killings (C.Z. Codreanu's assassination and that of his comrades — n. ns.) assumed the roles of martyrs and avengers of the crimes. Between 1938 and 1940, they became the executors of the "accomplices" of Carol II, thugs and assassins used to physically annihilate their deadly enemies — Jews, communists, and royalists. In context, they abandoned their idealism and their plans for a national reform of villages, factories, and bureaucracy. The Romanian fascists lost their original political identity, and with it, their political sense, between the end of 1938 and the fall of 1940, when the *Guard* defeated its main enemy, Carol II, and finally came to power" (*ibidem,* p. 118). See, by the same author, *Fascism, Communism and the Jewish Question in Romania,* in Bela Vago, George L. Mosse, eds., *Jews and Non-Jews in Eastern Europe, 1918-1945,* New York-Jerusalem, 1974.

[147] Cf., *The Background of Romanian fascism,* in Peter F. Sugar, ed., *Native Fascism...,* pp. 101-111.

[148] See *Garda de Fier, Carol al II-lea și Hitler. Din istoria fascismului, monarhiei române și a politicii externe,* Chișinău, 1970, 344 p. (original edition from Russian, Moskva, IMO, 1968, 328 p.).

[149] See *Fascismo Italiano e Guardia di ferro,* in "Storia contemporanea" (Bologna), nr. 3/1972, pp. 505-548 and, especially, *La Guardia di Ferro,* in idem, nr. 3/1976, pp. 507-544, an interesting critical study about the historic literature of Romania and from abroad that was dedicated to the Legionaries.

[150] See *The Rise of Fascism,* Berkeley-Los Angeles, 1969, pp. 181-193 (cap. *Anti-Semitism and Anti-Communism: The Iron Guard*).

[151] See Hugh Seton-Watson, *Eastern Europe between the Wars, 1918-1941,* ed a II-a, Cambridge, 1946; Henry L. Roberts, *Rumania. Political Problems of an Agrarian State,* Yale, 1951; Henri Prost, *Destin de la Roumanie (1918-1954),* Paris, 1954; Rene Ristelhueber, S.D. Spector, *A History of the Balkan peoples,* New York, 1971; P. Shapiro, *prelude to Dictatorship in Romania: The National Christian Party in Power, December, 1937-February, 1938,* in "Canadian-American Slavic Review", nr. 1/1974, pp. 45-88; Michelle Rallo, *România în perioada revoluțiilor naționale din Europa (1919-1945),* București, 1933 (Original edition — Roma, 1990, with special concerns about the history of the Legionary Movement).

[152] See S.M. Carrington, *Recuerdos de la Guardia de Hierro,* Madrid, 1969; Carlo Sburlati, *Codreanu il Capitano,* Roma, 1970; idem, *Codreanu el Capitan,* Barcelona, 1970; Paul Guiraud, *Codreanu et la Garde de Fer,* Rio de Janeiro, 1966 (Original edition — Paris, 1940); Ewald Hibbeln, *Codreanu und din Eiserne Garde,* Siegen, 1984; Jean-Paul de Longschamp, *La Garde de Fer ou l'historire d'une bande d'assasins,* Paris, 1975; Gerald F. Bobango, *Religion and Politics: Bishop Valerian Trifa and His Time,* Boulder, 1981.

The Trial of Corneliu Zelea Codreanu

The results of the efforts of these foreign specialists in studying the Legionary Movement created, like a summum of sums, three solid monographs, which at the moment are true works of reference for the subject in our attention. These authors are the American Nicholas M. Nagy-Talavera[153] (originating from Romania), the German Armin Heinen,[154] and the Spanish Francisco Veiga.[155] A result of their systematic work that required deep thinking, and, when it comes to the last two, required elaborate investigations in the German, Spanish, Italian, and French archives, the mentioned works constitute, not just a model, but also the basis for continuing the study of Legionary history and doctrine.

The Green Shirts and the Others by Nagy-Talavera is considered, when it comes to Romania and comparing it to the situation in Hungary, a quality piece of scholarship. Unlike Francisco Veiga, Nagy-Talavera shows a preference for the history of the Legionary Movement, not for analyzing the Legionary ideology. The American historian pictures essential details that outlined the Legionary evolution: the fact that the Legion wanted to remain, and did remain, *a movement*, and *didn't operate as a political party,*[156] just like all the other equivalent fascist groups in interwar Europe; also, the Legion was the only Fascist movement that was profoundly religious and that that used the icon of St. Michael[157] as a protecting symbol, or as part of the opposition, the Legionaries expressed their *faith*, not *a plan.*[158] According to Nagy-Talavera, Corneliu Zelea Codreanu rejected the idea of dictatorship, being a follower of *authoritarianism,*[159] and the nationalism they followed had a mystical nature.[160] The author pictures the political actions of the Legionaries

---

[153] See *The Green Shirts and the others. A History of Fascism in Hungary and Rumania,* pp. 246-344 (especially).

[154] See *Die Legion "Erzengel Michael" in Rumanien...,* cited edition, 558 p. (represents the 1st volume from the series *Sudosteuropaische Arbeiten,* edited by the famous *Sudost-Institut* in Munchen).

[155] See Francesco Veiga, *Istoria Gărzii de Fier, 1919-1941. Mistica ultranaţionalismului,* Bucureşti, Editura Humanitas, 1993, 383 p. (Original edition *La mistica del ultranacionalismo. Historia de la Guardia de Hierro. Rumania, 1919-1941,* Barcelona, 1989).

[156] Nicholas M. Nagy-Talavera, *op. cit...,* p. 266.

[157] *Ibidem,* p. 265.

[158] *Ibidem,* p. 267 and the next.

[159] *Ibidem,* p. 270.

[160] *Ibidem,* p. 271.

with their groups the *Iron Guard* and *All for the Country*, the three dissolutions ordered by I. Mihalache, the Iorga-Argetoianu government, and I.G. Duca, the participation in the elections in 1931-1932, the assassination of I.G. Duca, etc. The years 1934-1935, with the relations between King Carol II, prime minister Gh. Tătărescu, and the Legionary Movement, seemed rather "suspicious"[161] to the author. 1936-1937 — which we knew from other authors as well — were the years of *full ascension* for the Legionary Movement,[162] during which they enjoyed the victory on the 20th of December 1937 in the parliamentary elections (3rd place after P.N.L. and its allies, and after P.N.Ț.).[163] Nagy-Talavera, as well as Andreas Hillgruber earlier[164] and Armin Heinen after him,[165] *didn't discover any evidence related to Hitler financing the Legionary Movement*. On the question: who did it? the author stops at Malaxa, Auschnitt, etc.[166] relating to the situation of the Legionary Movement in the fateful year of 1938, the author doesn't miss the attempts of King Carol II to assassinate Corneliu Zelea Codreanu in February of 1938.[167] By arresting the Captain and a few thousand Legionaries in 1938,[168] including "the whole Legionary elite,"[169] it gave the obvious signal for a "violent persecution," that ended with the crimes of November 1938.[170] Horia Sima, Nagy-Talavera suspects, had a role in this outcome, considering he didn't follow the recommendations the Captain gave them from prison, telling them not to challenge the authorities.[171] The American specialist also focuses on the events between 1938-1940: the assas-

---

[161] *Ibidem*, p. 288.

[162] *Ibidem*, p. 290.

[163] *Ibidem*, p. 293-294.

[164] Cf. Andreas Hillgruber, *op. cit.*, p. 13.

[165] Cf. Armin Heinen, *op. cit.*, p. 322 and the next.

[166] Nicholas M. Nagy-Talavera, *op. cit.*, p.291.

[167] *Ibidem*, p. 298.

[168] *Ibidem*, p. 299.

[169] *Ibidem*.

[170] *Ibidem*, p. 301.

[171] *Ibidem*, pp. 299-301.

The Trial of Corneliu Zelea Codreanu

sination of Armand Călinescu and the reply of Carol II: "the bloodbath," the "massacre" of over 250 Legionaries, among them, the engineer *Gh. Clime*, the leader of the *All for the Country Party* (after the death of General Zizi Cantacuzino-Grănicerul in 1937); *M. Polihroniade*, the expert of the Legionary Movement when it came to problems of foreign policy, Prince *Al. Cantacuzino;* the brilliant lawyer *Alexandru Tell*; Moța's and Marin's armed comrades in Spain — *N. Totu* and *Bănică Dobre;* the lawyer and doctor *Ion Banea*, "probably the most admirable man in the Legion after Codreanu;"[172] the student or youth leaders *Gh. Furdui* or *Gh. Istrate,* and others. Nagy-Talavera concludes: "After this massacre, the Legion was 'like a potato... the best part of it was underground.' *The Iron Guard* was decapitated, with no leaders, when almost a year later it came to power..."[173] A chapter is dedicated to the Legionary-Antonescu Government[174] that ended following the rebellion in January 1941. As a result, "the Legionary Movement — concludes Nagy-Talavera — disappeared from the Romanian scene almost instantly. Grozea and 16 of his companions were tried and executed for participating in the murders at Jilava. In May (1941), the Military Courthouse in Bucharest sentenced 225 Legionaries: 30, including a lieutenant, and 15 police officers received a life sentence; 23 — between 5 and 20 years in prison, and 138 — sentenced for shorter terms; 33 of them were acquitted."[175]

---

[172] *Ibidem*, p. 304.

[173] *Ibidem*.

[174] *Ibidem*, pp. 309-330.

[175] *Ibidem*, p. 329-330. Related to the circumstances in which the assassinations in November 1940 were carried out and the rebellion in January 1941, the Antonescu cabinet later decided to open some investigations, try to punish the guilty ones, as well as publish the results in multiple "white books" (see Președinția Consiliului de Miniștri, *Pe marginea prăpastiei*, I-II, București, 1942; ed. A II-a — 2 vols., București, Editura Scripta, 1992; Comandamentul Militar al Capitalei, *Asasinatele de la Jilava...*, Snagov și Strejnicul. 26-27 Noiembrie 1940, Bucuresti, 1941; ed. A II-a- București, Editura Scripta, 1992). We suggest the reader compare the numbers communicated by Eugen Weber, Nagy-Talavera, etc. With the ones given by the daily paper *Universul* from Bucharest on the 25th of February 1941 (more precisely: 4,638 Legionaries arrested in Bucharest and 4,714 in the rest country) and in the named volumes (especially *Asasinatele...*). Dimitrie Grozea, for example, who was a notorious Communist starting in 1933 and who became a commander in the Legionary Worker's Corp in 1940-1941, was an active participant in the assassinations at Jilava and in the rebellion, and disappeared in January 1941, Bucharest gathering information about him and concluded he fled to... Moscow (*ibidem*, p. 11-12). Therefore, D. Grozea was only sentenced, but not executed, as Nagy Talavera pretends. The documents gathered by Eugen Cristescu (the leader of the infamous S.S.I.) after the rebellion, shows the role D. Grozea had in the Legionary Movement. So, from a source it is

Romanian Crucible

The monograph of the German historian Armin Heinen[176] surpasses, not just through its size, every scientific work on the subject, but also through solidity given by an exceptional documentation, by an adequate layout of the material and the theme presented, by an objective and irreproachable analyses of events and ideas, by the ability to picture essential elements, and communicate conclusive ideas. The structure of the work is ideal for permitting a global discussion on the Legionary Movement: historiography;[177] Romania in the nineteenth century, during World War I and in the interwar period, focusing on the social and political movements and conflicts, on the specific doctrines of the various stages;[178] student antisemitism, LANC and the birth of the Legion (1919-1927);[179] the path of the Legion towards masses (years 1928/1930-1933);[180] the Legionary Movement wins over the masses (1934-1937);[181] Carol II and the Legion (1938);[182] the social "profile" of the Legion;[183] Germany and the Legionaries (1939-1945)[184] and, finally, conclusions, historiographic debates and the Iron Guard in tables, annexes, complete bibliography.[185] Armin Heinen manages to create an excellent analysis of Legionary doctrine in relation to the currents of those times (liberalism, communism, antisemitism, etc.), after the way he precisely captures *all the steps/stages that marked the evolution/decline of the Legionary Movement* in the 1920s until 1945; another special merit of the author is that he consistently delimits the Legionary Movement from the actions of its political groups, and these from the rest of the fascist parties

---

revealed that Grozea, who "had stood out" in the strikers' fights at Grivița in February 1933, had brought the majority of his Communist friends in the Legionary Workers' Corp (see *Osobâi Arhiv,* Moskva, fond 492, opis I, dosar 26/I, f.9 — Safety note from 1ˢᵗ of February 1941).

[176] See *Die Legion "Erzengel Michael" in Rumanien...*, cited edition.

[177] *Ibidem*, pp. 17-39.

[178] *Ibidem*, pp. 40-113.

[179] *Ibidem*, pp. 114-150.

[180] *Ibidem*, pp. 151-256.

[181] *Ibidem*, pp. 257-356.

[182] *Ibidem*, pp. 357-379.

[183] *Ibidem*, pp. 380-414.

[184] *Ibidem*, pp. 451-463.

[185] *Ibidem*, pp. 464-552.

The Trial of Corneliu Zelea Codreanu

or the right-wing ones from Romania. Also, Armin Heinen precisely set the Legionary Movement among the fascist movements of those times. The fundamental conclusion Heinen came to is clear: "In the interwar era, from among all the movements (parties), only the Legion could have been considered as rightly *fascist*. It was the only one that found itself in fundamental opposition with socialism, and in equal measure, with the bourgeoise-capitalist order. Only the Iron Guard had a concept about the new man that was comparable with the fascist one, it was the only one who aimed for a mobilization of masses and made itself known, through words and actions, through the use of force as a political instrument."[186] Reconfirmed by Francisco Veiga on the fact that the Legionarism ended up representing a "mass movement,"[187] Armin Heinen, meticulously confronting the most trustworthy sources, managed to establish the numerical evolution of Corneliu Zelea Codreanu's "militants," more precisely: 1,000 in 1929; 6,000 at the end of 1930; 28,000 in December 1933; 34,000 in May 1935; 96,000 in January 1937, and 272,000 in December 1937.[188] We only stopped on this for a moment to highlight what the distinguished historian Florin Constantiniu declared about Armin Heinen's book, calling it "the most solid foreign research on the Legionary Movement."[189]

Francisco Veiga's book, as mentioned, was translated into Romanian, even though it is the more recent contribution to the history of the Legionary Movement. From the perspective of occurrence, the author proved to be loyal to the older approaches on the history of the Legionary Movement: Greater Romania after World War I — 1918-1919; the Communist danger and the antisemitic turbulences 1920-1922; the establishment of the "new Romanian right" — 1923-1927; from the *Legion* to the *Iron Guard* — 1928-1930; the "heroic years" 1931-1932; Romanian intellectuals and Legionary doctrine — 1932-1933; its implication in state politics — 1933 and the "traumatizing rebirth" of the Legion, 1940-1941. We will mention for the reader some opinions of the Spanish historian that were expressed with the

---

[186] *Ibidem*, p. 461.

[187] Francisco Veiga, *op. cit.,* p. 10.

[188] Armin Heinen, *op. cit.,* p. 382. Cf. Francisco Veiga, *op. cit.,* p. 346 (Heinen's table is reproduced). For those numbers, Heinen also indicates the number of *Legionary nests*: 3,495 in December 1933; 4,200 in May 1935; 12,000 in January 1937, and 34,000 in December 1937 (Armin Heinen, *op. cit.,* p. 382).

[189] Cf. Florin Constantiniu, "Garda de Fier — ieri și astăzi," in *Timpul* (București), nr. 29/1993, p. 8.

48 Romanian Crucible

occasion of a broad study about the history of the Legionary Movement. Thus, Veiga shows that the "Legionary Movement was never a transposition on the exact model of foreign fascism,[190] even less, it didn't even fulfill the role of a "Fifth Column" of Berlin in Bucharest;[191] right from the start, from before they became Legionaries, Corneliu Zelea Codreanu and his comrades were treated with brutality by the Romanian police, which was a common practice in Bucharest;[192] to this, Codreanu's "response" — considers Veiga — was surprising: the assassination of Manciu, about whom — years later — he won't speak of anymore to his followers, but he "never showed any regret;"[193] the decision of Carol II to assassinate Corneliu Zelea Codreanu was taken immediately after his meeting with Hitler, and after the 30th of November 1938 he started the "silent fight" to control the Legionary Movement, which led to the final disaster.[194] The idea of revenge for the Captain's death obsessed the Legionaries, who plotted numerous times to kill the King or Armand Călinescu. On the 21st of September 1939, the prime minister was assassinated by a Legionary squad and Carol II gave them an "excessive" retribution, even by Balkan norms of the twentieth century: within a few hours, the gendarmes shot 252 Legionaries, meaning every head of command."[195] For Veiga, the Legion stands out from a historical perspective as "the most representative and popular" among the far right movements in East-Central Europe," and, finally, appears as having a trajectory "crossed by... contradictions and inconsistencies, and with all these, it formed a *coherent whole, a specific political movement* [italics added]."[196] We consider it appropriate to end our comments on Francisco Vega's book with the portrait of Corneliu Zelea Codreanu made by the Spanish historian.[197] "At 21 years old, his essential personality traits were already defined. His extremely good-looking physique was a sound recommendation: he was tall in a country of short men, athletic,

---

[190] See Francisco Veiga, *op. cit.*, p. 163.

[191] *Ibidem*, p. 10.

[192] *Ibidem*, p. 78.

[193] *Ibidem*, p. 79.

[194] *Ibidem*, p. 257.

[195] *Ibidem*, p. 261.

[196] *Ibidem*, p. 327-328.

[197] *Ibidem*, p. 51.

The Trial of Corneliu Zelea Codreanu

of a classic beauty that was foreign in those times. In a way, all these characterized him as a man of action; he told a militant that lived with him for a time, that "he would prefer to chop wood than write." He never got to be a *zoon politikon*: his most extensive decisions were always impulsive and never clever. In reality, instead of walking past the events he preferred to respond to them: this doesn't necessarily suggest he was naive. His personal file from the Military School in Botoşani defines him from a military point of view, something that labeled him for the rest of his life, as "determined in action and energetic" and qualifies him as a "good troop commander." In other words, he is described as a tenacious man and a good organizer: simple, flexible plans and clear ideas. Among these skills, we can count those for linking and utilizing various influences, ideas and attitudes of different origins that were poorly expressed. Sometimes he appeared to be an especially complex man. In reality, his great success was always owed to his simplicity in conception and achievements."

***

We are obviously convinced that these introductory words, that aimed to capture events, processes, and the ideology that constitute the elements of the Legionary Movement as they appear in the Romanian and foreign historiography, or as we perceive them, have the role of a bibliographic inventory. In the following lines, we want to draw the reader's attention on one of the most important works published in the country, at the time after the collapse of the Communist regime in 1989. First, when it comes to editing documents, we must mention that this activity is only at its beginning,[198] contrary to editing memorialist literature, a situation valid either when it comes to former personalities of the Legionary Movement,[199]

---

[198] See Iuliu Maniu, *Testament moral politic*, ediţie Victor Isac, Bucureşti, Editura "Gândirea Românească," 1991; *Iuliu Maniu în faţa Istoriei*, ediţie Gabriel Ţepelea, Bucureşti, Editura "Gândirea Româneasca," 1993; Duiliu Sfinţescu şi colab., eds., *Corneliu Zelea Codreanu. 1899-1938*, ed. A III-a, f.l., Editura Fundaţiei Buna Vestire, 1933 (on the cover the title is different: *Din luptele tineretului român, 1919-1939. Culegere de texte;* [Liga pentru Apărarea Adevărului Istoric], *Horia Sima şi raporturile lui cu Mişcarea Legionara. Documente*, Bucureşti, 1993, Horia Sima, *Pour la conaissance de la verité. Declaration du Mouvement Legionnaire 1990*, Paris, Editura Dacia, 1992; *Testamentul lui Moţa*, Timişoara, Editura Gordian, 1993 (colecţia "Documente istorice sechestrate"); V. Arimia şi colaboratori, eds., *Istoria P.N.Ţ. Documente, 1926-1947*, Bucureşti, Editura ARC, 1994.

[199] See Nae Ionescu, *Doctrina legionară*, Bucureşti, 1993; Corneliu Zelea Codreanu, *Pentru legionari*, I, Timişoara, Editura Gordian, 1993 (printed edition after the original one, collection "Documente istorice

Romanian Crucible

or to Romanian political leaders of other orientations.[200] The *Journal* of King Carol II (1937-1951) is also available, and has already been used by one of his successors for biographical purposes.[201] When it comes to re-editing, we mention Ştefan Palaghiţă[202] and Horia Sima,[203] or the excelled *Almanah 1994* of "Gazeta de Vest":

---

sechestrate"); Mistor Chioreanu, *Morminte vii*, Iaşi, Institutul European, 1992; Nae Tudorică, *Mărturisiri. În duhul adevărului. Mişcarea Legionară şi Căpitanul aşa cum au fost*, Bacău, Editura Plumb, 1993; Petre Ţuţea, *Între Dumnezeu şi neamul meu*, Bucureşti, 1992; Mircea Eliade, *Memorii*, I-II, Bucureşti, 1991. After Romania was occupied by the Soviet troops and the Communists started taking over the country, the Legionaries started acting through various methods, including fighting with weapons in their hands against the Soviets, and they stood out through the power and will to resist in the Communist dungeons (see Cicerone Ioniţoiu, *Morminte fără cruci*, I-III, Munchen-Freiburg, 1981-1985); Filon Verca, *Paraşutat în România vândută. Mişcarea de rezistenţă, 1944-1948*, Timişoara, Editura Gordian, 1933; Ion Gavrilă-Ogoranu, *Brazii se frâng, dar nu se îndoiesc. Din rezistenţa anticomunistă în Munţii Făgăraş*, I, Timişoara, Editura Marineasa, 1993; Dr. Teofil Mija, *Am fost coleg şi prieten şi Ionel Golea. Pentru memoria lui şi a luptei comune*, cu Prefaţă de Horia Sima, Miami Beach, 1993; D. Bacu, *Piteşti — Centrul de reeducare studenţească*, Bucureşti, Editura Atlantida, 1991 (The author insists on the myths about Iuliu Maniu and C.Z. Codreanu that appeared during the years of Communist oppression and that were carried on by prisoners in the Romanian gulags. Mr. Bacu says about C.Z. Codreanu that "over years of oppression he had become a symbol hard to shatter from the hearts of those students who had been imprisoned, exactly for having accepted to serve his idea of moral healing of the Romanian nation. Both of these personalities [Iuliu Maniu and Corneliu Zelea Codreanu] symbolized for youth the most precious thing the country offered...," p. 107).

[200] See Armand Călinescu, *Însemnari politice, 1916-1939*, Bucureşti, Editura Humanitas, 1990; *Cine a fost Armand Călinescu? Mărturii*, Bucureşti, Editura "Presa Naţională", 1992; Nichifor Crainic, *Zile albe — Zile negre, Memorii*, I, Bucureşti, Casa Editorială "Gândirea", 1991; Mihail Manoilescu, *Memorii*, I-II, Bucureşti, Editura Encilopedică, 1993. Without having manifested a preference for a political party, Radu Lecca played an important role when it came to the connection between the Romanian-German secrets in 1933-1944 (cf. *Eu i-am salvat pe evreii din Romania*, Bucureşti, Editura „Roza Vânturilor," 1994). In his work there are numerous mentions and details about the ties the Legionary Movement had with Berlin, including categorical statements about the Legionaries receiving financial support from the Nazis starting with the 1930s. Lecca didn't have an excellent opinion about Codreanu, whom he had known personally (*ibidem*, p. 86-87), revealed the role that King Carol II played in the assassination of the Captain (*ibidem*, p. 134), and about Horia Sima whom he claimed was an informer for M. Moruzov, the SSR chief (*ibidem*, p. 136).

[201] Cf. Paul al României, *Carol al II-lea, Rege al României*, Bucureşti, Editura Holding Reporter, 1991 (Original edition — London, Methuen, 1988). The same person recently revealed another new writing by King Carol II (*În zodia Satanei. Reflexiuni asupra politicii internationale*, Bucureşti, Editura Universitatea, 1994), finished in 1945. Over the course of multiple pages, the ex-King described, from his point of view, the "Nazi" activities of the Iron Guard and the measures he took against them. (*ibidem*, pp. 90-96. 131-133).

[202] Cf. *Istoria Mişcării Legionare scrisă de un legionar*, cited edition (Bucureşti, 1993).

[203] See *Menirea naţionalismului*, Bucureşti, Editura Vremea Inex, 1993 (colecţia "Fapte, idei, documente").

The Trial of Corneliu Zelea Codreanu

Legiunea Arhanghelului Mihail de la trecut la present.[204] Among the works of analyses and synthesis, we mention the most representative ones[205] that were published before 1989 and were authored by Mircea Muşat and Ion Ardeleanu,[206] Florea Nedelcu,[207] and the late Al. Gh. Savu[208] and Aurică Simion.[209] As we close this introduction, we remember the summary of the Ph.D. thesis presented by Dragoş Nitipir-Zamfirescu on the 25th of February 1944 at the Faculty of History of the University of Bucharest.[210] With great pleasure with reveal the original contributions of a few American historians (Larry L. Watts[211] and Kurt W. Treptow[212]), who carefully examined certain chapters in the history of the Legionary Movement between 1936-1941.

There are many documents and new information (many of them fundamental) that focus on the past of the Legionary Movement, studies and articles, memorialist pages and portraits, bibliographic news, debates, etc. The reader can find them in a series of magazines, such as *Formula As, Noua Dreaptă, Dilema, Cuvântul, Nu,*

---

[204] Timişoara, Editura Gordian, 1993. In *Almanah* are also published more recent materials about the Legionary Movement.

[205] For an account of the period, cf. Teodor I. Amon, *Guardia di Ferro,* cited edition; I. Agrigoroaiei, *Noi rezultate în analiza critică a fascismului în România,* in "Anuarul Institutului de Istorie şi Arheologie" "A.D. Xenopol," Iaşi, t. IX/1972, pp. 511-522.

[206] Cf. Mircea Muşat, Ion Ardeleanu, *România după Marea Unire,* I, *1918-1933;* II. *1933-1940,* Bucureşti, Editura Ştiinţifică şi Enciclopedică, 1986-1988.

[207] Cf. *De la Restauraţie la dictatură regală. Din viaţa politică a României, 1930-1938,* Cluj-Napoca, Editura Dacia, 1976.

[208] Cf. *Dictatura regală (1938-1940),* Bucureşti, Editura Politică, 1970.

[209] Cf. *Regimul politic în România în perioada Septembrie 1940 - Ianuarie 1941,* Cluj-Napoca, Editura Dacia, 1976.

[210] See *Legionarismul românesc — fenomen de extremă dreaptă. Sincronism european şi aspecte specifice,* Bucureşti, 1994, 30 pg. dact.

[211] Cf. Larry L. Watts, *Romanian Cassandra: Ion Antonescu and the Struggle for Reform, 1916-1941,* Boulder-New York, East European Monographs, Columbia University Press, 1933.

[212] Kurt W. Treptow, *Corneliu Zelea Codreanu and Carol II,* in "Europa XXI" (Iaşi), I-II/1992-1993, pp. 61-64.

Romanian Crucible

Zig-Za, Totuşi iubirea, and especially in *Gazeta de Vest,*[213] *Mişcarea,*[214] and *Învierea*[215] or in the short-lived *Garda de Fier.*[216]

***

Before we end this introduction, we consider a historical sketch of the political context in which Corneliu Zelea Codreanu's trial occurred in May 1938 would prove useful for the reader.

The elections in December 1937 and the annulled elections scheduled for March 1938, signaled the end of the quasi-democratic political system in Romania. A decisive factor in these events was the relationship between the Legion of Archangel Michael and its leader, Corneliu Zelea Codreanu, with King Carol II during this period — years of significant importance in the history of interwar Romania.

The democratic political system in Romania ended at the command of King Carol II, who unilaterally revoked the Constitution of 1923 and established a royal dictatorship on the 10th of February 1938, an idea that obsessed him ever since he took the throne in 1930. Hoping to establish a royal dictatorship with support from the population, the King tried to reel in the Legionary Movement that was gaining influence in the 1930s. As Constantin Argetoianu noted in his journal, starting from 1934, "the King talks approvingly about the Iron Guard and about the Legionary current; he considered this could be channeled in order to popularize an activist government."[217]

While Carol was impressed by the growing power of the Legionary Movement, Codreanu was becoming an open opponent of the obvious corruption of the royal

---

[213] Edited in Timişoara, 97 numbers 1990-May 1994. Director — Ovidiu Guleş; Editors — Mihaela Marin, Emil Lungu, Adrian Onea, and Radu Dan Vlad.

[214] It's publication started in March 1992, in Bucharest, with the slogan "Publicaţie a noii generaţii" (Publication for the New Generation). Editor — "Mişcarea pentru România." First-editor — George Roncea; Secretary editor — Bogdan Munteanu.

[215] Two numbers were published at once — nr. 1/ Ianuarie-Martie 1993; nr. 2/ Aprilie-Iunie 1993. Editor: Dr. Şerban Milcoveanu.

[216] Only one number was published with the mention "Ziar al Mişcării Legionare — Legiunea Arhanghelului Mihail — Garda de Fier," 1991. We suspect this was a pirate number, through which they aimed to compromise certain political groups in contemporary Romania.

[217] ISISP, Constantin Argetoianu, *Pentru cei de mâine*, partea VIII, anul 5/2, colecţia 8,608, pp. 3,123-3,124.

The Trial of Corneliu Zelea Codreanu

circle. Argetoianu noted in 1935, after the birth of the political party *All for the Country*, that "the Legionary Movement was seriously leaning towards Maniu's plan, and distancing itself from His Royal Majesty."[218] This evolution didn't stop Carol from trying to bring the Legionary Movement over to his side in his effort to establish an authoritarian dictatorship. He started increasing his secret financial support for the Guard's activity — especially during the Congress of Legionary Students that was held in Târgu Mureș in April 1936 — hoping to win Codreanu over to his side. Shortly after this Congress, the King invited the Legionary Movement's leaders to a secret meeting, an invitation that was refused on the spot, with the explanation that "the Guard doesn't conduct secret activities."[219] Carol persisted in his efforts and, in February 1937, Codreanu finally accepted to meet secretly with the King. Codreanu described the meeting to Zaharia Boilă, one of the PNȚ leaders:

"A few weeks ago, I was called for an audience with the King. It happened during the night, at a private residence. The King told me, before anything else, that he is sympathetic to our Movement, and he thinks about dismissing the government, installing a personal absolutist governing, based on the Legionary Movement. The King asked me to declare him as the 'Movement's Captain,' with me being his sub-lieutenant and that he'd name me the leader of the government.

I told him I'm delighted with his kindness towards our Movement and I'm extremely humbled by his favorable appreciation, that was even exaggerated, that he expressed for my person, but, however, I cannot accept his offer. I consider that enthusiasm and discipline are not sufficient to assume the responsibility of holding government, that we're not yet ready, that we don't have the experience, and that when it comes to the problem of leadership, we consider the King as the highest factor, an arbiter over all of us, but that we can't consider him as the movement's or the party's leader, considering the Legionaries swore fealty to me and not to someone else, that this faith, this attachment, can't turn into an

---

[218] Quote from Florea Nedelcu, "Pactul de neagresiune electorală — origini și consecințe asupra evoluției vieții politice," in *Împotriva fascismului*, edited by Ion Popescu-Puturi and Valter Roman, București, 1971, p. 73.

[219] ISISP, Constantin Argetoianu, *Însemnari zilnice*, colecția 104, dosar 5615, p. 828; also see Florea Nedelcu, "Carol al II-lea și Garda de Fier: De la relații amicale la criză, 1930-1937," in *Studii: Revistă de Istorie*, XXIV:5 (1971), p. 1,019.

Romanian Crucible

object of political traffic. Carol II tried to convince me that my perspective is wrong, but, even if he spoke to me a lot, bringing arguments to support his idea, he couldn't convince me."[220]

Shortly after his failure to convince Codreanu to join him, Carol II created a Ministry of Public Order, naming the chief of the Bucharest police at its helm, Gabriel Marinescu. Marinescu's mission, as Armand Călinescu noted in his journal, was to "suppress Codreanu and other 30 main figures of the Guard. He formed teams of 20 convicts [each], which he used to lead an attack during a night. He was convinced that if they don't attach them through the element of surprise first, he and the King would fall victim to them."[221] Codreanu realized he was in danger after refusing Carol's proposal and wrote his political testament in which he declared:

> "When I won't be with you anymore, listen to this man [Iuliu Maniu]. No matter what ideological differences you have, this man is the most enlightened and the most just. Maybe the only just one. It would be terrible to be left as gifts in the arms of men that are artificially close to our ideology, but dishonest at heart and false. This decision remains for you with the power of a testament."[222]

While relations with the Royal Palace were getting worse and worse, the relations with PNȚ and the All for the Country Party were becoming closer as elections neared, ending with an electoral pact on the 25th of November 1937.

> "Between the undersigned parties an accord is created with the purpose of defending freedom and ensuring the fairness in elections. These parties sign a pact of nonaggression for the time of the current elections, for the suggested purpose.
>
> The nonaggression pact means eliminating violent acts and speech and disparagement; but it doesn't prevent stating their own ideologies and proper debates.
>
> The other parties will be notified to join this pact as well.

---

[220] Zaharia Boilă, *Memorii*, in *Din luptele tineretului român, 1919-1939 (Culegere de texte)*, cited edition, pp. 237-239.

[221] Armand Călinescu, *Însemnari politice, 1916-1939*, cited edition, p. 338-339.

[222] From a letter from Dr. Ciorogariu and Dumitrescu-Zăpadă to Iuliu Maniu, quote from Pompiliu Pop-Mureşan, *Adevărul despre Iuliu Maniu*, Bucureşti, 1946, p. 123. Also see *Procesul conducătorilor fostului Partid Naţional-Ţărănesc*, Bucureşti, 1948, p. 18; Larry Watts, *Romanian Cassandra: Ion Antonescu and the Struggle for Reform, 1916-1941*, ed. cited, p. 152; Elizabeth Baker, *British Policy in South-East Europe in the Second World War*, New York, 1976, p. 76.

The Trial of Corneliu Zelea Codreanu

A joint committee will establish the way to proceed and the steps that will need to be taken for possible future violations."[223]

This pact represented a great blow to King Carol II, because it included a great number of the parties in opposition, first, the National Liberal Party, Gheorghe Brătianu's wing and Agrarian Party of Constantin Argetoianu. Even the Jewish Party led by Wilhelm Filderman was affiliated with this pact.[224] Despite the statements of recent historiography, this electoral pact didn't discourage the democratic opposition, rather it strengthened it — a prelude for the failure of Tătărescu's government to obtain 40% of votes it needed to maintain its majority in Parliament.

Carol realized the National Liberal Party was in danger and, before organizing the elections, which were mandatory after a period of four years according to the Constitution of 1923; he suggested that Ion Mihalache and the National Peasants' Party form a government and organize the elections. The King noted in his journal:

"At the end of November finished the legislature, the first that has fulfilled the normal and legal term of 4 years for many years past. This means new elections have to be organized [...]

Considering that personal relations didn't allow a good collaboration with Maniu, I called for Mihalache, asking him to form the government, giving him one condition to collaborate with some of the right-wing nationalist elements, like the ones grouped around Vaida-Voevod. I did this and explained why, because in these moments, when the extremist elements of the Iron Guard are taking off, I consider a nationalist side should be present in the government, but this mustn't be the Guard, so that it could be dissolved. Mihalache however, makes the mistake to leave my home in the morning and consult with his friends, and before I contacted Vaida-Voevod, he refused my proposal that evening. It was a stupid political maneuver, because I'm convinced that Vaida wouldn't have agreed to collaborate with elements that are too democratic, knowing his opinion around Mihalache and Maniu. He would have been the one to appear in a bad light in front of me. He wouldn't have called to the nationalist elements, who, refusing, wouldn't have had the right to consider themselves cast aside. Pure national-peasants would have had in this way the most powerful weapon

---

[223] Apud V. Arimia și colaboratori, eds., *Istoria P.N.Ț. Documente, 1926-1947*, cited edition, p. 173-*174*.

[224] Larry L. Watts, *Romanian Cassandra*, p. 155.

56   Romanian Crucible

for their governing. The relentless Maniu-Madgearu, their lack of political suppleness made this plan of mine to fall in the water [...]

So, I decided to call Tătărescu to continue the governing and organize the elections; with all the opposition from Dinu Brătianu and, even though there were considerations that pleaded against it, after 4 years the party [P.N.L.] was worn out, and even like that he agreed and the elections happened in the middle of December."[225]

Because the parties that organized the elections in Romania didn't usually lose them, Carol believed the liberals could keep their place in the elections that were relatively free. It was a decision that he would come to regret. We mustn't think the elections in 1937 occurred in a completely free environment, because the government tried to somehow influence the results in its favor. For example, Armand Călinescu noted in his journal on the 13th of December 1937:

"The national-peasant meeting in <<Marna>>, where Maniu was supposed to have a speech, is prevented with tear gas by the police officers."[226]

General politics allowed the elections to take place relatively free, in an environment that was improved through the nonaggression pact between Maniu, Codreanu, and Brătianu. And more so because of certain changes in Tătărescu's government before the electoral campaign began: "Franasovici was brought to the Ministry of Internal Affairs through a shuffle," Carol II stated in his journal; "he was an internal state sub secretary during the time of Ionel Brătianu and Duca, he was familiar with this job, but he was also supporting the withdrawal from the government. It seems to me that he didn't try too hard, giving the excuse his recommendations for the elections to be fair and the result was the defeat of the government."[227]

The election results from the 20th of December 1937 were as follows:[228]

---

[225] Carol II, *Jurnal (inedit)*, volumul I, Centrul de Istorie și Civilizație Europeană, Academia Română — Filiala Iași, pp. 98, 100.

[226] Armand Călinescu, *Însemnari politice*, pp. 361-362.

[227] Carol II, *Jurnal (inedit)*, vol. I, Centrul de Istorie și Civilizație Europeană. Academia Română — Filiala Iași, p. 99.

[228] C. Enescu, *Semnificația alegerilor din decembrie 1937 în evoluția politică a neamului românesc*, in *Sociologia românească*, II: 11-12 (November-December 1937).

The Trial of Corneliu Zelea Codreanu

National-Liberal Party	1,103,353	35.93%
National-Peasant Party	626,612	20.40%
All for the Country Party	478,368	15.58%
National-Christian Party	281,167	9.15%
Hungarian Party	136,139	4.43%
National-Liberal Party (Gheorghe Brătianu)	119,361	3.89%
Radical-Peasant Party	69,198	2.25%
Agrarian Party	52,101	1.70%
Jewish Party	43,681	1.42%
German People's Party	43,412	1.42%
Social-Democrat Party	28,840	0.94%
People's Party	25,567	0.83%
Labor's Front Party	6,986	0.23%
Other 53 groups and independent lists	11,145	0.36%
TOTAL	3,026,140	98.52%
Cancelled ballots at the end of the election	45,555	1.48%
Total voters	3,071,695	100%

After the surprising failure in the elections for Tătărescu's liberals and because it was impossible for him to collaborate with Maniu or Codreanu, Carol II assigned the poet Octavian Goga to form the new government, despite the fact that the National-Christian Party had won only 9% of votes and had a strong antisemitic plan.[229]

We must mention that for Codreanu and the Legionary Movement, antisemitism wasn't a primary focus and from areas with a large Jewish population, with a long

---

[229] See Carol II, *Jurnal (inedit)*, vol. I, Centrul de Istorie și Civilizație Europeană, Academia Română — Filiala Iași, pp. 101-102.

tradition for antisemitism, the All for the Country Party received a very small percent of votes, while the National-Christian Party had the greatest success in those regions (especially in Bessarabia and the counties in north of Moldova).

The new Goga-Cuza government instituted censorship, forbidding newspapers such as *Adevărul, Dimineața,* and *Lupta,* and adopted a series of Anti-Jewish laws.[230] With the King's permission, they started a campaign of violence and terror against the Legionary Movement, a fact that made Codreanu and his party withdraw from the electoral campaign on 8th of February 1938.[231] After being assured protection from the Minister of Defense, General Ion Antonescu, Codreanu promised not to challenge them. It was a policy he publicly declared in Bucharest on the 21st of February:

> "We announce to our members that starting today 21st of February 1938, the All for the Country Party is no more.
>
> The entire leadership agreed that the reason for the Party's existence ended [...]
>
> We agreed to act within the law, manifesting our beliefs.
>
> If we can't do this, and if every act of faith is forbidden to us, the reason for our party's existence was put to an end.
>
> We don't want to use force.
>
> We don't want to use violence.
>
> For us it is enough the experience from the past, when without our will, we were dragged on the path of violence. To whatever violence comes our way we won't retort: we bear it. Even when the whole Romanian nation is treated like a herd of senseless animals.
>
> We don't want to overthrow the government.
>
> Through the essence of our ideology we are not against this system. It is a sudden attitude of an external nature, while we expect our victory to come from the people's souls, through a process of human perfecting.

---

[230] Armand Călinescu, *Însemnări politice,* p. 365.

[231] This plan to use violence against the Legionary Movement during the electoral campaign was initiated by the Minister of Internal Affairs Armand Călinescu (see Armand Călinescu, *Însemnari politice,* pp. 368-373).

The Trial of Corneliu Zelea Codreanu

We will not use these means, because the youth of today have the conscience and responsibility of its historic mission too embedded in its heart, because it resumes reckless acts, which could turn Romania into bloody Spain.

Our whole generation sees well the glove that was thrown to it.

The thrown glove will, however, remain on the ground.

We refuse to pick it up.

The hour of our victory didn't yet come. It's still their time. If the generation of our elders thinks it's better this way, we cannot interfere to lecture them.

They are the ones to the blame in front of God and history."[232]

Unsuccessful in trying to provoke Codreanu to violence, which would have allowed for a reciprocal response, Carol II continued his campaign against the Legionaries through intermediaries, such as Nicolae Iorga, who, after condemning the Movement's activities, especially the Legionary trade, received a letter from Codreanu, in which he accused him of having a "dishonest soul:"

When 15 years ago the youth noisily rallied against the Jewish domination (none more noisily than Mr. Iorga in 1906), the men of today, these men from today's government, were telling us: 'This is not the way to solve the Jewish problem. Start trading. Trade like they do.' So, we started doing it. With hope in our hearts. With a mind for work. However, when you saw us starting, when you saw that we're fair and capable, that our work is blessed by God, you all come and destroy this Romanian trade in its infancy, maybe the most serious one of our time, you come without mercy and suppress this attempt, along with all our enthusiasm and all our hope."[233]

Because Iorga was a minister in the government led by the Patriarch Miron Cristea, the internal affairs minister, Armand Călinescu, suggested that Zelea Codreanu should be sued for slander. The leader of the Legionaries was arrested on 16 April 1938, tried, and sentenced to six months in prison.[234] A month later, between 23 and 26 May, followed the famous trial of Codreanu for treason, where

---

[232] See Circulara nr. 148 from the 21st of February 1938, in *Legiunea Arhanghelului Mihail de la trecut până în prezent*, Gazeta de Vest — Almanah, 1994, cited edition, pp. 197-198.

[233] From Codreanu's letter to Nicolae Iorga, 26th of March 1938, (see annex I). See *Legiunea Arhanghelului Mihail...*, p. 200 and *Din luptele tineretului român*, pp. 109-111.

[234] Armand Călinescu, *Însemnări politice*, p.388.

60 Romanian Crucible

he had, as witnesses for his defense, Ion Antonescu and Iuliu Maniu, a trial that ended with a sentence for the leader of the Legionary Movement to ten years of forced labor, despite any evidence of treason.[235] Finally, at the end of November of the same year, Carol II decided Codreanu must be executed, and he was executed on the King's orders, along with 13 other Legionary leaders, under the pretext of trying to escape while they were transferred from the prison in Râmnicu Sărat to Jilava.[236]

The loss of their leader profoundly marked the activity of the Legionary Movement. The violent evolution of the Iron Guard, under Horia Sima's leadership, can be directly attributed to the Royal politics from 1937-1938. The political maturity shown by Codreanu during these times was never seen again while Horia Sima led the Guard. The American journalist R.G. Waldeck observed in 1940 that after the Legion's royal persecution in 1938-1939 *"almost nothing was left of the Guard's leadership; they were mass murdered in the last two years and the only ones left alive were the third and fourth rank leaders... Basically, the entire elite of the Movement was killed."*[237]

Finally, we agree with the American journalist Waldeck who noticed that *"Carol's jealousy with Codreanu caused the vicious circle of revenge and violence that stained his rule... The wild jealousy of Carol stemmed from the fact that C.Z. Codreanu was and did everything that Carol wished to be and do. Even from 1920, when it was first heard of Mussolini, Carol wished to create a fascist movement in Romania. But Codreanu was the one who created this fascist movement. Carol wished to be loved by his people, especially by the youth. But Codreanu was the Prince Charming that stole the hearts of his people, especially of the youth. Carol wished to be a tribune in the Romanians' imagination, instead of being a king. But Codreanu was the tribune who was a martyr as well as a prophet in the Romanians' imagination... The path to the collapse of Carol's reign can be followed back,*

---

[235] For details about the "trial" in May 1938, see Faust Bradesco, *La Garde de Fer et le terrorisme*, cited edition, pp. 167-175. The sentence was communicated to Corneliu Zelea Codreanu on the 27th of May 1938, at 4 o'clock. (see Anexa II, *Însemnări de la Jilava*).

[236] *Din luptele tineretului român*, p. 179.

[237] R.G. Waldeck, *Athene Palace*, New York, National Travel Cluj, 1942, pp. 36, 197.

The Trial of Corneliu Zelea Codreanu

through the darkness of blood and hate, to the King's jealous for Corneliu Codreanu. "[238]

***

In conclusion, we must say that the problem with the history of the Legionary Movement is a much greater than one might be tempted to believe, or as those interested would rush to suggest. The renowned literature on the subject, if uneven, is vast. Adding to this the fact that the internal archives are barely just now starting to be investigated, we can conclude that the true history of the Legionary Movement remains a future objective, one that is absolutely necessary. Fulfilling this scientific objective definitely requires abandoning, before anything else, the approach to Legionary phenomenon and Legionary ideology by using only one of two colors — either white, or black. Unfortunately, this simple and unscientific approach has been used too often up to now and it has compromised even serious historical research. We do not believe that even a skillful combination of these two colors would change the situation. The only way to get at the truth is to confront the history of Legionary Movement objectively, within global parameters and in segments, while studying it from a Romanian and European perspective, with an interdisciplinary spirit and with the conscious thought of risking to discover white where black predominated, and vice versa!

This volume represents, in the editor's mind, a first step to one such approach to the history of the Legionary Movement. The transcripts of the trial are taken from two main sources: the Bucharest newspaper *Universul* (an account that was censored by the Carol's authorities) and the book secretly published by the Legionary Movement in August 1938: *Adevărul în Procesul Corneliu Zelea Codreanu.*[239] Because it was created using multiple sources,[240] this text represents the most complete and balanced version of Corneliu Zelea Codreanu's trial published to date.

---

[238]R.G. Waldeck, *Athene Palace*, p. 29.

[239]The book was republished in a complete edition after 40 years: Mişcarea Legionară, *Adevărul în procesul Căpitanului*, colecţia "Omul Nou", Miami Beach, 1980, p. 250.

[240]We also suggest that the reader consult the text included in the volume *Din luptele tineretului român*, 1919-1939, pp. 273-411.

The editors want to thank the following people for their help with getting this volume ready for publication: Corina Luca, Stela Cheptea, Marcela Vultur, and Marius Bucur. For the English edition, we would also like to thank Diana Livesay for her work on the translation from the Romanian original.

The Trial of
Corneliu Zelea Codreanu
May, 1938

FINAL ORDINANCE

for the Arraignment of Corneliu Zelea Codreanu for Treason, Conspiracy Against the Social Order, and Rebellion

Ministry of National Defense
Military Courthouse of Army Corps II
Cabinet 5 Instruction

Year 1938, Month May, Day 16

We, Major Magistrate Dan Pascu, instruction judge of Cabinet 5 from the Military Courthouse of Army Corps II: given the prosecution order nr. 30,066 from the 7th of May 1932 and the prosecution order nr. 30,596 from the 12th of May 1938 of the General Commander of Army Corp I; given the instruction documents gathered and presented against Corneliu Zelea Codreanu, 38 years old, born in Iaşi, lawyer by profession, married, residing in Bucureştii Noi, Nicolescu Dorobanţu Street, Nr. 38, currently serving a sentence of 6 months in prison for contempt,[1] prosecuted for treason and the public reproduction of documents threatening state security, provided and compiled in art. 191, points 1 and 2 of the Penal Code of Carol II, combined with art. 190 of the same code, the offense of conspiring against the social order provided and compiled by art. 210, paragraph 1 P.C., all combined with art. 101 in P.C. and Royal Decree Nr. 856/938, regarding the state of siege.

Considering the indictment by the Military Prosecutor, which suggests the defendant be arraigned in the Military Courthouse of Army Corp II, for the crimes shown above;

On the established facts we ascertain:

Romanian Crucible

In fact, during the search made at the residence of the defendant, Corneliu Zelea Codreanu, from Bucureștii Noi, Niculescu Dorobanțu Street, nr. 38, at the Green House (*Casa Verde*), the headquarters of the former All for the Country political party, they found information and documentary materials that reveal the nature, means, and purposes of Corneliu Z. Codreanu's political activity, as well as the organizing means and activities of the organizations led by the defendant. During the raids and the searches made at the residences of various leaders of this political organization, in the Capital and in the rest of the country, they found informative material that shows the same situation: the existence of a vast political organization, under different forms, under the leadership of Corneliu Zelea Codreanu, directed from the headquarters in Bucureștii Noi, Casa Verde, and from Gutenberg Str., Nr. 3, Bucharest.

From the examination of the discovered evidence, the following facts and states of fact were precisely established: the so-called Legionary organization within the whole country, in nests and bigger units than these, has an occult nature, secret, and is only known to a small minority of Legionary leaders. In truth, the evidence of secrecy is made not only by the police officers and gendarmes who observed it, but also by documents shown by Legionary leaders. For this, we quote: "Nr. 37 circular for the leaders of regions and counties," regarding the organization, and that has an output number matching the headquarters on Gutenberg Str, specifically 60/936 (file Nr. 14 res. Col. C. Stănescu, p. 114). This circular contains the following fragment: "So, I ask you to read and carefully study the next template belonging to the so-called battle order of each unit, made after the army's mobilization system, whose work has to be, of course, absolutely secret." Another example from a circular belonging to All for the Country Party, from the organization in Vlașca county (file nr. 15, Eng. Clime, p. 259), says the following: "No nest will keep its own archives, but they will be given, through the leader of the nest, to the county center." "Also, the unit leaders, aside from the elements that are absolutely necessary, they cannot keep any report or document regarding the situation of the Legionaries and our organization, therefore they will send everything on to the county center. Explanations will be given in person by the undersigned. It is preferable for every piece of correspondence to be sent through a courier."

As contradictory as it might seem, it is a well-established fact that the defendant, Corneliu Zelea Codreanu, as a leader of the Legionary movement, tried and man-

The Trial of Corneliu Zelea Codreanu

aged, to some extent, by copying the Communist system in organizing the red pupil, to organize secretly among the pupils of middle school within the country, groups of the organization called the Brotherhood of the Cross (*F.D.C. — Frăția de Cruce*). To exemplify it, we'll refer to file Nr. 17, Stoia Gheorghe, p. 30. Through a Report, the chief of F.D.C. group Nr 14 to the F.D.C. Commandment says: I use this way to report the actual situation and the activity of F.D.C. group Nr 14. Group Nr. 14 contains the F.D.C. groups from six schools from the 4th Green Sector, and the situation is as follows:

1. The Superior School of Arts and Crafts Polizu has: F.D.C. Nicador serving from last spring and with a group of six brothers of the cross. A group of 15 friends, among which some are qualified to join the F.D.C.

2. Marele Voievod Mihail High School, with a group of 5 friends, among which 2 have been serving for one year.

3. Gheorghe Lazăr High School has a group made of 5 friends, among which 2 are former members of the old F.D.C Sterie Ciumetti, which was dissolved.

4. National College Sf. Sava has a group of 3 friends.

Sf. Iosif, which is mostly attended by foreigners, is signaled to be sympathetic to the cause, but they didn't form the group yet.

Aurel Vlaicu High School doesn't have any organized group.

However, all these F.D.C. groups work according to the F.D.C. regulation. On the day they celebrated the Legion they held a festive meeting."

On page 20 of the same file, we find: "The picture of the situation of the 8th grade A students, by origin and intellect."

On page 28 of the same file, we find a sheet — monthly report on the statistical situation of the Sterie Ciumetti group.

On page 78, we find a report signed by Alexandru Păunescu, "the leader of the group of friends from Sf. Sava, to the commander of Group 4," that contains a table with the names of students from different classes together with their residence addresses.

Another secret Legionary organization was founded on the 13th of January 1938, through the constitutive act written and signed by the defendant Corneliu Z. Codreanu, an organization called the Moța-Marin Legionary Corp, that consisted of 10,000 members.

On the 6th of November 1936, another secret association was born, called Friends of the Legionaries, an association that proves its inclination to conspiracies in its own statutes, where, in the chapter called 'Conditions for Registration,' the following rules are written: point III says about the friends of the Legionaries: "they don't know each other, and they never meet up;" point V: "the first meeting of these people will be held on the day of victory. Then they will be summoned by their name by the leader of the Legion, will be known by the Legionaries and celebrated by the entire nation," and at point VI: "they have an order number and a password" (file nr. 12, Al. Cantacuzino, p. 130).

This organization, according to its spirit of conspiracy, recruited members that were hiding under fake names and numbers, also bringing financial support to the Legionary Movement in the same way.

To emphasize the fact that the Legionary Movement and its leader, Corneliu Z. Codreanu made a habit of using secrecy and hiding their identity; we mention that even after the Iron Guard was dissolved on 9 December 1933, its activity did not stop, and it kept working through the same methods that caused it to be dissolved in the first place; more than that, its leader, Corneliu Z. Codreanu, openly showed the same nature of terrorism and conspiracy when he founded the new group All for the Country, as we are going to prove with documents released by the defendant Corneliu Z. Codreanu.

Therefore, through the agenda Nr. 1 from 25 September 1934, signed by Corneliu Z. Codreanu (file nr. 15, Eng. Clime, p. 155), circular that the defendant admitted to, he communicated the decision taken by the Honorary Council of the Iron Guard through which Mihail Stelescu was permanently removed from the Guard for "high treason."[2] Through the same agenda, point III, the defendant Corneliu Z. Codreanu says: "through the power given by my position as leader of the Iron Guard, I give Stelescu the right to, etc..."

Also, Corneliu Z. Codreanu signed the agenda Nr. 2, dated 25 September 1934, through which the Legionary Cotea Vasile is removed from this organization (file nr. 15, Eng. Clime, p. 200), and through the agenda Nr. 3, Corneliu Z. Codreanu gives a whole series of orders to dissolve some of the cores of the Iron Guard and remove other Legionaries for a period of three years: Tcaciuc, Petrescu, and Mazilescu (file nr. 15, Eng. Clime, p.201). These orders were admitted to without reserve by the defendant Corneliu Z. Codreanu.

The Trial of Corneliu Zelea Codreanu

The evidence of the secret activity of the dissolved organization the Iron Guard is also given by the call from 1934 of the now deceased General Cantacuzino,[3] through which they announced the establishment of the political party All for the Country on 10 December 1934, a document that starts: "My political leader, Corneliu Z. Codreanu, told me: Mr. General, on 10 December 1934, the legal term was fulfilled, after which you had the right to request an electoral sign and establish a political party. Therefore, I ask you to found a new party, for all those who believe in a new Romania, in order for them to have legal political activity". "I keep my old position — today illegal — in the Iron Guard, as I can't leave it, because I consider it was dissolved unjustly and without any legal justification."[4]

In the status of organization of the All for the Country Party (file nr. 14, rez. Col. Stănescu, p. 111) a double organization of the Legionary Movement is found. One with an electoral political character, organized by functions, with the following hierarchy: nest leader, leader of more nests, garrison leader, team leader, planning leader, county leader, and political party leader, with various other side functions: general secretary, secretary, Legionary judge, clerk, and archivist.

Parallel with this organization on functions, which had an electoral nature, the statute has an organization on ranks, which is the disguised side of the Iron Guard, which in the past was confused with the Archangel Michael[5] organization. The ranks of the disguised organization of the Iron Guard provided by the statute are: member, Legionary, Legionary instructor, assistant commander, Legionary commander, member in the Legionary Senate, commander of the Legion. The leader of the political party All for the Country was General Cantacuzino, and after him, Engineer Clime,[6] but the leader of the Legion remained Corneliu Z. Codreanu.

The evidence of subordination of the legal electoral political party to the real and illegal political party, meaning the subordination of the All for the Country Party to the Iron Guard or, more precisely, of General Cantacuzino at first and of Engineer Clime later to the Captain, Corneliu Z. Codreanu, results in the entire functional mechanism of these two organisms. Is sufficient to say that every order, report, decree, etc. ends with the slogan: 'Long live the Legion and the Captain.'

Besides, the defendant himself admits to being the leader of the Legionary Movement and that there is a dependency of the party leaders on their leader. As a result, it is certain that, since Corneliu Z. Codreanu admits the whole political, economic, and cultural activity of All for the Country Party was subordinated to him; it is suggested that the one in discussion was maintaining the activity of the Iron

Romanian Crucible

Guard as he chose to maintain it, "from the old position" — illegal — of the Iron Guard which he stated he couldn't leave. Therefore, he continued the secret activity of an organization that had been dissolved, for the purpose of putting in danger the security of the State and the internal order. We mention as a final and irrefutable proof that the defendant Corneliu Z. Codreanu was the sole leader of the entire Legionary Movement in all its activities the following two pieces of evidence:

1. A circular written and signed in his own hand by Corneliu Z. Codreanu, on 22 August 1937, with a mention from General Cantacuzino — Predeal, a circular that was sent to newspapers to be published by Corneliu Z. Codreanu, in the name of General Cantacuzino. This circular couldn't have been signed by substitution by Corneliu Z. Codreanu, without General Cantacuzino being a subordinate to him. From this, it results that the whole leadership of the Legionary Movement was so focused around C.Z. Codreanu, that even the orders signed and sent by General Cantacuzino had to be written and signed by C.Z. Codreanu as well, but under the name of General Cantacuzino.

2. The second piece of evidence that shows General Cantacuzino's subordination to Corneliu Z. Codreanu is the photograph that we can find in file Nr. 19, in which you can see Corneliu Z. Codreanu awarding the leader of All for the Country Party. Of course, General Cantacuzino must have been a subaltern of the one that was awarding him, an act done by C.Z. Codreanu by disregarding the Constitution and the laws of the country. As a result of the conspiratorial activity unleashed in the middle of the Legionary Movement, we show as an example the following phrase found in a report of the nest leader Alcazar, from Romanați county (file nr. 19, p. 328): "Either way, people know a new king was chosen: Codreanu." In pursuing the ultimate goal of the Legionary organization and activity: the Legionary revolution, the defendant C.Z. Codreanu did not organize military units, as a formation, as well as training and discipline. The foundation of the Legionary Corp Moța-Marin, in 13 garrisons of the Legionary corps, in military formation and discipline, as it clearly results from *Îndreptarul Corpului Legionar Moța-Marin*, with annotations from C.Z. Codreanu; the establishment of the Legionary corps of former soldiers, as well as the fact that all nest leaders had military training, proves that with paramilitary organizations they wanted to suppress the legal authority with violence at the right time.

To complete their arsenal that would be used to overthrow the government or to start a Legionary revolution, the defendant used the last method to suppress the

The Trial of Corneliu Zelea Codreanu

state: terrorism, which is a distinctive mark of the political regimes that have been overthrown in decades past. The terrorist training of the Legionaries was done by the defendant, especially when it came to its financial component. The moral, psychological side of terrorism, was conducted up to now through the following acts and doings:

1. The Nicadors' promotion,[7] the assassins of Prime Minister I.G. Duca (Constantinescu, Belimace, Caranica) at the rank of commanders in the Buna Vestire Legion, The promotion to the same rank of two of ten of the assassins of Stelescu. The facts were admitted to by the defendant.

2. Honors were awarded to the Nicadors (Constantinescu, Belimace, Caranica); a fact that was also admitted to by the defendant.

3. Material rewards for them (file nr. 1 and 16, Ogrinja)

4. The Nicador's Song:

> *All three we started in a thought*
> *And bound ourselves by oath*
> *To avenge our comrades*
> *And save our country.*

> *V*

> *The Archangel helped us*
> *To punish the culprit.*

5. The Legionary oaths: the Iron Guard Legionary oath.

"I swear in front of God to pursue, until the end of my days, these killers, their families, to give them the punishment that they deserve in front of God and in front of the Romanian nation" (file vol. IX, Casa Verde, p. 806).

6. The circular with instructions and exhortations for violence.

A way of thinking specific to the Legionary leaders concerning the use of violent acts, had to be present in the mind of all Legionaries, a morbid thinking, that's why in all the correspondence between the leader and his subalterns we can find orders, reports, and recommendations for violence. The files for our cause serve us with strong evidence. We quote the circulars from file nr. 15 p. 61, file nr. 15 p. 9, file nr. 16 order 37.

7. Memoirs. Through a memoir from 5 November 1936, signed by Corneliu Z. Codreanu, the defendant referring to certain European powers, he makes the following solemn statement:

"I declare in the open that all of us will shoot with our revolvers in all who brought us there and because we won't be able to desert, so that we wouldn't cause dishonor, we will kill ourselves."

8. The black lists with political outcasts of the current regime of the Romanian State.

9. Graves, the measurement system of Legionary heroism.

In a letter addressed by C.Z. Codreanu to Stelescu, he says among others: "All our suffering combined is valued as much as ten graves... And the quantity of our suffering that is necessary for our victory, is valued around 200 graves."

10. Shooting exercises. Aside from the moral and psychological training of terrorism shown above, they tried to physically train them in terrorist tactics. Therefore, Alexandru Cantacuzino,[8] in his attribution granted by C.Z. Codreanu, dedicated an important part of his training schedule, as commander of the Legionary Military Corps Moța-Marin, to shooting exercises. As an obvious consequence of maintaining this environment, every Legionary tried — either by fulfilling commands, or from individual impulse — to acquire the necessary weapons needed for violent manifestations. From the report nr. 8,556 from 21 April 1938, the General Inspector of Gendarmes brought to the attention of the Ministry of Internal Affairs, that during the searches run in the rural areas, the following weapons and materials were confiscated: 16 military weapons, 14 rifles, 57 hunting guns, 2 saloon pistols, 16 automated pistols, 137 revolvers, 1 baton with a revolver, and a knife, an unloaded grenade, 11 pieces of dynamite, 67.70 meters of explosive fuse, 237 rounds of ammunition, a military weapon, 12 rifle rounds, 57 rounds for hunting weapons, 40 rounds for automated pistols, 124 rounds for revolvers, 2 loaders for military weapons, 20 tubes of rounds for military weapons, 28 tubes of rounds for hunting weapons, 8 boxes with 700g of gunpowder each, 100g of pellets, 20 bayonets, 6 daggers, 1 knife, 2 swords, 7 brass knuckles, and a machine gun. Besides, the moral and technical violent training of the Legionaries, using the methods we showed above, is nothing more than the continuation of the processes that culminated in time with: the assassination of Vernichescu,[9] student, the assassination of the police prefect from Iași, Manciu, of the police inspector Clos, the assassination attempt of

The Trial of Corneliu Zelea Codreanu

the state subsecretary C. Anghelescu, and, recently, the assassination of prime-minister I.G. Duca and the Legionary commander Stelescu.[10]

Our country, that has rarely seen political assassinations, had to endure the defiant beginning of terrorism after the war, based on the use they made of people's naivety, which after a short time gained them a significant number of victims. This is exclusively due to the ill state of mind caused by Corneliu Z. Codreanu's propaganda, who through a personal unsanctioned act — the assassination of the police prefect Manciu — served to encourage his recruits.

In order to achieve its objectives, the Legionary Movement made use — disapproved of in theory — of financial means, which expanded the movement's reach exponentially. The millions coming in, obviously can't be explained by the support from its members and the donations collected through the requests made using the press. The unusual wealth and the way they spent huge sums of money, can only bring us to the conclusion that the origin of this money is not only suspicious, but completely compromising,[11] because it forces us to presume an occult source that supports the Movement, conspiratorial and terrorist, in order to endanger our state.

This suspect origin of the funds that were put at the Legionary Movement's disposal is evident from the circumstances in which the leader commanded the destruction of the accounting archives, as admitted to by the defendant, who states that "if he didn't give this express order to destroy this archive, he, however, imposed measures for its destruction, to not cause trouble for certain people." So, the defendant admits that in order "to not cause trouble" for certain people, the Legionary archive needed to be destroyed. If the subvention was legitimate and not following a certain purpose, the donor would not have any trouble with the law — and this is exactly where the issue lays; the source of the funding was hidden because it put the Movement in a compromising situation, receiving and using those funds for purposes imposed by the donor.

But the tentacles of this organization that tried to get hold — and actually did for a time — of the whole state organization through violent means are also shown by the proven fact that the Legionary Movement maintained a vast informational network in the General Staff of the Army, the General Defense of State, the Capital Police Prefecture, and other institutions.

Romanian Crucible

Circular orders, whose authenticity was admitted to by Codreanu, found in file nr. 2, Casa Verde, are evidence of the existence of such an informational network. We quote:

"To the Legionaries and members in the Capital. All the informers in the Capital's Police that are part of nests are invited to come to me personally to receive directives between 19 and 25 June 1937. The informers of other particular services, on the day of 26 June 1937. Those who don't show up will reveal that they want to deceive the Legion, to sell us out, and to betray us. You can be in our service without deceit, without selling out your brothers, without betrayal, and without breaking your oath." (ss) Corneliu Z. Codreanu.

One thing is certain, such maneuvers describe only conspiratorial and terrorist organizations. The defendant Corneliu Z. Codreanu claims that he gathered the informers and the agents of the General Staff, of the State Defense, and of the Capital's Police Prefecture, so the workers of these institutions that were affiliated to nests, for the purpose of "saving the moral situation of certain youngsters" or to "tell them they can give any information to the defense or the Police, without staining their conscience."

First, it is surprising that functionaries of the State could uphold their oath sworn to the State, as well as the oath that tied them to the Captain, who had the power to gather them in order to give them "directives." However, from what we showed above, you can see that the political interests of the organization led by Corneliu Z. Codreanu were in conflict with the security interests of the State, and then these double agents had either to execute their work obligations or fulfill the directives given to them by Corneliu Z. Codreanu. But from the way the circular concludes, it results, in the opinion of C.Z. Codreanu, that these functionaries had to be first devoted to the Legion — otherwise, they would be punished. In truth, the circular published in the brochure called *Circularele Căpitanului*, on page 25 it is categorically mentioned that "those who won't show up will be punished." The defendant chose to use State functionaries for the political objectives of the Legionary movement, which is strongly shown in the memoir found at the residence of C.Z. Codreanu — file nr. 9, Casa Verde, the content of which shows that "an undercover informant" of C.Z. Codreanu is a public worker.

What was the objective of this information service? This can be deducted from the structure of the service, its elements, and from the institutions in which it was operating. The explanation to which this was used to intercept certain persecution

The Trial of Corneliu Zelea Codreanu

measures planned by political adversaries doesn't make sense. Otherwise, why did he organize information services in private institutions? What political relationship existed between them and Codreanu's Movement? Weren't these services a significant form of espionage? Why did he need informants in an airplane factory that works for the state's defense? Why did he have informants in the Railway institution? It's obvious this was not about political trickery.

And more than that. How would the defendant claim that this was related to electoral battles when he organized an espionage service in the General Staff of the Army? What did the defendant want to learn from this institution, whose sole purpose is to defend the country? What purpose did he have in looking for information or documents in this military institution? Who benefited from this? These are the questions that stay at the basis of these many accusations.

This fact — of maintaining an informational network in some of the most important public services — explains, in large part, the fact that C.Z. Codreanu illegally owned a series of documents concerning the security of the State, which gravely show the dangers the country was put in by allowing this Movement to use them, and whose leader didn't think twice about resorting to traitorous actions against the State's interests.

Concretely, the material evidence found until now proves the defendant committed two crimes legally classified in art. 191 P. C. King Carol II, sanctioned as treason, paragraphs 1 and 2 — for which a public action was opened and the instructions were followed. Possession of documents concerning the security of the State is proven by the documents found at the residence of the defendant C.Z. Codreanu, documents obtained from the superior authorities of the Gendarmes and from the country prefectures, documents addressed to the subordinated institutions, either through their form or their service order being secret or confidential, some of them even coded in order to preserve their secret.

In this sense, we mention the following documents:

1. Order nr. 54 from 30 August 1934 belonging to the Legion of Gendarmes from Argeş, addressed to the rural gendarme units in their subordination (file nr. 3, Casa Verde, p. 516);

2. Information order nr. 64 from 4 October 1934 belonging to the Gendarme Inspectorate in Bucharest, addressed to the Legion of Gendarmes in Argeş (file nr. 9, Casa Verde, p. 79);

Romanian Crucible

3. The secret order nr. 16 belonging to the Gendarme Inspectorate in Craiova, transmitted by ciphered telegraph to the subordinated units (file nr. 9, Casa Verde, p. 79);

4. The ciphered telegraphed order nr. 586/938 from the General Inspectorate of Gendarmes, to the units in their subordination, signed by D. General Bengliu (file nr. 14);

5. The strictly personal and confidential order, nr. 198, from 11 October 1936, sent by the Prefecture in Ilfov County to the praetors, through which they are given a copy of the confidential personal order nr. 61,096/937 of the Ministry of Internal Affairs, The General Direction of Police;

6. The personal-confidential order nr. 116 from 27 June 1937, sent by the Prefecture of Prahova County (file nr. 14, Col. in. Res. Stănescu).

The public reproduction of these secret documents concerning the security of the State, consisted of the fact the defendant reproduced in the Legionary circular nr. 131 from February 1938, the telegraphic order nr. 586/938 sent by the General Inspectorate of Gendarmes, and reproduced in circular nr. 94, order nr. 198/936, sent by the Prefecture of Ilfov County, indicated at point 5.

The defendant admits in the examinations that the named documents were found during the search made at his residence at Casa Verde; also, he admits to publishing a part of those documents concerning the security of the State in various circulars he issued.

Therefore, the defendant himself admits the offense regarding possession of the documents, as well as the reproduction of some of them in the Legionary circulars. He claims that those documents were not concerning the security of the State and that he did not obtain him personally, also that the majority of those documents contained incorrect information. Regarding the procuring of documents, we reveal that the law punishes their possession, therefore, it is not necessary for the one who is indicted as the one who possessed these secrets to have procured them. But it is hard to believe that the defendant had in his possession so many orders from authorities that came to him through unknown people, who have not been asked to do this. The explanation can only be given by the conclusion that the main objective of maintaining an informative device in public services was to spy and use possible moments of weakness by the authorities to plan a revolt. The informer agents, the

The Trial of Corneliu Zelea Codreanu

public functionaries, were the people that made it possible for the defendant to obtain these documents concerning the security of the State.

It is not possible for these documents to have come into the defendant's hands by mistake, especially when he made public use of their content, so he found them useful for the interests of his future activities. So, there was mutual relationship between the ones who obtained these documents and the defendant, especially because the public functionaries were forced by their political leader to provide them in his interest for the activities of the public service.

When it comes to the truthfulness of the documents found in the defendant's possession, this is undisputable, otherwise the defendant wouldn't have used documents he knew to contain false information and that he published in his circulars claiming the information was real. Regarding the nature of those documents, if they indeed concern the security of the State or not, we will document our claims under this report, in the context of art. 191, point 1 and 2, combined with art. 190 P.C., regarding legal considerations.

***

The representative of the public ministry, in accordance with provisions of art. 204 C.M.J., having the case file, found from its contents that the defendant C.Z. Codreanu also committed the offenses specified in art. 209, point 4 and art. 210, paragraph 1 P.C., as it results from the piece found in the file, vol. 3, page 520, and in the documents contained in the material evidence found on the members of the Legionary movement.

Adding our opinion to the accusations of the military prosecutor, a public action was opened against the defendant for the offense presented above.

The offense of conspiring against the social order, classified in article 209, point 4, P.C., consists in the fact that the defendant, in 1935, got in touch with a foreign organization,[12] for the purpose of receiving instructions and support of any kind to plan a social revolution in Romania. During the examination, the defendant did not admit to this accusation, even though he cannot contest that the incriminating piece of evidence was found at his residence.

The imputation proves conclusive through the content of the piece of evidence, and naturally, the defendant won't admit his guilt because the evidence is extremely

Romanian Crucible

important in setting the defendant's activity of blatantly contravening the repressive law's provisions.

This is what the defendant, C.Z. Codreanu says, in a few conclusive paragraphs, to a foreign organization, in order for them to help him wave the flag in Romania in the following year:

"The central committee of the national-socialist Legionaries of Romania, debating on the problem of the realization of our plan for the campaign in 1935, which we had planned for the future economic and political alliance with..."

Therefore, this organization was preparing a campaign to obtain a political and economic alliance with a foreign power. Of course, this alliance would have been done without the approval of the legal government of the county, so through an act of violence.

And further on:

"Solidarity in our moral interests, first of all, that ties us in an indestructible manner, forces, and commands us to respectfully inform you of our wish.... Postponing the war will make it possible for the flag to wave in Romania also..."

From the given passages, it results that the "realization of our plan for the campaign in 1935" was dependent and strongly related to the "solidarity of our interests" the Legionary Movement had with a foreign organization. Then this indestructible manner related to the war being postponed — after the defendant's suppositions — would make it so in the following year "the flag would also wave in Romania..."

Therefore, peace was not as important as victory to Codreanu. The war was only supposed to be "postponed," in order to give him the chance to establish a new regime in Romania, one similar to a foreign regime that inspires him, with which he has mutual interests, and for which he wishes consolidation and complete success.

As a matter of fact, the defendant's intentions, as they are revealed in this document, are confirmed and strengthened by a second piece of evidence, which is the telegram sent on the date of... to a foreign power. The existence of this piece, as well as its expedition, is not contested by the defendant. Its content and the way it was sent is completely identical to the first piece. A fragment is conclusive: "...to which nobody will be able to resist."

The Trial of Corneliu Zelea Codreanu

This material of impunity proves beyond a doubt its classification in the provisions given in art. 209, point 4, Penal Code Carol II, which sanctions the act of contacting a person or organization from abroad with the purpose of receiving instructions and funds for preparing a social revolution.

The last offense, which is the crime of revolt, classified in the provisions given by art. 210 P.C., consists of the fact that the defendant Corneliu Z. Codreanu established deposits of weapons in different parts of the country, armed the members of the Legionary Movement, and formed paramilitary organizations. The defendant wanted to create a national uprising, to unleash a civil war, which would help him achieve a Legionary revolution and take control of the State.

From the factual evidence described before, we can conclude that the defendant, through a personal act, founded the organization called Legionary corps Moța-Marin, a military organization with a wide reach in the country, having a membership of 10,000 people. The whole structure of this organization shows the defendant wanted to use it for a Legionary revolution. The precise evidence that this organization planned to use armed force is shown by the fact that its members were enrolled in "shooting exercises," as can be seen in file nr. 12., p. 17 — Cantacuzino.

Besides, the defendant himself said, during the interrogations, that this organization had a paramilitary character; but, of course, it is hard for him to admit the whole truth.

But finding so many weapons on the members of the Legionary Movement indicates the defendant's methods through which he wanted to obtain political power at the right moment by arming them.

"The undercover police, as well as the uncovered one, meaning all of those who formed this police body, were armed with revolvers or knives, having the following instructions:

The undercover police were traveling through the country and whatever they would observe that could endanger the life of the Captain or of a Legionary commander, they had to react and, if it was the case, sanction them on the spot, using their weapon if necessary.

The uncovered police had the mission to catch thrown flowers, poppers, or bombs if necessary, and be the only ones that lost their lives; if the Captain or the commander were attacked by a mob, a bigger group would interfere, formed by both types of police, who were in the immediate vicinity of the Captain, subduing them with their firearms if necessary."

A concrete fact that proves this offense is that from the circumstance and time of the raids and searches made recently, within the country and at the residences of various members of the Legionary Movement, they found important deposits of weapons and materials, that could not have another purpose other than arming the rebels with them, in order to unleash the civil war that the Legionary Movement wanted, and to prepare for the revolution that was to follow.

Using this material evidence, we undoubtedly prove the crime of rebellion, provided and sanctioned by art. 210, penal Code Carol II.

In law:

Seeing that from the documents in the file and the following instructions, it is found that the defendant was in possession of documents and publicly reproduced them, even though he didn't have the right to possess them and even though they were part of the category mentioned in art. 190 P.C. Carol II.

In order to prosecute the crime of treason, provided by art. 191, points 1 and 2 P.C., the following constitutive elements are required: the offender must be a Romanian citizen; the offender must have procured or possessed documents from the category provided in art. 190 P.C.; the offender must not have the right to be aware of these documents; criminal intention. For the offense provided by art. 191, point 2, the following elements are required: Romanian citizenship; the material evidence of public reproduction of the documents, the documents must belong to the category mentioned in art. 191; criminal intention.

Regarding the first element that refers to the offender having Romanian citizenship, it doesn't need debating, as the defendant undoubtedly has it;

Considering the analyses of the second element, we must refer to the content of art. 190 P.C., which relates to art. 191 that describes the character of the documents;

Seeing that art. 190 P.C. contains and expressly refers to the documents and information that concern the security of the State, the second element is completely proven if we remember that the documents possessed by the defendant and partially publicly reproduced concerned the security of the State;

Considering that the doctrine makes the following enumeration of the main superior interests of the State: ensuring the existence, integrity, and independence of

The Trial of Corneliu Zelea Codreanu

the State; ensuring the social order in the State, ensuring the good international reports of the State (Dongoroz — special part of the Penal Code p. 51); That all the infractions against the security of the State have as their juridical objective "protecting the superior interests of the state." So, everything that would go against the "political order of the state" and the "social order of the state" would concern the security of the State. Considering that the doctrine also shows the "State's right to create state secrets, is not only lawful but also necessary. These secrets concern the security of the State" (Dongoroz, special part, p. 115).

Further on, the same author shows that "the State can create a secret whenever and in whichever field, raise it to the rank of state secret, therefore imposing the ones that know the secret to not divulge it under certain circumstances. The will of the state to impose the secret can be legally manifested through rules, decrees, or administrative documents" (Dongoroz, special part, p. 115).

Seeing these documents found at the residence of the defendant Corneliu Z. Codreanu are issued by the superior authorities of the Gendarmes and by the county Prefectures; that these documents are addressed to the units in their subordination, by their form and content being service orders, secrets, or confidential, some even coded in order to preserve their content; taking into account that all these institutions belong the executive power of the State; considering the most important institution to exercise power, according to the Constitution, is the Ministry of Internal Affairs, and this department has two types of attributions: some concerning local and general administration of the State, and others concerning public order and the security of the State — meaning police attributes; considering the police duties are divided depending on the law of organization of the general police of the State on three levels: administrative police, judicial police, and the police of the security of the State; considering the duties the police of the security of the State are shown by art. 2, letter C from the law or organization of the general police of the State, and they are fulfilled by the urban police officers from the general police of the State and by the rural police officers — meaning by the gendarmes — and through the county prefects and praetors. Considering that, from the content of the documents in the defendant's possession from his residence, we can categorically determine they concern the duties of the State's security police, meaning they are documents referring to the security of the State, provided by art. 190, Penal code Carol II, combined with art. 2, letter C and art. 12 from the law for the organization of the State's general police;

The state is composed of three elements: sovereignty or political power, population, and territory; therefore, the ordinances given and fulfilled to defend any of these three elements refer to the security of the State;

Considering that the State's sovereignty is defended internally, usually by the police, and exceptionally by the intervention of the army — and every measure taken for this purpose can only be characterized as measures concerning the security of the State; these measures can be documents with police decisions or other documents sent and fulfilled by them, however, it was, in order for them to have the desired effect, they must be exclusively known by the agents that were designated to defend the State and its public order, for whichever reasons, whatever their form, they are secret documents as long as that authority gives them this public character;

Given that the means of defending the State impose either as a repression, or in general, whichever measure ordered in terms of the State's security, to be known only by the agents that execute or order these measures;

If they acted in another way, it would mean they couldn't reach their target, and the security of the State would be severely endangered;

This easily explains the vital character of secret police measures when it comes to the security of the State, which are necessarily defined in the provisions of art. 190 P.C.;

Given the fact that the techniques used for the State's defense must adapt to every new situation used by the enemies of the State, which characterize the offenses against the security of the State in the years after the war, are conspiracy and terror, which automatically involves secret tactics from the institutions that defend the State in order to ensure their efficiency; therefore, the defendant was not asked to give his opinion about the secret character of the measures ordained by the authorities of the public order; also, that his claims that the measures and orders contained incorrect information were false; that the measures ordained by the authorities through the documents obtained and possessed by the defendant cannot be considered, as he claimed, as "simple police measures that don't concern the security of the State," because the right to qualify and appreciate them as public or secret, belongs solely to the legal institution that ordered that measure, and in no circumstance belongs to the leader of an organization suspected of acts against the security of the State, especially when these measures concerned the members of a dissolved

The Trial of Corneliu Zelea Codreanu

political organization, thus an illegal one, the Iron Guard, which the defendant through his own statement, did not want to leave, preferring to remain on his old position in the Iron Guard.

Even more, the defendant, by intercepting the ordered measures against an illegal organization, reveals his interest in knowing the content of the documents that he obtained for the illegal organization, and furthermore, endanger the security of the State; then, given the offense of possession of documents that concern the State's security, and that in general, the offenses against the public safety are dangerous offenses, thus it is not important if the offender achieved his goal by possessing documents or if he caused any real damage to the State by the imposed fact; that, by determining the documents possessed and partially published by the defendant are of the character specified in art. 190 P.C, the existence of the second element is highlighted;

Given the third element of the offense provided by art. 191, point 1 P.C., which says the defendant must not have had knowledge of the content of the documents that form the subject of the crime;

Given in this case that we must not insist on this element, because it is shown the defendant did not have any right to be in possession of documents concerning State security;

Considering the fifth element refers to criminal intention;

That, according to the doctrine, for the nature of this case is only required the simple generic role, which results by default from the material evidence and from the existence of the other concrete elements; that, since the defendant had the representation of the unlawful document, meaning he willingly completed the criminal act, the intention exists (Tanoviceanu-Dongoroz, vol. I, p. 588); in this case, it is indubitable that the defendant consciously sought to possess documents issued by the State, documents among the ones specified in art. 190 P.C, meaning he wanted to reach a conclusion sanctioned by the law; and, also consciously, he published a part of these secrets concerning the State's security that he possessed — highly resulting that the defendant had criminal intent to commit the imputed crimes; therefore, this element being also proven, we must look for the legal classification of the offense in art. 191, P.C., point 1, to see if the only element that is different from the others that were analyzed in the offense classified in art. 191, point 1, P.C., that of public reproduction of documents concerning the security of the State, exists or not in this case;

Or, the defendant himself categorically admits that he reproduced in the circulars nr. 94 and 131, the coded telegraphic order nr. 586/938 issued by the General Inspectorate of Gendarmes and the top-secret-confidential nr. 198 from 11 October 1936 issued by the Prefecture of Ilfov County; therefore, proof of existence of this element as well is complete; in consequence, the offense classified in art. 191, point 2, P.C. is determined in charge of the defendant.

Given that the crime of conspiring against the social order, provided and sanctioned by art. 209, point 4 P.C., is a crime of prevention, that has the purpose to protect and conserve the social order existent in Romania;

The text of law imposes as evidence the simple contact with a foreign person or association, that proves concluding to the incriminated piece, from which it strongly results in this relation;

The text also requires for this relation to have the purpose of receiving instructions or support of any kind in order to prepare for a social revolt;

The terms of the law are very broad, and refer to "any kind of support;" or, the defendant shows in his call to a foreign power that, in this case, there's at least a moral solidarity and common interest; therefore, even when it only comes to moral support, the demands of the law are satisfied, as we repeat the text of the law that says "any kind of support;"

In this case, for the purpose of receiving support and aid to "wave the flag in Romania as well...;"

So, this element is strengthened in this case, because the call to help the Legionary Movement by an association from abroad was made to change the social order in Romania, by establishing a regime led by the Legionary Movement;

When it comes to the international element, we do not have to insist, because the broad text of the law doesn't have a special role for the existence of this offense, and this element is highlighted and revealed by the material evidence;

Given the crime of rebellion provided by art. 210, paragraph I, P.C. Carol II, the text of law imposes as material evidence, the arming of the locals;

This element is strongly highlighted in this case by the discover of weapon deposits that belonged to the Legionary Movement, and by the fact that its members

The Trial of Corneliu Zelea Codreanu

were armed on the order of the defendant, as is proven by the weapons found on a large number of members — a situation confirmed by the testimony of the Legionary Ghiocel Dumitru, as well as through the paramilitary organization that focused on the secret task of arming them; we mention the law in this sense says that even if the weapons are deposited in order to be redistributed, the arming is done from a criminal point of view (Penal Code annotated Dongoroz, vol II, p. 210);

The purpose of arming: to promote civil war is pointed out by the intention of the defendant to found a Legionary State through violence and revolution, by choosing to justify his means and always supporting the terrorist acts of the Legionary Movement;

The intentional element is gathered in this case, because the defendant willed, accepted, and acted by instigating the nation, in order to unleash the Legionary revolution, to establish the Legionary State; but from these two crimes, one, conspiring against social order and the other, rebellion, prove their existence in the charges against the defendant Corneliu Z. Codreanu, factually as well as legally.

For these considerations: in conjunction with the final conclusions of the military prosecutor, we declare:

That in this case the defendant Corneliu Z. Codreanu is to be judged by the Military Court of Army Corps II for the crime of treason, through the possession and public reproduction of documents concerning the security of the State, provided and sanctioned by art. 191, points 1 and 2, combined with art. 190 Penal Code Carol II; for the crime of conspiring against social order provided and sanctioned by art. 209, point 4 Penal Code Carol II, and for the crime of rebellion provided and sanctioned by art. 210 Penal Code Carol II — on the basis of the Royal Decree Nr. 856/938 establishing the state of emergency;

We pronounce:

The court files will be forwarded to the General Prosecutor's Office of the Military Court of Army Corps II, to be adjudicated.

Given in our instruction office, today 16 May [1938], in Bucharest.

Military judge,

Major magistrate,

Dan Pascu

Day One
Monday, 23 May 1938

The proceedings of the trial of Corneliu Zelea Codreanu began in front of the Military Court of Army Corps II.

It was known in advance that the courtroom of the Military Courthouse in Malmaison, which has been renovated and nicely decorated in the past months, was to be overcrowded for a trial that was being followed with special interest.

That's why the Military Prosecutor took measures and precautions a few days ago, in order to forbid entrance into the courtroom of people that were not instructed to assist in the trial, other than the accredited representatives of the Romanian and foreign press, the lawyers, and relatives of the defendant.

Starting this morning, around six o'clock, these measures began being applied in the area, under the supervision of the first military prosecutor, Lieutenant Colonel Zeciu, order being maintained by numerous police agents, working under the leadership of a military prosecutor, Captain magistrate Ştefan Tărtăreanu.

Entry into the Military Courthouse is done through a long alley of approximately 50-60 m long and 6-8 m wide. At the entrance gates, they posted gendarme commissaries and soldiers. This is where they check identification cards and entry tickets.

The courtroom is full up to the last seat. Aside from the professionals, a few representatives of the international press are positioned in the room.

In a corner sits the mother of the accused, Ms. Eliza Codreanu, and next to her, the wife of Corneliu Codreanu.

We note a few among the members of the defense: Mrs. Lizetta Gheorghiu; Sebastian Radovici, Ranatescu-Călăraşi, C. Henţescu, Lică Zamfirescu Fuss, Horia Cosmovici, and Mihail Apostoleanu. The appointed counsel for the defense is Captain Teodorescu Gheorghe.

The Court Enters

The hearing opened at 10 am, with the Court being composed of the following panel of judges: Senior President Colonel Magistrate Dumitru Constantin, assisted by Colonel Lieutenant Ionel Nicolae, Major Grumăzescu Dumitru, Captain Bărdacă Gheorghe, Captain Dumitrescu Nicolae, Senior Prosecutor Magistrate Ionescu Radu, and Registrar Tudor D. Petre.

After that, Mr. Registrar Tudor read the order to the General Commander of Army Corp II, through which the Judges of the Court were appointed.

They proceed to interrogate the defendant. After the formality of swearing the oath by the magistrates, done by the President of the Court, on the holy cross, the panel of judges is formed.

Mr. President Col. Mag. Dumitru C-tin: What is your name?

The defendant Corneliu Zelea Codreanu: Corneliu Zelea Codreanu.

Mr. President: How old are you?

Defendant: 38 years old.

Mr. President: Where were you born?

Defendant: In Iaşi.

Mr. President: Where do you reside?

Defendant: Bucharest. Casa Verde.

The Defense Raises an Objection, Asking for a Delay.

Immediately after the oath is sworn, Lawyer Lizetta Gheorghiu, in the name of the defense, raises an objection worthy of delaying the trial, basing it on the fact that multiple case files have not been forwarded by the prosecution.

The ordinance was given by the county instructor on 17 May, along with the decision of the prosecution. Therefore it was impossible for him to take note of the ordinance in order to submit the respective memoir, to which he was entitled according to the Penal Code.

She then quotes the report of the reporting adviser, which said the defendant would have admitted to the offense.

The Trial of Corneliu Zelea Codreanu

The Major Prosecutor Radu Ionescu replies that the objections raised by the defense are unfounded.

He also mentions that he will base his claims on a limited series of documents, as did the prosecution, documents contained in volume I of the case file.

It is true that procedural law provides certain deadlines that can't be exceeded. But these have been respected.

Lawyer Horia Cosmovici starts by showing that, given the importance and the gravity of the trial, the defense wouldn't have brought up an objection that was legally unfounded.

The prosecution suffered the same lack that we suffer today: they didn't have some of the case files. The prosecution only had 11 files out of 20.

The decision of the prosecution must contain a detailed account of the offense, and this cannot be done if the files are missing.

The decision of the prosecution is null, therefore so is the notice.

There are documents and files quoted in the indictment, which don't exist.

Major Prosecutor Radu Ionescu, replying, showed that the Court cannot dismiss the decision of the prosecution that invested him with overseeing the trial. He must, therefore, go along with the trial.

After a debate that lasted 10 minutes, the Court reenters, and President Colonel C. Dumitru declares that the objection was overruled.

The Second Objection

Lawyer Lizetta Gheorghiu brings up a second objection; showing that the defense was not given certain documents and files, and she requests a new term, in order to prepare the defense, which is entitled to know their content.

Prosecutor Magistrate Radu Ionescu maintains his conclusions for rejecting this objection as well, and shows that, either way, the defense could have gotten knowledge of the files' content.

Lawyer Sebastian Radovici, in reply, shows that in a trial where a man is accused of the most serious crimes, nobody could have an interest in not making a complete investigation and defense.

Romanian Crucible

And Lawyer Cosmovici communicates the wish of the defendant to know the documents that form the basis of the accusations against him because his defense can only be done this way.

After deliberations, this objection is overruled as well, for reasons that will be given at the time of sentencing.

Lawyer Gheorghiu brings up a third objection, showing that among the witnesses for the prosecution, only one was notified legally; the others were informed of the trial the previous evening, but not notified legally. She asks for the trial to be delayed, based on art. 254 P.C.

Major Prosecutor Radu Ionescu, basing his answer on the same text of law, disputes the objection and states that, if it is determined that these witnesses were not notified legally, he relinquishes them, and prefers to interrogate them merely as informants.

Lawyer Horia Cosmovici shows that the interest of the law was to allow the defendant to choose his own witnesses. But he didn't have the chance to choose them.

Major Prosecutor Radu Ionescu: But you cannot deny that any person deemed necessary can be asked to come to Court, according to art. 309 P.C.

Lawyer Lizetta Gheorghiu: But we reserve our right to ask you to notify witnesses, by virtue of your power, and eventually to ask you to bring the criminal records of the witnesses for the prosecution.

The Court documents the decision of the prosecution to renounce those witnesses and will decide during the debates if it will be necessary to bring them in as informants.

Lizetta Gheorghiu, Lawyer: Mr. President, the undersigned defenders who make this request, have the honor to bring up the following objection in favor of a delay.

Mr. President: This cannot be done until the witnesses are called.

Lizetta Gheorghiu: Mr. President, according to art. 336, after the defendant's identification, this delay can be set. Maybe calling the witnesses would be a formality that would unnecessarily tire the Court...

Mr. President: The Court never tires.

The Trial of Corneliu Zelea Codreanu

Lizetta Gheorghiu: According to the law, we are entitled to elaborate the delay proceedings.

Mr. President: Mr. Prosecutor, do you have anything to object?

Prosecutor: I don't have anything to object.

Lizetta Gheorghiu: In order to be short, I will read the objection, which I will then leave in two copies, according to the text of law, on the table of the Honorary Court.

Mr. Senior President,

The undersigned lawyers, defenders of Mr. Corneliu Zelea Codreanu, in virtue of the provisions given by art. 294 and 336 of the J.M. Code, we have the honor to bring up the following objection concerning the flawed notification of the Court and disregard of the right to defense. In fact:

According to the final indictment of the military Prosecutor Mr. Gheorghe Athanasiu with the NR. 20 from 6 May 1938, as well as according to the final ordinance NR. 38547/938, 17 May, of Major Instructor Judge Mr. Dan Pascu, the arraignment of Mr. Corneliu Zelea Codreanu was made on charges based on documents contained, as is shown in the indictment and in the final ordinance, in a number of 20 files, to which the reference is expressly made. Or, also according to the address NR. 213 from 16 May 1938 of the Instruction Office to the Military Prosecutor's Office, p. 105, file 2,785/938, as well as address NR. 17,130 from 17 May 1938 of the Prosecutor's office of the Military Courthouse to the Prosecution Chamber, shows that the honorable Prosecution did not receive all the files, meaning all the volumes of the case, the file missing being NR. 12, 14, 15, 16, 17, and 18. In law:

According to the provisions given by art. 200 of C.J.M. concerning crimes, the public ministry will forward the files to the Prosecution with a deadline of three days from receiving it. Or, undisputed in this case, all 20 volumes formed the case file, and all of them must have been given to the Prosecution, so it can decide with a full knowledge of the facts. Art. 276 Rules of Criminal Procedure, also shows that the indictment is being convened only after it is in possession of all the documents and pieces that constitute the case file. Especially in this case, through the fact that pieces found in the volumes that constituted the case file constituted evidence of guild for the instruction judge and the military prosecutor, these not being allowed to be absent from the prosecutor's deliberation, then by flagrantly disregarding the law, which results in the nullity of decision NR. 17 from 17 May 1938 of the Prosecutor Chamber of Army Corps II. Nullifying this decision attracts the flawed notification of the Court, so we request resending the files to the prosecution, so they could proceed according to the law. We also consider the Court's notification to be completely flawed, and the Prosecutor's decision null for the following two considerations. In fact:

The final ordinance of the instruction judge was given on the date of 17 May 1938, with the NR. 38547, and the decision of the Prosecution was given on the same date of 17 March 1938 with the NR. 17. It is undisputable the fact that the last examination, provided by art. 201 of C.J.M. was done to the defendant on 16 May 1938. So, it was a material impossibility for the defendant to be aware of the Final Ordinance before the Prosecution pronounced their decision. In law:

Art. 221 from C.J.M shows that the procedure followed by the Prosecution of the army corps concerning military courts of justice is the same one provided by the criminal procedure code. Art. 276 in the Penal Code says in paragraph 9: The public ministry, the civil side, and the defendant have the right to submit written memoirs. So, the text of the law says they have the right, therefore, we have to repeat, it is a right of the defendant. But what sort of right is in this case when the Final Ordinance is given on the same day as the Prosecution's decision, and of course, the Final ordinance must first go through the public ministry because this is the institution that forwards the case file to the prosecution? What kind of memoirs could the defendant give? He didn't even know a final ordinance was given, he couldn't have had knowledge of its content, nothing was communicated to him, and he was not summoned by the Prosecution. Therefore, the right of the defendant was blatantly ignored, and the decision of the Prosecution, made under such conditions, cannot be sustained. We also reveal, in fact:

In criminal cases, the reporting advisor of the Prosecution must mention in the report he makes, the collected evidence, the legal qualification, etc. In this case, we can see from examining the report, a surprising statement from the reporting advisor, that the defendant admits his own guilt. Is sufficient to read the transcript of the examination of the defendant to see how wrong this statement is, and the way it presented a completely false situation to the Prosecution. Of course, an acknowledgment that the documents were in my possession does not prove the existence of a crime, but acknowledging the illegal act itself means acknowledging the imputation. But, probably starting from these completely wrong premises, the Prosecution

The Trial of Corneliu Zelea Codreanu

is content with repeating summarily the content of the final ordinance and the prosecutor's indictment, without concern for the defendant's defense. In law:

Art. 281 from the Penal Code is applicable to every military court of law, according to art. 221 C.J.M, categorically shows that when making a decision, the Prosecution Chamber is required to decide on the means of defense provided by the content of the instruction. The last paragraph of this article then shows that every provision of this article is provided under the penalty of nullity. Therefore, it is clear that the Prosecution's decision, through which the defendant's right for a defense is removed without any reason, cannot be on a legal basis. In this case, the Prosecution did not even want to know or to discuss the defendant's defense. With this process, a man cannot be accused of a crime and sent to trial. In consequence, the decision of the Prosecution Chamber, through investing in the Military Court of Army Corp II, by flagrantly disregarding the law, we ask you to consider it flawed, to notify the Military Court, and send it to the Prosecution, so they can make a decision in accordance with the law. Regards, (ss) Lizetta Gheorghiu, lawyer.

Lizetta Gheorghiu, lawyer: In consequence, Mr. President and Honorary Court, I ask you to take into account the objections brought to your attention, which we will leave in two copies on the table of the Honorary Council.

Mr. President: The prosecutor has the floor.

The reply of the General Prosecutor.

Senior-Prosecutor Major Magistrate Ionescu Radu: Mr. President, Honorary Council, I consider from the start that the objections raised by the honorary defense lack legal basis for the following considerations:

Regarding not sending the case files to the Indictment Chamber, I have to mention from the start that the final ordinance, as well as us, will not base considerations and conclusions on a certain limited series of documents, found in the mentioned files in the objection requests, documents that can be found in copies legalized by the instruction judge in vol. I, which was debated by the Indictment Chamber. In other words, the Indictment Chamber, if they didn't have all the documents, had however the necessary material, the material on which the final ordinance and the written indictment found their conclusions, meaning the given decision was pronounced in conformity with the law. Regarding the other objections, for all of these, we have the same argument: it is right to say the procedural law, the military

Romanian Crucible

one as well as the common criminal procedure to which C.J.M. refers, provide certain mandatory deadlines which cannot be exceeded. The obligation of the Prosecution Chamber is not to do this within three days, meaning to let three days pass and only after that set the term for the trial of the case. No. It is sufficient to respect the term set by the law within these three days and is considered as a fulfilled procedure. As such, the decision given by the Prosecution Chamber is legal, and for this reason, the objections are overruled.

Mr. Cosmovici, lawyer: We respectfully ask for our right to reply.

The defense asks again to speak.

Mr. Senior President: You can reply, but please be brief.

Mr. Cosmovici: Mr. President and Honorary Court, I take the floor specifically to oppose the beginning of the conclusions brought by the General Prosecutor. "From the start, they lack legal basis" — that's how they started. This "from the start" bothers us, first, because we're the defense in a serious trial, so we wouldn't allow ourselves to start with an objection that is outside legal bounds and not founded on the law. This is why we essentially believe — we'll only talk about one part of the petition — that today you are not legally notified. According to your organic law, C.J.M., in criminal business, the final ordinance follows to be communicated to the Indictment Chamber, and the Indictment Chamber is the one that notifies you. Look, I'll read paragraph 220: "Whichever would be the conclusions of the final ordinance in a criminal case, the Public Ministry will forward the case files to the Prosecution Chamber within three days from receiving it, and, in case of other crimes, directly to the Court, together with all the annexes and the list of proposed witnesses." The procedure from the Prosecution is the one provided by article 221 of the organic law, as follows: "The procedure of the Prosecution Chamber is the one provided by the criminal procedure framework for the respective Prosecution Chamber, in the extent applicable for military courts of law and if it doesn't contravene, to the express provisions given by this code." And the Penal Code, art. 270 has the following content: "If the offense is considered a crime by law and the Prosecution finds sufficient evidence and clues against the defendant, he must be sent before a jury" — meaning before you, the Honorary Court, by substitution and by sending the Code of Military Justice. Therefore, you are notified by the decision of the Prosecution, in this case through decision nr. 17 from 17 May 1938. Or, what do we find? We find that the Honorary Prosecution Chamber or Army Corps II endured the same lack that we, the defense, endured until today,

The Trial of Corneliu Zelea Codreanu

meaning the case files — there are 20 that, according to the law, make a whole file — have not been sent. Therefore, we say, if the Prosecution finds me guilty of something, it's my right to know: did you read every piece in the files? Otherwise, you can't accuse me. The address on which these documents are sent mentions, even in your instruction file, that only 11 files were sent. And then we say: Honorary Prosecution Chamber, you cannot bring me here for a crime, if from 20 files you only read 11. Almost half the files still haven't been researched. This is our argument, the argument of law on which you judge according to the Constitution: in every case, the Indictment Chamber is obliged to rule, for each of the defendants brought before it, on every offense that results from the case files. Well, where are the instruction documents if they're not in the files? The honorary prosecutor said: there are certified copies. I will come back to this. The nullity provided by art. 281 interferes here, which is required of you: the decision of the Indictment Chamber must contain a detailed display of the committed offense. Well, when the text of the law requires a detailed display of the committed offenses I want to know if with 50% of the files it can be called a detailed display? Certified copies? From 10 files to only have as much as one file? Only this, and it is sufficient to say that there are no certified copies in the file because you can't put copies of nine whole files in one. It is a material impossibility. But anyway, let us go on. The Indictment Chamber is required to decide upon the essential means — and I will prove there are essential means and those are missing, because the file in which they can be found is missing. Further on: each of these dispositions are prescribed under the penalty of nullity. Therefore, we say: if the decision given by the Indictment Chamber is null, and if you are notified through the Indictment Chamber's decision, your notification is also illegal. What is null doesn't exist. You can't rule, because you were not notified by the Indictment Chamber. And now, because I don't want to plead unfounded things from the start, we want to show that the ordinance takes responsibility for the final indictment, the following documents are considered essential when it comes to the final indictment in the case files. Filer nr. 14, p. 114; please, file nr.14 doesn't exist; file nr. 15, p. 254 — doesn't exist, file nr. 17, p. 50 — doesn't exist. I'll stop because you stopped me. They're all the same, the files don't exist. And then we say: since the Indictment Chamber, like us today, couldn't have knowledge of all the files, the Indictment Chamber according to art. 221, 227 from P.C. could only give a null decision according to the law. As a consequence, you are not notified, because what is null doesn't exist. You don't have a notice. This has been our serious objection right from the start.

Senior Prosecutor Major Magistrate Ionescu Radu: Mr. Senior President, a few words only: I fully maintain my first conclusions, adding that the Honorary Court is facing the decision of the Indictment Chamber, a decision which invests the Court with judging this trial. If the decision was given justly or not, you do not have the standing to reject this decision and not judge the trial. That's why you are required, from this point of view, to judge the trial, even though, again, I repeat, my conclusion is that the objection is unfounded and must be overruled.

Lizetta Gheorghiu, lawyer: Mr. President, our conclusions in this objection are the following: you are invested with discretion; considering the decision of the Indictment Chamber is null, this decision must be returned to it.

Mr. President Magistrate Col. Dumitru C-tin: We'll adjourn for deliberations.

The hearing is adjourned.

At reopening.

Mr. Senior President Col. Magistrate Dumitru C-tin: For reasons that we'll present later, the Court overrules the objection.

Another objection brought by the defense.

Mrs. Gheorghiu: Mr. President, please allow me to present the following objection, in accordance with art. 294, final paragraph, and art. 336 C.M.J. of the 13 documents given in the final indictment with the title Theft and possession of documents concerning the security of the State, only 9 were found in the files that were given to us to study and organize our defense. Two of these documents could not be found at the indicated pages; or, two could not be found, because the files containing them were not given to us. These documents are considered as material evidence and served as the basis for the charges from the military prosecutor, as well as the instruction judge. The two documents that are wrongly indicated are:

1.   Secret order no. 16 of Gendarme Inspectorate in Craiova (file no. 9, Casa Verde, p. 515).

2.   Secret brochure no. 8 of the Gendarme General Inspectorate (Lugoj file, p. 1).

The two documents that were not given to us are:

The Trial of Corneliu Zelea Codreanu

1.   Telegraphic coded order no. 586/938 of the Gendarme General Inspectorate (file no. 14 col. Stănulescu, p. 87);

2.   Personal-confidential order no. 116 from 27 June 1937 sent by the Prefecture of Prahova County (file no. 14, col. Stănescu, p. 100).

Mr. President and Honorary Court, we, the defense, did not receive those files by 9 pm when we left here; instead, we had the honor to find that these files had been requested by the honorary commission after they were claimed by the criminal investigation body. So, instead of serving for the defense, they probably served for the prosecution's inquiry last night instead of being used to prepare the holy right of defense. In consequence, based on the provisions given in art. 335 C.J.M., we request a new term, so that both the defense and the defendant can prepare the defense in due time, after we receive all the documents that form the case file, especially when these documents are the ones that initiated this trial, and which are considered as evidence of guilt. Therefore, they cannot be excluded from the defendant's examination and the defense.

Senior-President: Mr. Royal Commissary has the floor.

The Royal Commissary requests the rejection.

Senior-Prosecutor: Mr. President, Honorary Court, I maintain the same reasons and conclusions I had for the first rejection of this objection as well. The defense cannot complain in front of you for not having knowledge of the incriminating pieces, pieces that form the whole foundation of the indictment in this trial. They were part of file no. 1 in copies certified by the instruction judge, meaning you cannot complain today that you haven't had the possibility to acknowledge them. All this being said, according to the information we had, this problem, and especially the requests you've made during the case file study, were brought to your attention.

Lizetta Gheorghiu, lawyer (defense): When?

Senior-Prosecutor: I don't know this, but in any way, I know you had the chance to get acquainted with all the pieces of evidence that will be used by us and the instruction judge to form our conclusions.

Mrs. Gheorghiu: Mr. President, we cannot accept this offense, because we had never stated inaccuracies.

Romanian Crucible

Senior-Prosecutor: That's why, Mr. President and Honorary Court, please consider overruling the objection.

The defense intervenes again.

Mr. Sebastian Radovici, lawyer: Mr. President and Honorary Court, I believe nobody has the interest in a trial where the most serious accusations are brought against a man, a trial that keenly interests the public opinion of this country, to be judged differently than with the correct instruction and — I must highlight — with a complete defense. It is indisputable that from the files that were supposed to be put at our disposal that a few are missing, especially the evidence that should be found in file 14, evidence which is the most serious, because based on it, the defendant Corneliu Zelea Codreanu, is sent to be judged by you for the crime of treason. Then, Honorary Court, I ask myself how is it possible for us to respond to this accusation without knowing the evidence? Mr. Senior-prosecutor said that these pieces of evidence can apparently be found in the instruction file. Well, I refuse to acknowledge copies when we are supposed to work with pieces that constitute the material evidence itself, when they allegedly constitute the alleged committed crime. In such circumstances, these have no value if they are not given to us in the original. Besides, we believe that for the judicial and ethical value of the sentence you must give, our request must be admitted, and we respectfully ask you to admit it.

Mr. Senior-President: Mr. Cosmovici has the floor

Mr. Cosmovici, lawyer: Mr. President, Honorary Court, please allow me to make an observation from the defendant; it's not mine as a lawyer. This observation is the following: if there are pieces missing from the file and if he didn't have the file, the defendant was personally deprived of his right to a defense, because, only knowing the pieces in the file and having the file, we can know what witnesses to propose and what evidence we must use for the defense. So, the wish of the defendant is to add the following statement as an argument: I don't know how to defend myself if I don't know what I'm being attacked with. I insist upon the original pieces, because the defendant wants to see the originals. Do you know what were the first words we, the defense, were greeted with when the defendant was brought here from Jilava?

"Please show me the originals."

Those original documents don't exist.

The Trial of Corneliu Zelea Codreanu

Mr. Senior-President: The court will deliberate.

The hearing is adjourned. The Court enters deliberations.

At reopening:

Mr. Senior-President: For reasons we'll show later, the Court rejects the second objection as well.

On the problem of some witnesses:

Mrs. Lizetta Gheorghiu, lawyer: Mr. President, please allow me to raise briefly another objection.

Mr. President, the undersigned defenders of Mr. Corneliu Zelea Codreanu, we have the honor to raise the following cause for a continuance, for disregarding the right to defense: According to art. 254 C.J.M., Mr. President, with the occasion of fulfilling the formalities provided by this text, the defendant should have been notified of the witness list, the informants, etc., which the prosecution requests to be brought for oral deliberations. In this case, with the occasion of fulfilling the formalities provided by art. 254 C.J.M., the defendant has only been notified about one witness, Ghiocel, who was proposed by the prosecution on the 22nd of May, at 6 pm. On the eve of the trial, the registrar communicated, without the quality to do so, a new list of witnesses for the prosecution. It is only natural for the defense not to be able to administer the counter evidence and, either way, this notification is unregulated and completely against the law. We ask you, based on art. 335, 336 C.M.J, to kindly postpone the trial, in order for the prosecution to propose witnesses in a timely fashion and to do things properly from every point of view. Mr. President, there are 5-6 witnesses that are part of a separate list in the file. These witnesses were only communicated to us last evening, randomly. We could not come up with any counter evidence against these witnesses, and no type of counter-list for the defense.

Mr. Senior-Prosecutor: Mr. President and Honorary Court, my opposing argument for the same deposition from the same text of law brought up by the honorary defense for the admission of the third objection that was raised just now; which is, the final dispositions of art. 254 from C.M.J., which talks about the requirement to present the witness or informant list, on the occasion of fulfilling the formalities provided in the first part of art. 254 from C.J.M., and we are having the faculty – by "we," I mean me and the defense — to propose witnesses until a certain deadline, the only cited people will be the ones with a complete shown address, and that list will be proposed 5 days at most after the President completes the formalities provided by art. 254. Either way, I declare that these witnesses, if you consider they have not been notified legally, I renounce examining them, and I ask the Honorary Court, with the power of discretion that law gives it, to allow them to be examined as informants.

Mr. H. Cosmovici, lawyer: Mr. President, allow us to add the following: there are two types of evidence in a trial. There is the evidence that results from my initiatives, but there is counter-evidence, or as it's called in the text, the General Prosecutor kindly read, informants, expert witnesses. In other words, you present me with certain evidence, you drop them on my back. Well, let me analyze them... This is the meaning of paragraph 2. I don't have from where to know what you present me with; allow me, after I acknowledge it, to propose my own expert witnesses. This is the purpose of the text.

Mr. Senior-Prosecutor: Honorary Council, I formally declare that I renounce the examination of these people as witnesses. But if no text gives me or the defense the right, Mr. President is the only one allowed to decide if, during the debates, we can propose to be brought to Court in any type of way that could be useful in finding out the truth. Gentlemen, I declared from the start that I give up on the examination of these witnesses: but I ask in return for the dispositions of art. 309 to be applied, which say: "The office president or at the requests of the sides, can call during debates to examine as informants any people that seemed necessary to be examined in order to find out the truth, even giving an order for the witness to appear in court if necessary." That's why I consider that, in conclusion, I followed the law.

Mrs. Lizetta Gheorghiu, lawyer: We will also refer to the discretionary powers of the honorary President, asking him to allow us counter-evidence against these witnesses, and especially, allow for us to be brought a list of these witnesses from the criminal records.

Mr. Senior-President: We adjourn for deliberations.

At reopening.

Mr. Senior-President: The Court takes note of the waiver of examining the witnesses proposed on the previous list, waived by the public ministry, and will assess during debates if it is necessary for other informants to be examined. I overrule the objection.

The Trial of Corneliu Zelea Codreanu

The Witnesses

At 11:15 begins the calling of the witnesses. The following are called: Mr. Ghiocel, Ion Crăcăuanu, prof. Ion Zelea Codreanu, Lawyer Mihail Polichroniade, lawyer Al. Chr. Tell, Prof. Ion Dobre, Col. Zăvoianu, Dorin Hasnaş, Traian Cotigă, Gh. Stoenescu, Gh. Ciorogaru, Ilie Negoescu, prof. Dragoş Protopopescu, absentees, Prof. Nichifor Crainic (present), Lawyer Crânganu, Arnold Roth, Carol Becker, Henri Ghica, Prof. Ion Dumitrescu, Eng. Voicu Popescu, Dr. Ion Cantacuzino (present), Prof. Vasile Cristescu, Nicolae Totu, Victor Gârniceanu, Col. Gh. Polihroniade, Col. Petre Bolintineanu, Paraschiv Gheorgescu (present), Admiral Teodorescu, General Dr. Popovici, General Dr. Pharmacist Grinţescu, General Dr. D. Constantinescu (present), Prof. Mihail Manoilescu, Prof. Dan Rădulescu, Iuliu Maniu (present), Prof. Ion Găvănescul, Ion Mihalache, Prof. Simion Mehedinţi (present), Prof. C. Giurescu, Lawyer Jean Naum, Col. C. Bolintineanu, Ilie Gârneaţă, Traian Brăileanu, Nelu Ionescu-Iaşi, Emil Zgoanţă (present), Ion Banea, Lawyer Petre Pogonat, Col. Const. Stănescu, Prof. I. Frollo (present), Mr. R. Ioaniţescu, Prof. Em. Antonescu (present), Prof. Gr. Forţu (present), Prof. Dr. Mr. Gerota (present), Lawyer Mr. Popa, Priest Ion Moţa, Prof. George Murnu, Dumitru Livezeanu (present), Alex Hodoş, Prof. Vintilă Dongoroz, Eugen Petit (present), Gh. Solomonescu, Nic. Georgean, Mr. Al. Vaida Voievod, Gr. Iunian, Col. Const. Malamuceanu, M. Sândulache, General M. Racoviţă (present), General N. Rujinschi, Prof. Nae Ionescu, Eng. Clime, Alex Cantacuzino, Priest Gr. Cristescu, Col. Rez. Cristescu, General Arthur Vătoianu, C. Argetoianu, Col. Emil Pălăgeanu, General Ilie Şteflea, General Dl. Coroamă, General Virgil Bădulescu, Major Florin Rădulescu, Dl. Stoicescu, Alex. Vergatti, Gr. Manoilescu (present), Lawyer Crângaru, Vasile Iaşinschi, Gh. Furdui, Priest Andrei Miăilescu, Prof. Radu Gyr, Sima Simulescu, Rng. Eugen Ionică, Bănică Dobre, Col. V. Piperescu, General Gabriel Marinescu, Gr. Coandă, Eng. Fotiade, Ion Foti, Const. Iarca, Prof. Pantazi (present), Prof. Chirnoagă (present), Lawyer Dl. Gerota, Dr. Raneţescu-Câmpina (present), Dr. V. Trigu, Traian Herseni (present), Ernest Bernea, Prof. N. Pop, General C. Iacob, Col. Const. Luca, Eng. Ion Gigurtu, Eugen Demetriu, Neagoe Flondor, N. Ulrich, Dr. P. Topa, General Stănătescu, General Ştefan Ionescu.

From 117 witnesses for the defense there are present 27.[13]

Lawyer Emil Zgoanţă is removed from the list of witnesses, and he joins the defense.

Romanian Crucible

Four informants that were proposed later are absent.

Mr. Senior-President: Mr. Prosecutor has the floor regarding the witnesses.

Mr. Senior-Prosecutor: Mr. President, Honorary Court, I'd ask you to give the floor to the honorary defense, because I only have one witness, and he is absent as well. I'd like to listen to the defense regarding the absent witnesses, so I can give them a reply and at the same time, to make my own objections when it comes to my witness.

The defense intervenes.

Mr. Senior-President: The defense has the floor.

Mr. Cosmovici, Lawyer: Mr. President, Honorary Court, regarding the witnesses, we have to notice from the start that there are two categories — even though all of them, when the objection will be considered, the Honorary Court remembers it, we will show that because of the fact that we did not have the files, it is part of only one category, — but, however, we consider them as being from two different categories. The first category contains the outside witnesses. In what sense? Meaning the ones that through my client's quality[14] — which he doesn't contest and he admits — as the leader of the Legionary Movement and spiritual leader of the party All for the Country, I came into contact with. In this sense, there is a series of witnesses that I can place in the category of those beside me. But the most important category is the second one: witnesses who were not beside me, the witnesses that were next to me — because, you see, it cannot be denied that if I didn't tell the truth here, in front of you, by virtue of which you claim — and is right — to judge, we would not do it right. Well, the defendant today, Corneliu Zelea Codreanu, if he had been alone, he would not be here today. He was the leader of a party and a movement. Well, whichever way we'd do this, the ones that were next to him, the ones that helped and understood him, the ones that fulfilled whatever he believed in and commanded, we want them to be here. It's a legitimate request. This second category of witnesses is called the category of witnesses, in fact, of witnesses that know things others from the outside cannot know, only in the amount that contact with them allowed certain things to be known. Therefore, I conclude this first idea in the following way: You judge me for a political activity that I couldn't have done by myself. However I did it, however, I fulfilled it, or infiltrated it in the souls of the ones that supported me, they are the ones that need to tell you this. They are, in

The Trial of Corneliu Zelea Codreanu

fact, the witnesses. You cannot deprive me of them. And I believe you will understand the reason for our arguments. Now, because of the exceptional measures, we are in a new judicial position, that has not been seen until today. There are those who were part of it — some were, some were not; it's unknown, because we don't have a way to know and didn't have a way to acknowledge this, — they are those witnesses that today are under house arrest, meaning the people who, by virtue of an order of the Minister's Council and the Ministry of Internal Affairs, are forced to stay put in a certain place: in this case, Miercurea Ciucului. This use of force was done at first in three different places, but at this moment is only in one place: at Miercurea Ciucului. Well, this is a new legal issue that you must judge, and I insist on it more while the ordinance, as well as the indictment handle and analyze — even though we don't contest the way in which they analyze — the three State powers. You represent one of these three State powers, according to the Constitution and the laws of the country. However, according to the Constitution and the laws of the country, and according to the new Constitution given by King Carol II, art. 1, even though divided under this aspect, you are, however, unitary, because you represent the State, which can only be unitary. This is why this action in art. 1 of the new Constitution is so important, and it says: "The kingdom of Romania is a unitary state and indivisible." It is a whole. Well, if it's a whole, however, it manifests its power, either judicially, administratively, or through executive power, because it is a whole, you are an integral part of it — regarding these measures taken by the Romanian State — so you are one. Or, this is a measure: home arrest. You force a person to stay in a certain place. If that's forced, that is not his home. And if the executive power forces him to remain there, the judicial power, which is one with the executive power, cannot deny that the person is there because that's how the State wants it. Well, we gave you the addresses from Miercurea Ciucului for the witnesses that are being held there. The notices should have been sent. We cannot even be called negligent or be told we lack zeal. Therefore, we are in the impossibility to bring them. I conclude, combining the second part with what I said in the beginning: these are actually my witnesses. It's difficult and, in fact, impossible for me to defend myself. So, understanding the role of these witnesses, I request you to send for them to be brought here, and until then, if we can follow what the text says, actually we're forced to do so, art. 290, because we want to remain constant in this trial, contrary to other people's beliefs, that we want to judge. Then, I ask you to apply art. 290: "If the procedure is not fulfilled for one of the called

Romanian Crucible

witnesses, this won't prevent the defendant's examination, listening to the other present witnesses, or taking other measures, after which the Court will decide if they need to postpone judging the case." So, we make use of the right given to us by art. 290. We will proceed with the interrogations, we will listen to the present witnesses, we will do everything, but these witnesses in fact need to be brought, because we do not have the power to do it. This is why we respectfully ask you to listen to our conclusions and postpone the trial until these witnesses are brought.

Mr. Senior-President: Mr. Senior-Prosecutor has the floor.

Mr. Senior-Prosecutor: Mr. President and judges, I agree with the honorary defense when it comes to the conclusions, but I don't agree with their considerations. It would be pointless to elaborate the arguments that prevented me to agree with the justifications given by the defense, in order to reach the conclusion on which they stopped; which is to ask the Honorary Court to apply art. 290 from C.J.M. Since you, as well as us are encouraged to proceed with the trial on legal basis, I consider it would be pointless to waste the time of the Honorary Court since I agree with the honorary defense.

Mr. Senior-President: We took note. The hearing is adjourned for deliberations.

The hearing is adjourned.

At reopening,

Mr. Senior-President Col. Magistrate Dumitru C-tin: After deliberations on the last objection, we join the objection to the cause. The absent witnesses will be brought by telegraph orders. The witnesses will be called Tuesday 24 May, at 8:80.

Final Ordinance

Mr. Registrar P. Tudor reads the final ordinance of arraignment.[15] The reading of the ordinance takes place from 12 to 12:50. As it is known, the ordinance ends with the decision for the defendant to be tried for the crime of treason (art. 191 P.C.), the crime of conspiring against social order (art. 209), and the crime of rebellion by the military indictment chamber.

Mr. H. Cosmovici: Mr. President and Honorary Court, we respectfully ask you to kindly take note of us, lawyers of the defense, as we have in our briefcase materials and books that you daily judge: we're talking about Legionary literature that was sold in bookstores until not long ago. As our homes can be searched whenever

The Trial of Corneliu Zelea Codreanu 105

and by anyone, we ask you to note our statement, for if we were to appear in front of the Honorary Court in other qualities than lawyers, let us have an established jurisprudence.

Mr. Senior-President: If anything like this were to happen, we promise you our support.

Mr. Cosmovici, lawyer: I hope not in the same way as it was with Mr. Codreanu.

Mr. Senior-President stops the hearing at 1, announcing the future hearing for 4:30 in the afternoon.

The Afternoon Hearing

Mr. Senior-President Dumitru: Now that the Final Ordinance and the decision of the Indictment Chamber have been read, the law gives you the right to propose everything you find useful for the defense.

At the same time, I warn the honorary bench of defense, that according to art. 291, it is required to express a deferent attitude towards the Court.

Mr. Prosecutor Ionescu: Mr. President, before the defendant can start on elaborating his means of defense, I'd ask you to allow me to inform you, and please, at the same time, to kindly organize my future interrogation, because the defendant, being sent to trial for three different crimes, which were: treason, conspiracy against social order, and rebellion, will systematize the statement that he must give, whereas, regarding the crime provided by art. 209, which is a conspiracy against social order, a secret hearing follows to be held, according to art. 274 from C.J.M.

Mr. Radovici, lawyer: On the request of Mr. Senior-Prosecutor, Mr. President, we, the defense, having a part of the files, we studied them together with the defendant and made sure, suspecting the observation that Mr. Prosecutor did, to systematize the explanations for which he came here, and he has the right to give before you. So, the defendant, taking into account the ordinance and the main accusations, will reply precisely to each of them and will not try to take more time than necessary for his complete defense.

At the same time, we want to declare that nothing he will say will be likely to cause secret hearings, on the contrary, I believe that this trial in broad daylight has the interest to find the answers that the defendant will give.

Romanian Crucible

The ordinance of indictment was published in every newspaper, is known from one end of the country to the other, and it would be odd, even bizarre, for a person being accused of such serious offenses to only be able to give explanations in a secret hearing, knowing that the debates will not reach the public opinion. This measure would be unfair and illegal.

You have the sovereign power that, if you will find contrary to our declarations that through the declaration the defendant makes, he will touch problems concerning state affairs, so serious that a secret debate would be necessary, to take the measures you find right at the right moment. But until then, please listen to the examinations in the public hearing, in front of the country's public opinion, listen to the explanations that the defendant will give to you, precisely and with an open heart.

Mr. Cosmovici, lawyer: Mr. President, two words only. The conclusions of the senior-prosecutor are in a complete contradiction with the invitation you kindly made to the defendant. You told defendant Codreanu: you know the accusations brought against you, you have the right, according to the law, to defend yourself.

Or, Mr. Senior-Prosecutor would want for this defense to be done according to how he wants.

Mr. Senior-Prosecutor: No!

Mr. Cosmovici, lawyer: But then, regarding the systematizing of material, whoever talks about it being systematic, talks about it being organized in a certain way. If you request for the material to be systematized, it means you request for the plea to be made instead of the one whose duty it is to make it. You accused the man however you felt like doing it, in whichever order you believed to be good and useful, but let him defend himself in the order he believes is right for him to do it. The interrogation, in the sense of pleading, is something strictly personal, and he will defend himself as his conscience dictates, as his head, and only his head, helps him.

We, the defense, believe that we won't have much else to add after Corneliu Zelea Codreanu's defense. Now, regarding the secret hearing, it is only motivated by one single thing: what is said must remain a secret. Let him say what he has to say, and then decide if it must be secret or public. We, who had the great ease of studying together, allowed the defendant to come with his own defense and examined his plan, which we will also form after his plan, and we can tell you nothing

The Trial of Corneliu Zelea Codreanu

will give you a reason to open a secret hearing. And then we ask you, in the same way in which we worked and collaborated, and we were accepted by the defendant to offer him a defense today, we know there is so much cleanness and as much said with reason as it must be, every risk as much as it should be, no more than it's necessary, that anything that would motivate a secret hearing would probably be some embarrassing fact, and I honestly tell you that it upsets us. You won't hear anything that would motivate a secret hearing. If you will, you are the sovereign to decide it, but only afterward.

Mr. Senior-Prosecutor Major Magistrate Ionescu: Mr. President, I'd like only to give an explanation. When I made that request to you, I didn't mean to create hardships for the defense in presenting their defense methods to the defendant. I was probably misunderstood. I only want to bring to the attention of the Honorary Council about the time when the discussion will reach the offense provided by art. 209, which is the conspiracy against social order, you must then decide if there will be a reason for a secret hearing. Otherwise, without a doubt it would be something against my conscience to impose a Council, something that I cannot do, to impeach the defendant's defense. These were the explanations I wanted to give.

Mrs. Gheorghiu, lawyer: Mr. President, Honorary Council, I believe the final ordinance which was published and broadcast, as well as the indictment, are not secrets, our defense being based upon them.

Mr. President Dumitru: The council will decide at the right time if a secret hearing will be necessary. Please, talk based on the order of the articles, so you talk about art. 209 last. You have the floor.

The Defense

Mr. Corneliu Zelea Codreanu: Mr. President, Honorary Council, Mr. Senior-prosecutor, during the search that I was subjected to on the night of 17 April, on my desk, on the last page of the block note, a note was found. What did that note say?

From 1 November 1933 until 1938, salaries, rents, personal debts valued to 40 million lei. Underneath, Mihail Manoilescu, director, 72 thousand monthly, delegated administrators: Grigore Manoilescu, 52 thousand lei monthly, and Mircea Manoilescu, 42 thousand lei monthly. During interrogations, that note was put in front of me, and I was asked: where are the 40 million lei you've spent from 1

108   Romanian Crucible

November 1933 until today? I was astonished. I've never had so much money, neither myself nor the Movement.

That's not possible, he said, and I'll show it to you. And he showed me the note. I immediately gave the explanation regarding this note, even though Mr. Senior-Prosecutor who interrogated me, had the gentleness and courtesy not to set that note as evidence against me, neither in the indictment, nor the final ordinance. However, it was noted that I apparently had the funds, that the movement spent huge sums of money, and that this money could have only come from obscure foreign, illegal sources, and that I was trying to cause a civil war in Romania, a revolution, etc., to arm the population, to buy and deposit weapons. Even though in the Final Ordinance and in the indictment this sum didn't appear and is not mentioned, it was mentioned on the Radio, and in the Romanian and foreign newspapers.

Mr. President and Honorary Council, I'm not on trial for this fact, so I am not defending myself against it to discharge a possible sentence. No. I'm defending my organization and my honor, and for this I ask you to allow me to briefly insist on this matter, after which I will talk about the crimes of which I am accused.

Mr. Senior-President Dumitru: Without limiting your right to defense, please keep in mind that the organization is not on trial, and this is about limited facts. Without denying you any freedom of defense, please keep in mind that your defense is determined by the law and by the charges. Therefore, please go over these problems and let's come back to the trial.

Mr. Codreanu: Mr. President, I won't abuse this matter, but please allow me, as my honor is on the line, and this problem was mentioned before. What happened then? I explained myself. A week or three days before this search, a delegation of workers came to me from the mines in Șorecani, owned by Mr. Manoilescu. I didn't know them.

They said: "Mr. Codreanu, we came to report something. Is Mr. Manoilescu part of your organization?"

"He's not, but I know him," I said. Please forgive me if I use the name of a family to defend myself, but this is the situation.

"We haven't been paid since before Christmas. No factory worker was." I asked why. "Is the industry having problems?" "It doesn't," they said, "but they earn so much and don't give us any. We went to the Industrial Credit and took ownership of this mine. We came to tell you as well. From 1 November 1933 and until today,

The Trial of Corneliu Zelea Codreanu

they owe 40 million for salaries, rents, and personal debts. The directors earn over 72 thousand a month, and the delegated administrators earn 52 thousand and 42 thousand a month."

I didn't believe it, so I said: "I'll note this down and I will ask, because I don't believe these numbers are accurate."

How could these people be worth 40 million? I wrote the note. After that, I heard that indeed the Industrial Credit took possession of the mine. So, you see, Mr. President and Honorary Council, what was I interrogated about and how these 40 million were attributed to me?

I asked the director, the engineer of the factory, to be my witness, to bring the three men that came to me and to the Industrial Credit, men I don't know, to have them say if they came to me and if these sums were accurate.

I talked about this, but it's not enough. The Honorary Council must know my opinion in this matter and that's why I'll tell them to you.

In my book *Pentru Legionari*[16] (*For My Legionaries*), where all my beliefs are written down honestly and fairly — because I didn't write them for this trial, but for the history and for the people — look what I said (*he reads*).

But, Mr. President and Honorary Council, the charges that are being brought to me today through the final ordinance I've seen before, and it always seems to be connected to these movements of moral and national rebirth that are being used as reasons by those who hate them, with all the invectives, bringing against them every accusation possible. Look what happened to us a few years ago. This is what the foreign press was writing about us.

Mr. Senior-Prosecutor: Please mention the page you'll read from.

Mr. Codreanu: Pages 444-447.

The way we are seen: "A movement of disorder, of anarchy, of breaking the law, and terrorist," after that, the article called "În slujba străinilor" ("In the Service of Foreigners"), says on page 444: "For a time, not knowing what to charge us with, the Jewish press accuses us of taking money from Mussolini. That we pretend to be nationalists, but in reality, our purpose is to extort money from whoever comes our way. We now found Mussolini and we extorted him." Time and time again we were astonished about: "we are in the service of the Hungarians who are getting smarter;" "we are in the service of Moscow...;" "we receive Jewish money." We

Romanian Crucible

weren't even spared this ridiculous accusation. In the Jewish newspaper called *Politica*, from 10 August 1934, there's a significant fragment from an article called "Max Auschnit şi Garda de Fier": "So, in our country the phenomenon is proven as well and it is well known by everyone that the most significant fascist movement in Romania, the Iron Guard, was created and supported by the great capitalists." And this is where the sensational, that is not quite that, comes in place: the Jew Max Auschnit[17] supported and directly founded the Iron Guard. This statement was repeated by two serious and responsible men: Mr. Minister Victor Iamandi,[18] and the renown publicist Scarlat Callimachi.[19] After the above explanations, this fact appears as obvious. Who doesn't know that Hitler was financially supported by the great Jewish capitalists in Germany as well? On page 446: Hitler wants to take Transylvania from us. But we, the Romanian nationalists who want to be rid of the Jewish curse, are more or less with Hitler, so we want to give Transylvania to the Germans. But we reply: let us assume that Hitler wants to take us to war and take Transylvania. We, Romanians, in order to protect Transylvania from the Germans, we must be rid of Jews. We must resolve the Jewish problem as well. We must strengthen the positions of our nation that have been extorted by Jewry, an inert nation that is in the impossibility to defend itself. Because of the Jewry that poisons us and sucks our blood we won't have weapons, or a soul, or meat on our bones. Finally, we receive money, we are supported, we are on the payroll of the Hitlerites. We reply: A.C. Cuza has been fighting against the Jews since 1890, and us since 1919, 1920, 1921, and 1922, from a time when we didn't even know who Adolf Hitler was. Poisonous snakes!

But not much time passed and a new campaign started against us. Our enemies found a new financial source for the factory of fake banknotes from Răşinari. The sensational discovery filled the pages of political and Jewish newspapers. I'll give a few examples; I'll only quote the titles: "The Iron Guard and the fake banknote factory from Răşinari; The source of propaganda funds. At Răşinari, the commune near Sibiu, a sensational discovery was made that had the purpose of presenting a whole political organization in a bad light, against which the government, which now owns crushing evidence, will have to attack with all its might."

The fake banknote factory of the Iron Guard: "From the undertaken research it was found, to everyone's astonishment, that this time is not about a gang of gypsies or lunatics going against the law, but the Iron Guard itself, a political organization led by Mr. Codreanu, who in recent times gave up on the most shameful campaign

The Trial of Corneliu Zelea Codreanu

against the government and against all the other political parties in Romania. For those who have knowledge about the activity of the Iron Guard, with their groups that scout the country from one end to the other, a fact that seems natural: in such circumstances they especially need money. Or, it's known that the propagandists from the Iron Guard had numerous funds available to them, which allowed them to travel to villages, as well as print newspapers, and arm their supporters with everything necessary to conquer as Hitler did."

It was continued: "Lawyer Liveanu discovered sensational compromising material that reveals that the money factory in Rășinari was exclusively serving the subversive political purposes of the Iron Guard. Among the confiscated correspondence, they discovered letters from different organizations, especially from an organization in Iași, in which Mr. G... was asking me for a big sum of money to buy a truck. The police officers made a series of arrests and took all the compromising material, together with the devices used to forge the money. The investigation continues with much diligence."

Another article: "To the stakes with the forgers!" Another paper! This is how the conspirator association, called the Iron Guard, did it: "It pretends to act in the name of nationalism. This hypocrisy must be unmasked in front of the public opinion. Nationalism, in order to be served, doesn't need occult organizations, secret associations, and especially doesn't need the methods that the Iron Guard uses. Nationalism is a belief that must be defended in broad daylight, open, honest, and sincere, not by an association that serves nationalism through secret orders, invisible nests, occult cells, and especially, it doesn't need methods such as those used by the Iron Guard, such as forging money like ordinary criminals. The Iron Guard is only a handful of secretly grouped adventurers, who try to seize power in the State with violence, with an exaggerated and shameful demagogy. All of this in the name of national ideas."

I feel like I'm reading fragments of a court order: "The discovery of the gang in Rășinari shows the real colors of the Iron Guard. People wonder from where they get all this money or organization, for buying trucks, for travel, for maintaining cars. From where? The factory in Rășinari indicates the source: money forgery. The Iron Guard is a gang of forgers and cannot speak in the name of nationalism."

This is what happened to us. This is only one episode, to see what happened to us, in our lives, when mud was thrown at our souls, because nothing written here is true. They didn't even investigate it; we weren't even called for an interrogation. Nothing.

But now, allow me to tell you how my life has been. It's only natural for me to show it. Where can you see it? Give me file 1, page 210.

This is a circular from General Cantacuzino. When I speak this name, I want to share with you the conviction I have had living with our old General, a conviction which I believe any good faith Romanian has: that General Cantacuzino-Grănicerul was a man with a fair soul even when it came to money, that I don't believe anyone in this country could accuse him of something like this. Well, find out Mr. President and Honorary Council, that the General, up until his death, was the treasurer of our organization. He wanted to administer everything by himself.

He was the president and the treasurer of this organization.

This is what General Cantacuzino wrote in a circular for all the regional leaders: "Please keep up to date with the shares from icons, fliers, dues, etc., and think about this, if every member paid 5 lei monthly, that equals 60 lei a year, at 50,000 members we'd have 3 million a year, which would cover all of our expenses, because we don't live in luxury, and we don't waste the money." This is a circular given by prof. Vasile Cristescu[20] to the county of Vlaşca: "We know that our Movement is very poor. A new request was made to the sacrificing spirit of the Legionaries. It was decided that every county must help the center. Under no circumstances should the contribution be less than 500 lei a month. This will be gradually raised, depending on the organization, to 2,000 lei a month. I believe the spirit of sacrifice that the people of Vlaşca have shown every time will not deny our request this time either."

Mr. President and Honorary Court, everything I've written is contained in this book, and there are other circulars that are not listed here, either because the men couldn't find them when they printed these books, or they were given after that, and there are also interviews.

These are my doings, this is what I wrote, and for which I can respond with my whole honesty and power. I cannot respond to something that others write about me. I can only speak about what I've written. You'll see in a bit.

This is the circular from 31 May 1925: "Everything that is sent in writing from the center — orders, circulars, manifestos, brochures — must not be given to anyone for free. They will be sold for 1 leu per sheet."

The Trial of Corneliu Zelea Codreanu

Honorary Council, I don't know if you are aware that in politics, a lot of manifestos and brochures are printed by every political group, publications that are normally shared for free. This is the custom. This is the first time in the political life of Romania when the manifestos you were seeing stuck on streets and which belong to us were all paid for.

Each of our manifestos was bought from our headquarters or from bookstores — because they were also shared to certain kiosks. Whoever wanted to do us good — whether they were members of the Movement or not — came to us with 5 lei, and we gave them 5 manifestos, or came with 100 lei, and we gave them 100 manifestos, each took them and each paid.

"...will be sold for 1 leu per sheet."

Notice how much care and work everyone had! I didn't do all of this for a trial.

Further on, we had the great problem providing food for 15 Legionaries. See here: p. 37 in *Circulari*:

Monday, 7 October 1935

The Legionary Canteen

A great problem: how could we accommodate 15 Legionaries that work in different functions at the Head Office. They work for the Movement. They need a place to eat and sleep. Until now, they stayed in the guard barracks and had their meals at the Center. In very harsh conditions for the organization. This year, once we turned the guard barracks into a cooperative, we were required to find a solution. This meant we had to establish a Legionary canteen. In order to do this, we found a house a week ago. The Legionaries dealt with all the repairs needed, a bit too many since the poor house was almost in ruins, forgotten in the center of the Capital. The Legionary men and women repaired the walls with much care, disinfected, repaired the floors, and painted the walls. We have four rooms: two for sleeping accommodations (shared beds like at Jilava); two for cooking and dining. The hotplate and some of the dishes belong to my wife. We'll buy the rest. The tables and the dishes, a part was lent to us by Stelian Georgescu. The meals will be cooked everyday by the Legionary women on duty and our friends who want to do a good deed. Ms. Vran will lead and direct the Legionary women who are not familiar with those duties. A meal will cost 6 lei and will consist one well-cooked course, clean, tasty,

Romanian Crucible

and filling. With all the necessary bread. In the evening, it is better to serve polenta with milk (half a kg. per person). At this restaurant we will strongly recommend consuming onion and garlic in significant quantities. The food will be bought through the Cooperative at wholesale prices. The Cooperative will help with firewood and with the rent. 30-40 Legionaries will be able to eat here, and those are:

A) the ones working at the headquarters;

B) the ones working at the Cooperative;

C) the ones in different functions for the Movement:

For example: the leader of Brotherhoods of the Legionary Center, Student Center, and the Citadels;

D) the couriers arriving from within the country;

E) the poorest of our active Legionaries.

Every one of them will have to contribute. The ones from points a, b, c, d, will have to pay directly to the organizations. The ones from point e will be asked to work and earn 12 lei a day. No work is shameful. We will tell them: it's better to chop wood and carry water than to beg. We have to banish this disease from among us, this miserable mentality, to be an honor for us to be able-bodied and rational in order to earn our food by using our own strength. And all this is not in a poor country, where, indeed, earning one's existence would be heroic, but in a rich country like ours, that was blessed by God, where money is so easily earned. All those who cannot earn 12 lei a day are imbeciles that don't justify their existence.

Mr. Senior-President Dumitru Constantin: Please resume your story, because it's already been an hour, and we haven't started discussing the charges. The Court has a brochure and they will read it.

Mr. Corneliu Zelea Codreanu: Why do I insist on this matter? I want to show that this wasn't an isolated case.

We started a trade. Everything we build, except the iron parts, is made by our own hands: masonry, woodwork, plaster, painting. We started this with 73,000 lei, a sum we made during the camp at Carmen Sylva.[21] We spent over 60,000 on repairs, and that's why on the 16th of November 1936 we did not have much merchandise — we did not have groceries because no wholesaler wanted to accord us credit, not even 5,000 lei.

Another circular:

The Trial of Corneliu Zelea Codreanu

Bucharest, 12 November 1936

Changing the Staff

"To the regional and county leaders:

On 1 January, the old staff will turn over leadership to the new staff.

The regional and county leaderships will be classified based on their ability to lead and their activity, and on their fairness when it comes to handling money. These days we started the painstaking work of classification. Unfortunately, I found that, even with the Legionary school, with all our persistence from the last year on the idea of a fair man, we are still far from fairness. We cannot expect to have rights, presence in the government, we cannot critique or be infatuated with politics if we are not fair.

To those who ask me: "when will we start our political activity for government," I answer them "when the county and regional leaders report that in their organization there are no unfair men left."

Unfair doesn't necessarily mean a thief — it also means insufficient care, order, delicacy, or severity when it comes to money that doesn't belong to you. Concerning this last aspect, when we started working on the classification, we found some organizations that cared for brochures, photographs, calendars, *mărțișoare* etc. (from the propaganda service, some taken a year ago) that still haven't paid their dues to this day. Please remember: we are not asking for donations. This is about something else: you took the goods, sold them, so you have to turn over the money for the goods. Combined, these organizations owe the Propaganda Service 200,000 lei, enough to paralyze it. It is impossible to print. Faced with this situation, I was forced to suspend the work on classification and offer a month's time, meaning until 15 December, for these organizations to pay what they owed. Not only for this material matter, but also for the principle of honor and harsh fairness that every Legionary must show."

When Moța and Marin died in Spain, I gave the following order (reads): p. 102 from *Circulări*.

Bucharest, 15 January 1937

Legionaries!

Romanian Crucible

Ion Moța, founder of the Legionary Movement, honorary president of the Romanian students;

Dr. Vasile Marin, Legionary commander, the leader of the organization in the Capital, both of them, after 14 years of suffering, beatings and prisons, endured for their faith in the Romanian nation, forever fell asleep on the front in Majadahonda, in defense of the faith in our Lord Jesus Christ. The heartbreaking news fell like lightning on us. It will make any Romanian tremble. We gave God the best children this nation could offer.

General Cantacuzino leaves tomorrow to bring back their bodies. Because he needs a great sum of money, I must ask those who have them to contribute telegraphically for these holy bodies to be brought back to their country.

Sunday, 17 January 1937, the churches will have religious services.

May God receive their sacrifice!

Corneliu Zelea Codreanu

Fortunately, the people, all Romanians, helped, and we could bring them.

We reached the electoral period, where it's said we've done so much. This is an urgent notification published in *Buna Vestire*:[22]

Legionaries, the All for the Country Party submitted its lists for the Chamber in the whole country and for the Senate in 47 counties. 19 counties were left unpaid for the Chamber and the Senate. These fees came to 230,000 lei. Neither the counties, nor the center has money left. There are three days left until 10 December,[23] and if we can't pay the fees the lists are lost. I make an urgent call to every Legionary and friend to contribute telegraphically, as much as they afford, to pay the fees for the lists for these counties, or those can lend us the money, with our promise to repay it.

Signed (ss) N. Totu, chief of the electoral office.

The leadership of the Movement tried to obtain a loan for a long period of time from various entrepreneurs, because we had urgent need of woodwork and heaters. We thought we could obtain a new loan, — and there are more circulars here for that, which I won't read.

But I want to tell you, Mr. President and Honorary Court, I finished with my first idea. So, Mr. President and Honorary Council, I'll continue with the trial, because this trial has three layers: a part that is judged outside this court, in the press

The Trial of Corneliu Zelea Codreanu

and on the Radio — which I cannot do anything about, — another part consists of a whole series of accusations like the one before, but the indictment from Mr. Prosecutor and the Final Ordinance does not list them as charges, even though I'm accused of them but not put on trial for them, and finally, the actual charges I am being tried for.

Now I'd like to go straight to the center of my trial. I'm charged with treason. At the foundation of this charge is a false document and one of my circulars that has been misunderstood completely.

Which is the false document and what do I understand by that? When I think about a false document that doesn't belong to me, that I've never seen before, that hasn't even been found in my home, a document written by someone else, that I couldn't find it written down and ask what that is. What is this document that was found on Negoescu, the painter from Casa Verde? It's an informative memoir. Mr. Senior-prosecutor brought it to me, put it in front of me, and asked me: What's this? At first glance, I said: I've never seen it in my life. I said that without hesitation, so no. I've never seen it, and it was not found on me. It might have been planted by someone on the painter, some instigating agent. And then I started reading it. What did this document want to prove? First, that I had activity from the spring of 1934 until the fall, meaning the exact time when I wasn't allowed to have activity. For what? Because I asked for dues. He says: you gave me an order to make a history of this matter. This is the history: contributions are made only from that time. I didn't understand at first, but later on I realized that someone thought that my trial should be founded on this; meaning the secret continuity of the so-called Iron Guard in a time when it wasn't allowed and in relation to the party All for the Country, making it sound like the All for the Country Party was the Iron Guard in disguise. The gentleman who wanted to do this kindness to me thought well about this.

The second point, which follows to be proven by that memoir: it says that he is a hidden agent for me and that I employ undercover agents; this is where all the problems with the undercover agents started.

But I'm lucky. My luck is that he uses my name to earn credibility; there were 15 pages that had to be filled, so then it was very difficult to write in the report the dates between which he had activity: he had to use names, and there's where my luck stands.

Romanian Crucible

This is the memoir (vol. Instruction, file 9, p. 64, statement)

Gentlemen, I'm not an expert, but please, with a bit of thinking — possibly ask someone else — see that this paper and this writing are from 1935, if it wasn't recently written. The ink is so fresh, that it can only be dated — I say in my defense — from the 31st of December 1934. This is what it says: "For me your order remains the same as from 1927, you remain covered". Further, it talks about receipts and displays these earnings — look, gentlemen — made at the time when I was calling on everyone to give 50 lei each...

Mr. Senior-president Dumitru: You only address the Court.

The defendant: Yes, Mr. President.

This is the receipt from 1934 for the sums given by the supporters of the Iron Guard during that year:

No. 10, 25,000 lei a month

No. 24, 3,500 lei a month

No. 13, 12,000 lei a month

No. 21, 18,000 lei a month

No. 17, 9,000 lei a month

No. 25, 11,500 lei a month

No. 23, 8-9,000 lei a month

No. 14, 9-10,000 lei a month

No. 19, approximately 9,000 lei a month

And the last one, without a number, 6,000 lei a month.

We have never received such donations from the time we started our activity: the maximum amount has been 1,000 lei a month. But this is what it says further on: "and this is the reason, with its multiple sub reasons, that determines me to ask you, Captain, at the beginning of this memoir, to continue covering me and allow me to keep staying concealed."

I will stop for a second on this idea because secrecy is a criminal word, it's a derogatory word, and it is the word required by law that allows me to be called a criminal. So, he's not content with just saying he's covered, but also has to mention concealment. Nobody would say they are allowed to be concealed or use the word concealed in a random context, they wouldn't use the criminal derogatory word.

The Trial of Corneliu Zelea Codreanu

This is a lead for me, as well as for yourselves. Then, he split the Movement into classes: worker, commercial, intellectual, and authoritative — a classification that never existed, because it can be proven the workers' movement was founded by the General[24] only in 1937 in Azuga, through the first worker's corps; the commercial movement was founded by me last fall, by founding the Legionary trade; the intellectual section never existed, neither did the authority section, — what is the authority, I don't understand, but let's continue. One of the fragments in here says that I sent him to the Chemist-Engineer Crângaru. He doesn't exist. Lawyer Crângaru is listed here as a witness; he can tell if I sent him to forward anything or not. Finally, one of the pages here says that I ordered this gentleman to give me the history of a conversation that took place. And it also says, among other things, that I made a secret code. I have made a joke about a secret code during my student years at the University, or when I was 18 years old. Other than that, it's not part of my way of thinking. You imagine I couldn't make a secret code to discuss with him such matters without realizing what that meant?

On 16 May 1934 it says: "You allowed me to turn into a chronology the memorable dialogues you've had with the leader of youth of the 250 million nationalists, with Professor Dragoş Protopopescu and with professor Crainic, where I had the pleasure to assist, as well as the others that I had the permission to briefly note down when I was walking around by myself." So, this gentleman says he assisted in a discussion between me and Mr. Crainic, Prof. Protopopescu, and him, with the leader of 250 million young nationalists in the world — 250 million written with letters, not with numbers. From here, newspapers made their conclusions and published about me having an undercover agent.

Mr. President, I'm not a man to not take responsibility for my actions. I've been this way my whole life, and the whole world who came in contact with me knows this; everyone knows that I'm not the man to take a step back or only admit to half the truth. My education was done this way: for my actions, I take all the responsibility and keep going forward; if it's mine, I admit; if I tell you it's not mine, then it's not.

And now, the wrong interpretation of one of my circulars.

Mr. President and Honorary Court, let's look at the circular regarding informants.

Romanian Crucible

Hounded every day by a whole series of agents that infiltrated our numbers, people that might have been bought from my Movement, distressed constantly, every day, and urged by friends who showed us we had traitorous agents among us, I grabbed my pen and made a circular for all the Legionaries and the members in the Capital, and I said: the security agents must come to me on a set day; those who are from the Police prefecture to come to me on a set day. I explained what a private service was; they're the police next to important personalities, such as Max Auschnit and others, in the service of these private people. This is why I made the circular.

The circular — I said — will be signed by every nest member in the Capital to show they took note of it.

This is the exact copy of this circular: "To all the Legionaries and nest members in the Capital: Every informant from the Capital Police that is part of nests is invited to come to me personally in order to receive directives between 19 and 21 June; informant agents from security or the Great Major State, must come between the 21st and 25th of June 1937; the informants of other private services, on 26 June 1937.

This order will be read in every nest by the nest leaders, and every member will sign it."

Therefore, this order is addressed to all the Legionaries and members in the Capital and had to be read in every nest by the nest leader; and each member of the nest had to sign they were notified. Further, I said: "The order, once signed, will be brought to me by the sector leaders or other units. The ones who won't show up will be seen as trying to betray our Movement, to sell us and deceive us. Services can be done without deceit, without selling out anyone, without betrayal, and without breaking the oath."

Therefore, this order was addressed to them, thinking in my heart, that they would come to me and will admit to being agents in the way shown above.

As for me, I proffered them to come to me and tell me that to my face rather than sell me out. Besides, I was never against the agents coming straight to me. If I was against something, I was against cowardice, and I didn't want to be sold by my brother, the one that ate with me at the table, the one that drives with me in the car, just to sell me afterward.

The Trial of Corneliu Zelea Codreanu

Look, Mr. President, what the point of this circular was. Besides, I will prove it with the chief of Security that I proposed as a witness, Mr. Cernat. I showed him what was happening to me, I showed him what I was being charged with, and he knows all of this. He came and told me, Mr. Codreanu, I have such and such information. He came to my home whenever, because my home was open to everyone, and I always kept in touch with him, even though I'm standing accused that I'm against the security of the State, I kept in touch with the chief of security, so I can eliminate every reason for gossip.

Well, I constantly kept in touch with the chief for State Security, who came to Carmen Sylva to see me, because I couldn't abandon my work, who was in my home, who also visited engineer Ionică where he met me, who repeatedly saw me at Constantin Iarca's place, and every time he needed me, he looked for me and found me. In these circumstances, I don't think this man could tell you that it's not true and that I wasn't always fair to him, sincerely telling him: this is how it is; this isn't how it is.

During the time that we kept in touch, General Cantacuzino always kept in touch with General Gabriel Marinescu, who I asked to be my witness in this matter, also because of these informants, people that sold us, who would interfere and give all sorts of wrong information.

That's the time when I sent this circular. Nobody showed up. Two weeks later, I wrote another one. I can't find it in the file at the moment, because I didn't have when to see them within the past two days. I remember that either one or the other was published in the journals. From the first moment you said during instruction: there are two orders we've sent. I thought I would have them by now. Everyone signed it, even the nest leaders, after reading it. Why did I want everyone to sign it? I wanted to see if anyone said they didn't know about it. I had my suspicion about 3 or 4 men, and I wanted to see if they would sign. I can prove with witnesses how this order was understood. You mean I gave an order to my agents that I apparently had at Security? Honorary Council, let's presume I had agents. How many could I have? Two in Security, two in the Prefecture, two in another place. I'm not even talking about the General Staff. There would be no way. There are officers there. How could I enter the heart of a Romanian officer? This would be impossible. Ten in total. This would be the logical step when trying to gather 10 of your informants? With noise? To search all nests and all their members? This is how it's

Romanian Crucible

done? It was being discussed about selling brothers, betrayals, and oaths? This is how others would proceed?

I would have said: go to such and such house and street and call the man to me because I have something to tell him. But I wouldn't give an order for all the nests and mention at the end about selling brothers and betrayal.

What purpose would I have of phrases, if I only needed to see certain people? No purpose at all; I didn't have a reason to have everyone sign it. Only the one whom it was meant for should sign it, not everyone in the Capital. But you see, that's how our people interpreted this circular.

They are workers; they aren't intellectuals. They're simple men. On page 3,425: "Peneş Curcanul Nest, sector I: Dumitru Coforola, Bălaş Alexandru, Dumitru Ioan, Vasilescu. All these members took note of the order given by the Captain on the day of 15 July 1937, and we all take responsibility." Therefore, each of them understood and none of them is an informant agent.

Cavalerii Crucii Nest sign no. 1, 2, 3, and 4. At no. 5 it says: "military regional auto-traction Bucharest; I'm not part of any secret organization." And there is the proof that he was in the military service, at no. 6, where it says: "Stanciu Ilie is noted to be on leave, being in the military."

There is a second order I gave. I couldn't find it during these two days of freedom. I don't know where it could be. However, I remember that — I stated it in the instruction — the second order is even clearer. My precise words in it are: "Dog, you eat with me at the same table and you sell me. I know you." The second order was even more categorical than the first one. It could happen to find the second order, but I haven't found it so far. I know one of them was published. In this case, I believe there's sufficient evidence that I didn't announce through the journal that I was looking for informants.

Either way, I talked to others when I gave these orders. They asked me: Did anyone show up? I talked to Virgil Ionescu, to Polihroniade, to Totu, to the boys at my office.

P. 89 vol II:[25] Members of the Daco-Romanian nest: "Mihai Moraru, Victor Slăteanu, Gheorghe Mateescu. Comrade Gh. Mateescu is traveling to Poiana Ţapului, so I'll answer for him, because he's not part of the ones targeted above."

Meaning, these people understood precisely they weren't agents, and they're assuming the responsibility.

The Trial of Corneliu Zelea Codreanu

Mr. President, before going forward, please pause the hearing for a few minutes.

The hearing is adjourned.

At reopening.

Defendant C.Z. Codreanu: Mr. President and Honorary Council, I found the other two-three signed orders in the same way, with the warranty that the one who signed was not an agent.

For instance, the Legionary nest in Green Sector IV, signed that they acknowledge the order about the informer agents: Iancu Drăgănescu was traveling to the bath houses. In front of number 3 — there are 10 who signed — it is mentioned: "soldier, he's not an informant, attested to by the nest leader."

The man was not there, he was serving in the army, doing his military service, and the nest leader mentioned it above. So, the order was understood perfectly. This document is on page 59, file 225.

Mr. President, if possible, I'd ask you to make it so that the witnesses in the camp are not brought here. They can't make contact with anyone. I'd ask you to form some sort of rogatory commission to go there and ask them what they understood from the orders about the informants. They can't contact anyone to know what was discussed here. They don't need to come here as witnesses, let someone go there and ask them about this matter — I'd give the names of those who know this — so you can ask them what they understood by it.

Mr. Senior-Prosecutor: They will say the same thing you just did.

The Defendant: I believe so because it can't be another way, even though I had no contact with them.

Prosecutor Ionescu: Of course. There's no need for a rogatory commission.

Defendant C.Z. Codreanu: The conclusion is terrible. Meaning, an entire network of informants at the Police Prefecture, at the Major State, in plane factories, and in a series of private institutions. What can I reply to this charge? That's all I have to say: the order given by me was misinterpreted. Why would I have such a network of informers? Why? To get information? In a country where with the education we have, it is not possible to tell a secret to someone, to a friend of yours, and not be known two hours later or two days later by the whole Capital, or your whole city. In this country, nobody needs to have any informants. Where did I take my information from? The journalists were bringing it to me.

Romanian Crucible

Gentlemen, let me tell you a thing that is a bit comical. There are three locations here in the Capital, which are Capşa, Corso, and Athenée Palace, where there is every type of news, internal or external.

Prosecutor Ionescu: Only in the imagination of those who frequent them.

H. Cosmovici, lawyer: We have witnesses as well.

The Defendant: Those are not shameful locations, but places where people gather and a whole series of journalists as well. For instance, every day Ion Folea would come to the General[24] with notes from Capşa, and after that he'd come to me, telling me what events happened today from the information that journalists had. I met journalists every day because I was part of a political movement, and from every piece of information I was getting, I sorted half because some of them made no sense, some were real, but I received no information without sorting it. This way, I always got the information I needed from journalists and newspapers.

Then a question arises: how did you come across those orders? And I think I can prove definitively that my state information service falls. Let's look at the original orders; I'd ask for patience on your part, so we can study this order, for example (reads):

This is the original of another order. This is its content (vol. 9, p. 79):[25]

(Information Order of the Gendarme Inspectorate in Bucharest addressed to the Legion of Gendarmes in Argeş)

All subunits,

Information order no. 64 from 04.10.1934

"You are given a copy of address no. 13,243/934 of the Regional Inspectorate of Police in Bucharest of which you will take note and urgently start investigating, intensifying the information services and closely monitoring all members of the former organization called the Iron Guard. You will report until 10:10 am, if a new organization called The Lighting was established on around the perimeter of your section. I don't admit negligence, and I ask for much ambition from each rank, to be on top of everything that is planned in order to take measures in due time."

Commander of the Argeş Gendarmes Regiment,

Major...

Copy.

The Trial of Corneliu Zelea Codreanu

"We are informed that the members of the dissolved organization the Iron Guard are establishing a new formation called The Lighting, having a framed lightning bolt as a symbol. The new rules of the organization provide that every commune must form a committee of five members chosen among the best-trained ones. The instructions are sent from the Center by a Legionary courier. By bringing this to your attention, we ask you to take action and verify this information, communicating to us the results in due time."

Inspectorate of Regional Police I-a

(ss) Bogdan

Filer no. 3, p. 51,525 (order sent by phone to the subordinated units of the Craiova Gendarmes Inspectorate.

"After my secret telegram no. 16, the Craiova Gendarme Inspectorate is informed that the members of the former organization called the Iron Guard are making a new political plan:

1.   To place a hundred uniformed students in every county — blue shirts. Lawyer Ionescu from Caracal has already ordered these uniforms.

2.   They have the intention, before their arrival, to help General Averescu to form a dictatorship, and after his death, his place would be taken by Corneliu Zelea Codreanu.

The section commanders must take measures to discover these intentions."

But what conclusion can we come to from seeing this? That the whole issue with informants falls. Why? Because these orders are clearly not sent by the General Gendarme Inspectorate to me, by the Security Service, or by the Ministry, where I have been accused of having agents, but from the bottom of a village, which shows they were received occasionally and by chance. And that's natural. In four years, two orders were found on me from Argeş, one from Craiova, one from Prahova, and two that I published in the circular, one from the Security Service and one from General Bengliu.[26]

This is the deciding proof that rejects the statement of informants. Torn and deteriorated orders, kept in the pocket of who knows what notary or mayor or thrown away during the move of a gendarme post. They are not orders taken from the Center by me. Another proof: they are signed by the secondary authority, not by the central authority. So, they were sent to me occasionally. What do I want to

126 Romanian Crucible

prove with this? That once they are sent by the second authority, as it can be seen, I cannot be accused of taking them from the institutions where I am accused of having informers.

Now let me get to these orders. Yes, I admit to them, I admit they were found in my home. I admit I saw them. I admit that a part of them, two or three, weren't published, but I published another part of them. And now I'll justify it. If I'm guilty, I will take responsibility and suffer the consequences. I admit: what is mine, is mine. But I don't want someone to accuse me of something that isn't mine. And then, this is how I motivate the issue with the orders.

Their content. You've seen the content of these orders. It's not important. Have I ever thought about these endangering the State's security? No, I've never in my life thought about that. One of them from Craiova, another from Argeş, local, couldn't endanger the State's security, but it could employ an issue from those communes, a public issue, but under no circumstance the State's security. So I kept them.

But this is the content of the other order (reads):

Ilfov County Prefecture   Strictly-personal, confidential

(Administrative Service)   no. 198 Reserved 11.10.1937

Mister...

"We have the honor to send you the copy below, the personal confidential order no. 61,096/937 of the Ministry of Internal Affairs, a Police Circular regarding the order measures given on the propaganda expansion and Legionary organization in Ilfov County.

You will make sure to stop every Legionary attempt to penetrate the county and the communes. Those who don't listen to these words will be arrested and sent to their homes.

Every attempt of this kind will be immediately reported to the prefecture."

Prefect...

Copy

Mister...

"Following circular 956/12 August of this year, I have the honor to report the following:

The Trial of Corneliu Zelea Codreanu

Regarding the propaganda expansion and Legionary organization in Ilfov County, Prof. Sima Simulescu, the head of the Black Sector from the Capital's organization of the party All for the Country, commissioned all the nest leaders in his subordination personally to travel to the communes in Ilfov County, part of the Black Sector where, meeting with the leaders of local organizations, would collaborate towards the expansion of the propaganda and county organization.

Each nest leader was given a list of communes, where he is required to travel during the holidays for this purpose. Aside from this, each nest will hold at least one weekly march in the Sector's suburbs, and the whole Sector will organize at least four larger scale marches a month in the county.

By informing you of the above, we ask you to kindly order measures for executing the instructions in the circular we mentioned for the purpose of stopping such marches."

For Minister (ss) Cernat

I considered such an order to be illegal, an abusive order, which could serve me a purpose. In what way? First, by suing its author, because through it they are denying my right, my legal patrimony given to me under the law. I am a legally formed party and I have the right to propaganda. You can only follow me around, but you can't stop me. At one point, you can tell me: you're not legal, I'll take away your authorization, but you can't tell me: "look, you're legal, go do your propaganda," and on another hand, prevent me in so many ways. I told myself: this is a problem, a political and electoral chaff, as it happened many times before in every party. When a certain party is in the government, they try to prevent all the other parties. But that doesn't mean you can hide away your responsibility about illegal things you do when you give such orders, to hide yourself behind the words strictly personal, confidential, or even coded writing. No! And then, what can I do? I can publish it and show the public opinion: "Look what injustice they're doing to me", or I can take it to the Parliament. Why? To show them their injustice.

Besides, every political man that leads organizations gets such orders. They send it for every political man, because we have correspondence with the world, with people from everywhere, and they're sent to us: "look what abusive order was sent against us from such and such location to... ." All of them have them. I called a whole series of witnesses here, political men, almost all of them are political leaders, so they can state if they have these types of orders or not.

Romanian Crucible

But let's move on. Let me read you an order that I can't find in the file, an order from Prahova, from the brochure in which I published it, p. 16,527. A confidential order, personal, from the Prahova Prefecture. This was published (reads):

"A confidential order of the Prahova Prefecture. Address sent to the following factories: clothing factory, beer, glass, and cement from Azuga.

Prahova county Prefecture   Personal-confidential

State Service   no. 116 from 22 July 1937

Mr. Director,

I have the honor to bring to your attention that the officers in our subordination, found that the workers of that factory, which is named on the back, are guilty of agitations that disturbed and still disturb the public order.

For these considerations and as an example of intolerance towards such manifestations, please remove them from service."

Next, the names of 36 Romanian Legionary workers are listed, who were fired for their beliefs.

These are their names:

Clothing factory: Braga Ambrozie, Cioc Mircea, Irimia Al., Prian V., Crici Ioan, Irimescu Gh., Nedelcu Anghel, Bițoiu Ștefan, Prian Mihai, Talianu Ion, Talianu Mircea, Olteanu C., Pițoiu Gh., Prahoveanu Gh., Ghilberdicu Gh., Pitic Ioan, Pitic Nicolae, Turea Nicolae, Prian Nicolae;

Beer Factory: Banu Alexe, Crețu Gh., Toma Iosif, Moș Gh., Drăguș Nicolae, Păcuraru Tudor, Iordache M., Pavel Șerban, Ancu Nicolae, Cojocaru Anton, and Duia Ion;

Glass Factory: Vrabie N., Spiru Panciarele, Godea A., Stoian Tudor;

Cement Factory: Ciobanu Eliaș, Diaconu Nicolae.

I am being called a traitor for possessing such an order, a Romanian nationalist leader, and whatever mayor, whatever notary, can keep this in their pocket or in their home? I believe any order that Mr. Armand Călinescu can carry in his pocket, or that Mr. Madgearu can carry in his pocket, that whatever post chief, commissary, praetor, mayor, notary can carry, then I can as well, without someone telling me that I commit treason and jeopardize the State's security.

The Trial of Corneliu Zelea Codreanu

Mr. Prosecutor Ionescu: Mr. President, please request order no. 55, which I'm about to read, to be set on your table, so you can decide if it can be read in a public meeting or not, following to be the main subject of our discussion. I ask the Honorary Court to first acknowledge the content of this order, at least the final part of it.

Secret Hearing

Mr. Senior-President Dumitru: The Court decided to hold a secret hearing. The public is asked to leave the courtroom. The only ones remaining will be the defense lawyers.

Mrs. Gheorghiu: Mr. President, please insert in the minutes of the hearing of the Honorary Court, at the request of Mr. Senior Prosecutor, that he considered this piece is secret and that you requested a secret hearing.

Mr. Radovici: I request the floor.

Mr. President Dumitru: The court has decided.

Mr. Radovici: Mr. President, I ask you to kindly note in your report that you decided without letting the defense speak on it.

Mr. President Dumitru: This is noted in the official document. I adjourn the hearing until the courtroom is cleared. The hearing is adjourned. The secret hearing starts.

At reopening, in the secret hearing, Mr. Corneliu Zelea Codreanu gave explanations on the following:

1. General Bengliu's Order with the following content: The gendarme units in the country received the following coded telegram:

No. 586/938

"Take supervising and moral quarantine measures on the troops and especially on those suspected of being members of the Guard, Communists, or sectarians. Also, supervise the attitude of the officers."

General Bengliu

This order was reproduced in circular no. 131 with the following content:

"Okay nationalist brother, on one side you tell me the theory of brotherhood and unity, and on the other side you sent coded telegrams to have me supervised

Romanian Crucible

like a dangerous enemy of the State? I was expecting you to supervise all those who plunder the public money, all those who got rich through fraud, all the conspiring Jews in the army. I'm the one needing to be supervised? How ironic?!"

The circular wasn't only shared, but also displayed at the headquarters on Gutenberg Street.[28]

2.   Letter addressed to His Excellency Adolf Hitler, found in file no. 3, p. 52,025, with the following content:

"To His Excellency Adolf Hitler

The General Committee of the National Socialist Legionaries in Romania, debating on our program for the campaign in 1935, which we have been planning for a long time for the future economic and political alliance with the German nation, we decided, together with all the homages and wishes for complete victory, to also send you the Romanian echo of the ongoing European events:

1) Your Excellency's Government appears in the eyes of the Romanian people as the main disturber of peace among nations. Public opinion, which is profoundly influenced by the great press financed by the Jews, is afraid of a new war and doesn't support Your Excellency's regime in the same way, accusing it of causing it. The legend that says Germany is the country that destroys civilization and must be abolished.

2) The plebiscite in Sarre is concerning everyone. People expect a great catastrophe on 13 January. Hitlerism is harshly criticized. The enemy press presents you as the arsonist of Europe. Confident in the Nationalist-Socialist ideology, we firmly reject the insult brought to the German nation for preparing a war. We know the regime established by your Excellency, which we take as an inspiration for our future campaigns, involves more humane means, more efficient and permanent means for an economic, political, and social expansion.

3) As bearers of the National-Socialist flag in Romania, we watch with interest and special attention at the Jewish-Masonic maneuvers of revenge against Your Excellency's regime. Solidarity of moral interests especially, that indestructibly binds us, requires and commands us to respectfully inform you of our wish to strengthen Your Excellency's Government and make peace among the nations of Europe.

Right now, a war might mean destruction to us all. Postponing the war will allow the National-Socialist flag to wave in Romania as well.

The Trial of Corneliu Zelea Codreanu

Thanks to a new economic system of mutual enrichment, which we call an automatic economy, we'll be able to achieve our professional, national, and international goals.

Accomplishing this saving social-economic plan (which we'll tell you at the right time) demands, however, peace between the European nations, at least during 1935.

Confident in the wisdom, ability, and noble feelings of Your Excellency's Government, we send you the fraternal and enthusiastic greeting of the National-Socialist Legionaries in Romania".

Captain

So far, the author is not known. However, Mr. Codreanu keeps his belief that God will help him find him eventually.

This letter has been analyzed, first of all, from a technical point of view, and showed that, in the context of political economy, the phrases: "mutual enrichment," "automatic economy," and "economic solidarity" have not been used before and do not represent the ideological characteristics of the author. In this order of ideas, they compared the styles and proved it was foreign to the way of thinking of Mr. Corneliu Zelea Codreanu, as well as foreign to his way of speaking. Then, the author of this letter is not part of the Legionary Movement, because this Movement has never had a central committee, and have never called themselves national-socialists. As for the hope that one day the national-socialist flag would wave in Romania, it's an impossibility in the Legionary conception. This wish is a blatant contradiction for the best people, such as Moţa and Marin, who sacrificed their lives wrapped in the Romanian flag.

3) To receive foreign influence, in the mind of Corneliu Zelea Codreanu, is impossible. First, because the origin of the Romanian national movement starts – as it's shown in the book *Pentru Legionari*, pp. 132-144 — from Vasile Conta, Vasile Alecsandri, Milahil Kogalniceanu, Mihai Eminescu, Ion Heliade Rădulescu, Bogdan Petriceicu Haşdeu, Costache Negri etc., all of them from a time when in Germany anti-Semitism wasn't a problem, but they actually took precautions to protect the Jews. Therefore, we were imposed by the Germans to sign the Berlin Treaty.[29] Secondly, during the two manifestations: with the occasion of the meeting between Hitler and Mussolini at Stressa, and the anti-Semitic congress in Nuremberg, the attitude of Corneliu Zelea Codreanu kept a line of dignity and national

Romanian Crucible

pride, which was still unknown in our country. For this purpose, the telegram was sent in Italian, German, and Romanian, showing that Romanian was equal to the language of the other two states; the invitation received — contrary to Mr. Cuza and Mr. Goga who accepted it — was refused by C.Z. Codreanu, who didn't want to look small in front of the other states, and to be considered a representative of the nationalist movement in Romania. These two attitudes clearly reflect the impossibility of the defendant being the author of the letter but also the impossibility of him even having such a conception. Anyway, the signature Captain shows again the author is foreign to the Legionary Movement, because its leader has never signed with anything else but his own name, Captain being a nickname received from Nicolae Totu, and adopted by the other Legionaries. It was unacceptable for the leader of a serious movement to sign using a nickname.

4) The socialist revolution, as it's presented by the prosecution, doesn't make any sense for a Movement that, after obtaining 70 seats in the Chamber, had the perspective of doubling during the next elections in which it was to take part, it didn't need any violence. The leadership was given to it through normal ways. Besides, power has never been the main goal of the Legionary Movement. What scared the author of the Final Ordinance, about the Legionary conception, has a completely other meaning. Victory, or how the Final ordinance says: the Legionary revolution, is not obtained with the use of violence, but from the perfection of man's interior. Corneliu Zelea Codreanu has said these things countless times, and everyone understood his words. He reads the replies given by different personalities of our public life, during the investigation led by the newspaper *Buna Vestire* with the following title: Why do I believe in the Legionary victory? Replies given by university professors, generals, officers decorated with the Mihai Viteazul award, and so on. He especially insists on the reply given by Mircea Eliade in *Buna Vestire*, on 17 December 1937, highlighting the following phrases: "Today, the whole world sits under the sign of revolution, but, while other nations live this revolution in the name of class struggles and economic primacy (communism) or of the State (fascism), or of the race (Hitlerism), the Legionary Movement was born under the sign of Archangel Michael, and will emerge victorious through divine intervention. That's why, while all contemporary revolutions are political, the Legionary revolution is spiritual and Christian. While the purpose of all contemporary revolutions is the attainment of power by a social class or a man, the Legionary revolution has a supreme purpose: the nation's salvation, reconciling the Romanian

The Trial of Corneliu Zelea Codreanu

people with God, as the Captain said it. That's why, the purpose of the Legionary Movement differs from everything else that has transpired throughout history, and the Legionary victory will bring with it not only the restoration of the virtue of our nation, a worthy Romania, dignified and strong, but also create a new man that corresponds to a new type of European life. The new man was never born from a political movement, but always from a spiritual revolution, from internal transformation."

In the same order of ideas, Mr. Corneliu Zelea Codreanu painted the following picture: "Fascism, without neglecting the other sides of social life, is especially concerned with the State, Hitlerism, without neglecting all its other main preoccupations, gives special attention to race. The Legionary Movement embodies something deeper, being concerned with the soul. In other words, Fascism's outer shape would correspond to a man's clothing, Hitlerism gives precedence to what we find underneath the clothing, meaning the body, while the preoccupations of the Legionaries go beyond the clothing and the body, reaching deep into the human soul."

The public hearing reopens.

Mr. President Dumitru: Please continue.

The Defendant: Mr. President and Honorary Court, the second part of the Penal Code talks especially about crimes and offenses. This title is also split into two chapters: crimes and offenses against the exterior security of the State and crimes and offenses against the interior security of the State. I was charged based on art. 190 and 191 for crimes and offenses committed against the exterior security of the State. I was not charged based on the articles that concern the interior security of the State, but the exterior ones, meaning treason.

The essential and final element of treason is this: the crime of treason is that offense through which a native conspires against the exterior security of the State or in the interest of a foreign power. That's why, in the Penal Code there are no words such as Romanian citizen, except here. Why? Because if I was not a Romanian citizen, the guilty one would be charged with espionage. That's why the quality of citizenship is required.

Therefore, this is about sending orders that I supposedly possessed, to a foreign power, to endanger the exterior security of the Romanian State.

The hearing adjourns at 0:30, announcing the next hearing for Tuesday at 8:30 am.

Day Two
Tuesday, 24 May 1938

The hearing starts at 9:20 am.

Mr. Senior Prosecutor Col. Magistrate Dumitru Constantin: Judges, do you have any questions?

Lawyer S. Radovici: Mr. President, if you allow me, before we continue with the debates, I have to make a request for the defense.

Mr. President, Honorary Court, you allowed extensive publicity for the judging of this trial, which we, the defense, are deeply grateful for. At the same time, we want to thank the press, the vast majority giving objective descriptions about the debates in this trial. I however have to bring to your attention a fact, that for us, from a professional point of view and for our auxiliary role in justice together with the magistrates, is of great importance. The press that takes part in these deliberations, has to be decent and objective. I repeat: most prestigious newspapers in this country respected this condition. However, I surprisingly read — and this is an offense brought to the defense — in a gazette called *Capitala*, the following lines: "The replies of a weak defense on one part by incompetents, and on the other, by missed carriers...," "the defense, unsupported by an ammunition of sufficient judicial culture, pleads for Codreanu in this trial, presenting a desolate aspect with lack of honesty and conviction..."

Mr. President, we are here to play a role that is well-defined by law. We are under your protection as auxiliaries of justice, together with the magistrates. The people who dare to speak this way are reckless and abusive. Abuse can be committed against a magistrate.

Mr. Senior-President Dumitru Constantin: Mr. Prosecutor has the floor.

Mr. Senior-Prosecutor Major Magistrate Ionescu Radu: Is the defendant a lawyer?

I'm asking because in the book *Pentru Legionari*, on page 346, he says he didn't work as a lawyer, but the late Moța and others practiced as lawyers, and from their income they supported you as well.

Defendant C.Z. Codreanu: I was part of the Iași Bar in 1922. I practiced as a lawyer in Iași, and for a year I had an office in Ungheni, in 1929. I pleaded multiple trials in Ploiești and Putna, in Satu Mare and other cities where I was required to go. That doesn't mean that I spent my life practicing law.

What are the Brotherhoods of the Cross?

Mr. Senior-Prosecutor Major Magistrate Ionescu Radu: The Brotherhood of the Cross organization was founded, with the purpose of moral and patriotic education of the youth, as the defendant calls it. Did he take into account the lack of professional ability of the teachers and the inefficiency of the measures taken by the Ministry of National Education?

Defendant C.Z. Codreanu: No. I believe in the teacher's abilities. But aside from the education a young person can receive from his parents, he can receive another type of education, good or bad, from others.

Mr. Senior-Prosecutor: Did the defendant think that through these organizations he interfered with the Ministry of National Education and later on, with the National Guard, and through this he commits an illegal act?

Defendant C.Z. Codreanu: Yes. At the moment when I founded the Brotherhoods of the Cross the National Guard didn't come into discussion.

Mr. Senior-Prosecutor: But it did later.

Defendant C.Z. Codreanu: Yes, much later. Yes, it's true, but my conscience had to choose between committing a small crime or seeing the whole youth of our high schools becoming Bolsheviks.

Mr. Senior-Prosecutor: Were the teachers and the superior leader bodies of the Ministry of National Education not able to fulfill this role?

Defendant C.Z. Codreanu: As long as Bolshevism and Communism were spreading among these students and gaining proportions, it meant the teachers and the authorities had missed the chance to keep it under control.

Mr. Senior-Prosecutor: In what quality did you raise yourself to the rank of moral educator of youth?

The Trial of Corneliu Zelea Codreanu

Defendant C.Z. Codreanu: I didn't want to keep any secrecy and I don't think this is shown by anything. The file shows that these associations exist, but not that they're secret. My books, where I clearly wrote about the Brotherhoods of the Cross, as well as the trials I've been through, clearly mention them, so they exist, but it says nowhere that they're secret.

Friends of the Legionaries Organization

Mr. Senior-Prosecutor: Why was the member's activity secret in the Friends of the Legionaries Organization? Looking at the conditions to join from point 3: they don't know each other and never meet. And point 6 it says: they have an order number and a password.

Defendant C.Z. Codreanu: The question is: why was the secret kept about the activity of these members of this organization? Once these members never meet up, and they don't know each other, means there's no activity and these members literally helped a lawful movement. We imposed this on the people, either because of their work, or because of their class — there are people who want to help, but they don't want anyone to know that, — they didn't want this to be known, they weren't committing any crime, they just wanted to help discreetly. There's no crime in discreetly helping someone. The man has the choice of discretion when he wants to do good to show it or not.

Mr. Senior-Prosecutor: Who imposed this discretion in the name of the members of the Friends of the Legionaries.

Defendant: As you will see from the witnesses, this is a choice of each member. There are members who said: I'm a friend of the Legionaries and I don't intend to be discreet about it.

Organization of the Legionary Corps Moța-Marin

Mr. Senior-Prosecutor: In the regulations of the Legionary Corps Moța-Marin, art. 1, it shows the purpose of the Corps was to "severely educate and heroically inspire its members." How unprepared were these members, that, in order to join it, they were required to be at least 30 years old and have high spiritual qualities, according to art. 16 and 17 of the rules?

Defendant: They were not required to be 30 years old, on the contrary, they were to be at most 30 years old. You'll ask me why. Because we've realized that after 30 years old a man is inclined towards a certain mentality and is not susceptible to new education. Starting with the age of 30, the man becomes somehow stiff. He hardly accepts a new education, while those under 30 can still receive it. This is the proof that we are concerned with this problem.

Mr. Senior-Prosecutor: If the Corp was built on a commemorative foundation, why does the oath in art. 19 require the members to have virtues of sacrifice and death?

Defendant: The oath is a phrase, as I said before, from one of Moța articles called "On the Verge of a Red Storm," and the words are there as a commemoration to Moța.

Why Were They Trained to Shoot?

Mr. Senior-Prosecutor: For what purpose were the members destined for piety and glorification of the dead of the Legionary Corp Moța-Marin trained to shoot?

Defendant C.Z. Codreanu: I didn't give such a disposition and nothing shows that I commanded them to be trained to shoot. But shooting exercises are part of an educational system as well. If someone learns to shoot, he can't be immediately accused of wanting to kill someone. Therefore, for example, there are state societies abroad — in Poland, Germany, France, and Italy — where any citizen is called, and, for a small fee, he is given the option to learn how to shoot; it's in the interest of each country's defense for their citizens to know how to use firearms. There is such an organization in our country, led by General Bădulescu. He told General Cantacuzino: "send the boys to us, because the interest of the state and the country is to teach the youth how to shoot." I myself have gone to the General and was trained, as other active officers are and those in reserve, who train their shooting constantly. Alex. Cantacuzino had the initiative to write a simple note saying they will be trained to shoot; he will explain this matter. It's not part of my program, but I can justify it if necessary.

Mr. Senior-Prosecutor: Is it the same thing to have shooting exercises as part of the activity of a state institution, or do this in a private corps of ten thousand members?

The Trial of Corneliu Zelea Codreanu

Defendant C.Z. Codreanu: I let you know that this corps, when Al. Cantacuzino gave orders for the shooting exercises to be held, had, I think, around ten members. This was the effective, not ten thousand. I said ten thousand maybe over 10-15 years, when this corps would have reached its maximum organizational power, but back then there were only around ten people. And if they decided to do shooting exercises, I didn't know, because I didn't talk to Al. Cantacuzino and I can't explain this matter. He gave the order; I didn't give any order in that direction. I only tried to justify the general idea, meaning it's not a crime for someone to learn how to shoot.

Why Did the Defendant Continue to be Part of the Iron Guard After It was Dissolved?

Mr. Senior-Prosecutor: Why did the defendant continue his activity in the Iron Guard after it was dissolved? During the interrogation, he stated that he remained to further lead the spiritual side of the former organization.

Defendant C.Z. Codreanu: I said during interrogations that I remain in my old position, today illegal, because I want to obtain legality for my Movement, I'm in the process and, being in the process I want to obtain the symbol and the name of the organization, but in the new group I deal with issues related to education, and Mr. General, in his gentleness said: "No, I'll form the Party[31] with one condition, for us to call you our spiritual leader." I replied to the General, if that is your condition, then I'll accept it".

Mr. Senior-Prosecutor: Does the defendant know of any case in which the enrichment of the spiritual side is done through a political organization?

Defendant C.Z. Codreanu: Our organization is completely different from all other political organizations, and you can see that from my circulars and from the order I gave you. No political man deals with the moral side of the individual. They only care about votes, but I'm concerned about man as a moral value.

Mr. Senior-Prosecutor: How about agendas Nos. 1, 2, 3 from September 1934, through which, with the power you had as the former leader of the Iron Guard, you eliminated Stelescu, Cotea, and others from the organization? Was that in the context of morality and spirituality?

Defendant C.Z. Codreanu: Yes, it was in the same context, because those agendas treat a different type of treason, that of trying to have me assassinated.

Romanian Crucible

Mr. Senior-Prosecutor: The All for the Country Party was founded, I believe, in December 1934. Agendas 1, 2, and 3 were given in September 1934.

Defendant C.Z. Codreanu: Yes.

Mr. Senior-Prosecutor: Do you admit that through it you conducted illegal activity?

Defendant C.Z. Codreanu: Yes, but I'll explain. First, I was in the following situation: a dissolving act, a unanimous acquittal on this matter from the Council of five generals; the statements of all political men, confirming that my organization was illegally dissolved, and a pending trial at the Court of Appeal on this matter. So, what did I do? I didn't have political activity, as the law requires, but I stood my ground, waiting for the decision of the Court — the same thing my men are doing. Meanwhile, something happens: an internal attempt from our part, not a political manifestation on the outside; an internal attempt at revolt inside the organization. And then I was arrested. But I am not being judged for this problem, which I just want to make right.

Mr. Senior-Prosecutor: No, but because it was talked about in the final ordinance, and because you considered it necessary to explain it, I'll ask questions.

Does the defendant have knowledge that in 1934, through the law of State Defense, the Journal of the Ministry Council from December 1933 by which the Iron Guard was dissolved, and by it, as a governing act, the hope to win the trial was lost?

Defendant C.Z. Codreanu: My hopes of winning the trial are not lost even today, because, whatever the executive power decreed, it was found — I don't know now, in the new regime — always under the power of the decision of the judicial system. I, against a decision of the executive power, can always call on the Judicial system if I feel like I was treated unfairly; if I'm right, I know I'll win, because Justice always prevails.

Violence as Method

Mr. Senior Prosecutor: Does the defendant admit that violence is one of the methods used by the organization to attain certain goals?

Defendant C.Z. Codreanu: No, no. When you say: the method used to attain a goal, it means that the initial objective has been set initially when you state this,

The Trial of Corneliu Zelea Codreanu

and, if violence was a part of our life, this was not due to the principles that I've established, but determined by self-defense, maybe during unfortunate events. But it was not one of our principles. A misfortune can happen in the life of a man. During a moment of anger, he might act violently. It might happen within his family, within his home, but in a political battle?

Mr. Senior Prosecutor: During yesterday's hearing, the defendant stated that in his book *Pentru Legionari* he wrote his beliefs — and I noted — written fairly and honestly. They form the principles. What sort of beliefs, and especially, principles, can the defendant's statements in this book prove, for example, on page 95: "To these politicians, whose betrayal of their nation is so terrible, if they're alive, the nation should gouge out their eyes; and if they're dead, the nation should pull them out of their graves and burn their bones in public squares. The nation should seek the fortunes of all their children and grandchildren, confiscate them, and stigmatize them with the phrase children of traitors."[32] Further on, on page 168, when you planned the student's plot from 1923 — plotting is not an act of violence? — you were saying here, or better showing what Moța was saying: "We must obtain revolvers and shoot them, and give a terrible example that would remain in Romanian history. What would happen to us afterward, we would die or be left in prison our whole life, that doesn't concern me."[33] And you reply: "I agreed that the final act of our fight be, with the price of our defeat, a punishing act against the pygmies who, using the positions of responsibility, have humiliated and exploited the country."[34] And further, on page 169, you were saying: "We agreed upon a few elements found on the line of treason and chose six ministers, led by George Mârzescu. Finally, there came the hour at which the ones with filthy attitudes, who never imagined they would be held accountable for their actions, in a country where they saw themselves as supreme leaders, over a nation incapable of any restriction, were to answer with their lives." On page 172, you show that during the search conducted, the only revolvers found were in the home of Moța and someone else. Later on, however, you say, after suspecting someone was betraying you: "There, they put a few of my letters in front of me, and two baskets in which there were all of our revolvers that had been hidden in a good place." And when Moța shot Vernichescu, you were on his side. On page 188 of your book, to complete an idea that was already the object of a question regarding the Brotherhood of the Cross, you say: "we'll start from there [...] by organizing the whole country's youth, the boys and girls of the superior high school classes, even the inferior ones, the normal schools,

Romanian Crucible

the vocational schools, commercial schools, and the lads from the countryside." On page 212, you are on Moța's side saying: "We all stand in solidarity with Moța."[35] When the student Beza shot the state secretary Angelescu,[36] you seemed to brag that you were defending him, and when the note appeared in a newspaper that was saying — I believe — that you repudiate Beza's actions, that you will take measures against these assassinations, you immediately denied it in the same newspaper, saying: no, I will sign up to defend Beza, even though, from your letter and from your statement from back then, you showed that you didn't know Beza very well. That's all for now.

Defendant C.Z. Codreanu: It's true that I told my story in the book as I said before: fairly and honestly, about my life, and indeed, everything you read is written by me, fairly and honestly. If it wasn't right, I wouldn't have said those things, and if I wasn't honest, I would have looked for ways to avoid matters that could bring me displeasure at some point. No, I wrote them to reflect what happened. But all these matters have been judged at their time.

Mr. Senior Prosecutor: Of course, they have been judged, for showing the principle, because there was a chain of such actions, not isolated incidents.

Defendant C.Z. Codreanu: Yes, there was a chain of events over the past 15-20 years. But there was a trial, and the authorities judged it. This matter could be brought up against me by anyone, aside from someone in the justice system who cannot go above the authority of a judged matter. Secondly, you must take into account every factor, including the age of someone. Think about it, I was 20-22 years old, I was a child, and I was seeing things at that time with a childish mentality. But when a man starts living and until his life ends, he gains wisdom. At first, the man judges in another way, he thinks he's great. There are steps in the development of the human mind and actions, which 20 years later, you see in a different light. Maybe 20 years ago I would have created a secret alphabet, because that's the age that urges you to see things in the way that I've seen them at that time. But since then, a long time has passed. It's noticeable from my attitude, that is almost completely opposite to the initial one myself and my friends had. It's opposite because of my age. But someone can't be followed his whole life for things he dreamt about in his childhood, when he thought he could fight against the whole of Europe. I don't believe in this. Regarding Beza, that happened in the following way: at one point, a young man appeared that I had met two evenings prior. It was Beza. He

The Trial of Corneliu Zelea Codreanu

told me he wanted to be part of the Vlad Țepeș League,[37] but he wants to be accepted in the Guard. I told him: my dear, wait a bit longer, because I didn't know him, and I wanted to get to know him first, before accepting him. The following evening, he came to me again and said: you don't deserve to sleep at my place. Why not, I asked — because I didn't have a place to sleep that night. On my way, someone asked me to go sleep at their place, why wouldn't I go to the other guy's place? So, I went, and the next day, around 12, I read in the newspaper that someone shot sub-secretary C. Angelescu. Later on, I found out it was Beza. Of course, I was shocked at what might have happened if I had gone to his place to sleep. It would have been a misfortune for which I wouldn't have had any way to defend myself. They would have said that I taught him. I was called in for interrogations and I said: I know him from that day... this is what happened, I don't have any connection to him because I fight on the Jewish issues and on the question of the Bulgarians from the Quadrilateral. They let me go. The following days the newspapers say: Corneliu Codreanu called for interrogations on the headlines in *Dimineața*; in conjunction with Beza's actions.

Mr. Senior Prosecutor: I kept reading your book. Especially because, at yesterday's hearing, you said that your beliefs are written fairly and honestly and that they form principles. I am the first defender of the authority of the judged matter, but I don't defeat this principle since I am only reading your principles.

Defendant C.Z. Codreanu: Allow me. A book contains events and principles. We must not confuse the events with the principles because retelling events is one thing, and principles are something else. Confusion shouldn't exist here. What you brought up in the discussion were events.

Why Were the Assassins of Duca and Stelescu Decorated?

Mr. Senior Prosecutor: Now, the defendant stated in front of us, aside from the authority of the judged matter, through which his actions have been settled, that they were due to his childhood and he lacked the maturity and experience that he has today. How does the defendant explain today, after 15 years have passed, and we are all of a mature age, the defendant continues to reward with high ranks, dignities, and decorations, those who recently caused the terrible assassination of Prime Minister Duca and Stelescu.[38]

Romanian Crucible

Defendant C.Z. Codreanu: I explained this matter yesterday. I accepted then, not their deeds, but the suffering of the men who stay in prison and endure in name of the belief.

Mr. Senior Prosecutor: How do you calculate Legionary heroism, with "graves" for measures, as you've written to Stelescu?

Defendant C.Z. Codreanu: I explained yesterday. I said: through the amount of suffering.

Mr. Senior Prosecutor: It's right. Does the defendant know of any organization or formed corps in our country that has their own decorations and insignia?

Defendant C.Z. Codreanu: Yes. All associations have their own insignia and distinctions of various types.

Mr. Senior Prosecutor: They have. How about decorations?

Defendant C.Z. Codreanu: We wanted ours to be called The White Cross and The Green Cross. The Green Cross was for the ones that supported us financially. The White Cross was for internal attitude, for enriching one's soul.

Mr. Senior Prosecutor: Does the defendant know what an informer is?

Defendant C.Z. Codreanu: Yes. It is a man who informs another one.

About the Informers in the General Staff and the Security Service?

Mr. Senior Prosecutor: How do you explain conveying the informers from the General Staff and State Security, through the well-known circular. For what purpose? To give them instructions?

Defendant C.Z. Codreanu: The convocation was not addressed to informers from the General Staff or the Police Prefecture, but it says: "for all Legionaries and members in the Capital." Therefore, it's addressed to all Legionaries and members in the Capital. Not to the rest. I called them in this sense.

Mr. Senior Prosecutor: How would the defendant know the General Staff was handling the activity of the Legionary Movement?

Defendant C.Z. Codreanu: Someone came to me. Let me openly tell you the whole issue. I'll give you the name as well.

The Trial of Corneliu Zelea Codreanu

Mr. Senior Prosecutor: Of course, give us the name.

Defendant C.Z. Codreanu: Someone came to me and told me that he suspects someone named Bâca Gheorghe of being an informer for the General Staff, who is spying on us.

Mr. Senior Prosecutor: Why would the General Staff spy on you?

Defendant C.Z. Codreanu: I was only informed. If you ask me, I answer.

Mr. Senior Prosecutor: It seems paradoxical to me.

Defendant C.Z. Codreanu: I tell you what it was. And then, at that moment, I indeed wrote the circulars to see if this man would sign or not... the man signed that he was not. This was the whole story.

Mr. Senior Prosecutor: Why would the I.A.R., S.T.B., and others, especially S.T.B. and I.A.R. to spy on you?

Defendant C.Z. Codreanu: I forgot to talk about this matter yesterday, even though it was listed on the plan of defense. I had Legionary organizations everywhere, just like all the other political parties. It was common. So, then I sent these orders, of course, to everyone in the Capital. I sent them to the workers at CFR, to the Tram Society, and the STB, and at IAR, everywhere. It was a normal thing. This proves, if you wish, the existence — which I don't deny — of a Legionary Workers' Association founded by General Cantacuzino. But you cannot pull the conclusion from this that we have informers there. Besides, I wasn't even interested in this. Why would I need informers working for the railways or other societies?

Mr. Senior Prosecutor: The defendant claims he is afraid of betrayal. This was the purpose for calling the informers through those circulars.

Defendant C.Z. Codreanu: I'm not afraid of betrayal, but the idea of it terrified me. There's a difference.

Mr. Senior Prosecutor: I'm asking: legally, isn't the term betrayal more correct when it comes to the State, to which these workers had sworn an oath, than as it relates to his organization?

Defendant C.Z. Codreanu: I didn't tell them: don't give me information. I precisely said: give me information but give me the correct information, not like the memoir that was thrown in my file now, which was probably created by one of my people.

Romanian Crucible

Mr. Senior Prosecutor: If the defendant claims that his organization had a line of dignity, gallantry, and patriotism, he should tell us the names of a few of the informers called through the mentioned circular. Just now, you wanted to read from a circular you said you used to call the informers.

Defendant C.Z. Codreanu: No. I said: if someone from the Police comes and wants to get information, call him inside, and invite him to the hearing. This is what I said: whoever comes from Security, call him inside, open the door for him.

Mr. Senior Prosecutor: If by any chance you didn't know their names, then how could you know you had supporters in the State's institutions?

Defendant C.Z. Codreanu: This is not deduced from anywhere.

Mr. Senior Prosecutor: Yes, it is deduced, from the moment you call them with the circular. In the circular you say: all the informers in the General Staff, State Police, Security, etc. will come to me — and you gave them dates.

Defendant C.Z. Codreanu: I was not replying to the spiritual probity of some people, of whom I knew are surrounding me from every direction and spying on me. I was telling them: come and tell me to my face, straight forward. I am such and such an agent. I said it in this sense.

Mr. Senior Prosecutor: That is what I was asking.

Defendant C.Z. Codreanu: I called them, trying in this way to determine them to come. But they didn't come!...

Mr. Senior Prosecutor: Does the defendant admit to having a secret police and that he ordered members of the organization to be armed?

Defendant C.Z. Codreanu: No, this is not true. What happened? I'll tell you openly. During the funeral of Moța and Marin — because I have said I didn't want protection, that I didn't need protection, because I am protected by God, and I didn't want people to follow me in their cars, and make my adversaries think that I was afraid of being put in ridiculous situations — the boys, without telling me, they thought I was going to pass by different houses, railway workshops where there were many communists, and they were afraid someone was going to throw a bomb at me. And then, they organized a police service. That was the situation. If someone came and tried to kill me, of course my men would have intervened, and they wouldn't have relied on the law to let me get killed and then sue the assassin.

The Trial of Corneliu Zelea Codreanu

Dues and Funds of the All for the Country Party

Mr. Senior Prosecutor: I ask the defendant to tell us what sums were collected yearly from the dues and donations made to the organization

Defendant C.Z. Codreanu: I can't state that, because I'm afraid I'll be wrong, but this can be found in various newspapers, because the press published it — and I read yesterday — sufficient information. The different issues related to loans, dues, and donations were published. For instance, we asked for 2,300,000 for the house. We chose the idea of an internal loan, meaning each member from the organization or friend gives 1,000 lei and takes a ticket, and whenever they need the money, they come and say: here's my ticket, give me my thousand.

Mr. Senior Prosecutor: How much did the elections from 1937 cost, and how much did you spend on the election propaganda in 1938?

Defendant C.Z. Codreanu: I couldn't say, but I imagine? Maybe the manifestos were around 3-4,000,000 lei.

Mr. Senior Prosecutor: In the whole country?

Defendant C.Z. Codreanu: We made the manifestos, and let the counties decide to make their own. But we made typical manifestos, which were suggested to me and I approved them, because nothing was done without my approval. We sold them here, in the county organizations, which also had the choice to make theirs using the same model, and we sold them in the Capital, as I said before, for 1 leu each, especially photographs, because we especially made photographs.

Mr. Senior Prosecutor: Tell us the names of the donors and what sums they contributed, aside from the 300 from the 15,000 members who were paying dues. Aside from these dues, were there any other sums collected from donations? We would like to know their names and the sums donated.

Defendant C.Z. Codreanu: There's a small confusion. Before the Guard was dissolved, before 1933, five years ago, they asked me in the interrogation and I said: that we were 15,000 total members and of those around 300 were paying dues, peasants and young members. That was five years ago. The situation is different now: we're not 15,000 members. The General says that in 1935 we had 50,000. I never calculated it, because I was never interested in this fact, but I think our number is now around 200,000. In the last elections, we had 450,000 votes — of course, half of those were not members of our organization — therefore, the number of the

Romanian Crucible

signed-up members should be over 200,000. What I said before is related to a matter from six years ago.

Mr. Senior Prosecutor: In a statement in the interrogation, you said that you suspected harsh times are coming, and you decided to dispose of the archives — the accounting one as well as the political ones. Why would you have these archives destroyed, if they only contained clean and honest documents?

Defendant C.Z. Codreanu: First, I have to tell you what I said: I stated that I charged Engineer Horodniceanu with liquidating the headquarters and giving the house back to the owner, and second, what I considered useless or could make someone uncomfortable, should be destroyed, and the rest to be stored for safekeeping. Therefore, I didn't order the destruction of the archives for being dangerous to the State or to us. I said: destroy what could bother someone. Allow me to find ways to present them in front of you. If you allow me, I'll do everything in my power, through my men, to do so.

Mr. Senior-President: Either way, it would be useful to give them to Mr. Prosecutor.

Defendant C.Z. Codreanu: I will try to have them brought to you, because I don't believe those folders are destroyed.

Mr. Senior Prosecutor: Please, Mr. President, I asked this question because I was genuinely surprised to know the archives were destroyed, if it was built on honor and respect for the law. What purpose would justify hiding these registers — assuming they are not destroyed? This is the purpose of my question.

Mr. Senior President: Regarding the donors that preferred to remain anonymous, you stated that you considered it necessary to make a special organization inside the party; you said it is an association composed of donors who preferred to be anonymous.

Defendant C.Z. Codreanu: Yes, and I also explained why. Because the man should always know, in time, all the ones who wished him well, and a movement like ours wanted to know and be close to those who supported it.

Mr. Senior President: Regarding the documents found on you, you said you considered that if these documents could come from a post chief or from a mayor, they can come to you as well, as a party leader. I ask you: in the political system of Romania, is a party leader an authority?

The Trial of Corneliu Zelea Codreanu

Defendant C.Z. Codreanu: From a legal point of view, the party leader is not an authority; but it is incontestable that he has a role that holds something of the patrimony of national sovereignty.

Mr. Senior President: National sovereignty can be held by anyone however they want?

Defendant C.Z. Codreanu: Yes, I speak from the point of view of the legal mechanism.

Mr. Senior President: I know the idea of authority is connected to the idea of power in the State, and that State Powers are organized under the Constitution. While you were a deputy, you were part of the judicial power, and during that time, you could say that you were invested with a sovereign power. I ask myself, however, if the leader of a political party can be considered as having power in the State.

Defendant C.Z. Codreanu: Undeniably, as authority, no. But it is no less true that he has a relationship with this type of authority.

The hearing is suspended for ten minutes.

Witness Interrogation

Mr. President Col. Magistrate Dumitru Const.: We will begin the hearing of witnesses.

Witness Ghiocel Dumitru is absent.

Lawyer Iacobescu: Mr. President, when it comes to our witnesses, we have a respectful request to make. For a better administration of justice, and to shorten the time and for a logical chronology of events, we ask the witnesses for the defense to be called in the courtroom following the list that we compiled.

Mr. Senior Prosecutor Major Magistrate Ionescu Radu: Regarding the witnesses for the prosecution that are absent, please allow them to be called at the end, according to the provisions of the law.

The Testimony of Iosif Frollo

Witness Iosif Frollo is called.

Romanian Crucible

Lawyer Paul Iacobescu: Was the witness a candidate on the list of the party All for the Country, in Roman county and Bacău, in the last elections. What urged him to do so?

Mr. President Col. Magistrate Dumitru Const.: Were you a member of All for the Country Party?

Iosif Frollo: No.

Mr. President: Were you a candidate in the last elections in December?

Mr. Frollo: Yes, I was a candidate for the Senate in Bacău and Roman.

Mr. President: Not being a part of the All for the Country party, the lawyer wants to know — briefly — what was the motivation that urged you to become a candidate on the list of this party, that you are not a part of?

Mr. Frollo: It was a great problem for me, moral and national; I was a politician before the war in the Conservative Party, together with Nicolae Filipescu, and at the end of the war[39] I resigned from politics, because I understood it was impossible, as a member of that party, to work towards an ideal, knowing for sure that's what I'm working for.

So, I followed Codreanu's nationalist movement, even from before he became its leader. Of course, I followed it from a distance, without being close to any of the people that were part of the Movement. The Movement grew, many events happened with great repercussions for the public, one of them being the first trial of Codreanu for killing Manciu in self-defense, then the great event happened, Duca's assassination, then Stelescu's assassination. This was an account for me: on one side, the great ideal of the national movement, on the other side, these events that — I've been writing in my own newspaper for years — I was condemning.

A friend, I forgot his name, told me that Mr. Codreanu would want me to be a candidate on the lists of the All for the Country party. Then, I told myself, it's very serious, especially because I would stray away from my peaceful career. I read the book *Pentru Legionari* and *Cărticica şefului de cuib*, I highlighted them and I asked myself about every ideal of the Movement. I was asked to be a candidate for the Senate. And then I had a long talk with Mr. Codreanu, during which I told him about all the problems that I was interested in from a moral point of view. Then I got to better understand some things, that for me had been black points and foreign to the Movement and to Codreanu's person, and to his way of work. I asked him how could I enjoy the results of the work of so many Legionaries who sacrificed

The Trial of Corneliu Zelea Codreanu

themselves? When I realized there was no chance for me to be elected in those counties, I accepted his proposal. I found this Movement sacred in everything. I was part of the electoral campaign, and I got to see the Legion in all its splendor. Everything written in the book *Pentru Legionari* and *Cărticica șefului de cuib* was true. I realized the Legionary Movement was not a political party, but an organization of high moral standards.

Lawyer Iacobescu: If by participating in the electoral campaign of last year, the witness saw, knew, and found the means by which the members of the Movement reacted to the whole government pressure that was made?

Mr. Frollo: They endured. They didn't react. I realized they were following a high ethical concept of social life, and they were not a far-right wing party, neither far-left, but a party of extreme honor that fights against extreme dishonor.

Mr. Senior-President Col. Magistrate C. Dumitru: The witness gave an indirect answer to this matter.

Mr. Senior-Prosecutor Major Magistrate Radu Ionescu: The witness stated that when he was offered to become a candidate for the Senate in the two counties, he thought about the bad side that could have influenced him not to accept the offer, which were the assassinations of those times. The witness then stated that the two assassinations, which were going against his initial attitude, were outside the All for the Country organization; he then accepted. I ask you: today, how do you find the defendant's decision to award a high rank in the Legionary Movement to those who killed Duca and Stelescu?

Mr. Frollo: These days, the one who killed Dolfuss was named a national hero in Vienna. Obviously, I personally, wouldn't have proclaimed him a national hero for this, as I repeat, I condemned it when I wrote about it and I will always condemn the assassinations of Duca and Stelescu. Not of Manciu, because that was self-defense. I answer the question with the following: assuming these actions are separate the Iron Guard, the fact that they were all awarded with distinctions of which I only know from the newspapers — but let's assume it was that way — I don't doubt that, given the psychology of the Guard, and Codreanu's way of thinking, they didn't look at the crime itself, but at the sacrifices of those who committed them, to become convicts for what they believed to be good. Because, you see, in my opinion, the worst thing happens when people start believing that Duca's assassination was a good thing. This psychology, which is wrong for a man who has objective judgement, is an explainable psychology for those who act quickly and impulsively. If one gets the idea that justice cannot be attained through the justice system, he starts believing that it is heroic to act in this manner. Naturally, it's immoral and inadmissible, but no less true that it requires a certain degree of bravery. But it's bad when one gets the idea that courage is the deciding factor, instead of allowing his mind to reflect and decide.

Mr. Senior-Prosecutor Major Mag. Ionescu Radu: Another question: by rewarding sacrifice for murder don't you think that is the same as rewarding the murder itself?

Mr. Frollo: Rewarding sacrifice for murder means rewarding murder? See, that's exactly what I just said. If murder is considered as a heroic act, not as a crime, rewarding him would be for a heroic act. If the killing is considered to be a crime, then that would be a glorification of the crime. For example: when one kills another, he robs him and then comes and shares the money, and you praise him for stealing, then you glorified the murder. If you believe that person did an act of high justice, that means you glorify the act of justice. It's a matter of mentality. I told you what my mentality was. You judge.

Mr. Senior-Prosecutor: If murder is qualified as a crime, you say?

Mr. Frollo: Morally.

Mr. Senior-Prosecutor: This killing was considered morally and judicially a crime, through a final sentence. Where does your answer stand then?

Mr. Frollo: In my judgement, or course, it isn't commendable.

Mr. Senior-President Col. Mag. C. Dumitru: The defense asks what impressions you had from the things said in the book *Pentru Legionari*.

Mr. Frollo: My impression was the following: it creates the idea that killings are acts of honor. This was my impression. I saw, and this was the reason why I was conciliated with Codreanu's person, the way he talks about Manciu's killing, however, he is not a person who takes pride in this gesture. The chapter is even titled *Ziua Fatală* (*The Fatal Day*), as a fatality that snatched away what happened.

Mr. Senior-President: The witness spoke, I believe, about a psychosis of these people who sacrifice themselves. Could you tell us what reasons would cause such a psychosis?

The Trial of Corneliu Zelea Codreanu 153

Mr. Frollo: It might be caused by everything happening daily, by the impossibility to choose a path. And then, of course, the whole atmosphere of the times.

Lawyer Horia Cosmovici: I was asking if the witness knows, that from the trial of Duca's killing in which Mr. Corneliu Zelea Codreanu was judged, it resulted that the events were under the aegis and warranty of justice, and was said it was true? Does he know this?

Mr. Frollo: I didn't know this, because I didn't follow the trial.

Mr. Senior President: Do you believe the defendant C.Z. Codreanu to be capable of rebelling?

Mr. Frollo: Definitely not, absolutely not.

Lawyer Iacobescu: But of treason?

Mr. Frollo: I wouldn't put my trust in anyone, but Mr. C.Z. Codreanu.

The Testimony of General Dr. Constantinescu

The witness General Dr. Constantinescu is called.

He is asked to take the oath.

Mr. Senior President Colonel Magistrate Dumitru Constantin: Do you personally know anything else about the activity in the book the defendant wrote, other than what was shown today?

General Constantinescu: I am not a part of Codreanu's political group, because until last year I was part of the army, I couldn't be a part of any political party. But, even if I had motives to join after that, I wouldn't have done it, considering that I was a part of the army for 39 years and I didn't want my affiliation with a political group to be misinterpreted.

Mr. Senior President: Therefore, you are not aware of other political activity.

General Dr. Constantinescu: I am only familiar with what is written in the book. C.Z. Codreanu's activity was not occult or concealed, because he presented them with honesty in his book.

Lawyer Paul Iacobescu: Were his means conspiratorial and his goals illegal?

Mr. Senior President: The witness states he was not part of the Movement; he did not take part in its activity in any way, and he couldn't be aware of something other than what he had read.

Do you have other questions?

The Defense: No

The Testimony of Colonel Gheorghe Polihroniade

Witness colonel Polihroniade Gheorghe from Bucharest, Gutenberg Street Nr. 3, enters the courtroom.

Lawyer Iacobescu: Does the witness know the Movement and its leader? Does he know this Movement to be lavished in material opulence or to struggle with hardships?

Mr. Senior President Colonel Magistrate Dumitru Constantin: What knowledge do you have of this Movement and its funds?

Colonel Polihroniade: I know this movement as a pure-nationalist one, without suspicious activity, without anything being concealed in broad daylight.

Mr. Senior President: Are you a member of All for the Country party?

The Witness: Yes, from the time when General Zizi Cantacuzino was its leader, and the leadership of Zizi Cantacuzino for me was the best guarantee of truth, honesty, and frankness. I joined, convinced that I have to fight for the Romanian nation.

Mr. Senior President: The question was if you were aware of the ways in which this Movement was earning its income, the way it was spending it, if the Movement was rich, or if it was struggling.

The Witness: My answer is: Romanian poverty. This and nothing more. Their income was earned from dues from poor people, who would give 1, 2, 5 lei to help this organization, because everyone knew they wanted the supreme good for the nation and the monarchy. I gave the Legion a loan of 6,000 lei and I know the Legion is indebted.

The Defense: Does the witness know that for the house the Legionary Movement is building in Bucharest...[interruptions]

Mr. Senior President: I will not allow any type of manifestations. The questions are for the witnesses, not for the public.

The Trial of Corneliu Zelea Codreanu

[The one who interrupted is to be removed from the courtroom.]

A Voice: I am a lawyer on the list of the defense.

Mr. Senior President: If you are a lawyer, you can't speak from the back of the courtroom, it is an indelicacy towards the Court.

The Defense: In the name of the defense, please allow the gentleman who interrupted to come here, in order to ask his questions, in the name of the defense.

Lawyer Iacobescu: For a better and more efficient interrogation of witnesses, we agreed to organize the way in which the questions are asked, and which questions must be asked.

I repeat the question: Does the witness know that to complete the construction in Bucharest, the Movement had to remain open to the engineers who provided the construction materials?

The Witness: I am not very familiar with this matter, but I know from my discussions with one of the leading architects of the building, who told me: we don't have money, the small sum we had is gone. We might have the chance to get some more from the iron we'll sell. If we can't sell the iron, we'll be stuck.

Lawyer Iacobescu: Do you believe the defendant C.Z. Codreanu is capable of treason?

The Witness: Never, he would never betray his country.

The Testimony of Prof. Eugen Chirnoaga

Lawyer Paul Iacobescu: Does the witness know the Legionary Movement and its leader?

Prof. Chirnoaga: Yes, I know them.

Mr. President Dumitru Const.: How do you know them, are you a party member?

Prof. Chirnoaga: Yes, I'm a party member. I've known the Movement since 1937. Until 1934, I was an opponent of this Movement, because I lived abroad for a long time, around six years, studying, and during this time I only got my information from newspapers. That's why I ended up having a completely wrong opinion when it came to this Movement. I returned to Romania with the thought that Mr. Corneliu Codreanu is an ordinary criminal. I had believed this for years, until

Romanian Crucible

I came to see the reality in the country. I was deeply moved in 1937 when I had my first contact with the Legionary spirit at Carmen Sylva, where the work was directed. I considered this Movement to be our country's salvation, and I can say the Legionary Movement has never attempted to take power by overthrowing the government. The student movements have had a suspicious mentality. They were used as a tactic by the political parties. Ever since the Legionary Movement entered the student life, I noticed, day by day, a change of spirit in the schools, as well as on the outside. I congratulate them for this attitude. The best of my students are Legionaries, because the defendant C.Z. Codreanu urged them to focus on studying.

Lawyer Iacobescu: Does the professor think the defendant C.Z. Codreanu is capable of treason?

The witness: No, honestly.

The Testimony of Priest Ion Moţa

They proceed with the hearing of witness Priest Ion Moţa.

Mr. Senior President Dumitru Const.: Do you know the defendant?

Priest Ion Moţa: Yes.

Mr. Senior President: Are you related to him?

Priest Ion Moţa: Yes. My son is married to his sister.

Mr. Senior President: Is the prosecutor opposed to hearing him as a witness?

Mr. Senior Prosecutor Major Magistrate Radu Ionescu: No, but please keep in mind that they are related.

The witness is asked to swear the oath.

Mr. Senior President: Does the defense have any questions?

Lawyer Iacobescu: Because some ill-wishers stated that Corneliu Codreanu intentionally sent Moţa to die in Spain, what can the witness tell us about the departure of Ionel Moţa to Spain?

Mr. Senior President: I'm the one asking the questions.

Lawyer Iacobescu: We'll withdraw the question.

The Trial of Corneliu Zelea Codreanu

Then, because the priest knows the Legionary Movement, he should tell us if he knows this Movement to work in an occult, underground way, with illegal purposes and an aim to overthrow the government.

Priest Ion Moța: For as long as I've known the Movement — and the Movement is not that old, so I've known it from the beginning, I've had a good opinion about the Legionary Movement, because it was supporting those things that I was wanting as a Romanian and as a priest. They were building churches, crosses, places of culture, and they were aiming for a national awakening; regarding their funds, they were gathering money, coin by coin, from people to support the Movement.

Mr. Senior President: You are asked: what opinion did you have about the Movement itself and about its leader?...

The Witness: Mr. President, I have been a political fighter for 40 years, and always — even in former Hungary — I followed the far-right. Everyone was a far-right wing extremist there, and we couldn't even be something else, because we couldn't keep our nationality if we were not.

The Testimony of Dr. Raneţescu-Câmpina

Lawyer Iacobescu: I'd like to know if the witness knows the Legionary Movement and the defendant, C.Z. Codreanu, and what opinion does he have about the organization that he leads.

Dr. Ranetescu-Câmpina: I've known the Movement for three years, from the point of view of a supporter, from what I've read, and from what I've discussed with the Legionaries. I'm convinced it's a Movement of order, unhidden, and my opinion is that Mr. Codreanu cannot be accused of treason in any way. Mr. Codreanu's main goal is not power.

The Testimony of Professor Traian Brăileanu

Professor Traian Brăileanu, the witness for the defense, enters the courtroom.

Lawyer Paul Iacobescu: Mr. President, please ask the professor, who knows the Legionary Movement, what he thinks this Movement represents for our country, in relation to the other existing political parties.

Mr. Senior President: Were you a part of the Legion?

Romanian Crucible

Prof. Brăileanu: I was a Senator in the Legion.

Mr. Senior President: For how long have you been a member?

The Witness: Starting with after the Union,[40] I was a politician, just like all the other intellectuals in Bucovina, and I believed that in my political activity I had to pay attention, first, to lifting up the Romanians from Bucovina. That's why I started doing politics. Mr. Nistor[41] and other liberals from there were my friends, and at one point I got close to them. When I saw their fight against the foreign element in Bucovina didn't have any result, I walked away from them, and leaned towards Averescu's party. Later on, I found they were making national compromises, and because I am not a politician just to be in politics, but an intellectual who wants to help, first, by promoting Romanian interests, I left this party just as it came to power.

Following that, to give you my whole political biography, I joined Iorga's party,[42] which had a beautiful reception among the people of Bucovina. Iorga's Movement in Bucovina was led by me. Mr. Iorga had, back then,[43] in the national program, an unbending point of view, so I embraced it. But following the fusions that were made,[44] I stopped liking this type of politics, because it became party politics in the end. Finally, right at that time, the League of Christian-National Defense was formed in Bucovina. I was familiar with Mr. Cuza's[45] politics from my time as a student at the University in Cernăuti. Mr. Iorga and Cuza were at Cernăuți back then, and they held conferences that were much appreciated among the students. Because divisions started interfering in the League of Christian-National Defense as well, I gave up on being a candidate, and I was left without a party, choosing to write a series of articles in Mr. Cătuneanu's magazine in Cluj.

Meanwhile, I became friends with Mr. Ion Zelea Codreanu, who led the whole propaganda of the League of Christian-National Defense in Bucovina. I met Mr. Ion Zelea Codreanu. Following that, I got to see the movement of the youth that was formed after the League was divided. On this occasion, I met Mr. Corneliu Zelea Codreanu. I approached the organization, which at that time was called the Iron Guard.

Finally, the idea of participating in the elections came up, and I remember the precise statement of Mr. Codreanu, to eliminate the belief this organization was illegal and aimed toward some secret goals, it had to join the elections, to show that it was legal, even though it wasn't illegal even before that. So, they were looking

The Trial of Corneliu Zelea Codreanu

to enter politics in a normal way, even though this organization did not have the required power to fight against the existing political parties. And so, the events that everyone knows about unfolded.

Lawyer Paul Iacobescu: Does the witness know about the income of this Movement? Did it have important funds? And, if yes, how did the Movement spend this money?

Prof. Brăileanu: I don't know all the details, because I didn't have to deal with money in the organization, but I know precisely that the members had to pay their dues, everyone as much as they could afford — I contributed as well, not much — for the needs of the Party. But they didn't have important sums of money, especially obtained from other sources, because I know I struggled with the printing costs. From every conversation I had with Mr. C.Z. Codreanu, he didn't give me the impression that he was in a hurry to obtain power; from everything I've seen, the Movement was legal.

Lawyer Iacobescu: Does the witness believe the defendant C.Z. Codreanu would take action against the interests of the country?

The Witness: I am convinced that he, as well as the Legionary Movement, cannot be accused of actions against the country, against the nation.

The Testimony of Prof. Mihail Manoilescu

Prof. Mihail Manoilescu[46] joins the hearing.

Lawyer Iacobescu: Does the witness know the Movement and its leader, the conception and the ideology of this Movement?

Mr. President Dumitru: Professor, what could you tell us, briefly and naturally, about the Legionary Movement, its conceptions, tendencies, and purpose?

Prof. Manoilescu: Honorary Military Court, I know the Legionary Movement, not just as a Romanian movement, and not just judged as a Romanian phenomenon; I know it from the prism of my long studies on all the European movements that have a similar ideology to the Legionary Movement. Because, as much as we believed these movements are a result of the needs of a single nation, this is a European phenomenon, a global phenomenon. Every era has its own forms of political life, its own political instruments, its own political ideals, which create, what we call, a bit too delicately, conformism, identity, similarity of different movements.

160 Romanian Crucible

Lawyer Iacobescu: Does the witness know anything about their methods and purposes? Were their methods occult or insurgent?

Prof. Manoilescu: I confess that, to my knowledge, as a friend of the Legion, and as a candidate who won — which was extremely hard — an absolute majority in two counties in the elections for the Senate, I don't know the complete inner workings of the Legion, but I know its spirit. And, from this spirit and from what I know of Corneliu Codreanu, it uses methods that maybe sin through selfless excess. This Movement, its moral side, which regenerated certain nations: Italy, Portugal, Germany, is the phenomenon of the century. People stopped believing in the Parliamentary formulas. The Movement represents aspirations towards totalitarian and constructive nationalism, and it focuses on the man. Corneliu Codreanu considered we have to start with the man. In a future that will become true at one point, this form: man, and institution, will become one. It's a prophecy that will fulfill all my other prophecies. The Legionary Movement meets all the conditions to become a movement of purification. Mr. Corneliu Codreanu, as well as the Legionary Movement, are of a virtue of soul, of cleanliness, of a purity, sacrifice, and excess of loyalty that I've never met before.

Lawyer Iacobescu: Do you believe the defendant, C.Z. Codreanu, is capable of treason?

The Witness: I can't accept such an association with Codreanu, they exclude each other. I know the spirit of the Legion and I know Mr. Codreanu, who sins through an excess of honesty and loyalty. This doesn't blend with illegality. Mr. Codreanu considered, and considers, that it would be a dishonor for him to obtain to power by overthrowing the government of a minority. He wants to do this by earning the hearts of the masses. He could have done it, but he didn't want to. I want to add one thing that is interesting. I just arrived by train from abroad, and I bring with me the terrifying impressions of a European conflict that is about to start.

Mr. Senior President Dumitru: Please elaborate this fact in a public meeting.

Prof. Manoilescu: It is an interesting fact to set a certain atmosphere.

Mr. Senior President: Next witness.

The Testimony of Prof. Nichifor Crainic

Professor Nichifor Crainic[47] joins the hearing as a witness.

The Trial of Corneliu Zelea Codreanu

Lawyer Iacobescu: I'd like to know if the witness knows the Legionary Movement and the leader of this movement, and how he knows Mr. Codreanu. I ask this in relation to a fragment from a document that was found.

Defendant C.Z. Codreanu: If Mr. President allows me, I'd like to ask this question.

As you all know, it was planted in my home, well not in my actual home, but on the painter working in my home, a document that I stated to be forged from the first moment, and showed that it does not belong to me. I said: my luck was that the document contained names that I could use to prove this document as false. One of those mentioned was Professor Nichifor Crainic. This is what the text says about this document: "You allowed me to turn into a chronology the memorable dialogues you've had with the leader of the 250 million nationalists, with Professor Dragoş Protopopescu and with Professor Crainic, where I had the pleasure to assist."

I want to ask professor Crainic if he remembers — this is about memorable discussions — about a discussion between me, him, and professor Dragoş Protopopescu, the leader of the 250 million nationalist youth, a discussion to which the unknown author of this memoir assisted in 1934?

Mr. Nichifor Crainic: Honorary Council, Mr. Codreanu and I have not been in contact for the past three and a half years. We don't speak, we don't greet each other on the street, we've rarely met, but without speaking. Everything written in this document is pure fantasy. First, I find it quite comical: the leader of the 250 million nationalists! I don't understand this folly. We've never spoken of such things.

Mr. Senior President: The answer is clear.

Lawyer Iacobescu: Would you believe him capable of treason?

Mr. Crainic: I don't understand. What type of treason? Treason of a country? I was expecting serious questions.

Lawyer Iacobescu: This is in the final ordinance.

Mr. Senior President: It's not in the final ordinance.

Lawyer Lica Zamfirescu: Thank you.

Mr. Crainic: I believe him incapable of it.

Mr. Senior President: The hearing is adjourned until 16:30.

162 Romanian Crucible

The hearing stops at 13:00.

The Afternoon Hearing

The hearing starts at 5:25.

Senior President col. Magistrate Dumitru Constantin: May the defendant be brought into the courtroom. We continue with the witnesses for the defense.

Lawyer Paul Iacobescu: Mr. President, you should inquire if Ghiocel Dumitru, the witness for the prosecution, arrived, so we don't exhaust all of our witnesses.

The witness is absent.

The Testimony of General Constantin Petrovicescu

Witness General Petrovicescu Constantin,[48] 57 years old from Târgu-Mureş, residing in Craiova, enters the courtroom.

He swears the oath.

Lawyer Paul Iacobescu: General Petrovicescu was Codreanu's accuser in 1934. I want to ask how he met Corneliu Codreanu.

Senior President: General, you were the Prosecution's representative in the trial judged here in 1934. The question is: under what circumstances did you meet Corneliu Codreanu, the defendant of then and of today?

General Petrovicescu: I met him here, in the courtroom where I was working. I was a special Royal Commissary. Three days before the trial, he came willingly to the Council. I hadn't seen him before that. At the moment when he showed up, I had just finished my general lines of the indictment and I was about to continue, of course, with the oral instruction. However, I had a feeling not to make late changes. I then asked for a meeting with Mr. Codreanu here, so he can tell me the things I was interested in, for the purpose of completing the conclusions I had made by that point.

We talked for almost an hour. I noted down everything he told me, and I found that my conclusions were identical to what he had told me with his own mouth. It was perfectly identical. And so, I entered the hearing confused. I verified it for a

The Trial of Corneliu Zelea Codreanu

second time during the oral instructions, and it was shown that the events were the same as they were presented by the documents, without distortion. Therefore, I could do my job with perfect knowledge of the subject and without having to make changes to my indictment. During the trial, I saw him here every day. From the day of the sentence until today — more than four years have passed — I haven't seen him any time since.

Lawyer Iacobescu: The General should tell us if the instruction of that trial in 1934 was detailed, serious, challenging, and if it lasted for a long time.

Senior President: Every instruction is serious, because you can't send people to trial without a serious instruction.

Senior Prosecutor Major Magistrate Radu Ionescu: The instruction took a long time, because the large number of defendants required it.

Senior President: I ask the question. But a question must be asked in order to reach a conclusion, and I wouldn't like to ask questions that are not relevant to the case.

Lawyer Iacobescu: We ask the General to tell us if during the long instruction, he could find any acts committed by Codreanu that would imply he was following objectives against the interests of the State, through occult and subversive means, or if he wanted to cause a revolution or a civil war?

Senior President: I won't ask the question, but look what is happening: the General was a Royal Commissary then, so he was the representative of the Prosecution in the trial. The conclusions he reached were spoken out loud in the public hearing at the time.

Lawyer Iacobescu: These conclusions are very interesting, allow me to tell you why.

Senior President: I ask the question. What conclusions did you reach, General, following the research done in the quality you had in that trial?

The Witness: The instruction was done by General Instructor Ilie Bădescu. My role was as prosecutor. What I can speak about it is the way the oral interaction took place and how I reached my conclusion in the indictment. I found nothing, I found no evidence, and the conclusions at the end of the indictment where I requested the sentencing of the three assassins of Duca, and I let the Council decide upon the cases of Codreanu and General Cantacuzino. I asked for everyone else's acquittal.

Senior Prosecutor: If General Petrovicescu, in his quality at the trial of 1934, asked for the acquittal of the 47 Legionaries and asked the Court to decide the fate of defendant C.Z. Codreanu and of the late General Cantacuzino, does it mean that he made differences when it comes to guilt?

General Petrovicescu: I forbid such interpretations, Mr. Prosecutor. If I let the Court decide about Corneliu Codreanu, I did that because they, him, as well as General Cantacuzino, were the leaders of the Legionary Movement, and I considered it right to let the court make a decision on this matter.

Senior Prosecutor: Is the General aware that after the sentencing of the Prime Minister's assassins, whose conviction he asked for, as well as after the sentencing of the ten who assassinated Stelescu, the defendant gave them awards, raising their Legionary ranks to the highest one, giving them the Legionary distinction called The White Cross?

General Petrovicescu: I heard once on the Radio, between a commercial for Adesgo socks and another for Mott champagne, that these people were honored.

Defendant C.Z. Codreanu: Mr. President, I want my words to be interpreted correctly. I didn't raise the three in rank, I didn't reward them. On the day of Moţa and Marin's funeral, I raised two of the ten in rank.

Senior President: How do you appreciate the gesture made by the leader of the Legionary Movement, by awarding those that justice had convicted?

General Petrovicescu: I don't want to give the impression that I want to run before giving a reply. But in these circumstances, I can't respond to that, because it's a subjective matter. Since that trial until today, I didn't learn anything else other than what the newspapers presented.

Defendant C.Z. Codreanu: What does the General think about the subversion of the Legionary Movement?

General Petrovicescu: Considering that I held in my hand documents, books, etc. that could be bought in bookstores, obviously it does not have a subversive character, revolutionary, or seeking to provoke a civil war.

Defendant C.Z. Codreanu: Does the General think me capable of treason?

The Trial of Corneliu Zelea Codreanu

General Petrovicescu: I don't believe him capable of treason in his beliefs or ours, and I don't think anyone in his entourage would ever have that intention. If anyone had similar thoughts, he would have removed them.

The Testimony of General Ion Antonescu

General Ion Antonescu[49] joins the hearing.

Defendant C.Z. Codreanu: Mr. President, please allow me to ask my own questions instead of my defense team.

Senior President: Yes.

Defendant C.Z. Codreanu: If the General remembers a conversation[50] that took place at his residence, concerning my attitude towards challenges, during the time he was War Minister, and if my worries were towards public disturbances, because of our geographic situation, and what attitude did I have when we had this conversation?

Senior President: The question formed this way, can't be admitted by the Court, because it involves challenges your party might be subjected to. This is the decision of the Court, which is sovereign.

Mr. General, the question is the following: If during the elections, or around that time, Mr. Codreanu, during the conversation that he's referring to, confessed to you what his reaction would be if there would be any disturbances during the elections, in which he participated as well.

General Ion Antonescu: The conversation didn't take place before the elections, but during the elections, meaning when the elections took the form that everyone knows, and we were afraid we were heading towards a civil war. I then asked Mr. Codreanu — and Goga was agreeing with me — to stop this unrest in the country, because it can only threaten the security of our borders. Mr. Codreanu had a conversation with me, if I'm not mistaken, on a Friday, and two days later he met Goga at Mr. Gigurtu's residence — which I only found out about two days after that. And then, in front of me, Mr. Codreanu said he will resign from the electoral fight, and in front of Goga, I believe he said he would resign from the elections completely, which proved a great patriotic nature.

Defendant C.Z. Codreanu: Did the General conclude, from his discussions with me, that I was in a rush to come to power?

Romanian Crucible

General Ion Antonescu: On the contrary, from our discussions I concluded that he was not interested in this problem, but only in the good of the country.

Defendant C.Z. Codreanu: Does the General believe me capable of causing unrest or a civil war?

General Ion Antonescu: If he had given me this impression, I would have never had a discussion with Mr. Codreanu. Mr. Codreanu had a beautiful attitude towards the interests of the country.

Defendant C.Z. Codreanu: If I asked the General about what I could do with the weapons received in General Cantacuzino's last will and testament?

General Antonescu: To surrender them to the military authority. If I'm not mistaken, Mr. Codreanu, because I'm a man with activity in various realms, and I could forget.

Senior President: It was the Military Museum.

General Antonescu: Exactly. The Military Museum. That's what I said.

Defendant C.Z. Codreanu: if the weapons found during the searches within the country, on different citizens, can inspire the smallest fear of arming for insurrectionary purposes.

Senior President: I don't think the General can answer this question, because he doesn't have the necessary evidence.

Lawyer Paul Iacobescu: We'll put it at his disposal, if you allow it.

Senior President: This is not a question related to the General's situation and to his answers. He is not familiar with this matter, because he didn't have the documentation, therefore we cannot ask him a question to which he's unable to reply.

Defendant C.Z. Codreanu: If our organization could be considered illicit, conspiratorial, and if it could pose a threat to the security of the State?

Senior President: What organization is this question referring to? The Legionary Movement or the All for the Country Party?

Defendant C.Z. Codreanu: It's referring to the Party, because that was the human element.

Senior President: General, how did you see this organization: as a political party, with a certain title, or as an echo of an organization that seemed to have other types of activity? Because I can ask this question only for the All for the Country

The Trial of Corneliu Zelea Codreanu

Party, because this was the only one you were familiar with, during the time when you were part of the government. What was the opinion you had on this Party?

General Antonescu: I regret that I can't provide an answer to this question. I'm under military laws, and as a soldier, I can only judge the activity of my subordinates.

I know the All for the Country Party in the same way everyone else knows it, but I can't say I have a good or a bad opinion of it, as I can't have an opinion as a military man about a political party.

Senior President: Let us return to the previous matters.

Defendant C.Z. Codreanu: Mr. President, I am on trial for treason according to art. 190 and 191.

Senior President: For possession of documents concerning the security of the State and for publishing some of them, let's be clear about that, because the notion of treason has different understandings. For the public opinion and for the great public, the idea of treason has a completely different nature.

Defendant C.Z. Codreanu: Does the General believe me capable of treason?

General Antonescu: From all the elements I've had and have, I can say that he cannot be accused of treason. General Antonescu doesn't talk to traitors.

The Testimony of Professor Emanoil Antonescu

Lawyer Iacobescu: As a professor of law, how does the witness interpret art. 190 and 191 of the Penal Code?

Professor Antonescu: I am a professor of civil law, not criminal law, but I studied the Ordinance because I was interested in it. According to our Code, we must make the distinction between...

The prosecutor interrupts...

The President comes back to the discussion but doesn't insist.

Lawyer Iacobescu: If the documents issued by the gendarmes that were found on Mr. Codreanu touch on State security, and if he can be accused of treason.

Prof. Antonescu: No, because they are political documents, not security ones because...

168   Romanian Crucible

The President interrupts.

Professor Antonescu: I wouldn't have defended him if I believed he was capable of treason. We must pay attention, we must be patriots, the times...

The President interrupts.

Lawyer Iacobescu: Does the witness believe Mr. Codreanu was interested in causing unrest or a civil war?

Professor Antonescu: The documents don't say that he was causing a civil war, because this is about defense... If someone defended me, it doesn't mean that someone wants a civil war. I defended him twice, at section 2 and section 4 of the Ilfov Courthouse, where he was on trial for wanting to demolish Romania. A revolution is done in another way. Also, I do not believe that he is capable of treason, and my conscience dictates me to see it this way.

The Testimony of the Counselor at the High Court of Cassation Eugen Petit

Lawyer Iacobescu: In what circumstances did you meet the defendant Corneliu Codreanu?

Counselor Eugen Petit: I was a police prefect with a delegation in Iaşi in 1920, when Bolshevism was flourishing. I was a judge back then. There were red flags hung on buildings, I asked my agents to rip them off, but they wouldn't dare, because the buildings were tall, and they were afraid the Bolsheviks would shoot them. While I was talking to my men, I saw a young man: he climbed on the building, and although he was surrounded by Bolsheviks, he snatched the red flag, and set the Romanian tricolor in its place. It was Corneliu Codreanu.

Lawyer Iacobescu: Does the Counselor believe the defendant Corneliu Codreanu capable of any act of treason?

Counselor Eugen Petit: I consider any man honest until evidence to the contrary, because I'm a magistrate. But I've known Mr. Codreanu from childhood.

The Trial of Corneliu Zelea Codreanu

The Testimony of General Mihail Racoviță

Lawyer Iacobescu: For how long have you known the defendant C.Z. Codreanu and what opinion do you have on his activity?

General Racoviță: [51] I've known him since he was 18 years old, from Mehadia, when a pair of youngsters appeared, who made a good impression on me. I asked myself who they were, and I was told it was Corneliu Codreanu and his wife. Seven to eight years later, when power was held by the Maniu[52] government, and we were planning Prince Carol's[53] return. Mr. Maniu[54] and Vaida[55] didn't oppose it. I asked the youth as well and Mr. Tăzlăuanu told me to speak to Mr. Codreanu, who was the leader of the youth. At Tăzlăuanu's residence, around 9 o'clock, I spoke to Mr. Codreanu, who agreed with us. I was briefly part of two parties. Then I gave up on politics. I knew General Cantacuzino-Grănicerul. I saw that he had joined the Legionary Movement. I wanted to speak to Mr. Codreanu, so I spoke to him for about two hours, and saw that was the only place where something could be done about the interests of the country, so I joined them. Because the country's salvation will happen through him.

Lawyer Iacobescu: Do you believe the defendant capable, General, of treason? And if you reached the conclusion that his activity and the Legionary Movement's activity could be suspected of illicit tendencies?

General Racoviță: I swore on my human and military conscience to tell the truth. Never did either Mr. Codreanu, or his Movement have a subversive character or endanger the State. I think it's a joke for him to be accused of treason, and I don't even think you believe that, how would you expect someone who knows him to believe that?

The Testimony of General Constandache

After General Racoviță's testimony, General Constandache is brought into the courtroom.

The Defense: How does the witness know the defendant Corneliu Codreanu, and what could he tell us about his activity?

General Constandache: I know Mr. Codreanu from his trial in 1934. I was his judge. I can tell that the ideology he follows, Country, God, and King, ideology that everyone is familiar with, can only be a beautiful ideology.

The Defense: Could the defendant be accused of civil war or rebellion?

General Constandache: Corneliu Codreanu is not capable of this; he has so many followers and they would have abandoned him if that was the case.

The Testimony of General Dona

General Dona enters the courtroom, and he swears the oath

General Dona: I know Mr. Codreanu. I judged his trial in 1934, and I was in permanent contact with him afterwards. He causes a deep impression. Young, with a nationalist point of view. He didn't have any involvement in Duca's assassination. I judged the trial with my conscience clear. He's an honest man.

The testimony of General Comănescu

After General Dona, Mr. President calls for General Comănescu.

The Defense: If the General knows defendant Codreanu, and what can he tell us about his activity?

General Comănescu: I've known him since I was commanding the division in Bârlad. An incident had occurred. I wrote a letter to Mr. Codreanu, he understood me, and the incident ended. I judged him in 1934. I had contact with him regarding political matters of the National Peasant's Party. There were a lot of serious issues that came out in the open. We had contact again in 1936, at Carmen Sylva's. They were struggling in poverty. I sent them a barrel of cheese and other things. He told me that he was trying to lead the youth on the nationalist path, that he wasn't looking to gain power, and that he wanted to build character. He is not capable of committing acts against the security of the State, or a civil war.

The Testimony of Engineer Stelian Ionescu

Engineer Stelian Ionescu follows.

The Trial of Corneliu Zelea Codreanu

The Defense: What does the witness know about a conversation between him and Mr. Corneliu Codreanu, regarding a sum of 40 million lei?

The Witness: I was in the delegation at the mines in Șorecani [King Carol II], together with three other workers: Morar Sabin, Moldovan Ion, and Suler Gavrila, on the 4th or 5th of April 1938. The delegation hasn't been at the Industrial Credit. It was supposed to go after that. I told Mr. Codreanu that the workers are miserable and haven't received their salaries for a few months. I told him that I know Mr. Manoilescu had spent around 40,000,000 lei in a few years. He asked me what he'd spent this money on and I told him Mr. Manoilescu has 72,000 [*he's stopped by the President*]. Mr. Codreanu took notes. The note shown to me was written following my explanations.

The Testimony of Sabin Morar

The Witness: On the 5th of April I was part of the delegation from the mines in Șorecani, because we didn't receive our salaries. We went to Mr. Manoilescu and went to Casa Verde as well, with Engineer Ionescu, and we spoke to Mr. Corneliu Codreanu. Mr. Codreanu took notes about what Mr. Ionescu told him about the incomes, spending, and other great sums of money (the Manoilescu case) …

He is stopped from continuing.

The Testimony of Alexandru Hodoș

The defense asks if the Moța-Marin guide was seen by him before being published, as chief of censorship.

The Witness: The censorship depended on the Ministry Council presidency, I was a State Subsecretary, and in this quality I had the task to exercise censorship control, and I know I allowed for publication the preliminary instructions for the founding of the Moța-Marin Corps. They were not considered in violation of the law given at that time.

The Defense: What do you know about the meeting between the former president of the Ministry Council, Octavian Goga, and the defendant?

Romanian Crucible

The Witness: It was about the elections in 1938 — in the spring — a discussion I was not a part of, but Octavian Goga told me, a day before the Government was overthrown, that they talked about the way in which the electoral campaign was being done, and about the fallen victims; the dialogue, as it was reported to me, was dramatic in nature, in a sense that Octavian Goga brought up the unification between the two organizations. Octavian Goga told me what Mr. Codreanu said: if Octavian Goga considers the All for the Country Party to be an obstacle to the propaganda of nationalist ideas, Mr. Codreanu is ready to retire from the elections. I know this much. I'm ready to answer other questions.

The Testimony of Sextil Pușcariu[56]

The Defense: Are you familiar with the Legionary Movement?

The Witness: I'm not a member of the Movement. I've known it long ago and had much sympathy for it. I've never been involved in politics. The warm heart of these young people, necessary to this country, is what attracted me. The best students of mine were Legionaries. I liked the book *Pentru Legionari*. Codreanu is a skillful writer. I approached him because of his deep rigor, his love for the country, and his devotion for the throne. I wanted to see him and I saw him. My impression stayed the same.

The Defense: Could the Movement be dangerous for the security of the State?

Mr. Sextil Puscariu: I saw this Movement as something against corruption and abuse, under no circumstances as something against the State.

The Defense: Do you believe him to be capable of treason?

The President doesn't allow him to answer, considering he answered enough questions.

The Testimony of General Iacob Constantin

The Defense: Are you a Legionary?

General Iacob: I've met Mr. Codreanu on the 1st of February 1938. I asked to join the party. I didn't take part in the meeting of the Legionary Senate because I

The Trial of Corneliu Zelea Codreanu

wasn't asked. But after I became aware of the newspapers, I joined. It was a nationalist party. If I believed it to be subversive, capable of overthrowing the Government, of fighting against the State order, I wouldn't have joined it.

The Testimony of Gheorghe Pantazi

The Defense: How did Codreanu and the Movement behave during the electoral campaign? [*20th of December 1937*]

Mr. Pantazi: I'm not a member of this party. I was invited to be a candidate in Bihor for the Senate. I accepted it and traveled to Bihor. Before this, I went to the headquarters and asked: what do I need to say when I go to Oradea? I was told to not speak of any political organization, or of any political man, only about the Legion and the Legionaries. During the elections, the political parties had the most trust, knowing that a Legionary was behind it. The Legionaries did not respond to challenges and did not challenge anyone. At my age, I can say that I've never seen such elections before. Their patriotism, honesty, and loyalty were exemplary. This is what made me decide to campaign.

The Testimony of Mr. Nicolae Pop

The Defense: How did you interpret the second circular — about the secret agents?

The Witness: I've been a member of the Legion since January 1935. I read the circular posted at the headquarters. I asked myself if such people could be hiding among us. The members of the nest told me that none of those are part of our group.

The Testimony of Lawyer Dimitrie Popa

The Defense: What does the witness know about the second circular?

Mr. Dimitrie Popa: I've been a member of the Iron Guard and the All for the Country Party since 1929. I'm a lawyer, and I was a part of the Legionary legal department. Mr. Codreanu — I was there — was informed of agents that the Siguranța had infiltrated among us. I read the circular as well. I had a copy, because I was a nest leader. It was posted on the board. I led the electoral campaign in Argeș for two months. I know that one of the tendentious information spread around was

Romanian Crucible

that we were organizing a great manifestation in Argeş. I found 1,300 gendarmes under the leadership of Colonel Popescu and Major Cireş. All the precautions taken against our small projects were exaggerated. Personally, I never identified an agent from the Security or from the Police. The circular was strictly referring to the agents of Security and Police who would have infiltrated in our midst.

The Testimony of Traian Herseni

The Defense: What do you know about the origin of the Legionary funds?

The Witness: I've been a part of the Movement since 1936. Normally, we'd get weekly donations from 1 to 5 lei; those who had more money would give up to 100 lei weekly. We were collecting from friends as well, from 100 to 500 lei monthly. During the elections, because the spending was too great, we gave up on wine, cinemas, and pastries, saving up 500 lei to give the Legion. We were paying for the posters. We'd print brochures that we'd sell, and the money from it we'd give the Legion. I myself printed two brochures: *Mişcarea legionara şi ţărănimea* (*The Legionary Movement and the peasantry*) and *Mişcarea legionară şi muncitorimea* (*The Legionary Movement and the workers*).

The hearing stopped at 8:30 PM.

Day Three
Wednesday, 25 May 1938

The hearing starts at 10 in the morning.

Before continuing the witness hearing, lawyer Sebastian Radovici reminds them about the Senior Prosecutor's invitation to bring the registers of the former All for the Country Party. One of these registers is presented, the one for the Blue Sector that contains proof of income for the amount of 288,000 lei.

Lawyer Lizetta Gheorghiu protests because a newspaper claimed she was a lawyer for the Communist International and asks the President not to allow these libelous remarks.

Lawyer Colfescu also speaks about this.

Senior President Colonel Dumitru Constantin: The court will make inquiries on this at the Ministry of Internal Affairs, to clarify the testimony of General Constandache, and instructs the press to retell the debates accurately.

The defense requests for the following witnesses to be heard: Prof. Dobre, Col. Zăvoianu, M. Polihroniade, Prof. Ion Zelea Codreanu, Dorin Haznaș, Ciorogaru, Traian Cotigă, Ilie Negoescu, Dragoș Protopopescu, Lawyer Crânganu, Arnold Roth, Carol Becker, Henri Ghica, I. Cantacuzino, V. Cristescu, N. Totu, Victor Gârcineanu, General Dr. Grințescu, Iuliu Maniu, S. Mehedinți, R. Ioanițescu, Prof. Dongoroz, Al. Vaida-Voievod, Grigore Iunian, Engineer Clime, Al. Cantacuzino, C. Argetoianu, Gh. Furdui, Prof. Radu Gyr, Engineer Eugen Ionică, General Gabriel Marinescu, Ion Fotti, C. Iarca, Engineer Gigurtu, Dr. Topa.

Defendant C.Z. Codreanu: These witnesses are party leaders, movement leaders, ministers. I'd like to ask them if they had the documents that were found at my place. And if they protested with those documents in the Parliament or in the press. The second question would be, what type of document possession?... This is not about possession with intent. The witness must come and say the documents

176 Romanian Crucible

weren't held onto with any intent (Dongoroz, under art. 191, provides three hypotheses: a Romanian citizen that obtains and transmits secret documents, any citizen that, without having the quality, possesses secret documents with intent...and the case...)

The conclusion to this question remains to be decided by you, after consulting with the other members of the Court. Regarding art. 300, last paragraph from C.M.J: I'm interested in "intent," according to the doctrine...

Senior President: It is noted. We'll conclude on every question depending on each specific case.

The Testimony of Iuliu Maniu

Defendant C.Z. Codreanu: Why did we sign a nonaggression pact if our ideologies are so different?

Mr. Iuliu Maniu: [57] It's true, our and your ideologies are completely opposed, and I don't believe there are two other parties in this country to be more opposite than ours.

[*After he gives the apology of democracy, he continues*] The Iron Guard is totalitarian and against democracy... Codreanu's party is an antisemitic party!... Aside from this, we are different through the methods we use in the political fight.

Given these differences of ideology, the question is obvious: how did we end up having an electoral agreement?

The reason is double. First, we had a personal reason: I had not met Mr. Codreanu before we signed the nonaggression pact. However, I closely followed his activity and attitude. I found that he was honest in his actions, consistent, and tenacious, qualities that are rare in political life and not many political leaders have them. For these reasons, I gladly offered him my help. Aside from this personal reason, we had political reasons. Mr. Codreanu, as well as I, believes that for a healthy national and State politics, it is absolutely necessary to respect the national dignity. When Tătărescu[58] was named Prime minister, the national dignity was gravely attacked, as well as the spirit of the Constitution. That's why we had to join hands, to make our nation reject this attempt to break our national dignity. We were successful. Mr. Codreanu believes, as I do, that the national idea is the vital factor for the prosperity of a nation. He believes, as I do, that the State, with all its power,

The Trial of Corneliu Zelea Codreanu

must preserve the unparalleled beautiful qualities of the Romanian nation, supporting the State, and giving it the possibility to fulfil its mission, through material, cultural, and social methods. It's true that Mr. Codreanu, as I have shown, has an antisemitic element in his mentality, which I don't approve of, but the fundamental idea is identical. Aside from this, Mr. Codreanu is convinced, as I am, that without respecting the rules of private and public life, and without taking into consideration the Christian morals, you cannot ensure the survival of a nation; ignoring these factors could mean the same thing that it meant for other nations of the past: death and destruction. For this reason, we agree on imposing fairness, honor, and Christian morals, in personal, social, and public life, which today, unfortunately, so many disregard...

All of these facts were decisive when creating the agreement between me and Mr. Codreanu, and I'm glad we did it.

The Defendant C.Z. Codreanu: If the Liberal Party, when it had the power, used Police, Security, Gendarmes, and all the other State authorities to stop the electoral campaign of the opposing parties?

Senior President: He opposes this question.

Defendant C.Z. Codreanu: If in the practice of our political life, the opposing parties protested publicly, in the press and in the Parliament, against electoral interferences, and if they presented copies of orders issued by the authorities for their subunits?

Mr. Maniu: It's true, during all the elections, aside from the ones in 1928 and 1932 that the National Peasant's Party conducted, the government used the Executive Power, the Gendarmes, and the Security Service, for electoral purposes of the party in power, and they didn't only limit it to the State's security. The opposing parties have always tried to obtain secret orders, through which the public force was used to stop the opposition from carrying out their political activity. I, myself, in 1927, had in hand 18 secret orders, confidential, of the public authorities, through which the executive power was put into the service of the party in power. I even published these secret orders in newspapers. More than that, I went to the President of the Council of Ministers, Ionel Brătianu, and I showed them to him in a memoir as a protest against such interferences. Neither the Prime Minister nor the authorities charged me with anything because they couldn't, as obtaining and possessing

Romanian Crucible

such a secret order was a custom followed regularly by every political party in the opposition.

Defendant C.Z. Codreanu: If Mr. Maniu knows about me trying to come to power, or if from the conversation he had with me he understood that I'm rushing to gain power?

Mr. Maniu: No, on the contrary, from every conversation I've ever had with the defendant, I found this difference in attitude between us: I was aiming for our Party to come to power as a result of the elections, because it was our obvious right, and I found it necessary for the country. While Mr. Codreanu always showed that he's in no rush, that he has time, and his time hasn't arrived yet.

Defendant C.Z. Codreanu: If Mr. Maniu saw in me, and in the Movement I led, a man who aimed to overthrow the State order or to cause a civil war?

Mr. Maniu: If I ever suspected this, or saw anything that would make me believe that, I would have never shaken hands with you over a political campaign, because I've always believed, and still believe, that for our nation and for the Romanian State, the worst misfortune would be a rebellion, unrest, or a civil war.

Defendant C.Z. Codreanu: If I discussed with Mr. Maniu about foreign politics and if, during these discussions, I ever showed a personal interest or was driven by personal convictions?

Mr. Maniu: During our discussions, we talked about foreign politics twice. I came to the conclusion that we have opposing views on this subject, and I tried to convince him that the only correct foreign policy that corresponds to Romania's interests, is that of France, England, and the great democracies of the West. He talked about his considerations on the other side. He had an opposite point of view. The whole discussion was based on national interest, and I didn't see any personal interest on Mr. Codreanu's part.

Defendant C.Z. Codreanu: If Mr. Maniu believes the propaganda of my Movement was conspiratorial, occult, or illicit?

Mr. Maniu: During the electoral campaign I observed the organizations of the Iron Guard, who were in the open, combative, with energetic manifestations, sometimes too energetic for my taste.

Mr. Prosecutor: Does Mr. Maniu believe it would have been a good or a bad thing, if the defendant Codreanu had managed to gain power?

The Trial of Corneliu Zelea Codreanu

Mr. Maniu: Mr. Codreanu is the leader of a party, and I'm the President of another party, with a completely different ideology. Obviously, I wouldn't have considered it right for Codreanu's party to come to power. Every party wants the good of the country, but obtained through their own means. I think the only good option is the one presented by our Party. Therefore, I only consider the National Peasant's Party to be good for the country.

Finally, the wish of the nation is decisive for me, and the parties have the right to try to earn public support, but I can't allow for governments to be imposed on the country against the national wish. If the public opinion will be on my side, I'll come to power. If the public opinion will be with Codreanu, he'll come to power.

The Testimony of Constantin Iarca

Defendant C.Z. Codreanu: Is it true that I met Mr. Cernat, the former General Director of State Security at your residence?

The Witness: Yes, it's true that at my residence and at Carmen Sylva's residence there were meetings between Mr. Cernat and Mr. Codreanu. Mr. Codreanu was offered the government.

[*He is corrected by Mr. Codreanu, who brings to his attention that he wasn't asked about that, and it could be misinterpreted*].

Anyway, Mr. Cernat was the head of Security, and he asked me multiple times to facilitate meetings between him and Mr. Codreanu, and these meetings did happen.

The Testimony of General Virgil Bădulescu

Defendant C.Z. Codreanu: Is it true that you were my commander and educator? And do you believe me capable of acts that could endanger the State?

The Witness: I was the commander of the Military High School in Mănăstirea Dealului. He was my student from 4th grade to 8th grade. He was very good. I tried to inspire him to love his country. He was a very good student and loved by his classmates.

The Defense: Do you believe him capable of treason?

180   Romanian Crucible

The Witness: I can't have an opinion on this as a military man, however, from the way I know him, I don't believe he'd ever be capable of harming the State. My situation today doesn't allow me to express other opinions.

The Testimony of Sever Dan (former Minister)

The Defense: From your relationship with Mr. Codreanu, did you ever consider him in rush to come to power?

The Witness: I've known the Movement from the beginning, and in this quality, I was interested in every movement, especially the nationalist movement. In 1923, I asked to help the students. My connection with the Legionary Movement was established a few months ago, under the government of Goga. Mr. Alex. Vaida insisted (me being a member of the Romanian Front) to speak to Mr. Codreanu. I intervened and asked him to invite him to my home, where Mr. Vaida was. They talked for 3 hours. No political ties resulted from these discussions. The Goga government had fallen. A new regime came to power, one that Mr. Vaida had fought for a long time. I was curious to know what Mr. Codreanu thought about it. A letter was written regarding this matter [*he reads it*]:

Mr. Sever Dan,

"Thank you for the words you have written to me... it's not the case for the new government to be put into difficulty... let's leave it a year, maybe two, maybe even more... Please be assured we won't oppose this government. I don't consider it my time."

The Defense: This should be added to the case file.

Senior President: A copy of it will be added to the case file.

The Defense: Did the witness ever have secret documents in possession?

The Witness: Yes, even my friends had them under the old regime. The electoral fights were true civil wars.

The Defense: Were the secret documents issued by the Prefecture, Gendarmes, or Police?

The Witness: They were. They were also published and discussed in the Parliament.

The Trial of Corneliu Zelea Codreanu

The Testimony of Professor Carol Beker

The Defendant C.Z. Codreanu (asks the witness regarding the translation in German of his book, *Pentru Legionari*): Did you come to me with Mr. Arnold Roth?

The Witness: I was asked by a gentleman, who I've known for a long time, by Engineer Ionică, if I know of someone who could do corrections to the translation of the book *Pentru Legionari*. I suggested a German writer from Romania, Mr. Arnold Roth.

Defendant C.Z. Codreanu: Do you remember about me being upset with the German journalists?

The Witness: I know Mr. Codreanu had acted upset multiple times (about an article published in *Volkischer Beobachter*, probably inspired by Istrate Micescu); he had the feeling he was seen with a certain adversity, especially since they had refused to publish his reply to that attack. The newspaper is the official National Socialist Party paper, under Rosenberg's leadership.

The Testimony of Henri Ghica

Defendant C.Z. Codreanu: Do you remember that I was offended by an article from the newspaper *Volkischer Beobachter*?

The Witness: At the end of last December, Mr. Codreanu did indeed tell me that an article had been published, I believe, by Mr. Micescu, and he told me he wouldn't agree to see any more German journalists, because his reply had not been published. He told me about those things that were bothering him multiple times.

The Testimony of Doctor I. Cantacuzino

The Defense: Do you know who was writing General Cantacuzino's circulars? Was he writing them personally, or did other people do it for him?

The Witness: I know the General never allowed releasing something made by someone else. Everything he signed it was from his own mind. I know the General, at Predeal, couldn't write with his own hand, and had other people write them for him following his words. Constantin Reich told me he was present when this letter

("I fight death...") was dictated by the General to Mr. Codreanu. Mr. Constantin Reich also read in the newspaper that this letter had been attributed to Codreanu.

Lawyer Cosmovici shows that Codreanu is charged with treason because of violations against the foreign security. That there are witnesses who had been ministers or political leaders, and we want to ask them if, in this quality, if they ever received documents similar to the ones that Corneliu Codreanu is on trial for, even if they protested against the abuse done through them.

Secondly: this is about possession of documents with intent. The Court takes note and will decide depending on the testimony of each witness.

The defense renounces hearing Prof. Gerota, Engineer Gigurtu, Dr. Topa, C. Argetoianu, A. Roth, General Dr. Grințescu, Prof. Dongoroz, etc., and insists on hearing the other witnesses, among them Dr. Vaida-Voievod, and Dr. Dan Rădulescu.

Defendant C.Z. Codreanu: I especially insist on the witnesses from Ciuc to be brought. These are people I worked with, witnesses in fact and I need them here.

Senior President Major Ionescu insists on the hearing of a few informers. He gives up on witness Ghiocel Dumitru, following to read his written statement.

The discussion revolves around a few informers suggested by Mr. Prosecutor, and some of them give course to his call.

Lawyer Lizetta Gheorghiu states these informants haven't been notified until now, so it's inexplicable why they had shown up.

After the prosecution intervenes, the Court allows their hearings as informers.

Ion Hagiu is asked by the Prosecutor what he knows about the circulars addressed to the informers. He replies that he had seen the order the defendant gave to have Duca and Stelescu assassinated, that the Brotherhoods of the Cross were secret organizations. The witness gets confused in the answers, giving the impression he had rehearsed his statement; therefore, the Prosecutor stops asking him questions.

Not having other witnesses present, and because the defense was insisting on hearing some that were absent, the hearing stops at 12:15, being scheduled to continue on the following day, starting at 9 AM.

Day Four
Thursday, 26 May 1938

The Indictment

The morning hearing was dedicated to the inquisition of the Senior Military Prosecutor, Major Magistrate Radu Ionescu.

The representative of the Prosecution spoke for an hour and a half, supporting the grounds of the accusation.

Mr. Senior President and Honorary Court,

I consider that this is the moment when we are entering the actual trial. Why? For two days we have assisted to a long statement from the defendant, while he spoke about things that were not related to his charges; he spoke about some of the charges brought to him, describing them in ways convenient to him. After that, we were witnesses to a long parade of witnesses, all of them suggested by the defendant, most of them friends of his or party members, who answered general questions on things that were not related to the charges.

Therefore, these past two days were dedicated to long discussions that were outside the objective of this trial.

But you might ask yourselves, what for? Why would this be allowed? Why would we lose precious time?

Mr. Senior President and Honorary Court, I observed a very simple reason. We wanted to give the defendant the freedom to state his defense. He brought up the prosecution too often, he hid all the insufficiency of his defense behind excuses.

This game ends now. Otherwise, Honorary Court, what value would the defendant's statements have if they are outside the trial's objective. I'm not only talking about the fact that, obviously, no defendant would ever admit his responsibility, and as a result, they're partial from the start. But, in this case, we are facing a man

Romanian Crucible

with a well-known conception, which was already confessed to by his defense. In truth, allow me to bring to your attention a characteristic fact of this matter. The book written by Codreanu[16] has already been brought up countless times. The defendant himself had brought it up to support his conception and his feelings. Evidently, this book must be read in full, even when it's not in the favor of the author.

Well, this book contains a chapter that describes the plot made by Codreanu and his friends against a few ministers in 1923.[63] It shows the conditions in which the investigation happened then and the replies Codreanu gave to the investigators. This is about the weapons that were found and about the people following to be assassinated. What was Codreanu saying? First, he was asking himself: what could I do? To confess it or not? To tell the truth or not? What would be suitable for my interest? And then, a series of considerations upon the tactical advantages of one choice or another. Therefore, his statements are made depending on the momentary tactical interest, not based on the truth. This is his conception; this is the line we must follow.[64] In the same context, Codreanu was disappointed that his friend had adopted different tactics and they went in contradiction. So, this is the point of view, which was started by the defendant himself, which shows the truth of his statements.

Then, there are the witnesses, his witnesses: what value do these testimonies have? And first, what do they contain? Aside from the two Generals who are not involved in political fights, they brought party members, and they asked them what opinion they have on their leader. If they believe him capable of one thing or another, if his movement is illegal or not. Therefore, his party members are called to give testimonies for their leader. These people are asked to speak about the organization they represent, or in which they were members at one point. What do you want these people to say? Of course, most of them had preconceived beliefs.

And what did they say? Simple subjective opinions, simple personal appreciations. That's why, in these circumstances, allow me to state that neither the testimonies, nor the defendant's statements can be conclusive for the charges debated here.

This is why I say that the trial only starts from this moment.

The Trial of Corneliu Zelea Codreanu

Disturbing the Country's Peace

Mr. President and Honorary Court, what type of trial are we judging here today? Is this an accidental offense, is it a common crime? No, gentlemen, this is about a crime that a man initiated, that he premeditated, that he planned for years. The charges debated today are not isolated, and they can't be weighed separately if we don't include them in the whole case. What did this crime represent? A disturbance of the peace of this country, the corruption of youth, the corruption of souls, the undermining of the country's legal establishments. You might ask yourselves; how could this freely unfold? Why did Justice not sanction it in time? The defendant himself brought up his favors to the authorities. Yes, it's true. This happened because of weakness and tolerance. But this doesn't minimize the guilt; this doesn't justify the crime; this can't lead to permanent immunity. And because of the past experience and its serious consequences, today I impose severe repressions. Because, Honorary Court, can you imagine where we're at? He had undertaken an action of corrupting all the living forces of this country, through his ability of perseverance. They were slandering each other, wildly cursing each other, all the men who contributed to the development of this country. Nobody was spared. A man such as Marshal Averescu has been cursed so many times, a professor such as Nicolae Iorga has been gossiped about so many times, the country's Patriarch was insulted as well. Who was spared? Why were these people attacked in this way, people that brought their precious contribution to building our country over the years? Why were our national values discredited? What was with this action of rebellion of the country against their leaders, this unfortunate action of seeding distrust and suspicion? Did no one see that through this action they were causing the moral disintegration of the nation? What was the purpose of this criminal action? Of course, not of the country, but of its enemies.

Codreanu's Origins and His Training

And, gentlemen, who was the man that always assumed to represent Romanian nationalism, even reserving the national sentiments for himself? Where did he come from? What does this man represent? What personal value did he have? What high worth and qualities did he have, when he felt entitled to denigrate a whole generation which, no matter what others would say, prepared the bright future of

Romanian Crucible

this country, by fulfilling the millennial national ideal? A generation that bled on so many war battlefields? Who is this man who presumes this?

Interestingly, Honorary Court, we must pause on this subject for a bit. We must know the man!

Corneliu was born in 1899, his parents being Ion Zelinski and Eliza, born Brauner. I won't talk now about this family's genealogy. I won't tell you who are the ancestors of Zelinski. I won't speak about the Condac and Antec families. I won't analyze the racial or ethnic purity of these families. But I will mention two precise and incontestable facts. First, at the birth of the defendant, his father's name was Zelinski. Therefore, Corneliu's name was Corneliu Zelinski, which is the name he received in his birth certificate. Only two years later, in 1901, the father Zelinski requested to have his name changed to Codreanu — a change which, of course, would be passed on to his son as well. This is one fact. The second fact. When Corneliu was born, his father didn't have Romanian citizenship.[65] Therefore, his son was a foreign citizen. Only four years later, in 1903, Zelinski, after having his name changed to Codreanu, requests and obtains his Romanian citizenship through a special law on the 24th of March of that year. We don't know in what circumstances was this citizenship obtained. Of course, we all know how easy it was to pass these laws through the Parliament, and most times these things were done as favors. Today we can complain about how easy was to work in this field. And today we have a list of conditions on which the Romanian citizenship was obtained in this case. But we won't talk about that now. Therefore, Corneliu Codreanu was the son of Zelinski, who was a foreign citizen at the time of his birth.

Mr. Senior President and Honorary Court, we must highlight something regarding this matter, which is quite odd. No matter Codreanu's origin, his documents are Romanian. His mysticism, obscurantism that he shows, the acts of cruelty that he personally committed or inspired, the death threats against his enemies, women, or children, none of these have a Romanian character. The Romanian has an open nature, is happy, and eager to live his life, the Romanian is kind. These characteristics are part of organic or congenital foreignism, or of a randomly borrowed foreignism, but it is obvious that the son of Zelinski and of Eliza Brauner, brought to Romania foreign actions and habits, that are foreign to the soul of our nation.

But, Honorary Court, what is the training of young Codreanu, what teachings did he acquire? Nobody has ever claimed that he showed any special skills or inclinations towards learning. What did he do after he finished his studies? What

The Trial of Corneliu Zelea Codreanu

profession did he embrace? Did he persevere in practicing it? What social situation did he form after this report? Nothing. Absolutely nothing. You see, from the questions I asked him here, he brought up vague memories about some attempts at practicing law in some unknown courthouse, in a faraway province.[66]

Such a man, with such training, with such a stage of professional activity, more exactly, without any serious studies, without professional activity, such a man had the pretension to crush a generation of schooled men, who worked constantly and toiled? Well, gentlemen, it would be ridiculous if it wasn't sad. Besides, anyone could come to a natural conclusion. He would not come to gatherings; he would not address the nation. He was precautious, because he had a conservation instinct, a conscience of inferiority, so he always avoided debating problems in public. The reputation of Codreanu was never based on open activity, in public, in which with intelligence and talent he would face the difficulty of adversity. No. He was quiet, hiding, cultivating mystery, creating the law that was convenient to him.[67]

The intellectual manifestations of Codreanu are very few.[68] A few circulars, a few letters. He published a book, it's true. I would have been very curious to see its manuscript.[69] Until then, I found in these files a few reflections written in his hand. It's obvious that Codreanu was a philosopher during his free time. This is the result of these profound meditations, concluded in five ideas.

— Clean your feet.

— Open and close the door quietly.

— Use an appropriate tone of voice in halls and rooms.

— Don't touch the walls.

— Pick up a piece of paper wherever you see it.

In a word, ridiculous.

If Codreanu can't prove a capital of professional work though his culture or his talent, at least he could add other worthy assets to his activity. Let's look at this for a bit.

Mr. Senior President and Honorary Court, I'll open the book titled *Pentru Legionari*, the autobiography of Codreanu, and I'll stop, of course, on a chapter: "A revenge attempt to serve as an example to the coming centuries," on page 163.[70]

Therefore, revenge, what a characteristic symbol, what a stigma of the soul! A revenge to be known by the coming centuries. What cruelty, what sadism! This is how his career starts! What was this revenge all about? A thought-out conspiracy, prepared, and set to be executed. Against whom? Against certain ministers. It has been debated if the revenge was against the Jews, but following some theories, they decided on the Romanian ministers. They met up in the house of conspiracy, with revolvers. Anyway, they got caught, Codreanu admits that they wanted to kill the ministers. When he was asked "And do you regret it?", he replied, "I don't". This is how this man started his career.

But, with this fact, we must mention a second one, which was the consequence of the first one. It's characteristic, because it's found in an analogous circumstance. In truth, Codreanu and his friends believed one of them had denounced them to the police, causing them to get caught. After all of them were imprisoned in the prison in Văcărești, they plotted the assassination of Vernichescu, the one who was suspected of it. And Codreanu recounts: "A few minutes later we hear seven revolver shots and shouts. Moța had shot Vernichescu." What do you think Codreanu did after this assassination?[71] Did he try to help the victim? Did he condemn the crime? No. He alone continues: "I rushed to Moța's side to defend him, because he was surrounded by guards who were threatening him", and underneath, "we could see on the small window how they took Vernichescu out. We all started to whistle our hymn!".

Therefore, gentlemen, the soul, this is the man! This is the plot to assassinate the ministers. The arrest of the accomplices. The suspicion of having been denounced. The shooting of the suspected friend, followed by a sadistic explosion of satisfaction.

And all these are stated in a book published under his signature.

Gentlemen, only the fact that these horrendous things could be written and published, proved the perversity and cynicism of the author.

Look, Honorary Court, the first act in Codreanu's career, in 1923.

The Second Act: Manciu's Assassination

Let's move on to the second event, one that happened in 1924. After some conflicts with the Iași Police, Codreanu retreated to the Rarău Mountains. Why did he do this? What Romanian soul would do this? What did he plan on doing on the mountain?

The Trial of Corneliu Zelea Codreanu

This is his story: "We all considered leaving the country. To leave it and curse it." This is his patriotism, his noble soul! And, further on: "to wander the whole world... or to get back here with a weapon in my hand! To banish the beast that laid across in our way! I'll come down. I'll leave everything to chance. From now on, I'll carry my revolver. And I'll shoot. Nobody will make me change my mind." [72]

And it was true, Honorary Court, he shot. A few days later, Codreanu killed Manciu, the Police Prefect of Iaşi.

This is the second great act in this man's career.

The Assassinations of I.G. Duca and Stelescu

This is the third event. In 1934, Codreanu ended up being part of the group accused of being involved in killing Prime Minister I.G. Duca. Of course, Honorary Court, this man was acquitted in this trial, and I won't go into much detail about the trial. But I have to mention a few significant factors.

Duca's assassins were members of the Iron Guard; this is incontestable. They all admitted to it. They were members of an organization where it was known that nobody did anything without the leader's permission, without his command. The plot and the assassinations in 1933, are similar to the plot and the assassination attempt on the ministers, in 1923. The assassins were still members of the organization afterward. They were glorified. The Nicador Hymn was created after that. They are seen as honorary members, at the top of the organization. They were the subject of a general discussion. They were decorated with the Legionary award. There's no greater display of solidarity than that. Around the time of the crime, Codreanu wrote a letter to his friend Stelescu, which he doesn't deny, in which he asks his opinion about the situation, writing in the cruel terms that we're used to seeing, speaking of graves. I don't know whose graves he was referring to. Everyone can interpret it in their own way. After the plot in 1923, after Vernichescu was shot, after Manciu was shot, we could understand differently. Duca's grave would soon come, which strengthens this interpretation. After this, Stelescu's testament comes into play. Stelescu accuses Codreanu. Was it in the same way in which Vernichescu had accused Codreanu? Stelescu is murdered with unprecedented cruelty, in a hospital room, in his bed while he was suffering, when ten Legionaries shot him 40 times. They then struck him with an ax. Vernichescu denounced them and was murdered.71 Stelescu also denounced the accomplices, and now he was dead

Romanian Crucible

as well.[2] The cases are too similar to leave doubt of a strategy. The Iron Guard's strategy. Stelescu's assassins were also glorified. They are sung hymns, and they are awarded.

So, you see, Honorary Court, these are the 3rd and 4th acts, the assassination of Duca and the assassination of Stelescu.

Can there be any doubt about the recent manifestations, when faced with these precedents? Can't you see the letters, manifestos, Legionary circulars, where they all talk about death threats and punishments that could make future generations shiver?

This, Honorary Court, is the school of crime, this is the spilled blood, these are the horrendous acts of he who is the son of Zelinski and of Eliza Brauner.

Why is this called a national movement? Why is it considered a movement for moral regeneration? Is it supposed to strengthen the Country?

Gentlemen, we must cover our faces in shame. This is the most horrendous spectacle the history of this country has seen. It is the most erratic era our nation has ever known. This is the most horrible collapse some people could achieve.[73]

It's time to recover. It's time to leave aside everything related to personal enmity, to bad advice, and banish this dangerous element from our nation's body, that for a decade and a half, has constantly and systematically dug at the soul of our nation.

Actions through School Children

Mr. President and Honorary Court, the cruel man whose portrait and biography I sketched, the man who caused so much rage, the man who spilled so much blood, this man is guilty of an even more heinous act: he organized the corruption of children, he stole for his personal purposes all the school children from their natural environment, thus undertaking an action of compromising the future generation. A wretched man who impulsively acts only once to seduce a minor, is sent to prison. This man, who deliberately and systematically tried to own the children's souls, of all the school children, has immunity? This is inadmissible. What are all those brotherhoods? What is this disorder caused in schools? How could he pull the children away from their school education and away from their parents' authority? What could a child become, after he is persuaded to participate in secret meetings,

The Trial of Corneliu Zelea Codreanu

while having an order number, and who is subjected to a whole ritual imposed by the dangerous mysticism of a man? You must ask yourselves what would the future Romanian society become, if the youth is seduced in this way. Have you ever thought about the despair caused in those families? This, gentlemen, is what I found in the files: two letters from parents who were protesting against their children being perverted by "scoundrels who entice them."

File 15/8

Gheorghe Clime, page 87.

4th of November 1935, Bălteni.

"Eugen,

When I arrived home, I found your mother worried, because some gendarmes had been looking for you, to take you to the instruction judge in Slatina for an interrogation. I didn't see them, so I don't know what you did. So, that's how you ended up, to hell with your foolishness. You leave with scoundrels to satisfy a group of brainless fools. It's obvious the Prefect has denounced you to the Court, and now you have to be interrogated for death threats, and most likely they'll send you here at the Academy,[74] to instruct you and show you what you have done, following to be put in the service of — hell knows who — some men who are interested in enticing you and use you for their own purposes.

I decided not to go to Bucharest anymore, as I don't want to face those who know us; again, it's your business, I can't condemn you for it, but I advise you to come home, and take care of your fortune, so you can have a good life later on, and leave those scoundrels who are only interested in using you.

Deal with the Prosecutor and with the Academy, because they'll find out that instead of studying, you serve those brainless fools. I won't answer for your actions, and if necessary, I'll let the Academy know that I won't oppose your sentence, and that I'm not responsible for it. Instead of hearing of your good deeds, of praise, of you being a man of the future, schooled and everything, we hear that you have problems with the law, that you made death threats, and all the other mischiefs you were asked to do by those fishers of murky waters. Do you think you're going to be the one to right the country and the habits of the society?

All you're left to do now is pick up a weapon and follow in Doru's and Belimace's footsteps, because you think you have people to support you in Bălteni.

Romanian Crucible

Keep causing trouble and forget about us, this is all we're going to give you, since you don't want to listen to your parents thinking we're your enemies.

Your parents: Radu and Stanca."

File 15/8

Gheorghe Clime, page 86.

5th of November 1935, Bălteni

"Eugen,

I went to Slatina yesterday, and the judge told me you must go and give a statement, the same way you did, for the Prosecution.

He told me he'll send you to trial for violence, if the case won't become even more complicated, depending on the statements of witnesses. The whole town knows about it, even the villages know, that you threatened the Prefect, that you are the leader of the Iron Guard, and much more... to hell with your Guard. As I've told you in my previous letter, you joined a group of scoundrels who are using you and who will cause your demise. All said, they've seen you with Anastasiu, who is a leech and a scoundrel, as everyone knows, and it's a pity for the social standing you've had to end up in the hands of criminals. All the lawyers I've met told me of these deeds, and they were all surprised about the path you've chosen, to lose your future and standing in a society that, sinful as it is, however, can only be made better by people with a sense of responsibility and the masses that listen to them. All, absolutely all of them are shocked by the path you're on and by the bad things you're doing. It's bad, my boy, very bad how you ended up. I thought they were childish pranks, a way to lose your energy, but this has changed you and made you choose the wrong path.

Now you're not welcome here anymore, everyone will point at you, because that's how people are. You might as well go to the judge, and deal with your problems how you can.

Don't come to my house anymore because I have enough problems in my heart and enough misfortune, even if it's undeserved, there's nothing I can do about it. I'll suffer for my own actions.

All that's left now is for the Academy to find out about you breaking the law, and expel you from there as well.

The Trial of Corneliu Zelea Codreanu

Anyway, you won't see me there anymore. When you'll finish here, you won't have an income, so you can come home and take care of your fortune, administer what I'll give you, and everything we've earned for you. If you don't have a quiet life there, you'll have to come work in your hometown, can't you see you weren't made for another type of life?

If you think you'll be able to live in that society, following everyone else's advice, then ask them to take care of you and support you financially.

We've tried hard since we were young to ensure you had a good life and a good position as we thought fit, but you didn't listen to us, and did things your own way. This is not a passing sorrow or a fleeting moment, it is a painful decision for us, a misfortune for us all.

Pity of our work, pity of the illusions we've created.

Your parents, upset with your behavior."

How upset these parents must have been. I ask myself, how heartless must this man be, that after corrupting minors and receiving such letters, to not immediately put an end to his mission? How many of these family tragedies are still unknown?!

Well, Justice must protect Romanian society from such damaging actions.

Codreanu's Guilt in this Trial

Mr. Senior President and Honorary Court. Allow me to analyze the charges brought against Codreanu in the Final Ordinance. I won't recount all the details that have already been enumerated by the documents read during the hearing. I'll highlight only a few characteristics.

First, I accuse Codreanu of conspiring against the social order, offense provided and sanctioned by art. 209 in the Penal Code. This conspiracy consists of relationships with foreign organizations, for the purpose of receiving instructions and help of any kind, in order to prepare for a social revolution in Romania.

What is the evidence for this charge? Documents found during the search of Codreanu's residence, documents found in the case files, which have also been signed by the sister of the defendant who was present during the search. The defendant admitted to one of the documents. When it comes to another one, the defendant doesn't contest it being found in his archives, but he doesn't admit to writing it. Honorary Court, this charge is better defined if we frame it in the whole of

Romanian Crucible

Legionary activity. First, there is a series of commonly known prior facts, which are not only presumptive, but they are also constitutive elements of the crime. In truth, is there anyone who doesn't know the ideology of the Iron Guard doesn't have a Romanian origin, but is a foreign ideology borrowed from abroad?[75] Is there anyone who doesn't know that between the doctrinal and programmatic conception of the Legion and a foreign organization, there's a kinship with a perfect identity? Has Mr. Codreanu ever denied this?[76] And hasn't this been seen through outbursts of joy, whenever the foreign ideology from abroad would have a victory? Aren't they following a common victory?[77]

And aside from this, didn't Codreanu state that 48 hours after his victory, the country's politics would change, and he would affiliate it with a new political axis, meaning the one that inspired their ideology? Evidently, yes. But you might say, this might be a political attitude that any party could embrace, that another party could have embraced. Yes, if only he resumed this statement. Yes, if there were no documents to prove such an activity, concentration, and synchronization of efforts! Yes, if there was no document to show that the Iron Guard had an action plan for a determined period of time, disregarding the lawful government. Yes, if this document didn't contain a request addressed to the foreign organization, a request that, in order to fulfill it, needed the Guard to be victorious. Yes, this document shows that Codreanu's goal was to plant a flag in Romania, one that wasn't the Romanian flag.[78] Finally, this document demonstrates that communication with foreigners was customary for him.

Therefore, Honorary Court, the document you can find in the case file doesn't leave any room for interpretation.

Codreanu admits to this document's existence. He doesn't admit this was found in his archive or that he is the author. Why? Maybe according to his conception, the tactical necessity for defense prevents him from admitting it: it's obviously embarrassing, compromising, and crushing. Why? What importance does it have if he doesn't admit it? Because, gentlemen, aside from the fact that this document is confirmed by his activity and indicated presumptions, it's strengthened by a second document, by the famous telegram that Codreanu admits to.

The truth is that the content of the telegram and its recipient, as well as the transmission method, is identical to the first document. Thus, contesting it is futile.

The Trial of Corneliu Zelea Codreanu

What everyone thought, what everyone understood, namely, that the inspiration from abroad necessarily had to be accompanied by actions. This is confirmed, now, by the discovery of some very serious documents, documents that prove Codreanu's intentions and methods. And, Honorary Court, we must not forget one crucial thing: the evidence we are presenting in this trial is not everything that exists related to this.

What we choose to show is just an example. Because, gentlemen, we were very lucky to be able to intercept a few of the documents. We didn't find the whole political archive of the Legionary Movement just yet; Codreanu has hidden it, because it was in his interest to do so.

Immediately after the first charge, meaning the one related to conspiring against social order by entering relationships with foreign organizations, comes a second one, just as serious.

It's about possessing secret documents from the archives of the State security services, documents he didn't have the right to possess.

So, along with the connection to foreign organizations, the possession of secret documents stolen from the State archives.

You will understand what special significance these deeds have, as they seem to have a connection, to complete one another.

The Charge of Treason

The second charge, as I mentioned, is provided and sanctioned by art. 190 and 191 from the Penal Code.

What evidence do we base this charge on? On documents found during the search of Codreanu's archives. These documents were acknowledged and signed for by the defendant's sister, who was present. The defendant acknowledged these documents. What type of documents? During the interrogations, Codreanu tried to comment on the content of these documents, pretending they are of a lesser importance, and so on and so forth.

Honorary Court, such a defense is inadmissible. The defendant is not the one who must decide the importance of those documents. He doesn't have the right to decide about their secret character. And of course, the law does not give him the competency to determine this.

Romanian Crucible

When trying to guarantee the State's security, the law creates a serious offense for those who lack the quality or the right to possess documents issued by the authorities. And these are the types of documents found at Codreanu's residence. These documents' existence has not been contested. How were they obtained? Here the defendant tries to defend himself: "I received them. A sympathizer probably sent them to me."

Mr. Senior President and Honorary Court, assuming for a moment that their origin might be true — this isn't important — the law doesn't distinguish when it comes to the means of obtaining them. It's indifferent. It's enough for these documents to be obtained and held onto. The law sanctions this fact.

But, is the defendant's statement true when it comes to their origin? Unfortunately for him, no. Because a very serious fact intervenes here. In Codreanu's archives an order for informers was found. This is the text:

"To all the Legionaries and nest members in the Capital: Every informant from the Capital Police that is part of nests is invited to come to me personally in order to receive directives, between the 19th and the 21st of June; informant agents from security or the General Staff, must come between the 21st and the 25th of June 1937; the informants of other private services, on the 26th of June 1937.

This order will be read in every nest by the nest leaders, and every member will sign it.

The order once signed will be brought to me by the sector leaders or other units.

The ones who don't show up will be seen as trying to betray our Movement, sell us out, and deceive us. Services can be done without deceit, without selling out anyone, without betrayal, and without breaking the oath.

(ss) Corneliu Zelea Codreanu"

What does this order represent? What does it show? Of course, this is about an organization, just as all the manifestations of this Movement were being organized. Thus, deliberately. What is this organization? A system of information or contact with informers for this purpose.

What informers? Whose informers? It doesn't matter if the informers belonged to Codreanu or if they were in the service of the State.[79] One thing is for sure, which is: Codreanu had connections to these informers. He was gathering them for him. He was giving them instructions, obviously, with a purpose, which was receiving

The Trial of Corneliu Zelea Codreanu

information. That required a connecting agent, a state service, and the transmission of information. This is the system.

Why did he need informers?

Well, gentlemen, why did Codreanu need to maintain this network? These people certainly exist. The file contains a considerable number of examples of this circular order. And the examples of this order are signed by his employees, who were organized in nests. The defendant claims he wanted to verify if these people would betray him. Does he mean all his people are informers of the State?[80] And he wanted to test them all in this way? Or is it more plausible for his party members, who were functionaries and workers in services or establishments, were set up as informers, and had this mission given to them by Codreanu? Because it's clear that the defendant addressed the informers, and naturally, only they had the quality to acknowledge the circular addressed to them and to sign it. And where were these informers? What State services were they working for?

Let's consider the possibility that Codreanu was interested in finding documents related to his political activity. He wasn't allowed to do it. It's reprehensible. But let's assume it for a moment. If that was the case, why did he need informers in the General Staff of the Army? Because this category is mentioned in the circulars. "The informers in the General Staff...." What did the informers look for in this institution of national defense? What did the son of Zelinski and of Eliza Brauner want to find out? What did this man, who was communicating with foreign organizations, want to know?

Information from the General Staff

What purpose would information from the General Staff serve for him?

Mr. Senior President and Honorary Court, this simple fact of organizing an espionage network in the State services, is a condemnable act. And then, regarding this system that exists, that can be proven by documents, could we have any discussion upon the way in which Codreanu obtained these secret documents, that he possessed without any right to do so?

But, gentlemen, this was a system, and organism used not only for Codreanu's personal reasons, but also for other members of the Iron Guard. It was a spread-out practice. This is the only thing that explains why, during the searches, other similar documents were found in the homes of other members. At some of them, the

Romanian Crucible

searches found military maps of the regions where military tactics were being planned, they found scientific studies presented to the services of the General Staff. Why would they need to obtain such documents? Why did they hold on to them?

The Secret Character of the Documents

Anyway, regarding the main objection of the defendant, saying the documents didn't concern the security of the State, I oppose the following:

– the security of the State is maintained and defended by a complex system of measure and dispositions, some permanent, others temporary or occasional, which are decided by the authority determined by the state, meaning the Ministry of Internal Affairs, first, with all its instruments and annexes.

– the secret or public nature of a disposition is determined by the authority that issues it, under no circumstance by a personal understanding of individuals, who are under the obligation to submit to it, and not to divulge or disregard acts of authority.

– the documents found at the defendant's residence, as well as the ones reproduced in his circulars, had an undeniable secret nature, because, aside from the special title of the majority, such as top secret, confidential, personal, etc., their content was outlined in special dispositions, with limited and confidential instructions. If some of them were related to the organization led by the defendant, this doesn't eliminate the fact that they were secret and concerned the public order, proven by the preventative measures stated in them.

– therefore, the administrative document issued by a lawful authority, such as the Ministry of Internal Affairs, for the purpose of defending against an impending danger, or eliminating a danger that already occurred, concerning the territorial integrity, public sovereignty, and population of the country, is a document that is meant to defend the security of the State. The evidence found at the defendant's home incontestably has this character, and his denial can only mean a weak attempt at a defense, which won't impress the Court.

The Trial of Corneliu Zelea Codreanu

Qualifying the Offenses

Regarding the defendant's arguments, by which he tried to remove the existence of treason, saying that art. 191 orders it under the chapter of crimes against the external security of the State, and therefore, in this case, he would have been guilty of this only if we could prove that he transmitted these documents to a foreign state, we reply:

– the qualification and applicability of a crime is not decided by the title in the Code, but by the component elements determined by those texts, that synthesize the intention of the offender.

– article 191 indeed, in paragraph I, considers an offense regarding the external security of the State, by expressly conditioning its perpetration by the material fact of transmitting documents to the State of a foreign power, but, if we study points 1 and 2 under that text, we can clearly and undeniably see that they form other two other stand-alone offenses, that exclusively treat the internal security of the State.

Point 1 requires "the Romanian citizen to have obtained or possessed secret documents without the quality to do so." So, this is a purely static action within the country's borders, without having to go past them.

Point 2 requires "the Romanian citizen to publicly reproduce writings or documents." Of course, this concerns only the Romanian public because where the law wanted to condition the existence of the offense in connection with a foreign state, it did so expressly.

A final argument for our thesis is that art 190, which generally is a typical text on the crime regarding the external security of the State, we find a stand-alone offense in it regarding the internal security of the State, namely when "the public official obtained documents and forwarded them to any other person," that person which can be a fellow countryman.

On this charge, I consider, respected judges, that there's nothing more to add regarding this factual state, and his rightful charge is perfectly determined, meaning:

Treason, as provided by art. 191, points 1 and 2 P.C., requires the following elements:

– the quality of Romanian citizenship;

200 Romanian Crucible

– obtaining, no matter the means, of writings or secret documents concerning the security of the State, which has already been proven, both in terms of procurement, as well as the nature of the documents;

– the lack of the quality to obtain, possess, or publicly reproduce, which the defendant didn't claim to have. Their secret nature and their precise destination completely eliminate any discussion on the lack of quality of the defendant;

– possession of documents or their public reproduction are uncontested and proven facts;

– the criminal intent deduced from the whole complex of factual manifestations that fall within the law.

In conclusion, we consider the act of treason the defendant is charged with as fully proven and within the provisions of art. 191, point 1 and 2, following that you satisfy the law and the society for the serious violation against the social order that was committed.

The only objection the defendant could have made against the non-inclusion of his act in art. 191, would have been his violation of the law, which, under the same chapter, provided for different crimes, without thinking that there may be minds that confuse them

Therefore, Mr. Senior President and Honorary Court, it's proven by facts and by precise documents, which can be commented upon, which can be interpreted and misinterpreted, but which cannot be contested in their existence, which proved Codreanu is guilty of the crimes provided and sanctioned by art. 191 and 190 P.C.

Mr. President and Honorary Court, I'll now examine the third charge.

The Crime of Rebellion

We've seen the agreements with foreign organizations, we've seen the possession of secret documents from the archives of the authorities; we'll now look at the charge of rebellion provided and sanctioned by art. 210 from the Penal Code.

How is this crime proved?

Allow me to add that this point is well-known, and that the rebellions prepared and executed by Codreanu through the Iron Guard are so numerous and so striking that they identify with the purposes, means, and activity of the Iron Guard, they

The Trial of Corneliu Zelea Codreanu

became a common thing. Who doesn't know this fact? Who didn't have the opportunity to observe this activity? Who could ever doubt their character?

Maybe only their frequency and their immunity so far could give these people the courage to pass by these manifestations with such candor. But, Honorary Court, leaving aside the general atmosphere and the multiplicity of the acts that had scandalized the last years, which are enough to characterize and confirm the rebellion of the Iron Guard, I will highlight a few concrete acts that prove the methodical organization of the rebellion.

First, Codreanu used paramilitary strategies for the Movement. Uniformed soldier groups, movement in military cadence, and so on. Why would a political organization need military troops? What purpose did this instrument serve? What did they want to use them for?

Second, his men were armed and practiced shooting. The defendant asked: where are the weapons deposits? And he was making a big deal of the fact that he had donated some weapons, inherited from General Cantacuzino, to the Military Museum.

What is the connection to arming his party members? There are a few circulars issued by his party members, for example, the ones from Bucovina, in which the people were urged to pick up the weapons. Then, during the searches, absolutely all the members of the Iron Guard were found to have weapons without legal authorizations. A few hundred people were tried and sentenced for possessing explosive material. What weapons? More often than not, there were military guns. Therefore, there are conclusive facts that prove the members of the Iron Guard had weapons. Why did they need to hide them if they didn't plan to use them in acts of rebellion?

Military Organization

But the most important act of rebellion is the organization of the Moța-Marin Corps, under the name of Moța-Marin Legionary Corps, a quasi-military organization, where the ones accepted had to swear a special oath. This organization also had a hierarchy of ranks, advancements, and punishments.

In other words, while disregarding the heads of authority and the criminal law (art. 326 P.C.), the defendant organized a private corps, with its own discipline, and limited in number (10,000), which through its structure and designation could cause, at any moment, disturbances in the order of the State.

The justification for this organization's existence is given by the defendant using art. 1 from the Moța-Marin Legionary Corps Guide, which defines it as "a strict group of essence, severe education, and heroic inspiration...." It cannot be qualified as serious, while the guide requires the following joining conditions in art. 15 and 16: the members must be over 30 years old, worthy, and of a healthy soul, mind, and body etc.

If, after 30 years of age, the members of the Moța-Marin Legionary Corps, who had to have a healthy soul and mind, still needed severe education and heroic inspiration, then, of course, this purpose couldn't serve as an element of praise and pious remembrance of those in whose honor it was allegedly formed.

The oath in art 19, which partially contains magic words, is the one that shows us the real substrate for which it was created, a corps ready for sacrifice, not a pious organization.

To help you better understand, I'll read the oath: "And we don't have another ideal, than to grant God our joy to die ripped apart and tormented for the spark of truth that we know we have in us, and for whose defense we fight against the ruling powers of darkness, a battle for life and death. I stand ready to die. I swear."

Material Means

Mr. Senior President, Honorary Court, the analyses of the offenses attributed to Codreanu would not be complete, and the spirit in which the activity of this organization unfolded would not be completely outlined if we didn't add a few observations regarding its financial means.

In truth, gentlemen, this is an extremely important point. Because it's known that a political movement generally needs consistent funds in order to function and work. In this era, costs such as publications, manifestos, transportation, electoral campaigns are frequent. But if every party needs financial resources, the ones led by Codreanu had to be even more considerable. Why, gentlemen? Because the Iron Guard, unlike other parties, had special activities that required more funds. This party had, first, exceptional expenses for uniforms and for equipment, which makes it different from the other political parties. Then, all its members received compensation for their tasks. Where did they get all this money?

The Trial of Corneliu Zelea Codreanu

The defendant has already answered to these questions saying: membership fees! Membership fees? Well, gentlemen, in this country there were many political parties, parties in the government, who had many important members of high society, with good financial situations. And everyone knows these parties were not able keep up with the spending, and their membership fees didn't manage to cover even small expenses!

But the Iron Guard's fees were sufficient? How many fees? Codreanu's partial and confusing statements said that, at one point, he had three hundred paying members out of 15,000 members! Is he serious, gentlemen? Could anyone believe that a party that wasted money would be able to self-manage with the help of 300 members?

But here I have the proving documents that show the value of the fees; first, a report that shows what the organization lacked, that says: "the central treasury of the All for the Country party received 15,000 lei in regional fees for the months of November and December." Therefore, a whole region paid only 15,000 lei for two months. These are the meaningless sums they could get from fees. Besides, it's a well-known fact the quantum of these fees was 1 leu a week. Therefore, the fee cannot be accepted as a sufficient explanation to prove the money spent by the Guard. They had other important sources, that much is obvious. But what sources?

Where is the Archive?

I asked Mr. Codreanu to show us the accounting archive for the Party that shows the real income. This archive must exist. Smaller archives were found in smaller organizations within the country. It can't be missing from the headquarters. We found mentions of people who had donated great sums. Who are these people? What is their identity? What was the reason for mentioning them in another way? The defendant refuses to give an explanation, so we are entitled to believe this system was used to cover-up secret funds. There's no other explanation. There was a mention about the organization spending 40 million lei. The defendant offers one version of the story. I don't believe his explanations have solid ground. But of course, the defendant doesn't want to admit this mention was strictly referring to him. One fact remains certain: the defendant can't show, or doesn't want to show all the sources of the Party's income. Considerable sums have been spent, that's

204   Romanian Crucible

certain. The membership fees were not sufficient, they couldn't be sufficient, and this is proven by documents.[81]

The funds were indeed covered up. This is proven by the documents. The defendant refuses to give the names of the people. He refuses to procure his accounting archive. All these circumstances cast a suspicious light upon the actions of a man who had connections to foreign organizations,[82] a man who possessed secret state documents, and planned rebellions.

We Need Calm

Mr. Senior President and Honorary Court, these are the facts and their precise evidence and their legal classification. My conscience is clear. I know that in the limit of my powers and with deep respect for the law, I did my duty as a representative of society, whose normal course has been greatly disturbed by the defendant.

My role is finished, you are the ones in charge of applying the law, with all the severity and repression deserved by the one who is on trial, who, through his damaging actions against the order of our State — built on so many sacrifices — wished to defy the laws of peace and the progress of our nation.

The good conduct of the witnesses — the majority of them being former members of the organization led by the defendant, cannot influence your integrity or the power of the example that you must set. The time we live in and the international circumstances, which are not very favorable, impose all those who truly feel Romanian to join forces in harmony, not to disturb the peace, through misconduct and wishes for glory, and act against the healthy path our leaders have set us on.

In conclusion, I ask you to apply the dispositions provided by article 191, points 1 and 2, art. 209 point 4, and art. 210 of the Penal Code.

Mr. Prosecutor ended his indictment at 12:24.

The Afternoon Hearing

The hearing started at 5 in the afternoon.
The defense has the floor.

The Trial of Corneliu Zelea Codreanu

The Statement of the Defense.

The lawyers who spoke are Ranetescu-Călărași, Lizetta Gheorghiu, Horia Cosmovici, Paul Iacobescu, Caracaș, C. Hențescu, Sebastian Radovici, and Captain Theodorescu.

Lizetta Gheorghiu's Plea

Lawyer Lizetta Gheorghiu: Mr. President, Honorary Court, Mr. Prosecutor, there are two sides in this trial: on one side, there's the law, on the other side, there's passion; on one side, there's the truth, on the other, there's the indictment; on one side there's the directive, on the other there's violence. And this violence doesn't come from the true public opinion to be noted by the Final Ordinance, but it comes from the press subjugated by censorship or by the government, which continues to launch accusations, even though they have all been demolished in the hearing. These are miasmas that mustn't reach our hearts; defense and judge.

Debating, you must ask yourself, Mr. Prosecutor, from the top of what pyramid does Mr. Codreanu aspire to rule the country?

You say a speaker is not a simple court lawyer. Of course, not everyone has your oratorical talent, even while reading an indictment, however, I find that elocution is not what our country is lacking, a place where everyone speaks but nobody accomplishes anything. If being a good speaker means being a master at pedantry for the arbitrary tribunes against the Romanian state, or for the beneficiary companies against the budget of this nation, then you're perfectly right. Mr. C.Z. Codreanu is not a good speaker. As you also said, the pride of this country must not allow a Zelinski to rule us. How did you come to the conclusion that Zelinski is205ifferrent from Zelea? Since when do you allow yourself to be led by a Jewish press campaign without verifying the information? This is how Zelea Zelinski was and how his son, today, is the Romanian who brought the country together through 50.000 free votes in December 1937.

But, Mr. Prosecutor, do you want to learn the origin of this name?

By what we are about to show, we don't want to contribute to the offense brought without hesitation to some personalities of Romanian public life, people with foreign-sounding names.

Romanian Crucible

Those who publicly question the ethnic origin of Corneliu Zelea Codreanu's life, did they ever think that by doing so, they implicitly question the ethnic origin of an impressive number of the country's leaders? I wonder what would they be saying about this campaign, ministers Iamandi, Franasovici, and Canciov? Or the generals and superior officers of the Romanian army, such as Ilasievici, Gorski, Sidorovici, Macarovici, Cihoski, Iacobici, Dombrovski? What would others say, who even though they have Romanian names, they know they have enough foreign blood in their veins (for example, Professor Nicolae Iorga, who according to his own statement, has Greek origins). We ask ourselves, in any case, why is it so easy to look past them? We give these explanations about the origins of C.Z. Codreanu for the people of good faith.

On his father's side, Corneliu Zelea Codreanu gets his origin from a Moldavian family in the village of Igeşti, located in the land of Storojineţ in Bucovina. His great-grandfather on his father's side was named Simion Zelea (from the word *zale* meaning *chainmail*), who probably got his name from his ancestor's armor, who were Moldavian soldiers that fought in the war dressed in chainmail. During Austrian occupation, after 1786, when Bucovina became part of the Polish administration, becoming, as professor Nicolae Iorga puts it (*Historie des Roumains de Bucovina*, p. 61), "a simple district of Galiţa", this name of Zelea was changed by the authorities, during school or army service, into Zelinski, which had a Polish resonance. This operation of making names sound Polish was a general custom of that era in Bucovina. The system was part of a "systematic persecution against anything that reminded the administration, in schools, and even in the social life, of the era of Moldavian rulers" (N. Iorga, op.cit., p. 62).

The main objective of the Poles was to obtain, by any means possible, the abandonment of Orthodox faith and the conversion of Romanians to Catholicism. Professor N. Iorga says that Romanians couldn't become teachers unless they abandoned the Orthodox faith, and the ones that wanted to embrace this profession had to cross into Moldavia. The second objective of the Poles was to abolish the Romanian language, which they considered to be unworthy to be spoken, just like the language of Gypsies.

The Romanian language, an author tells us (Constantin Marariu, *Istoria Românilor Bucovineni*, p. 30), was rejected everywhere in Bucovina during the Polish occupation, and in the schools, "it was tormented and savagely mocked without limits." Keeping the Orthodox faith and the ancestral language was, for the

The Trial of Corneliu Zelea Codreanu

Romanians in Bucovina, during those times of humiliation, a national problem of life and death. And, of course, it was also the element that differentiated the Orthodox Romanians in Bucovina from the Catholic Polish and Austrians. Any person of good-faith who saw the copy of Ion Zelea Codreanu's birth certificate in the newspaper was struck by the four elements that prove, against the sensational titles written in small letters, his Romanian citizenship:

1. The document is written in Romanian. A Pole wouldn't have thought about using our "Gypsy" language for his son's baptism;

2. The first names of his father, grandfather, and child are purely Romanian, "Niculai, Simion, Ion";

3. His child is baptized in the Orthodox faith;

4. The birth certificate has the seal of the Romanian Consulate in Cernăuți (Czernowitz in Polish). The Romanian Consulate could only be used by ethnic Romanians with Austrian citizenship.

So, the only foreign element here is the Polish termination of the name Zelinski. This is what the author tells us about it: "the Polish were not just strangling the Romanian language, but also crippled the Romanian names of our people, turning the Romanian into Romanivicz, from Pietrar into Cietrarscki, from Andrei into Andriczuc, because, you see the 'vicz', 'ski', and 'uc' terminations are Russian, and the Polish were sticking them to the names of the Romanians in Bucovina, so they don't appear as Romanians anymore, and so others could say: those speaking Romanian are not Romanians because Romanovicz and Andriczuc are not Romanian names."

So that's how the great Polish administration, between 1786 and 1848, managed to change three-quarters of the Romanian names to Polish ones. They started being called: Pietrarschi, Samsovici, Scavinchi, etc., the Romanian bishops were named Andrievici, Ciupercovici, Blajevici, etc. As the Romanian poet wrote:

Our language, sacred language,

Language of the old struggles

That cry it and sing it

On their hearth, the peasants

His name that got Russified was Mateevici (in Bessarabia), and the Transylvanian writer, Samuel Micu was named Samuel Klein in German.

The generation present today in Bucovina, the one living in formerly oppressed villages, is characterized by the names with predominantly Polish resonance or termination.

Well, if the theory of those who claim these people are actually Polish, then Poland — if they thought about it — could rightly annex Bucovina to their territory since three-quarters of it is inhabited by Poles.

Perhaps then many of our scholars, who for now prefer to be hypocrites, would decide to protest against it.

But luckily for our national unity, the Romanian State has admitted to the situation of these foreign-sounding names, and offered its help to those who want to reclaim their former Romanian names. Here is the motivation of the law, given on April 8th, 1936: "In the connected provinces, the local Romanians who have been living there for centuries were forced, in order to quickly assimilate with their oppressors, to change their names, to ones with a foreign resonance."

And now let's go back to our story.

So, Simion Zelea had become Polish, under the name of Zelinski. His son, Niculai Zelinski was a ranger. Instead of Zelinski, as it was in his birth certificate, the village preferred to call him Pădurarul (The forest ranger), or more aesthetically, Codreanul (which is a synonym). Thus, they named him Niculai Zelinski Codreanu. From his marriage with the Romanian Maria Anticu, Ion Zelinski was born, who after crossing into Moldova became a teacher at the high school in Huşi, and married Eliza Brauner, an Orthodox Romanian (but with a German name), and in 1902 he requested for his name to be changed from Zelinski to Zelea, to have the Polish condition removed, keeping his ancestral name Zelea, together with his unofficial, but precious name of his father: Codreanu.

Corneliu Zelea Codreanu is his son. His mother, Eliza Brauner, is the daughter of the Romanian Mariţa Sârghi and of Carol (Costache as he was called) Brauner, and Orthodox Romanian after his mother, the son of Romanian Elisabeta Cernea, and German from his father's side, Adolf Brauner, of Bavarian origin.

So, in conclusion: from his father, Corneliu Zelea Codreanu only inherited Moldavian blood from the line of Stephen the Great and, from his mother, he inherited a small drop of German blood, from a river of pure Moldavian blood.

Here is, finally, the story of C.Z. Codreanu's origin. You can now compare the truth with the mysticism, and you'll understand how much filth was spilled, and is

The Trial of Corneliu Zelea Codreanu

still being spilled about the Legionary Movement. Because I consider it is cowardice to use against the great-grandson the same weapons used by his enemies against his great-grandfather. And for trying to remove Corneliu Zelea Codreanu from the Romanian life and soul by using such campaigns and arguments is a great and unwise illusion, equal to those who tried, in the past, to eliminate Mihai Eminescu, for being named Mihai Eminovici until the end of his life. Would you like to know what the newspaper *Glasul Bucovinei* was saying, the propaganda instrument for the political union of Romanians from all over, from Cernăuți, on the 29th of November 1918, on the page talking about the defendant's father? Evidence? Here: "ION ZELEA CODREANU, one of the most relentless idealists of our nation, unbent not even by the turn of time and fighting without reprieve and without a doubt for the rights of the peasant class, and whose clean figure the soul of the peasantry is always holding close, arrived in Cernăuți to enjoy the happiness of his country, for whose realization he's fought a lifetime. Urged by the flight of his Romanian soul, he left Suceava in 1898 after finishing his studies, and since then he hadn't walked on Bucovinian soil until the loud voice of Bucovina's land called its sons from every corner to take part in the celebration of its victory. Ion Zelea Codreanu arrived as a victor. He has the gentle touch of the brave fighter who finally sees the fulfillment of the idea for which he's been carrying a flag, never surrendering it to anyone. A Romanian major, the brave Romanian who has been decorated so many times for his glorious rigor on the front, the peasant son of this land, welcome back to us! (ss) D Marmeliuc — Liberal Mayor of Cernăuți."

Mr. Corneliu Zelea Codreanu, with his poor hands and Christian soul, built churches and crosses, destroyed and dishonored today after persecution. I believe that in this way, enmity is spread all over the country, and the hand that destroyed these can be accused of being anti-Christian, disloyal, and anarchist. He is guilty of being an inspiration to the youth, and in his beliefs, the youth strongly embraces the permanent flame of life. In the youth, he found his spirit, a righteous path, and a never-ending passion for truth. This youth will always be determined not to stray from their conscience. No matter how much time they'd have to spend in prison, they are determined to keep a national and moral structure until their death, by fixing and ranking the values of this country, following ethnic and Romanian precepts. Thus, in his youth, he decided to bind the future of this country to its youth, to uncompromising moral values, which cannot organically integrate with the profitable career of servitude. He searched for a superior way of life, one that would seek true meaning according to the moral ideals of this nation.

Does he resort to mysticism when leaving and choosing to retreat into the forests and mountains, Mr. Senior Prosecutor? I have the feeling you know nothing of the Romanian soul if you don't know that it always connects to the forest and that in isolation, good thoughts and the soul become clear, becoming one with God.

You also said that he corrupts the children and urges them to rebel. This is how he was urging the students who left home, on the 3rd of March 1937:

"1. A correct behavior.

2. A great propaganda of Legionary beliefs, but not by scandal, fights, and debates, but by confessing one's faith:

I believe in Romania's rebirth through the Legion;

I can take every hit;

I gladly endure every torment;

But I believe in the Legionary victory and the salvation of the Romanian Nation.

3. So, no fights, no rebellion, no contradictory discussions, but through confession: This is my opinion, but you can believe whatever you want.

4. In conclusion, I believe that, with the closing of the University, and your removal from the dorms, you endured a great injustice. Endure it with love.

There will be a time when the one who has treated you unjustly will be ashamed and humiliated.

(ss) Corneliu Zelea Codreanu"

Do you want to know how he was planning to overthrow the government on the 26th of February 1937? Here is the circular, if witnesses such as General Antonescu, Sever Dan, and Hodoş are not to be believed:

Circular Nr. 58

To all regional leaders

"Please communicate to the Legionaries:

Following Moţa's and Marin's funeral, the authorities became afraid, but not because of RIOTS, but because of ORDER, which was impressive and prevailed the entire time.

The Trial of Corneliu Zelea Codreanu

A few days later, the ministry started making declarations that lacked even the most elementary foundation. "We want to introduce order. We'll do everything in our power to reestablish order." I didn't understand. Why would you defend the order that nobody was threatening to break? There's a rumor going around now that the authorities would want to make provocations, in any way, to make searches and arrests, looking for green shirts in the homes of Legionaries. These might be simple rumors started in a café. However, my duty is to inform every Legionary:

1. The Legionary Movement will never accept this "idea of plotting" to obtain a victory or to overthrow a government.

That's foolish.

The Legionary Movement can only become victorious once the Romanian Nation fulfills its process of internal consciousness. When this process will complete in the hearts and minds of most Romanians, victory will come automatically, with no plots needed.

The victory that we're all waiting for, in this way, is so great and so bright that we would never allow it to be replaced by a cheap and ephemeral victory born from a plot or from overthrowing the government.

2. When it comes to searches, day or night, the Legionnaires will open their doors and invite the authorities in with the utmost courtesy. At the offices where Legionaries are present, when the authorities show up they will conduct themselves honorably.

3. If the Legionaries, their families and children will be shoved or struck, then, with calmness and serenity, they will say: GOD, for the victory of the Legion, makes us worthy of every suffering and of death such as it was for MOȚA and MARIN."

This order will be posted in every center in the country."

(ss) Corneliu Zelea Codreanu

This is the circular from the 2nd of March 1937, which shows the line of wisdom that every student must follow.

But surely, an accusation must have the right atmosphere while talking about an element in conflict with the authority and with the freedom of the country, a conflict with those who had the power to command.

It's important for us, as Romanians, to grow up free.

We must have the courage to look at the consequences of what we have healthy in our laws — the fundamental element of their use must be searched for in order and equity.

The abuse of exceptional measures is always a thing to fear, because the executive power easily inclines towards illegality, governs with the convenient help of legal decrees, makes its propaganda using the organs in the service of the Ministry of Internal Affairs, labeling abusive orders as top secret, confidential, and under this label it leads the authorities around the country against the opposition, preventing them from carrying out their electoral propaganda.

Mr. Maniu told us he had 16 such orders, which he had compiled in a brochure to show the Parliament the abuses committed by the governing party. All these orders were discussed in the Chamber with all their top secret, confidential labels, which you can see in the Parliamentary debate in *Monitorul Oficial*, Nr. 4, 22 June 1931, when this took place. How could we talk about treason regarding Mr. C.Z. Codreanu as the leader of the Legionary Movement? Is this serious?

Conclusions:

In law, from the wording of both the Final Ordinance and the Military Prosecutor's Indictment, we're not talking anymore about the decision of the Indictment Chamber, which is a pale rewording of the content found in the Final Ordinance and the Indictment. From the start, we find that the military magistrates have deliberately sought to create, before the defendant was even charged, a certain coloring and atmosphere of the trial. Besides, this atmosphere was methodically prepared by the authorities outside of the military magistracy, through official notices, short publications with the so-called compromising evidence, before Justice gave any sentence, and special radio commentaries that used all the official means to "prepare" the atmosphere for the trial today. It was natural for the military magistrates to "get a hold on" this wish of the superior authorities to pronounce themselves before the trial — which explains that three-quarters of the Senior Prosecutor's Indictment, as well as the Final Ordinance, focused on the atmosphere of the charges, and the rest on the charges themselves.

From the prosecution's indictment, you can see in extenso in every newspaper, the Final Ordinance probably being only the copy of this indictment, because whole chapters are dedicated to: 1. The secret organization system of the Legion, founded

The Trial of Corneliu Zelea Codreanu

on nests. 2. Concealed and conspiring activity of the Legion. 3. Paramilitary organization of the Legion. 4. The terrorist training of the Legionaries. 5. Luring the minors. Of course, all the statements contained in these "atmosphere" chapters are not related in any way to the charges of treason for possessing documents, the one the defendant was charged with until then. With the actual conclusions, it was examined what these chapters really represent; we refer to them as legal conclusions, only to emphasize that, being foreign to the charges subjected to trial, they are not part of a juridical discussion, especially because the right must be raised above the odious opportunistic calculations, in order to show justice and equity.

The charges brought against the defendant were classified under two chapters of the Penal Code: the first chapter talks about crimes and offenses against the external security of the State, the second talks about the internal security.

However, Corneliu Zelea Codreanu was considered to be a criminal only when it came to the external security of the State, then, after Mr. Prosecutor forwarded his indictment and had only one charge published in every newspaper, the one concerning possession of secret documents, later, the Final Ordinance said that he found two more crimes in the same case file: "rebellion" and conspiracy against social order, which he ends up charging the defendant with, and Mr. Instructor Magistrate decided to join these "subsidiary" charges. But it's significant how it was possible for the Military Prosecutor to have the same files, the same evidence — Because Mr. Instructor Magistrate didn't do anything else but interrogate the defendant. All the pieces and all the evidence were collected by Mr. Prosecutor, and even like this — if thought he found only one offense — he later added two more offenses on the list from his own initiative, as the Final Ordinance says, but with the same elements. It's well-known that the Prosecution is one and indivisible; so, it's not possible for a prosecutor to contradict another, while working on the same pieces from the same file.

This happened to Corneliu Zelea Codreanu: we repeat it because it's extremely important for this trial. Mr. Prosecutor forwards the Indictment for one offense, and then he states in the Final Ordinance, that Mr. Prosecutor, using the same file, found two other offenses, and Mr. Instructor Magistrate agrees to this new finding.

It's as obvious as the light of day, and a won point for this debate, that the last offenses were added on top of what the Indictment already contained and on what Mr. Prosecutor had already published in the newspapers as a result of the actions taken against the activity of the Legionary Movement, and it constitutes the genesis

Romanian Crucible

of the judicial trial. We cannot imagine that the prosecution wanted to cover these things up, but it is categorical they didn't come from nowhere, and the Final ordinance, which was an exclusive reproduction of the Indictment, using the same evidence, documents, and elements, of course, cannot retain two more offenses, except by distorting the facts and flagrantly disregarding the reality of things.

Therefore, the crimes against the internal security of the State are an add-on to that concerning the external security of the State, and the last one was considered treason. Treason means an action against the interests of your country, and in the interest of a foreign country. Treason cannot be assumed without that "animus hostilis" towards your country. You must be an enemy of your country, putting yourself in the service of a foreign state. Treason without the intention of divulging anything to anyone, without having a thought of using secret documents for a damaging purpose against the interests of the country, is not possible.

Art. 191 P.C. itself says that the traitor must have committed the material act of procuring, transmitting, or communicating to the enemy or its agents, or to a foreign power or its agents.

In this case, neither the Indictment, nor the Final Ordinance could find an "animus hostilis" against the country, they can't state or prove the possession of those documents was done for the purpose of prejudicing the interests of the country. So then, what is the label of treason for?

The offenses provided by art. 191, paragraphs 1 and 2, are about possession of documents concerning the external security of the State, and the partial public reproduction of these documents. We make a small detour to show the investigation, the indictment, and the decision of the Indictment Chamber only considers possession of documents as an offense, not their publication. But what is the interest in this case?

From the case file, we can see the defendant is charged with possessing 6 documents concerning the security of the State.

Mr. Prosecutor finds five component elements for the offense provided by art. 191, points 1 and 2 P.C: The Instruction Magistrate only found four component elements in the Final Ordinance but discusses each paragraph in part, considering points 1 and 2 from art. 191 P.C. contain two special offenses. Both military magistrates, however, omitted an essential element, namely that the document is part of the ones listed in art. 190 P.C. It should be noted that art. 191 doesn't say anything

The Trial of Corneliu Zelea Codreanu

about a secret or confidential document, so it doesn't matter if the document is labeled as secret or confidential. Art. 191, point 1 and 2, precisely talks about "plans, records, or documents mentioned in art. 190". So, it must be about the documents provided by art. 190 P.C., and this article says that not everything is forbidden to be shared, but only the documents concerning the security of the State, mobilization and concentration of the army, etc. Therefore, it's not enough for the defendant to be aware of the secret or confidential label of the incriminating document, but he must have been aware of the document containing information concerning the security of the State, the defense of the territory, etc.

In this case, not only is it not proven that the defendant knew the documents concerned the security interests of the State, but it's obvious those documents are based on fiction, which is why the very existence of the documents is doubtful. In any case, neither the prosecution's indictment, not the Final Ordinance, nor the decision of the Indictment Chamber, neither retain nor state the defendant knew the nature of these documents, meaning the security of the State. I repeat, it is not enough to see it and automatically know they're secret and confidential, because the law doesn't only deal with secret documents, but they must have content of a secret nature and concern the security of the State. On the other hand, art. 190 and 191 P.C. are integrated with chapter 1 of letter I in the Second Book of the Penal Code, which shows that it refers to "crimes and offenses against the external security of the State." But you might say that it's simple terminology, a label that could be wrong. Let's see what the authors of the law say. The authors of the law list themselves the offenses that refer to the external security of the State, and among them are the ones provided by art. 190 and 191 P.C. And for external security, the same authors show that the existence of the State must be endangered by "external factors." Nobody was accused of having "external factors" as a role in possessing secret documents that could have divulged the secrets of the State, when they are purely electoral in nature, and at most they indicated the abusive means of repression towards internal political organizations that had legal activity. If the documents don't concern the external security of the State, then they are not classified as documents provided by art. 190 P.C.

Documents whose content is fabricated, documents that dictated abusive measures against a legal organization, documents that didn't serve in any way to ensure the State or to conserve its existence, couldn't be considered as documents that concern the security of the State. As evidence of other organizations possessing such documents, who didn't have any scuffle with the law over this matter, the newspaper *Dreptatea*, run by the National Peasants' Party, who used entire columns to publish secret orders issued by the superior commandments of Gendarmes and of the Ministry of Internal Affairs serves as an example. No legal action has ever been taken against them, because it was obvious these documents were not considered as ones to concern the security of the State.

To call this possession of administrative documents treason and sanction it with forced labor, goes beyond any measure. Classifying these documents as ones concerning the external security of the State is a judicial monstrosity. Whoever got a hold of the letter addressed "To his Excellency Adolf Hitler," would be shocked to see it being used as evidence. However, it was framed in art. 209, point 4 P.C. This article describes a foreign individual or association. We insist on the fact that we object to this piece of evidence because it's forged and misleading; more than that, I asked for the author of this letter, Mr. Thamir, and I asked for graphic expertise, indicating the comparison pieces with the piece on p. 520, vol. III. But just as it is, it cannot, under any circumstance, be integrated into art. 209, point 4 P.C., or any other text.

Indeed, art. 209, point 4, sets the following legal conditions: the connection must be with an individual or association of an international character, the connection must be for the purpose of receiving instructions or aid in planning a social revolution.

What association of international character or an individual that serves such an association would the defendant have been in contact with? The Final ordinance from the Indictment Chamber hesitates to name it, and good for them because by publishing that fragment, they would have looked ridiculous. The evidence talks about German nationalism socialism, and even more: it's about the Führer of the German Reich, Mr. Hitler.

Or, to claim that a racist state — with a strong nationalist, even chauvinist ideology — has an international character is to disregard any common sense. So, the condition for the connection to be with an association with an international character doesn't exist in this case, therefore, art. 209, point 4 P.C. cannot be charged to the defendant.

The Trial of Corneliu Zelea Codreanu

The legislator who drafted the Penal Code, through the dispositions in art. 209, thought about communism, which does have an international character. Or, to apply a text that exclusively concerns the communist internationals to nationalists is more than impossible.

But the text requires instructions and aid. Are these given by the material evidence? No! So, even like this, the piece, forged as it is, doesn't have the characteristics of an indictment and does not apply to art. 209, which refers to the offense of conspiring against the social order, meaning it doesn't make sense. The last offense of rebellion, also, doesn't have any legal consistency for the defendant. It's true, the text says that the offender "must be armed." So, it asks for an offense personally committed by the accused. But there's no evidence the defendant armed anyone or gave any disposition to do so. Yes, there were worn-out weapons found at some of the Legionaries' homes, you heard the explanation for that: most of them were former soldiers, and how would the leader of a movement be responsible for locals having weapons? Something else must be proven; the fact that he gave them weapons or helped them obtain them for a certain purpose, for civil war.

But what proves a civil war occurred? Nothing, because it's not enough to just say you've found weapons, and it's ridiculous to state the weapons found were for engaging in civil war. But the actual conspiracy must be shown and proven — the agreement for a civil war against me, the one who supposedly armed you, and you, who agreed to be armed for a civil war. Where was such an agreement proven? There's no evidence for it. Same with the deposits; nothing and nobody proves the defendant established deposits for weapons. But the law requires this. The deposits are not actually deposits; if a few weapons were found in a certain location, it's absurd to say that it was a deposit.

Civil war requires an agreement between an instigator and the one provoked — but the defendant sees himself alone at trial — or is it possible to have a civil war with only one person accused? Think, gentlemen, is such a thing even possible?

If there really was a civil war, this courtroom would have been filled with accused people, because you can't have civil war unless you have an agreement between two parties, and then both must be sent to trial, the person who armed them, and the person who was armed and literally carried out the civil war. There's no civil war because I repeat: this is not about arming people because arming them is for war; so, the executor accepted my objective, me, the instigator, and must be by my side and take responsibility because he accepted to be armed and carry out the civil war.

This point of view cannot be debated because the things I've shown are not only based on the text of the law but also based on common sense. In conclusion, the crimes the defendant was charged with are not supported by the legal requirements imposed by the law. And the law must be respected, because think about the situation of a person who was sentenced above the law, illegally. A society can't accept this type of solution, based on someone's arbitrary and personal opinions.

Mr. President, please believe that, without getting into politics, I can't be blinded by interests and political passions. I'm only a lawyer, and my politics revolves around being a Romanian woman that respects the laws of my country, which I swore an oath on. In the same vain, I believe in the oath you swore as a judge and as a military man. I await the acquittal on all the unfair charges against Mr. Corneliu Zelea Codreanu.

Lawyer C. Hentzescu's Plea

Mr. President, Honorary Court! After my co-counsels' pleas, the judicial side of the trial seems clear to me. I won't insist on it anymore.

What I consider necessary to analyze is the political side of it. Because, even though the Indictment put together by the honorary Senior Prosecutor, this aspect of the trial is in the shadows, I am convinced that the political aspect of the case was determined by the criminal prosecution.

Corneliu Zelea Codreanu appears before you for the most despicable crimes in our penal code: attempting to start a rebellion, attempted revolt, treason; these are the astonishing offenses he must answer for today in this courtroom. Here are the charges brought against him.

Following the legal analyses of the trial, made so brilliantly by my co-counsels, let's see if the recent activity by Mr. Corneliu Codreanu would lead a man of common sense, objectively and honestly, to believe these charges have a weak foundation. We all know that the politics of the Iron Guard, and later the All for the Country Party, is a right-wing political organization, opposing the horrors of communism and social anarchy.

The Trial of Corneliu Zelea Codreanu

Ever since he was a small child, Corneliu Z. Codreanu has been raised in an environment in which discipline and the sense of rank stayed at the base of civic education. As a pupil at Mănăstirea Dealului, the exemplary high school established by the fearless patriot Nicolae Filipescu, Corneliu Codreanu formed his spirit in the uplifting atmosphere of permanent exaltation and self-sacrifice. But he didn't stay for long at the foot of the mountains, breathing the fresh air, because he was thrown into war by the whirlwinds of life from the time he was a child. The testimonies of the witnesses that came before you, corroborated by the defendant's statements, should have made you see how preoccupied he was with the fate of his country during those tragic times. He accompanied his father to the front as a scout, and he joined the war from the beginning, not leaving until his father made him face his responsibility as the elder son — the only man that could support the family. These are the initial characteristics of Corneliu Codreanu's personality.

What follows: fighting as a student at the University of Iași against the damaging communist propaganda, preached during those troubled times by the university professors themselves. The street movements to whip up public opinion, raising the tricolor flag instead of the red one, are the obvious consequences of the patriotic convictions, deeply rooted in the soul of this man.

You've listened to witnesses from the highest social ranks, who portrayed, in a very objective manner, the moral outline of the defendant, in his brave fight to accomplish his convictions sourced in a deep faith.

But, leaving behind this period of time, let's come back to his recent political activity, and analyze it in order to reach the required conclusions. As I said before, from the start, the activity of the youth in the Legionary Movement is inspired by nationalist doctrine, which focuses more on the national sentiment, leaving in shadow the social preoccupations that push for separation and intense fights. All we have to do is to watch the spectacle of the Spanish anarchy, to perfectly understand where doctrinal intransigence leads, when it doesn't care about safeguarding the social unity of a nation. Well, with every example, not just the one in Spain, but also those from Western countries, with a new superior civilization, where the rivalry between the right slipped on the land of personal enmity and fraternal hatred, Corneliu Codreanu knew how to maintain his right-wing Movement within the unified soul of the Romanian nation.

Although he was under the flag of national regeneration, he avoided starting a war against his own brothers, for he realized all too well this was what the foreign and the domestic enemies were waiting for, to give us a deadly blow. I'm not the one saying this, the defendant himself states it in his public declarations made in a time when nobody could think about him facing a Military Court.

But, a little more: remember the conditions under which the partial elections were held two years ago. Armed groups were disturbing the peace in villages, some supported one party, others supported another. Especially in Medehinţi, there was a small repetition of the tactics used in the civil war. Well, Corneliu Codreanu did not take part in these pre-anarchy games. And, when on the 2[0th]h of December the All for the Country Party was on the list of candidates, the first of Codreanu's concerns was to prevent the country's collapse, signing the well-known non-aggression pact with the National Peasants' Party and others, even thought he was fully aware that by doing so, he became a target of political attacks. However — out of true patriotism — Corneliu Codreanu protected Romania from those shocks that could have endangered its unity. If this man had looked for social revolution and rebellion, nothing would have been easier than that, he could have let the hate boil, take advantage of it, then finally give the Catiline blow. But Corneliu Codreanu was not a rebel, he was not an instigator that followed his political ascension by whatever means. He was guided by the supreme Romanian interests that required order, discipline, and harmony of the soul. The pact that was signed at the end of 1937, proves not only political maturity and civil bravery, but also a superior sense of personal responsibility.

Let's continue. Mr. Octavian Goga is called. New elections are announced. This time, the electoral campaign presents even darker aspects. In Moldavia, Bessarabia, and Bucovina, passions simmer, a wind of madness seems to blow over our country. In Ilfov county, a group of young Legionaries from the All for the Country Party, riding in a propaganda truck, come back with two corpses. What is the immediate reaction of Corneliu Codreanu? A thirst for revenge? No, he has a feeling of deep Romanian worry. Mr. General Antonescu, who was called as a witness, told you about his conversation with Corneliu Codreanu right after that event. What did the defendant do to push the country on the fatal slope on which it was engaged? Not only did he not do anything to enhance the anarchy, but he did one single gesture to defy it: he withdrew from the electoral campaign.

And, when he made direct contact with the Council president of that time, Octavian Goga, according to the statements of one of his private associates, Alexandru Hodoş, a former secretary of the Presidency, to the serious objections raised by the

The Trial of Corneliu Zelea Codreanu

late patriot, saying the national action could be completely compromised if the fight continued between the two camps of right-wing nationalism, Corneliu Codreanu, through an impromptu gesture, offered to withdraw from the elections.

What other party is capable of such sacrifice in the interest of the public peace and for the victory of his faith?

Well, I wanted to show the recent attitude of Corneliu Codreanu, to prove it is in absolute contradiction to the indictment and the charges brought against him, for he is far from preparing a favorable atmosphere for a rebellion and social war, having, on the contrary, the gift to calm spirits and defend Romania from being torn apart.

And, from this point of view, I can say with all my conviction that Corneliu Codreanu is well-deserved by the country.

But, Mr. President and Honorary Court, the very education of the Legionaries aimed for a completely new orientation of Romanian political life. What characterizes the youth gathered around Corneliu Codreanu is the contempt for material satisfaction. This is why in the electoral campaign we didn't see any requests for ransom, false promises, or incitement concerning mass poverty. So, the accusations brought against Corneliu Codreanu, claiming he was trying to provoke a social revolution, we consider unfounded.

What stirred up irreducible enmities against the defendant who stands before you is the fact that what characterized the normal life of political parties in this country is completely foreign to him. Starting from the idea that Romania wouldn't play the global role it was aspiring to, until the moment when we would achieve a superior conception of life, the Legionary Movement managed to pull the new generation from the bog of vulgar materialism. Manifesting itself through works of national interest, building dams and churches, the Legionaries proved they reached another plane of life, foreign to the self-seekers and scroungers who have invaded the Romanian politics. To form such men is indeed a danger of rebellion.

Mr. President and Honorary Court, the ceremony that marked the funeral of Moța and Marin in Bucharest proved that the activity of the Iron Guard had started to take root in the souls of many. I'm no more than an impartial observer. What I found was also found in turn by many other people of good-faith. But the acts of the martyrs from Majadahonda[86] didn't just have decisive repercussions on the public mentality, but undoubtedly opened the eyes of that man who held the direct responsibility for the Iron Guard: Corneliu Codreanu.

I'm convinced the good actions in the last months, manifested through electoral agreements, and later though the decision to withdraw from the elections, was determined by the horrific spectacle of the Spanish tragedy, which the survivors had brought or communicated to their loved ones at home.

Without a doubt, a man that manages to plant boundless faith in the souls of so many, and especially the power of sacrifice cannot be viewed with indifference.

The Legionary Movement can rightly be proud of these heroes. This is what terrifies all the Romanian political profiteers, all those who crawl like worms in garbage. This is the crime for which Corneliu Codreanu must answer for today in front of you.

If this man was driven by uncontrollable ambition, he would have embraced the intransigence of foreign ideologies; if, tormented by thirst for power, he would have let his political passions run free, if, in a word, he would have set fire to the country, no doubt we wouldn't be here now. The fact that he didn't serve such foreign forces, at the moment when he considered the peace of the country was endangered, the fact that he manifested on a national terrain rather than a strictly political one, brought him the fierce enemies who brought him here today, in this situation.

Mr. President and Honorary Court, there has been widespread publicity on Corneliu Codreanu's interrogation after the prosecution's Indictment had informed public opinion about the charges. Those organizing this publicity considered it as a supreme ability. But not only did the blow fail, it had a completely different effect. The lawyers were not the only ones who realized from the defendant's interrogation that the accusations brought to him are unfounded, but public opinion, the whole country is now convinced this trial is a just terrible setup.

This is the result. And after you caused this unanimous conviction in everyone's minds, how could we get out of this tragic debate with a sentence as a result?

Mr. President, Honorary Court, I didn't come to this trial to make a political manifestation. I'm not a Legionary. I was part of another political group than the Iron Guard. However, I'm here, and pleased to explain my presence by a deep worry about my country as a Romanian patriot. Dear military judges, the defendant played a determined role when it came to the university students. In a time when,

The Trial of Corneliu Zelea Codreanu

in other countries, the enthusiasm of the new generation manifests more as a social fight, when aspirations for equality and hatred toward social privileges guided the students — urging them onto the field of communist terrorism — Corneliu Codreanu waved the Romanian colors. The son of a professor who was voluntarily exiled from Bucovina, represents the middle class, the source of greatness, of common sense, and of social balance. Nobody denies the fact that this great clash bled on both sides. The defendant's guiding thread is, without a doubt, coming from the purest love for his people and for his Romanian country. This is the finding any objective man could proclaim without hesitation.

And now, Mr. President and Honorary Court, think what would happen to this new generation that grew up in the sentiment of the national ideal if Corneliu Codreanu was to become a convict tomorrow. Because you've come here to judge, not only the defendant's actions, but also his activity among the youth. The revolt would stir their souls in front of an unjust sentence such as this, and it would determine, not only a wave of despair, but also of contempt for the established order, that would push the new generation precisely on the slope from where conviction would want to pull it away. I speak honestly, from the heart, as a man fully aware of the importance of the spoken word in these moments. Don't create, dear military judges, something irreparable! Realize that if Greater Romania was established by conquering historical borders, it's not fully consolidated yet!

Many enemies watch us, not only from abroad, but from inside the country as well. Our duty as Romanians is to keep watch constantly, so the soul of our nation isn't destroyed by the cancer of sterile revolt. Your diligence can determine much. So, deeply reflect upon its consequences.

We're living the most dangerous age of universal history. The concepts regarding the life of states, individual rights, public freedoms, are violently clashing in the arena. By the position we hold in Europe, we are a sort of border stone of rival ideologies. As a country with common sense and tolerance, we must avoid entering the storm of internal conflicts. And, especially, we must not create a report of force between the state authorities and the citizenry.

Mr. President and Honorary Court, the problem this trial poses to your conscience, presents an aspect which I am obliged to show you. The movement of the Iron Guard represents, as I said, a young action, an action whose objective judgement only those who will come after us will be able to decide on. But even today it can be considered a normal reaction against parasitic foreignism and Romanian passivity. From this point of view, it deserves all the attention and all the support of true patriots. Don't dig an abyss between the generations that succeed us. Romania is the product of tireless work and of continuous sacrifices of the ones who preceded us. But if, in the course of our history, we were able to face the dangers and defeat cruel fate, this is only due to the full solidarity of our elders with the youth when facing the existential problems of Romanian culture. Don't cut the thread of our national tradition, don't ostracize from the political arena by the sentence you will give to the generation that came immediately after the fulfillment of our secular aspirations.

Corneliu Codreanu doesn't represent only his own person in front of you, but the restrained aspirations of the ones who will be responsible for our historic destiny. The ranks of the nationalists are shrinking. Think about what the future might hold for us.

That's why, I ask you, in the name of salvation of the country's soul and of the defense of our future as a nation, to unanimously acquit Corneliu Codreanu.

The Plea of Lawyer Horia Cosmovici

Mr. Senior President, Honorary Court, the defendant, Corneliu Zelea Codreanu, was sent to trial for treason, social revolution, and civil war, namely based on articles 190-191, 204, point 4, and 210 of the Penal Code.

While a science, law is no more than a science of words that involves me speaking and you listening. It is absolutely necessary to ensure we will understand each other. We must be certain that we speak the same language because, as a doctor who works with a corpse, we work with words, Discussions would be in vain if I spoke something and you understood something else. So, let's come back to the three charges and I will talk about each of them in part.

Treason! It is what the Indictment stated; The Final ordinance also stated treason; it was mentioned by the Indictment Chamber; the newspapers spread treason from one end to the other of the street; the radio talked about treason, and this is what you came here today to judge. So, Mr. Prosecutor is trying in vain to tell us today that this is about something else. No, gentlemen! This is about treason, the foulest charge, the one that proves the accused didn't have a place in his soul for the most natural attachment, for the most natural connection: the one with his country.

The Trial of Corneliu Zelea Codreanu

We don't understand what is with this last-minute turn from the honorary prosecution. In fact, this attempt — that denotes the lack of any basis from the prosecution — also presents another painful aspect of the sanctions required against the obvious detour of the word "treason," after throwing mud at this man for the most horrendous crime.

According to the new Penal Code, which maintains the system of the old Penal Code, the classification of offenses is: crimes, offenses, and contraventions. The classification is done through the punishment criteria. A crime is considered to be the one punished with a certain number of years, and so on, as it's provided by art. 22, 23, and 24 of the P.C.

I wonder who in this country didn't know the punishment for C.Z. Codreanu is from five to twenty-five years of forced labor. Then, if the punishment for the crime of treason is not legal — at least — to say something else because of embarrassment of being able to fit it in, then the decided sentence.

Gentlemen! Again, it is difficult for me to follow the methods of the prosecution, that not only does it pull a text from a code, but more, separates a few words from this text. This is not the way to do an interpretation. The first rule of interpretation given to a first-year university student, says a text cannot be ripped from the context and isolated. Like anything in this life that has a beginning and an end, the texts of law also have their heads and tails. Our penal code, in the second part, title I, regarding crimes and offenses against the State, distinguishes the crimes and offenses against the State, and puts them in two separate categories — crimes and offenses against the external security of the State, and crimes and offenses against the internal security of the State. Therefore, a first distinction is imposed, and it's imposed because between the theory of the Final Ordinance and the opinion of Professor Dongoroz expressed in a study from 1929, and the dispositions of the P.C. of King Carol II, we must — because there's no other way — follow the last ones.

Art. 191, points 1 and 2, like art. 190 to which we are sent to, contain the subchapter about crimes and offenses against the external security of the State; chapter II, which refers to crimes and offenses against the internal security of the State, only starts in art. 201. So, if you accuse me of doing something, it must correspond to an act against the external security of the State.

Romanian Crucible

We have two lines of arguments that prove this, all we have to do is look at these texts from the point of view of an international element. But let's come back to it: here is the content of the text — art. 191 point 1, for point 2 the reasoning remains valid: 1. the Romanian citizen who obtains or possesses, without having the right to do so, plans, writings, or documents mentioned in art. 190. What gives the criminal character to these offenses? Mr. Prosecution talked about possession. But, it is not the possession that gives it the note of criminality, as one can possess things even without the right to do so, as the text says, and that wouldn't make it treason. I can own, without the quality, a commission without thinking it would cross anyone's mind to accuse me of treason. I can have a bill of exchange, a letter, and so on. So, it's not the unlawful possession that gives it the criminal quality. Let's see what's left in the text; nothing more than the documents mentioned in art. 190. That means here is where we find the element of criminality.

Gentlemen! We must pay a lot of attention to this mention. The content of art. 191, point 1 doesn't refer to art. 190, except when it comes to the list of provided documents. This is the only connection between art. 190 and art. 191.

Contrary to the ease with which this list was looked over, we'll insist upon it, because we're not facing a useless list that contains 180 possible cases, which are here in this text, this list of 180 documents possessed without a right that could motivate forced labor between five and twenty-five years.

We are first given 9 documents, namely: plans, sketches, drawings, photographs, writings, secret diplomatic documents, information, and secret notes. I'll stop to mention that none of these 9 documents, in the case that I represent, cannot motivate any accusation. Possessing them without the right to do so becomes a crime at the moment when any of them would concern one of the 20 points listed in the continuation of the text of law. These documents must concern, meaning they have to refer to the country's defense, the security of the State, mobilization and concentration of the army, economic mobilization of the national territory, the state, the quality and quantity of the military material of any category, strengthened regions, forts, technical establishments, warships, aircrafts, weapon, ammunition, explosives, equipment or any other references to the interest of national defense. For this matter, we have 180 possibilities, 180 types of documents, and from the 180 you were not able to find one when it comes to C.Z. Codreanu. In a normal trial, if this was the only argument I'd have, I'd consider it a complete defense. But in this trial my instinct tells me something else. What documents did you find regarding

The Trial of Corneliu Zelea Codreanu

the territory and the external security of the State — I explained why it can't be about the internal security of the State –, mobilization and concentration of the army, military material, and so on? You didn't find anything! You can't just assume the Romanian State was endangered, not knowing which authority ordered Sima Simulescu to be prevented from doing electoral propaganda. For the respect of the court, we want to believe the external security of the State is something completely different.

The preparatory works of the Legislative Council that served to design the Penal Code, in the statement of reasons referring to the crime of treason, examining the difference between the external security of the State and the internal security of the State, from an objective point of view as well as from a subjective one, the imposed difference, received and consecrated by the Penal Code, says that the crimes against the external security of the State intend to destroy the nation's identity. So, no matter how much we'd try, we can't understand how abusive documents from the authorities, concealed because of abuse under the confidential label, sometime sent in code, and that could be considered as electoral interferences at most, we can't understand how they would endanger the external security of the State, chipping away at its independence.

Here is the second line of arguments: to give a punishment as required, my action should have endangered the external security of the state, namely its existence.

Gentlemen! We have two identical offenses that make no sense. They're identical in how confusing they are, and they don't differ except from the point of view of their criminal quality. They speak of treason and espionage. In truth, to get as close as possible to our Penal Code, I have to read from the reasoning explanation of the Legislative Council: "In consequence, considering this new doctrine as a criterion for distinction, the texts were thus composed to make the intention of the law obvious, in a sense that when collecting information for a foreign power, as well as forwarding such information or plans, secret agreements, etc., is qualified as a crime of treason for a Romanian, and, for a foreigner, the offense of espionage.

Therefore, it's the perfect structural identity between treason and espionage. When –and I believe everyone will agree with this — espionage is done for the purpose of endangering the external security of the State, in a serious logic which for me is correct, treason cannot represent another danger. In other words, for the victim state there's no difference between treason and espionage when it comes to

Romanian Crucible

its security. For the offender, there's one difference: he's either a citizen or a foreigner.

I conclude this first part contains two rows of arguments. Whoever says treason, implicitly speaks of endangering the external security of the State.

You don't have a document, because there is no document, no order of this nature, so I rightly ask myself: why does the word "treason" have such an echo, when you haven't even been able to speak it out loud?

Also, when it comes to this text, we must ask for your attention on the attempt — starting from the same separatist inclination in this trial to detach the word "possess", from art. 191, after the text of the article was removed — from the chapter containing it that provides for the crime against the external security of the State.

It says: the law says "any possession." Therefore, the law punishes the singular material act of possessing, no matter if you have intention, joining a curious theory to support it, the work of Professor Dongoroz from 1929, partially quoted and out of place. There are three considerations for the new theory of the Final Ordinance that cannot be accepted, namely: the content of art. 126 from the P.C., the comments under art. 191 of the P.C., also annotated by Professor Dongoroz in 1937, and an argument taken from art. 583 P.C.

Let's analyze them one at a time.

Art. 126 P.C. provides: "the crime is committed with intention." Therefore, treason, being a crime, must be committed with intention. In the same way, Mr. Ionescu Dolj's note under the article on treason, says: "following the system of the Penal Code, we focused on the intentional element, assuming that it exists for every offense mentioned in art. 126 from the general part." So, for the crime of treason that Mr. C.Z. Codreanu was accused of he must have had intent.

The comments under art. 191 P.C. analyze the hypothesis provided by the text: "the second hypothesis is for every citizen that, without having the right to do it, obtains or possesses secret documents, even without communicating their content further." So, when the law says "possesses" it doesn't imply intention, but says something completely different, which is: that even if they didn't forward their content, they are guilty of treason only for possessing them. So, in order to be accused of treason, C.Z. Codreanu must have had intent. The argument taken from art. 583 P.C., point 4, is even more eloquent. This is its content: "execution without permission from the military or maritime authority, and without fraudulent intent,

The Trial of Corneliu Zelea Codreanu

of photographs, plans, or typographic works in a forbidden area or in military or maritime establishments, is sanctioned with imprisonment from 5 to 20 days, and a fine from 100 to 1000 lei." Or, if by making the plan of a military or maritime establishment, by taking photographs of one of these establishments, is considered an offense and sanctioned with a maximum of 20 days in prison, then the one doing this serious offense didn't have fraudulent intent, how could anyone claim it for the same listed offenses in art. 190 that sent us to art. 191? The intent can't be investigated, unless one is thirsty for punishment and is afraid this serious offense will remain at most — and I don't exaggerate when I say "at most" — a simple contravention. So, for C.Z. Codreanu's charge there must be intent. But the intent doesn't exist. And especially because it doesn't exist, the honorary prosecution tried to eliminate it. There is no intent because, first, these orders were divulged by word of mouth for everyone who could hear. Second, they were reproduced in circulars and offered to the first hand that reached for it, because that's how circulars were shared at the Legionary center. Third, they were posted at the center. Fourth, they were published in newspapers, especially in *Buna Vestire*. Fifth, they were gathered and published in a book.

Well, gentlemen, I'll stop, because it is sufficient. The proof for lack of intent is loud and clear. Except only if we didn't admit that, after the documents were showed and divulged by the word of mouth, Corneliu Codreanu was not accused of treason, that anyone could have reproduced them and shared them as circulars, and, seeing that he wasn't arrested, they would have given orders for them to be displayed at the headquarters. But later, seeing the trial for treason was delayed, he sent them to the newspapers for publication, and disappointed by the lack of reaction from authorities, hoping for a charge, to publish them in a volume, showcasing them in one of the largest bookstores in Bucharest. It's impossible, not just for C.Z. Codreanu who is a clean man, but for the lowest of the men. This means pushing perversity to foolishness, and this can't happen!

But what did these orders contain to require a punishment as severe as forced labor?

Gentlemen! It's painful, but we have to say it. They all contained, under the safety of confidential and top-secret labels, abuses by the authorities, set up by the governing party against the Legionaries during elections. For the abusive documents issued by the authorities, the law allows me to complain to Justice. I have the right to do it. Why do I say that I have the right? Because the action of Justice

Romanian Crucible

is the action that characterizes a right! I have a law that provides me the necessary action against abuses from the authorities. With this action, as far as I can exercise, I have the implicit right to complain about the abuse, even if out of explainable prudence I found it hidden under the label of confidential, personal, and secret. And finally, I have actions put at my disposal by other special laws. Another method is the one I also used, after others have used it before me. I showed you the parliamentary debates presented by the *Official Monitor*, that revealed other such orders given by the representative of an affected party. I showed newspapers, such as *Dreptatea* from previous years, where the victims of abuses had denounced the content of such secret and confidential orders to public opinion. I brought to you valuable witnesses, such as Mr. Iuliu Maniu, who stated under oath, that they had received abusive orders from their acquaintances or from unknown people. Mr. Maniu has said: "only in 1927, I had no less than 16 secret and confidential orders, and nobody thought to accuse me, because they couldn't bring me any charge, because this wasn't treason." And then, we ask ourselves what connection is there between the external security of the State and the order of some authority that dares — by disregarding the law — to stop me from joining the electoral campaign? And even if it wasn't an abusive document, as a jurist, a man of law, I ask: is the external security of the State, meaning the very existence of the State compared to other States, the same thing with internal police measures?

There has been talk of maps. Gentlemen, this is painful, because it can't even be revolting anymore. Please, look at file 19, browse through it! It contains maps representing different counties, bought from bookstores and that are used by pupils. These were found at Mr. Clime's residence, which is why they were marked with a red pencil up top, and you can tell they were used for the electoral campaign. Would you consider this as a curious thing? It's natural for those who know the mentality and the thoroughness of the Legionaries. The Legionary propaganda was not done in the counties' capitals or in important cities. No! They were using the map of the county, and each member assigned to handle the propaganda was given a certain map. They were shown — after dividing the map into sectors — which was the sector where they had to go from village to village. That's how the Legionary propaganda was done. And with the map in their hand, every Legionary would start his journey singing, happy, with a clear mind, and with good thoughts, prevented from bringing any insult to anyone. Their instructions said there's no praise

The Trial of Corneliu Zelea Codreanu

in pointing out the mistakes and sins of others. Show them what type of Legionary you are. Your praise must be the cleanliness of your deeds.

It's true there are two more maps, set above. One has the title: Maneuvers from 1929, and the other is a touristic map of the Rucăr region.

But gentlemen, Mr. Clime, in addition to going to war, is also an officer in the reserves. The man might have done some maneuvers in 1929, and he has the map to prove it, in the same way as me having the map of the maneuvers in which I had taken part. For the touristic map of a mountain, at least from respect toward the Honorary Court, I take the liberty not to talk about it. This is the serious problem with the maps found in Mr. Clime's home, but listed, I believe, by virtue of inertia, just like the other essential pieces in C.Z. Codreanu's case. Finally, there's one more thing to talk about in this sad chapter — sad for the prosecution –, the informers.

Gentlemen, I wonder what else I could add — without risking any damage — to the honest and precise explanations of Mr. C.Z. Codreanu. First, the circulars were used to summon the informers of others in the midst of the Legionary Movement; it was published in newspapers and in the book. If you accused me of having an espionage system, I can rightly state, because it can't be any other way: that this accusation is unfounded, if I'm this stupid, because I have to be stupid when I'm involved in espionage and I chose to summon my spies for everyone to see and hear. With this the unfounded accusation fails. In fact, you read in the file what the Legionary population understood from it. These circulars were read in the nests, and for the ones who were absent, the nest leader wrote: "I guarantee that he is not part of the ones mentioned above." It's obvious that this was about the informers that others had in my organization, not about my informers sent to other places.[87]

And now, what's left of treason? What right do you have to drag me through the mud with such a vile accusation? Nothing and again nothing!

This is what this trial was based on!

Art. 209 has the following content: "it constitutes a crime of conspiracy against the social order...." Point 4: "getting in touch with any individual or association with an international character, from abroad or from within the country, for the purpose of receiving instructions or aid of any kind to prepare a social revolution."

Gentlemen, if something is grim, it can only be a result of having to plead the evidence.

Romanian Crucible

But let's try; in a normal trial, this attempt would be reckless from a professional point of view. Reckless, because we would uselessly engage in a defense, even though the prosecution brought no proof. The text has two parts. The first refers to the connection I must have with an individual or an organization with international character, from abroad or from within the country, from which I must receive instructions or aid; the second part requires — in order to issue an accusation — that all the information mentioned above must be done with the intention of preparing a social revolution. Which are the documents that proved that I tried to have such a connection to support your claim that I received instructions or aid? I ask the questions and you can't give me an answer.

Corneliu Codreanu, keeping the line of conduct he had during this whole trial, which corresponds to the moral attitude he's shown throughout his whole life, has told you with the simplicity that only the deep fairness of his soul could have: "I answer for my actions, however they are and however they are understood. I cannot run away from responsibility, but I cannot take responsibility for someone else's actions, especially when these are people that I have never met, people I don't know."

Perfect, to answer — and that's a big deal in this country — to the smallest fact, to the last fragment of my thoughts; but I can't answer to what others have written, to what others had thought! This isn't possible, gentlemen, to sanction someone for the actions of another legally — because I only deal with the law — is a monstrosity. From a human point of view, C.Z. Codreanu told you without revolt, maybe with reproach, if you want, maybe because of the simplicity I was talking about earlier; you've all heard it: "This isn't right. I wouldn't have done something like this." However, the prosecution did what I call, from a legal point of view, a monstrosity, and from a human point of view, Corneliu Z. Codreanu named it a thing that shouldn't be done. You remember the letter from the file, written by hand, addressed to His Excellency Adolf Hitler. From the first moment it was presented C.Z. Codreanu stated: "I don't know how you could find such a letter on me. I haven't seen it in my life." In the short time, extremely short time that we had available to study all the 20 files, about 2 days, because we never had all the files in the trial, we read and reread this letter so many times that today I could recite it from memory, if I wasn't afraid to fall into what we are terribly afraid of, because we don't like secrets. Meaning a secret hearing. Its content, as I saw when I raised an objection regarding this letter, is different, very different from C.Z. Codreanu's

The Trial of Corneliu Zelea Codreanu

clear and precise style. What grabbed my attention were two phrases, which in science we call concepts, that not only haven't been used until today, but we can attribute them to an attempt of innovation in the scope in which they were used, meaning political economy. You can search until the last page and you won't find them. I'm talking about: "mutual enrichment" and "automatic economy." Much has been done in this world: "automatic" pistols, machines, and much more; but I admit that "automatic economy" gets me thinking. Starting from these two characteristics, as well as side-by-side enumerations: professional, national, and international goals," I started researching. Of course, when C.Z. Codreanu was interrogated: "they will search and it is not possible for God to not help us find the person who wrote this letter," many probably smiled. The miracle, however, happened, because in less than two days, the original author was identified among 20 million people. Original not only when it comes to political economy; but original in his attitude when he was informed that because of "his automatic economy" he was going to be taken into forced labor, and he told us with revulsion: "Gentlemen, I am the one who invented the automatic economy and I don't understand why the result of my mind would be attributed to another person." This man is Mr. Rădulescu Thanir, a writer for the newspaper *Neamul Românesc*.[88] I brought you his book, a book written by a schooled man, called *Neocooperația*, with a subtitle on the cover: *Solidaritatea mutuala* (*Mutual Solidarity*), and underneath, on the cover, *Economie automată* (*Automatic Economy*). The author is Mr. Rădulescu Thanir, and his name is written on the cover. The book was published many years ago. So, this couldn't have been done during the trial. Besides, because the letter in the file is written by hand, the possibility of any doubt is removed, because from all the people on this earth, only one can write the letter in this way.

I submitted this evidence in time and added: Mr. Rădulescu Thanir is outside at the door. Bring him in and ask him. To the extent that we believe your purpose is finding out the truth, we have the right to state the evidence was sufficient and his hearing was no longer necessary, nor was the expertise in your mind as long as you refused our evidence. And then, I come back to what I was saying in the beginning: I am responsible for all my actions, but I cannot be responsible for someone else's actions. The way this concept came to be in our file doesn't mean we're trying to accuse someone of anything. In normal ways or abnormal ways, it is of no concern to us. It would have been possible to have arrived as many other things addressed to the leader did, others came addressed to the leadership of the party All for the

234 Romanian Crucible

Country, especially when they were similar to the letter in this case. Gentlemen, you must not forget one thing, that aside from being the leader of a political party, a man who always had the possibility to solve a problem within the State organization, C.Z. Codreanu, through his new air and the deep renewal of our social life, was seen by everyone as one among us who could bring to life any new idea, any original formula. From here it is very possible for this new project of reform of "professional, national, and international" life though "mutual solidarity" and "automatic economy" to have sought its author and make him end up, if possible, in the hand of the Legionary Movement's leader. That he didn't end up there, which is more than obvious, was because the idea was too original and certain sorting had to be done before it reached the leader. And, if the witnesses from Miercurea Ciucului had been brought, without question, the defense would have been fully successful. Finally, I repeat, and I could say it until the phrase became a shout if necessary: "I can only answer for my actions. The letter is not my doing." It's not possible and you can't accuse C.Z. Codreanu of writing it. But if those are my doings, which are my ideas in this matter, that I admit to in front of everyone and for which I chose to answer not just to you, but to anyone?

Gentlemen, if there is something that might embarrass someone from the life of this man, if there's something that for some — because it's not familiar to them— would motivate sanctions, is the sentiment of human and Romanian dignity, a man pushed to his limit of exigency. During the interrogations you've heard the explanations given to you regarding the congratulating telegram addressed to Hitler and Mussolini, with the occasion of their meeting, by C.Z. Codreanu. He told you then: "I sent the telegram in three languages, German, Italian, and Romanian. I also sent it in Romanian because, from a feeling of national pride, I wanted to set the language of my country as an equal to the languages of the States considered to be the great power of Europe." Well, how is it possible for a man like this to be accused of receiving aid, as mentioned in art. 209, point 4, or as he'd say, instead of text to receive alms?

Also, you were then shown that, when the international antisemitic congress was held in Nurnberg, the following were invited to attend: A.C. Cuza, Octavian Goga, and Corneliu Z. Codreanu. Mr. Cuza, as well as the late Octavian Goga, accepted the invitation and took part in the congress, Corneliu Z. Codreanu refused it and didn't join them at the congress, saying: "I didn't see the point of going there where everyone was so great, assuming the task of representing Romania, when I

The Trial of Corneliu Zelea Codreanu

knew from many sources that we were so small". I have the right to ask, I have this right in the name of Justice, how is it possible that, disregarding attitudes as high as these, to throw the mud of criminal texts saying they received instructions, and they could have received instructions like the ones listed in art. 209, pt. 4, from people or associations with an international character?

Something more: not instructions, we couldn't even receive inspiration from abroad, because we didn't have reasons to receive anything from abroad. The book *Pentru Legionari* was read to you, whole pages, and I repeat (what's the problem? I like repetition in this trial), this book was written in 1936, so it wasn't written to serve in the trial, whole pages that show that the inspirational sources for our Romanian nationalism were Simion Bărnuțiu, Mihail Kogălniceanu, Mihai Eminescu, and so many other philosophers, writers, poets, political men, all of them ours, from our blood, fierce and tireless fighters, doctrinaires of love for the Nation, so we didn't need other sources of inspiration, and in any case, we can't receive lessons from somewhere else, when during the times of these people of ours, who served the same precious flame as us today, the great states such as Germany imposed the Berlin Treaty on us that provided — against the wishes of the Romanian people — the right of equality for the Jews.

We don't conceive even a source of inspiration in the line of conduct of our pride. Gentlemen, it is not possible to be brought the painful accusation of having sat as beggars, begging for instructions from abroad. But, again, you won't find evidence for it in any of the 20 files, which contain the last trash from a man's house, trash raised to the rank of a page in a file with a number, when the most it can show is how a stern master dismissed his employees for neglecting their duties of cleaning the house.

As for the second part of the text, the one concerning preparing a social revolution, it falls for the simple reason that, if no evidence was brought — because we need evidence in a trial, not rumors and insinuations — no evidence that shows a connection with an individual or association with an international character from abroad or from within the country, with the purpose of receiving information or aid of any kind, I wouldn't be accused that I used those means that weren't proven for preparing a social revolution. However, we should keep in mind the problem of the social revolution, because we will discuss it together with the problem of the civil war provided in art. 210.

Romanian Crucible

Let's move on to art. 210, the crime of rebellion. Here we find two ideas, namely: arming the locals or urging them to arm themselves, one idea; with the purpose of starting civil war, the second idea. For the accusation of arming the locals or urging them to arm themselves, where is your evidence, Mr. Prosecutor? Show us one. The Final ordinance says: weapon deposits were found. Please, show us one of these deposits. The place where you found it. The person guarding it. The order I gave on this matter. Your reply is a great silence. The reply, from the point of view of the evidence, because the reply from the point of view of insinuations and free statements, just as a certain side of the press does, this reply, we can't use. There's nothing needed to be combated.

But in order to give the opportunity to that certain side of the press, that sometimes from an order, today the whole press can announce with big bold letters: significant weapon and ammunition deposits found at the members of the former political organization All for the Country. You started the searches and searched the whole country, says the Final Ordinance itself: "in the whole rural territory." And what did you find? Here and there, a poor Romanian with a rusty gun or a piece of a pistol without a trigger, or a dagger, not all together, but spread one for every man, some that were left from their grandparents, some from the war. Are these the important weapons and ammunition to be used to start a civil war in a country? And, more than that, from the order of this dangerous man?

If he's so dangerous, how can you believe the weapons he is responsible for are those old rusty toys found here and there?

Danger? How come? It would come about like this (I'll list the weapons in the Final Ordinance at my own risk): C.Z. Codreanu, thinking about a civil war, called the men and said: for yourselves, take these cartridges for hunting rifles and you will conquer Northern Bessarabia. For Southern Bessarabia, take this gun barrel with two boxes. It's harder to conquer Transylvania, so take these machine gun cartridges and this empty firecracker. Perfect, all that's left is Banat. Here, as this is our war industry, take these hundred grams of pellets. I'll stop, gentlemen, because I was raised to respect the law. It's hard for me to continue. I have the feeling I'm telling a story to some children, not that I speak before you about the worth, honor, and about the life of a man.

And why would I need a civil war or a social revolution if I promised to do it together. I was representing a top political party. We managed to have over 70 deputies in the Chamber. I went to the country's capital after the government,[90]

The Trial of Corneliu Zelea Codreanu

since the government doesn't matter in the elections during equal fights, as it has secret, confidential, and coded methods, the first party in the electoral force. In the upcoming elections we were sure to double our votes. You all know that. The whole future was waiting for us, and he promised us the understanding of those who were searching for something pure in which to believe. Why would I want a social revolution? What would have been its purpose?

But all these were in vain, because everywhere, even in the chambers of this court, the alarm of civil war was rung, the cry of the violent methods.

Violent methods? But why? Doesn't everyone know how the Legionaries were shot like dogs? And that the answer was always the same: "Give as much as you want, hit them as hard as you can. Don't be afraid. We won't react. Nobody can kill as many of us as we are ready to die for our faith. Our foreign enemies and the ones within the country, who believe the Legionaries can play their game by starting a rebellion, we tell them they are wrong." And so many died for this line of conduct,[91] we tremble at the thought that we're talking about rebellions and civil war.

No gentlemen, this is bad.

You understood and interpreted this man's life however you wanted, and through it, the life of the Legion.

You had no evidence, and despite all our evidence you have climbed to the last step on the ladder of unfounded accusations. Illegal movement. "Illegal" was the word used by the indictment, by the Final Ordinance, and the imputation was resumed by the Senior Prosecutor. I say imputation, because this fact, just like all the others that I will talk about, cannot receive any criminal classification from the law's point of view, and they have no purpose except for the thirst for defamation of a man's perfect cleanliness.

Gentlemen, what is illegal in the Legionary Movement?

Some whisper, because it's only a whisper, the sound of assumption, that the Legion is organized in nests. So what? What is illegal about this? The nest? Well, let's talk about the nest then.

What is the nest? If I told you myself, you would say I'm just doing my defense for the trial. But C.Z. Codreanu himself said it long before the trial. And not just to you for the Final Ordinance, where he already talked about it, he says it in the book called *Cărticica şefului de cuib*: you all know it as the booklet for which you gave prison sentences 6 months and up.

Let's start with the title. *Cărticica şefului de cuib,*[92] meaning the book of the first leader of our organizing cell. The nest, in the Legionary organization. Represents the family organization of the State. If you condemn daily those who possess it, you have somehow given it an official character. On the other hand, the authenticity of its content is reflected from the fact that, being a guide for the founding cells of the Legionary organization, to avoid risking seeing the organization undermined by his own activity, C.Z. Codreanu had to broadly include the lines of conduct of Legionary life.

We find the first elements on the first page: "The Legion is an organization founded on order and discipline. The Legion is guided by clean nationalism, sourced from the boundless love for country and nation. The Legion wants to awaken to battle all the creative energies of the nation. The Legion defends the altars of the churches the enemies would want to destroy. The Legion kneels before the crosses of heroes and martyrs of the nation. The Legion is the unbending shield around the Throne, from where the voivodes and kings have sacrificed themselves to protect the Country. The Legion wants to build a strong country from hard souls and strong arms, a New Romania."

The Legion also promises all this, first by keeping the 6 fundamental rules of the nest. We list them:[93]

"1) The law of discipline: you must be a disciplined Legionary, because this is the only way to emerge victorious. Follow your leader for better or for worse.

2) The law of labor: Work. Work every day. Work hard. The reward for your labors shouldn't be your income, but the satisfaction for putting a brick at the rise of the Legion and the flourishing of Romania.

3) The law of silence: use few words. Speak only what you should. Speak only when you should. What you say should reflect your actions. You must take action; let others talk.

4) The law of education: you must become someone else. A hero. Finish your education in the nest. Know the Legion well.

5) The law of mutual help: help your brother in need. Don't abandon him.

The Trial of Corneliu Zelea Codreanu

6) The law of honor: only follow honorable paths. Fight and you will never be a coward. Leave the path of infamy to others. It's better to fall on the path of honor than win on the path of infamy."

On page 9 of this book, which can be bought by anyone, from any bookstore, and known by anyone, he defines the nest: "The gathered nest is a church. By entering the nest, you abandon every small thing, and you dedicate one hour to your pure thoughts, and to the country. The meeting time of the nest is the time of the Nation."[94]

Now that we know what a nest is, we should know what is required of a Legionary to become a member of this church: "He must have a kind heart; he mustn't quarrel with anyone, or think about fighting, because in the nest members cannot fight each other.... Great and good things are done with a kind heart, because where there's a kind heart, there is God."[95]

You have been told, gentlemen, and you can find this especially in the Final Ordinance, about the Legionary oath. There was much talk on this matter. People didn't realize that a Legionary swears because he believes in the Legion, it is a sword because they are connected to the soul of the Legion. This oath caused envy and formed proselytes. Because the thirst for defamation was asking for it, there was no lack of interpretation on this chapter. The Final ordinance presented an oath whose exact form I don't exactly recall. As much as my memory helps me, you can correct me, or Mr. Prosecutor can do it, it sounded something like this: I swear that I won't follow such and such, all his life, him as well as his whole family. Now you can understand why I couldn't remember it word by word. A normal mind cannot remember such an odd formulation. However, we ask ourselves if this sensational discovery is due to the hard instruction and the eagerness of the searches.

If this book hadn't existed, though it wouldn't have been excusable, it would have been, however, an opportunity to explain the composition of the oath as I have reproduced it to you. But the presence of this book in every bookstore eliminates any motivation. This is the actual oath: "Let us pray to God, let us rise in thought to the souls of the martyrs: Moța, Marin, Sterie, Cumetti, and all our comrades who have fallen for the Legion or have died in the Legionary faith. Let us believe in the rebirth of Legionary Romania and in the collapse of the wall of hate and cowardice surrounding it. I swear I will never betray the Legion."[96]

Romanian Crucible

Put the oath in the Final Ordinance next to the Legionary oath that I just showed you. Please, look at them and you will feel, as judges, why we must refrain from any comments in order to maintain the Legionary line of conduct.

Oh! But the Legionary "march," what discussions, what investigations, what deductions created?! It was said they marched, and passing this idea through the filter of the most subtle analyses, it was categorically and severely concluded: They were training for the great march in Bucharest! It's something like this: conquering Bucharest by stomping your feet. But why, gentlemen, nobody wanted to understand what was written in the booklet on page 21: "On Sundays and holidays, every nest [...] must get used to marching. We don't know our country. Some don't even know their neighboring village. During holidays, on bad or good weather, we must go out into nature [...]. During religious services we must stop at churches on our way. Our comrades must stop in the neighboring villages. Marching is healthy. Marching rests and restores the human nerves and soul."[97] Therefore, you march to explore your country, to explore the neighboring villages, to be in nature, and to go to church; not to go to Bucharest. There's no other way to explain it to make someone understand.

It's painful, of course, everything that is happening, but everything is considered as part of the Legionary line of conduct. On page 53 of the book[98] we find the path a Legionary must follow in his Legionary life: "The Legionary life is beautiful. But it is not beautiful because of riches, parties, and luxury; it is beautiful because of the noble brotherhood that binds all the Legionaries across the country in a holy fighting brotherhood; beautiful because of the unyielding manly attitude when facing suffering. When someone joins the Legionary organization, they must learn ahead about the life waiting for him, and the path he'll walk on. This path goes through much suffering, then through the forest of wild beasts, and through the swamp of despair. The mountain of suffering. After a man enlists a Legionary, with longing for his country in his heart, he is not received with a rich meal, but he must receive the Savior Jesus Christ on his shoulders: "take my yoke upon yourselves..." And the Legionary path starts going up a mountain which people named: the mountain of suffering. At first, it seems easy. Later, walking up the path becomes harder, the suffering greater. The first beads of sweat start dripping from the Legionaries' foreheads. Then, a dark spirit that sneaked among the Legionaries that are following the path now asks for the first time: "Wouldn't it be better to turn back? The Legionary path is starting to become hard; the mountain is tall, and we can't see its

The Trial of Corneliu Zelea Codreanu

end." But the Legionary doesn't listen, he keeps going forward, even though it's hard. After a while, going up the endless mountain, he starts to get tired, and his powers seem to abandon him. His luck is that he finds a spring, clear as the tear of a friend."

Gentlemen, please try to remember about "mutual enrichment," "automatic economy," and "economic alliance," to feel how far from us these things are. But let's continue: "He cools off, he washes his eyes, rests a bit, and then continues walking up the mountain of suffering. He passes the halfway point and the mountain continues without water, grass, or shade, made entirely of stone and cliffs. When the Legionary sees this he says: I have been tormented so far, so help me God to reach the top. But the evil spirit asks him: "wouldn't it be better to turn back? Forget about your Nation. Can't you see how much you suffer if you love your Nation and your King? Your people and your land? And then: what do you gain from this? Wouldn't it be better to have peace at home?" But he keeps walking up the barren slope with unyielding faith. He's tired now. He falls. He scrapes his hands and knees, and sees the blood flowing for the first time. He bravely stands up and starts walking again. He's almost there. But the slope became steep and sharp. His chest is bleeding, flowing down the unforgiving cliff. "Wouldn't it be better to turn back?" he hears the voice of the evil spirit again. He starts thinking about it. But suddenly, he hears a voice crying from the depths of thousands of years: "Forward, children! Don't give up!" One last effort. The brave man reaches the peak, victorious, on the peak of the mountain of suffering, with his Christian Romanian soul full of joy and happiness: "You will be happy when they chase you away, and they'll say bad words against you." And they were leaving, joyful for being beaten in the name of Jesus. The Legionaries greatly climbed this mountain of suffering. A whole book would be needed to describe their suffering."[99]

"The forest with wild beasts." The one who wants to become a Legionary shouldn't imagine that his trials end here, on top of the mountain of suffering. It's good for everyone to know what awaits them, to know what path they're starting on.

The second trial: shortly after, the Legionary path goes through a forest people named: "the forest with wild beasts."

The howls of these wild animals can be heard at the edge of the forest. They can't wait for someone to enter, so they can rip them apart. After the mountain of suffering, this is the second trial all Legionaries must complete. Whoever is scared,

Romanian Crucible

remains at the edge of the forest. Whoever has a brave heart goes in, fights bravely, and faces thousands of dangers, on which he could later write a whole book. In this fight, the Legionary doesn't run from the danger, he doesn't hide behind trees. On the contrary, he shows up where the danger is greatest. After emerging out of the first he is awaited by another trial.

The swamp of despair. He loses the path and he must cross a swamp. This is called "the swamp of despair", because one must go through despair to reach the other side. Some don't have the courage to go through it, they start doubting the victory, thinking it's too far away, that they won't see it happening. So, many of those who conquered the mountain of suffering, who passed through the forest with wild beasts, drown in the swamp of despair. But true Legionaries don't lose hope, they swim through this trial as well, and come out on the other side in full glory.

There, at the end of the hard road of these three trials, starts the sweet work, the holy work for the foundation of New Romania. Only the one who passed the three trials, the mountain of suffering, the forest with wild beasts, and the swamp of despair, is a true Legionary."[100]

Under these circumstances, we are entitled to ask: which political organization has done so until today? What a Legionary was promised couldn't be found in another place. But we're talking about the small ways in which the Legionary Movement was organized, and about its methods of making itself known. Even though its leader was not obliged to do so, he wanted to show everyone the basis on which his Movement was founded. Even so, he was not spared the accusation of illegality.

But wasn't the process identical when it came to the "black lists"? What was understood from the Final Ordinance? The newspaper *Buna Vestire*, on the date of 26th of January 1938, contains on page 6 the circular of the party All for the Country from the 24th of January 1938. This is its content: "It was brought to our attention that in some counties there is forced labor, illegalities, arrests, even beatings against the Legionaries. The regional leaders will report each case as soon as possible: 1. Name and address of the persecuted, arrested, or beaten Legionary; 2. The name and address of the perpetrator; 3. Full details on the event; 4. Witnesses, if there were any."

The Final Ordinance says black lists were made at that time; a black list with people who had to be punished, while any man who saw the content of the circular

The Trial of Corneliu Zelea Codreanu

would understand, without effort, that the order was given for the purpose of stopping the abuse by legal means. They needed the name of the victim, the name of the offender, details about the event, and witnesses, if there were any. In other words, they were gathering all the information required for a trial. If, for those who build their existence on illegality, the circular could have been used as a way to compile "black lists," for the ones who pretend to be representatives of Justice, this was not allowed. The only black highlight on these lists that I can see, is the darkness of the abuse and the blackness of the recklessness of those who think their actions are justified, while promises are flowing. Not only with the black lists, weren't things the same when it came to paramilitary organizations? These were misinterpreted as well. Every word weighted by the gram and no chance to push away the insinuation. They were looking for words, because they wanted punishments. During his interrogation, C.Z. Codreanu explained and clarified, just as he would be able to do it, the orientation of his Movement toward corporatism, imposed by the way of things. In this way, as he had a workers' corps, an intellectual corps, and so on, he also had a corps for the former active military, adding that the presence of his corps in the organization should eliminate — without any other defense from his part — the accusations brought against him for apparently trying to cause a rebellion in the country, that the people who dedicated their lives, as the soldiers do — without reserve, to defend their country, men whose blood splattered across the whole country, couldn't, at the end of their lives and of such a glorious career, provoke or take part in what would be considered a collapse for our country: a civil war that would turn it into a bloody Spain. But everything was in vain. The storm of accusations continues, not sparing even the most perfect distillation of the sublimely named the Moța-Marin Corps. On one side, the Final Ordinance and the Indictment of the Public Ministry accuse; on the other side, the explanations and the evidence that couldn't be combated by the prosecution, by which the purpose of this Corps was precisely defined as a heroic attitude when facing life and death.

But as I said, words were taken out of context in search of punishments.

Gentlemen, you were shown proof concerning the education of C.Z. Codreanu, and that it took place at Mănăstirea Dealului. Raised there during the years that define the line of the whole life through the education received, in the military discipline, he kept in this way of thinking and acting, the military characteristic. First, this explains his perfect discipline — that even his enemies admit to — proven for the Organization in every circumstance.

Romanian Crucible

In the Legionary Movement, you will find respect and obedience for the ranks. Executing orders and trusting the superiors. Proper attire and even taking the upright military position when a superior talked to them. Finally, whenever and whatever is sought in the Legionary Movement, all that will be found will be in perfect order imposed by severe discipline. This, gentlemen, is the realization of the principles that the best military school in the country, through the brightest teachers, were made to exist in the heart and mind of C.Z. Codreanu.

Perhaps it is tragic to accuse him of what you taught him to do.

And now, here is the proof:

Gentlemen, for everyone, trade is trade. For C.Z. Codreanu, trade is a "battle." For whoever those needing collaborators for a trade are called functionaries; for C.Z. Codreanu the shareholders are called a "battalion." This is what you'll find in *Buna Vestire*, on Saturday, 4 December 1937, on page 6, written with capital letters: "The battalion of Legionary trade starts the battle. In Moldavia occupied by Jews FACE TO FACE WITH THE ENEMY."

It will be said perhaps — because what wasn't said in this trial? — that this is the title of an article. Well, I'll read you from an agenda, signed by C.Z. Codreanu and published on the first page of the newspaper *Buna Vestire*, on Sunday, 12th of September 1937. I ask you to stop me, those of you who are not soldiers, if you get the impression that I read a true agenda given on a battlefield, in the midst of a fierce battle. It seems the war was in full swing. And yet here is the title: "THE LEGIONARY TRADE." Let's move on to its content: "If the Legionary cooperative in Bucharest had the character of school, the summer trade at Carmen Sylva had the character of war, of an OFFENSIVE. The first Legionary trade offensive. After the season ended and the two establishments closed down, this OFFENSIVE STOPPED, resulting in a GREAT MATERIAL CONTRIBUTION and a GREAT MORAL CONTRIBUTION. In memory of this first accomplishment, which was truly a GLORIOUS LEGIONARY OFFENSIVE: a new distinction is established — the Final Ordinance accused him of giving awards — in the setting of our Movement, which will be named THE BATTLE OF LEGIONARY TRADE. IT SYMBOLIZES: 1. Fairness to blind trust; 2. Good manners and elegance. These, next to devotion and ability. Dear comrades!... Everywhere, trade is trade. For us, it is WAR. THE WAR of a race, which within 100 years lost all its economic positions in the favor of a foreign race, INVADING IN THIS WAR. STEP BY STEP, YOU, THE LEGIONARY, WILL CONQUER ALL THE ROMANIAN POSITIONS

The Trial of Corneliu Zelea Codreanu

THAT HAVE BEEN LOST, OVERWHELMING EVERY RESISTANCE. Soon, new BATTLES will await you: they will happen one after the other. VICTORIES and GLORY await you, which no conspiracy can darken. Here, everyone shakes your hand gladly, C.Z. Codreanu, Carmen Sylva, 12th of September 1937."

There are the paramilitary organizations. They were used for a civil war. No, gentlemen, nothing was understood or it didn't want for the life of this man to be understood.

Now, at the end — even though I was asked to be silent when it comes to this — I apologize for not doing so, but, what do you expect, I am revolted and, while waiting to be scolded, I'll talk about it, so you may feel my pain, as a man, about the "graves."

The surprised Final Ordinance said: "The measurement units for Legionary heroism are: GRAVES!" Really! I wonder what other unit of measure would be more justified than this. And I mourn those whose heroism would be valued differently. But what graves are we talking about? Someone else's graves? Or ours?

We are brought up in the cult of our dead that we love. It is natural to respect the death of others, if death found them in a moment of heroism. But our heroism can only be the aura of our graves.

Here is the proof:

If you remember, during Goga's government, because of the political fights – and it was a good thing that policy was abolished — a critical point was reached. Two Legionaries are shot: Mija Dumitru, a worker, and Popescu Florian, a student. They are brought to the Capital by their comrades, in which they were shot. The Capital was in turmoil. The legitimate reaction of the Legionary Movement was expected.

Buna Vestire was published on Wednesday, 9th of February 1938, with the following featured article: "Their Last Words." Legionary Mija Dumitru was shot in the head, while he was singing "Blessed Legionary Youth." "For the Holy Cross, for the Country, we defeat the forests and subdue the mountains..." — these were his last words. He then collapsed into the arms of his comrades. The Legionary Florian Popescu gave his last breath in the Colentina hospital. His last words were: "It hurts!," and when his uncle came to him crying, he told him: "Your father died at Turtucaia, to wake up now and see you shot by the gendarmes!," he replied: "Don't cry, uncle, because my blood was also spilled for the Country."

246   Romanian Crucible

The following day, after the meeting of the Legionary Senate at 11:30 PM, a special edition of the newspaper *Buna Vestire* was published, and even if 20,000 copies were printed, they were sold-out within half an hour. It contained the following Legionary Movement's response to the two new graves: "Nobody can kill as many as we are willing to die for our faith. The Legionary Movement, with its heart bleeding and mourning, won't respond to the lawless challenge to which it has been subjected. Attack us however you want; hit as hard as you want. We won't respond, so don't be afraid of a reaction. The foreign enemy powers, or the ones within the countries, who imagine that the Legionnaires will play their game by starting a rebellion, we tell them that they are mistaken."

I ask: isn't this heroism?

Were not those graves ours?

I asked for those who are forcibly detained in Ciuc to be brought. You rejected our request. But you can't prevent one of them from testifying. The poet Radu Gyr. On Friday, 21 February 1938, he tells you what graves are needed to measure the Legionary heroism in *Buna Vestire*:

> *"We have so many dead, so many bones,*
> *Our minds are heavy with their memory...*
> *We carry in our hearts the solar graves*
> *And our ribs hurt from so much light.*
>
> *So many dead, so many promises....*
> *Their myrrh blessing our temples*
> *And from us to their holy graves*
> *The golden moon brilliantly shines.*
>
> *So many dead, so many beloved graves...*
> *You see their souls walking in the gardens*
> *We feel their hot kisses on our foreheads*
> *Like an evening breeze smelling of lilies.*
>
> *They touch our hands and our words*
> *Just like the sun burning our faces....*

The Trial of Corneliu Zelea Codreanu

So many dead, so many bones
Topaz icons, lighting up our dreams.

So many dead, so many beloved graves...
Growing within us like holy icons
Just like our martyrs before them
Through bullets, storms and rain!...

So many dead sharpen the steel within us
The century shatters in shards of iron
Our sacrifices reach the stars,
Our wounds are now touching the sky.

We build the Destiny of holy walls
Not work with lime and stone
We plaster them with the white bones,
And rise the walls with wounds for bricks...

Molded from flint and oaths,
With burning eyes of holy mystery,
We watch, each day, new graves
Rising like eagles towards the sky.

The Country must have a steel foundation!...
We have so many dead, so many bones..."

It's late now. You will either say "yes" or "no." A word for an entire life.

But you should know that if you condemn him, along with Corneliu Zelea Codreanu you will imprison the soul of a whole generation!

Following the defense's plea, at 10:30, the Court gave the LAST WORD to the defendant CORNELIU ZELEA CODREANU.

The Final Statement of Corneliu Zelea Codreanu

YOU DON'T HAVE MY LIFE IN YOUR HANDS, WHICH I WILL GLADLY GIVE, YOU HAVE IN YOUR HANDS THE HONOR OF THE WHOLE YOUTH

OF THE ROMANIAN NATION. I BELIEVE IN THE JUSTICE OF MY COUNTRY.

I HAVE PROVEN WITH MY PRINCIPLES, ACTIONS, AND WITNESSES, THAT WE NEVER THOUGHT ABOUT STARTING A CIVIL WAR. BUT NOT ONLY THAT; WE DIDN'T EVEN THINK ABOUT CAUSING THE SMALLEST DISTURBANCE, AS THE DANGER FROM THE EAST WAS WATCHING EVERY MISTAKE, EVERY MOVE.

The hearing adjourned, and reopened at 11:45 PM, when the Court withdrew for deliberations concerning the objections brought up at the beginning of the trial, regarding the evidence in the trial.

After fifteen minutes of deliberations, the Court rejects the objection with a majority of votes.

At 12 AM, the debates are closed.

Mr. Senior President colonel magistrate CONSTANTIN DUMITRU reads the accusations, after which the Court withdraws again for deliberations, returning to the courtroom at 3 in the morning.

The Verdict

Regarding the accusations, the Court responded with the following:

1. Did the defendant, Corneliu Zelea Codreanu, a Romanian citizen, residing in Bucureștii Noi, Niculescu-Dorobanțu street, nr. 38, commit the crime of possessing secret documents concerning the security of the State, that knowingly and with guilty intent, he possessed order Nr. 54 from the 30th of August 1934, issued by the Argeș Legion of Gendarmes, addressed to the rural gendarme units in their subordination, an order found at his residence during the night searches of April 17th, 1938? Was the defendant aware of the secret nature of the document, and of the fact that it concerned the security of the State, and that he had no quality to possess it?

To these questions the Court answered YES.

2. Is the defendant guilty of committing this crime?

To this question the Court answered YES.

3. Does the defendant deserve mitigating circumstances?

To this question the Court answered NO.

4. Was the crime committed on a territory under siege?

To this question the court answered YES.

5. Did the defendant commit the crime of possessing secret documents concerning the security of the State, that knowingly and with guilty intent, he possessed the informing order Nr. 64 from the 4th of October 1934 issued by the Bucharest Gendarme Inspectorate, addressed to the Argeș Legion of Gendarmes, an order found at his residence during the night searches from April 17th, 1938? Was the defendant aware of the secret nature of this document, and of the fact that it concerned the security of the State, and that he had no quality to hold onto it?

To these questions the Court answered YES.

6. Is the defendant guilty of committing this crime?

To this question the Court answered YES.

250 Romanian Crucible

7. Does the defendant deserve mitigating circumstances?

To this question the Court answered NO.

8. Was the crime committed on a territory under siege?

To this question the court answered YES.

9. Did the defendant commit the crime of possessing secret documents concerning the security of the State, that knowingly and with guilty intent, he possessed the informing order Nr. 16 issued by the Craiova Gendarme Inspectorate, sent telegraphically in code to their subordinated units, an order found at his residence during the night searches of April 17th, 1938? Was the defendant aware of the secret nature of this document, and of the fact that it concerned the security of the State, and he had no quality to hold onto it?

To these questions the Court answered YES.

10. Is the defendant guilty of committing this crime?

To this question the Court answered YES.

11. Does the defendant deserve mitigating circumstances?

To this question the Court answered NO.

12. Was the crime committed on a territory under siege?

To this question the court answered YES.

13. Did the defendant commit the crime of possessing secret documents concerning the security of the State, that knowingly and with guilty intent, he possessed the coded telegraphic order Nr. 586/938 issued by the General Gendarme Inspectorate, addressed to their subordinated units, an order found at his residence during the night searches from April 17th, 1938? Was the defendant aware of the secret nature of this document, and of the fact that it concerned the security of the State, and that he had no quality to hold onto it?

To these questions the Court answered YES.

14. Is the defendant guilty of committing this crime?

To this question the Court answered YES.

15. Does the defendant deserve mitigating circumstances?

To this question the Court answered NO.

16. Was the crime committed on a territory under siege?

The Trial of Corneliu Zelea Codreanu

To this question the court answered YES.

17. Did the defendant commit the crime of possessing secret documents concerning the security of the State, that knowingly and with guilty intent, he possessed the strictly personal and confidential order Nr. 198 from the 11th of October 1937, issued by the Ilfov Prefecture, addressed to the praetors, through which they were forwarded a copy of the confidential personal order Nr. 61096/932 from the Ministry of Internal Affairs, the General Police Direction, found at his residence during the night searches from April 17th, 1938? Was the defendant aware of the secret nature of this document, and of the fact that it concerned the security of the State, and that he had no quality to hold onto it?

To these questions the Court answered YES.

18. Is the defendant guilty of committing this crime?

To this question the Court answered YES.

19. Does the defendant deserve mitigating circumstances?

To this question the Court answered NO.

20. Was the crime committed on a territory under siege?

To this question the court answered YES.

21. Did the defendant commit the crime of possessing secret documents concerning the security of the State, that knowingly and with guilty intent, he possessed the confidential personal order Nr. 116 from the 27th of July 1937 issued by Prahova Prefecture, found at his residence during the night searches of April 17th, 1938? Was the defendant aware of the secret nature of this document, and of the fact that it concerned the security of the State, and he had no quality to hold onto it?

To these questions the Court answered YES.

22. Is the defendant guilty of committing this crime?

To this question the Court answered YES.

23. Does the defendant deserve mitigating circumstances?

To this question the Court answered NO.

24. Was the crime committed on a territory under siege?

To this question the court answered YES.

Romanian Crucible

25. Did the defendant Corneliu Z. Codreanu, a Romanian citizen residing in Bucureştii Noi, Niculescu-Dorobanţu street, nr. 38, commit the crime of public reproduction of secret documents concerning the security of the State, that knowingly and with guilty intent he reproduced in circular Nr. 131 from February 4th, 1938, personally signed and addressed to the members of the Legionary Movement, so meant for publicity, the telegraphic order Nr. 586/938 issued by the General Gendarme Inspectorate, addressed to their units in a suborder, which was a secret document in nature concerning the security of the State?

To this question the Court answers YES.

26. Is the defendant guilty of committing this crime?

To this question the Court answered YES.

27. Does the defendant deserve mitigating circumstances?

To this question the Court answered NO.

28. Was the crime committed on a territory under siege?

To this question the court answered YES.

29. Did the defendant commit the crime of public reproduction of secret documents concerning the security of the State, that knowingly and with guilty intent he reproduced in circular Nr. 94 from October 20th 1937, personally signed and addressed to the members of the Legionary Movement, so meant for publicity, the strictly personal confidential order Nr. 198 from October 11th 1937, issued by the Prahova Prefecture, sent to the praetors, by which they are forwarded a copy of the confidential personal order Nr. 61096/932 from the Ministry of Internal Affairs, General Police Direction, which was a secret document in nature concerning the security of the State?

To this question the Court answers YES.

30. Is the defendant guilty of committing this crime?

To this question the Court answered YES.

31. Does the defendant deserve mitigating circumstances?

To this question the Court answered NO.

32. Was the crime committed on a territory under siege?

To this question the court answered YES.

The Trial of Corneliu Zelea Codreanu

33. Did the defendant Corneliu Z. Codreanu, a Romanian citizen residing in Bucureștii Noi, Niculescu-Dorobanțu street, nr. 38, commit the offense of conspiring against social order in 1935 by knowingly and with guilty intent contacting a foreign association, with an international character, which he contacted in order to receive help or instructions to prepare a social revolution in Romania, fulfilling the social program of the so-called Legionary Movement?

To this question the Court answers YES.

34. Is the defendant guilty of committing this crime?

To this question the Court answered YES.

35. Does the defendant deserve mitigating circumstances?

To this question the Court answered NO.

36. Was the crime committed on a territory under siege?

To this question the court answered YES.

37. Did the defendant Corneliu Z. Codreanu, a Romanian citizen residing in Bucureștii Noi, Niculescu-Dorobanțu street, nr. 38, commit the crime of rebellion by, between 1937-1938, with guilty intent arming a part of the Legionary Movement's members whose leader he was, depositing weapons in various points within the country and ordering the organization of an undercover armed paramilitary corps for the purpose of starting a civil war in Romania?

To this question the Court answers YES.

38 Is the defendant guilty of committing this crime?

To this question the Court answered YES.

39. Does the defendant deserve mitigating circumstances?

To this question the Court answered NO.

40. Was the crime committed on a territory under siege?

To this question the court answered YES.

The Sentence

The Court answered affirmatively to every question, and negatively to the questions asking if the defendant deserves mitigating circumstances.

The Military Court of Army Corps II finds the defendant Corneliu Zelea Codreanu guilty, a lawyer from Bucureștii Noi, Casa Verde, Str. Niculescu-Dorobanțu, Nr. 38, for the crimes imputed above, and sentences him to ten years of forced labor and six years of civic degradation, as well as a fine of 5,000 lei and 2,000 lei in court fees.

Communicating the Sentence
of Corneliu Zelea Codreanu

Yesterday morning, after the sentence of Corneliu Zelea Codreanu was pronounced, Mr. Military Senior Prosecutor, major magistrate RADU IONESCU, accompanied by the first registrar of the Military Court, Mr. Tudor Petrescu, went to the prison where they read the defendant his conviction sentence.

The Appeal

Yesterday afternoon, Lawyer Lizetta Gheorghiu presented herself at the Military Court registry on behalf of Corneliu Zelea Codreanu, and submitted the appeal against the conviction.

The Trial of Corneliu Zelea Codreanu

The reasons for appeal at the Court of Cassation:

Reason I

Violation of the right to a defense. Slander. Excess of power. Violation of art. 220, 221 C.M.J., combined with art. 276, 279 penal procedure and art. 305 combined with art. 270, point 3 of the last penal procedure and 275 point 4 of the same code. The objection was brought up before the Court.

The defense before the Military Court encompassed a part of the first objection and voiced the following:

1. The case files were not sent; therefore, the Indictment Chamber didn't have them when it gave its Decision Nr. 17. On May 17th 1938, fact that constitutes a flagrant violation of the right to a defense, by disregarding the categorical dispositions of the law.

2. Corneliu Z. Codreanu was put in the impossibility to formulate his memoir – which he was entitled to before the Chamber, a fact that, again, constitutes a flagrant violation of the right to a defense.

1.   The first objection

The indictment chamber did not have the case files available.

The proof: The address Nr. 213 from the 16th of May 1938 of the 5th Court Cabinet to the Prosecution of the Military Court, as well as the address Nr. 17 .130 from the 17th of May of the Military Court Prosecution to the Indictment Chamber, that show files Nr. 12, 14, 15 (2), 16, 17, 18 were not sent, a fact admitted to by the Senior Prosecutor, as well as by the Military Court, as shown from the appealed sentence.

Our argument: Art. 220 C.J., last paragraphs, says: "Whatever the conclusions of the Final Ordinance would be, when it comes to crimes, the Public Ministry will forward the file to the Indictment Chamber..." Therefore, the organic law of the Military Courthouse imposes the Public Ministry to forward the case file to the Indictment Chamber. In this case, the case file contains 22 volumes numbered from 1 to 20, files 15 and 19 containing 2 volumes each, namely 15 (1 and 2), 19 (1 and 2).

Six volumes were missing from the files, meaning the "case files" as provided by art. 220, last paragraph, was not forwarded to the Indictment Chamber, by this violating the categorical dispositions of the law.

On the other hand, according to art. 276 and 279 of the penal procedure that sends us to art. 221 C.M.J., reveals the same obligation of the Indictment Chamber to have the case files. In truth, the last paragraph of art. 276 says: "The President receiving the file..."; point 3 of the following talks about the Indictment Chamber being asked to examine the "case files in criminal cases," then, further on, the matter of the files is brought up again in the following fragment: "the distribution of files for the report is equally done among all the members of the Chamber." Art. 279, final part, talks about the Indictment Chamber's duty to rule on all the offenses that result from the "instruction documents;" to be understood as, all documents, and not just a part of them, must be judged upon by the Public Ministry.

Therefore, these texts reveal the same duty of the Public Ministry to forward the files to the Indictment Chamber, and for them to hold onto them. The fact that six files were missing was a violation of these categorical texts in this matter.

In this way, by violating the law, the right for a defense was violated as well, at the same time disregarding art. 277 from the penal procedure and the last paragraph of art. 270.

For a Court to judge a crime, the defendant must be sent to trial from the order — as the law says — of the Indictment Chamber. The Indictment Chamber, however, can also state though its Decision, according to art. 277, if there's "no need for prosecution," if they consider there isn't enough evidence to show guilt, or according to art. 226, last paragraph, "can order new information or investigations, assigning the instruction judge with this task, or another judge." But how can they find there is not enough evidence of guilt, or the investigations must be continued (based on pieces that were not withheld by the prosecution), if they don't have the whole case file? This possibility doesn't exist for me when the case file is missing.

In this case, the violation of the right to a defense by not having the whole case file is produced especially on two considerations which are:

1. Lack of original evidence

2. Lack of documents that were NOT retained in the indictment.

The Trial of Corneliu Zelea Codreanu

1. The lack of the original evidence. In criminal matters, the incriminated documents are the body of the crime. You can't use copies of these documents, unless the originals were lost, and even then, their restoration is done following certain rules, not by certifying them. The bodies of the crime must always be brought and presented in their material form. As an application of this principle are the dispositions of art. 305 in the penal procedure, as well as art. 270, last paragraph of the penal procedure code.

But, more than that: The Public Ministry is not a Courthouse, as neither the Instruction Judge, nor the Indictment Chamber are, as otherwise, it wouldn't be explained why, following the Final Ordinance or the decision of the Indictment Chamber, a trial must be held in Court. The Public Ministry is part of the trial. It represents society. While being part of the trial, it cannot have more rights than the defense. And then, it cannot certify copies, because it would be identical to reciting them. No! In criminal matters, the incriminating documents must be original. Especially when the defendant was accused of possessing the originals.

Here is an example from this case, that shows that, if we had been given a copy, and not the original document, the defense wouldn't have been able to do its job. This is the letter addressed to His Excellency Adolf Hitler. In its original form, the letter is handwritten. The consequence was: first, we were able to prove it wasn't written by the defendant, then, we were able to find its author, and, finally, proving the man we found was the author was absolute, because his handwriting was the same. If we had been given a copy of this — even if certified by the prosecution — all of these defense methods would have been eliminated by the lack of the original document.

2. Lack of documents that were not retained in the indictment.

For the defense before the Indictment Chamber, the interest was not in the pieces of evidence retained by the prosecution, but more in the pieces that were not retained by the prosecution. The reason is simple. The retained pieces are useful for the prosecution and the purposes of the prosecution. When it comes to the defense, I have to use the other pieces to prove my innocence, so I need the pieces that leave no possibility of discussion. Clear pieces that don't leave room for doubt and contradictory conclusions.

Romanian Crucible

Here is an example from this case, which clearly reveals that, if we had limited ourselves only to the pieces from the prosecution, regarding one of the most important charges, we couldn't have built the defense. This is about the circular with the "informers." Only the circular was retained by the prosecution. The defense can be conducted only from explaining its content as well; but the file contains replies from the members of the Legionary organization, which clearly show, precisely, and without debate, that the circular was referring to someone else's informers in the midst of the Legionary Movement, not to the Legionary Movement's informers in other places.

2. The second objection.

Corneliu Z. Codreanu was put in the impossibility to formulate his memoir – which he was rightfully entitled to do — before the Indictment Chamber, a fact that, again, constitutes a flagrant violation of his right to a defense. According to art. 276 of the penal procedure, the Public Ministry, the civil part and the defendant, HAVE THE RIGHT to submit memoirs, letters." The submission of the memoir is, therefore, an uncontested right of the defendant. Whoever is given a right must be allowed to exercise it. The right is not platonic. Or, when the Final Ordinance has the date of 16th of May 1938, so it was written within a day (the proof that it was written on the 16th of May is the last interrogation that took place on the 16th of May as well, when the Ordinance couldn't be written yet), was addressed to the Prosecution, the Prosecution addressed it to the Indictment Chamber, the reporter made his report, the Indictment Chamber studied the files and drafted its own decision, we assume to believe that only through a painful irony it could be assumed the defendant and the defense would have had the material possibility, effective, in due time, to write the memoir which was given as a right by art. 276 in the penal procedure.

The motivation of the Court and the faults for which is requested.

The Court, in dealing with this objection and taking it into consideration through excess of power, somehow distorts the way in which the objection was presented, because it says nothing about violating the right to a defense, while the objection was presented in that way, namely, in connection with the complaint, and for which we complained in the second reason for the appeal of violating art. 103 penal procedure.

The Trial of Corneliu Zelea Codreanu

On the other hand, by arguing the certified copies are sufficient and that the files are left to the request of the Indictment Chamber to be sent to it or not, it violates the right to a defense by disregarding the categorical dispositions of art. 220, 221 C.M.J. combined with art. 276, 277, 279 from the penal procedure, as well as art. 305 combined with 270 point 3, last paragraph and 275, point 4 P.C, from which results that the case files, as well as the incriminated originals must exist in the Indictment Chamber, with the possibility that through their analyses to be able to reform the Ordinance, in a sense "that the case doesn't need to be prosecuted."

Reason II

The violation and misinterpretation of art. 221 C.M.J. combined with art. 281, 102, 103, 109, 275 point 4, and 270, point 3 P.C.: the violation of art. 103 from the Constitution given in 1923, now art. 75 from the Carol II Constitution and art. 228 P.C.

The Military Court, feeling the weakness of the arguments in its considerations when addressing the objection raised in the first reason for appeal, tries to hide behind a misinterpretation of art. 221 from C.M.J., with it violating all the articles mentioned in the title of the present reason for appeal.

Indeed, the Military Court says: the last paragraph of art. 221 from C.M.J. says that "The Indictment Chamber rules as a last resort." If by ruling as a last resort – the reasoning of the Military Court continues — it means that however they ruled, within or outside the law, nobody can complain. If nobody can complain, it concludes that nobody can rule. It ends with the conclusion that they are part of "nobody."

However, the problem is much more serious than the Public Ministry believes, also denouncing in this objection the Military Court that receives it.

First, we note that the objection raised by us was dedicated to the flawed notification given by the Military Court.

Art. 105 P.C. provides that: "the dispositions...relating to Court notices are always prescribed under penalty of nullity." The text also adds: "this nullity cannot be removed under any circumstance; it can be suggested at any point in the trial and has to be pronounced by the office." Under this circumstance, the Military Court cannot refuse to address the objection raised by us, because it concerns its notice.

The notices given by the Military Court can only be done from the order of the Indictment Chamber, as shown by art. 270 point 3, 275 point 4, and 279 P.C.

Or, if the decision of the Indictment Chamber represents the notice of the Military Court and if according to art. 103 P.C. concerning this notice, it's provided that the reasons for nullity cannot be removed — and more than that –, they can be suggested during the trial at any time, having to be pronounced by the office, only by violating the categorical dispositions of these last texts, the Military Court embarrasses itself by misinterpreting and violating art. 221, last paragraph of C.M.J.

Why do we say the Military Court misinterprets and violates the last paragraph of art. 221 C.M.J.?

First, it confuses two well-defined notions: final decisions with irrevocable decisions. Art. 221 C.M.J. says: "The Chamber rules as a last resort." That's all it says. This doesn't mean it has to be understood as: not subjected to the law, or not subjected to the appeal. This is not possible because the right to appeal would be violated, which is part of art. 103 from the Constitution given in 1923, today art. 75 in the Carol II Constitution, which is a Constitutional order.

If such an interpretation was shown by the High Court of Military Cassation, we expressly reserve the right to appeal it before the United Sections of the High Court of Cassation and Justice, art. 221, last paragraph, C.J.M, as unconstitutional, for a special reason in accordance with the law, with this reason mentioning the matter of unconstitutionality before the Honorary Court.

Therefore, the decision of the Indictment Chamber is subjected to the appeal, which means that it is in accordance to what can be understood from art. 224, last paragraph, C.M.J., saying the Decision of the Indictment Chamber is final; but not irrevocable.

In this sense, as art. 282 P.C. rarely contradicts the dispositions in C.M.J. it remains valid and has all the power. The consequence of applying it is that Decision Nr. 17 from the 17th of May 1938 of the Indictment Chamber of Army Corps II, couldn't constitute a lawful notice of the Military Court, because it didn't fulfill its obligations toward the defendant by communicating the Decision and notifying the General Prosecutor before the Military Court as it did today, so the defendant has the right to appeal the Decision of the Indictment Chamber; the Decision can be revoked.

The Trial of Corneliu Zelea Codreanu

In any case, if applying art. 282 P.C. was refused, the next step is to apply art. 35 from the Organic law of the High Court of Cassation and Justice, which gives 30 days, not 5 days from communicating and notifying the Prosecutor.

We observe that art. 282 does not give the right to appeal. No! From the content of art. 282 it is revealed that the right to appeal exists; and it only speaks of this right when requiring the Prosecutor to notify the defendant that he has this right. This is the fragment: "The Prosecutor notifies the defendant that he has the right...." The only modification brought by the text is the one concerning the deadline, reducing it from 30 days to 5 days.

Under these circumstances, we ask: Could the Military Court's notification be considered lawful according to the law if it was based on an irrevocable decision?

The Military Court must learn and receive the nullity of its notice by the obligations — the nullity sanction being of public nature — imposed by art. 103 P.C., because of the null decision given by the Indictment Chamber.

The Indictment Chamber's decision is null, when it is given as it was given in this case, without having the "case files" as it's provided by art. 281 P.C. According to this text, the Chamber's Decision must contain a detailed explanation. What type of detailed explanation can be given without a file? More, according to the same text: "The Chamber is required to give a statement on the essential means of defense, brought up either during the interrogation or through a memoir." We ask: How can the Chamber fulfill this obligation, without a file, and especially, without the "memoir" as they did, the defendant being put in the impossibility, as shown in the first reason for the appeal, to give his memoir? All these dispositions are prescribed "under the sanction of nullity."

But, by applying the general principles found in the chapter about nullity in the penal code, the nullity of the Indictment Chamber imposes in consequence the nullity of the Sentence given by the Military Court. Art. 102 P.C. provides the nullity of the document when a document is declared as null, bringing the nullity of the prior documents, concomitant, or following it, as this nullity is "imposed by a causal connection." Therefore, the null Decision of the Indictment Chamber nullifies the Sentence given by the Military Court because of the intimate connection between the two: The Decision of the Indictment Chamber serves as the notifying document for the Military Court, the second not being able to rule without it.

262   Romanian Crucible

We conclude this reason by saying the Military Court was required, according to art. 103 P.C. to state the nullity of its notice, one hand, because the notice document, namely Decision Nr. 17 from May 17th 1938 from the Indictment Chamber still being subjected to the appeal could be reformed, still not being irrevocable (not even today), and, on the other hand, the notice given through a null document imposed thought the causality provided by art. 109 P.C. the same finding regarding the invalidity of its notice, repeating at the same time the matter of notifying the Court, implicitly art. 103, are of public order, being able to be brought up anywhere, in any state of affairs, even in the office.

Reason III

Violation of the right to a defense. Violation of art. 335 C.M.J. Fact distortion. Failure to state the reasons.

The defense revealed a concrete, indisputable fact to the Military Court, namely that it was given the same treatment as the Indictment Chamber, in the sense that it wasn't provided all of the documents, which caused it to be unable to prepare a full defense.

Art. 335 C.M.J. precisely shows that, in this case, the Defense is justified to ask to postpone the trial for the near future.

The Court, however, disputes the evidence saying: that the Defense had the files before the trial. Aside from the uncontested fact that, repeatedly, the files were requested through petition, and the absence of certain files was shown through reports — petitions and reports registered with the Background Court — proof of this absence also being constituted by the address Nr. 213 from May 16th 1938 of Cabinet V Instruction to the Prosecution of the Military Court, and especially by the address Nr. 17, 130 from May 17th 1938 of the Prosecution of the M[il]itary Court to the Indictment Chamber, which can show that a part of the files were sent to the Capitol Police Prefecture.

So, we can prove the files were removed from the Military Courthouse, and there is no proof they were returned in due time. The absence of these documents prevented the Defense from doing its job, by not having access to the original incriminating documents, and to the rest of the pieces that were widely explained as the first reason for the appeal.

The Trial of Corneliu Zelea Codreanu

The Military Court's statement that the Defense had the files, constitutes a flagrant distortion of reality, and implicitly, a flawed reason, violating, at the same time, by disregarding art. 335 C.M.J. (by lying, the files were not missing), by which we could have been granted a term. The violation of the right to a defense is obvious.

Reason IV

Abuse of power. Violation of art. 313 C.M.J. Flawed interrogation. Complete and incomplete questions. Violation and misinterpretation of art. 191 points 1 and 2, and 126 Penal Code. Lack of constitutive elements of the offense.

Violation of art. 314 C.M.J. Violation of the principle *"Nul poena sine lege"* (art. 1 Penal Code)

Wrong legal classification. Violation R.D.I. Nr. 856/938 regarding the state of siege, comb. With art. 110 and the next in C.M.J, and with art. 393 point 2 C.M.J. Incompetency.

Describing the reasons:

A. The questioning of guilt regarding the "crime of treason by possessing and publishing secret documents concerning the security of the State" are completely flawed, disregarding the substantial juridical conditions provided by the texts mentioned above. First, the questions of guilt must also contain and mention every factual element and every element of the law that characterize the imputation for which the defendant was sent to trial, as this indictment was determined and classified by the Final Ordinance and the Decision of the Indictment Chamber.

In this case, all these elements had to be revealed by the wording of the questions:

a. Were the secret documents part of those provided by art. 190 and 191 P.C.?

b. Were these documents secret for their content?

c. Do these documents refer to the external security of the State?

d. Were they of the nature that if, known by another State, to touch on the external security of our State, on its sovereignty, on our independence or on our relations with other States? (because otherwise, the "crime of treason" is impossible!)

e. Did the defendant have the intention to transmit these documents to a foreign power, with the intention of aiding that power in damaging our Country, meaning committing an "act of treason" (animus hostilis)?

But none of these essential elements were used, which makes the whole questioning completely flawed.

Another would have been the Court's solution, if the accusatory questions had contained, as the law requires, these elements, because, in this case, the answers could have been negative — the offense lacking its constitutive elements, because you can't have a "crime of treason" without the "documents" being part of the ones provided by art. 190 P.C. and without these documents being possessed with the intention of being transmitted to a foreign power, our Penal Code not recognizing crimes without international elements and crimes of treason without the intention of treason.

On the other hand, the questions are complex and the meaning of the word "intentions" is not mentioned enough, the general term being used instead of the one specific to the imputed crime.

In this way, through excess of power, the Court violated art. 313 C.M.J., as well as art.191, points 1 and 2, and 120 P.C. that were misinterpreted and wrongfully applied.

B. From the way the accusatory questions are formulated, it shows the Court changed –without discussing it with the parts and without putting it from the office, as art. 314 C.M.J requires "subsidiary matters"- the classification of the "crime of treason" by possessing secret documents concerning the (external) security of the State (which the defendant was on trial for) in "crime of possessing secret documents concerning the (internal) security of the State".

By doing so, the Court, through excess of power, violated art. 314 C.M.J, created a new criminal fact unprovided by the law, "the crime of possessing secret documents concerning the internal security of the State", violating the principle "*nula pena sine lege*" art 1. P.C.

C. The accusatory questions, knowing the fact of possession and publication of documents concerning the security of the State, doesn't include the element that this possession was done with the intention of committing treason, meaning, with the intention of possessing these documents to make them available for a foreign government or its agents.

The Trial of Corneliu Zelea Codreanu

The offense was included in the provisions of art. 191, points 1 and 2 P.C. combined with art. 190 to which it refers, regarding treason.

Or, this treason is not legally possible without "*animus hostilis*" towards the Country, the national criminal, this element being the essence of this crime.

Because this element was recurrently disregarded in the accusatory questions, and as it doesn't result from the whole content of the case file, the classification of the offense in the provisions of art 191, points 1 and 2, combined with art. 190 P.C. is devoid of any consistency.

And because the classification of the offense is a matter of law, which can be brought up before the Appeals Court, it follows to find the legal consequences caused by this lack of constitutive elements which qualify an offense.

The offense, legally, escaping the provisions of art. 191 points 1 and 2, combined with art 190 P.C., cannot receive a legal classification — given the nature of the orders claimed to have been possessed by the defendant, orders regarding the internal security of the State at most (being simple measures of internal police with an obvious political preoccupation) — being a simple police contravention, which doesn't justify, not even during a state of siege, the competency of the Military Court.

Because the decree to extend the state of siege in the whole Country, as well as the previous decrees, caused the Military Court to rule in trials for non-military offenders who commit crimes regarding the public order and the security of the State, and because the nature of the offense is one that sets the exceptional jurisdiction and not the article that classifies an offense, in this case, as that was a simple police contravention (see art. 583 P.C.), the Military Court was not competent to rule, and for these reasons we require the case to be sent to a normal Court, as neither of the other two offenses the appellant was charged with, also by misclassification, do not justify the competency of the Military Court, because they do not meet the component elements of the offense provided by the applied text.

Reason V

Violation of art. 137 P.C., of the right to a defense provided by art. 294 and 309 C.M.J; failure to state reasons; abuse of power.

During the oral debates, the defense has raised an objection in three parts, regarding the offenses provided by art. 209, point 4 P.C. and classified as "conspiracy against social order" in the following circumstances:

The appellant, Corneliu Z. Codreanu, never admitted, neither during the interrogation, nor before the Court, to be the author of the letter addressed to Adolf Hitler, a letter that constitutes the main evidence for the offense provided by art. 209, point 4 P.C.

This was followed by the constant efforts of the appellant, as well as of the Defense, to find the real author of that letter. From a happy circumstance and led by the repetition in the letter of some specific phrases, that were also a true obsession in a book called *Neocooperația*, written by a senior official named Rădulescu Thanir, the defense — after receiving a copy of the book with the signature of the author, the signature was identical to the handwriting of the letter the appellant had been charged with — contacted Mr. Thanir, who admitted being the author of the letter addressed to Adolf Hitler, and agreed to testify before the Military Court, thus joining the defense in the War Council.

Faced with this new situation, which could help with dismissing a serious judicial error, the defense, in due time, asked for Mr. Thanir to be heard as an informer, and the hearing of the person who was given that signed volume of his book, while both of them were waiting outside the courtroom. We also requested a graphic expert to prove the writing from the dedication on the book is the same as that from the letter addressed to Adolf Hitler, which the appellant was accused of writing.

The Military Court overruled the objection for reasons based on art. 309 C.M.J. The Court considers there is no need for the informers to give testimonies, and also, there is no need for the expertise requested by the defense.

Considering the Court adopted this decision through a flagrant abuse of power, our evidence was rejected by completely disregarding the right to a defense and by violating the texts shown above.

The evidence was meant finally to show the judges that the piece on which the imputation for conspiring against social order is based on, belongs to a third party, that has nothing to do with the trial, as that person takes responsibility for the content of the incriminating piece.

The Trial of Corneliu Zelea Codreanu

Such evidence is not likely to be dismissed. We don't believe there are records in the annals of Justice for a second precedent like the present one, namely: to indicate the real author of an incriminating piece of evidence that is the subject of the criminal trial. The person agrees to be brought to the trial and the Court refuses to hear him.

But the very formula used to overrule the objection is completely illegal. The President is sovereign when it comes to the people called to testify during the debates, but when a request to contest arises, as the whole panel of judges assumes its resolution, there is no more sovereignty. When the Court makes a decision, it must give reasons for it.

However, the statement of reasons implies not just simply stating that a request for evidence is not necessary, lacking opportunity, but it must show why the suggested evidence is not necessary.

Or, in this case, when it comes to hearing the suggested people, as well as the experts, the Court doesn't motivate why the testimony and the expertise are not appropriate, simply stating that it has sovereignty to make decisions, without giving the actual reasons as to why the defense's request is inconvenient and inconclusive.

The provisions of the law as well as the basic right to a defense were disregarded, meaning the sentence given under these circumstances cannot be valid.

Reason VI

Failure to state reasons; abuse of power; violation of art. 137 P.C.; violation of the right to a defense.

The appellant and his defenders insisted on the hearing of at least a part of the factual witnesses, who were necessary to prove his innocence. In this category of witnesses are included the former associates of Corneliu Z. Codreanu, who were arrested and kept by force in a residence decided upon by the executive power. The importance of these witnesses was essential. All of them were in close connection and had knowledge about events connected to the charges.

The Court rejected the request as "inconvenient." Flagrantly disregarding the right to a defense and violating art. 137, P.C., according to which evidence can only be rejected as inconclusive.

The Court has to give reasons on why it was not conclusive to bring and hear the witnesses as requested, witnesses who, because the Court admitted for them to be summoned again, were won in the debates and their absence could only be motivated by a serious event. Simple statements have never constituted a motivation.

Reason VII

Violation of art. 313 C.M.J, comb. With art. 209, pt. 4 P.C.; Incomplete and flawed questioning.

The matter of guilt must state the concrete material facts that result from the legal elements.

The appellant was convicted of the crime of conspiring against social order, when the question of guilt didn't contain any mention about material circumstances.

Nothing is specified, so the question of quilt is abstract, but the appellant is convicted for alleged concrete facts, which we don't see anywhere.

The question simply asks if he has ever been in connection with a foreign association with an international character. But what association is that and what would demonstrate its international character?

However, is it possible to support such a theory that the appellant had connections to international associations? Where does it say this in the case file?

Then where is the association? Nothing is mentioned. And he still was convicted of it.

But the question also states that certain help and instructions of any kind were requested; which are these instructions and help? Nothing is mentioned, but a person cannot be convicted for nothing.

It's always said that he wanted to change the social order. How and by which means, it's not mentioned, vague terms are used, simply copying the letter of the law, the appellant being convicted without any mention of material facts. Of course, such questioning cannot justify the conviction, and, for the reasons stated above, it has to be annulled.

The Trial of Corneliu Zelea Codreanu

Reason VIII

Violation of art. 313 C.J.M., comb. With art. 210 P.C.; Incomplete and flawed questioning; failure to state reasons.

The same total lack of mentioning the material facts is found when looking at the questions of guilt that refer to the crime of rebellion.

The text of law requires the offender to be the direct cause for arming the population, but where was this element proven in this case? It was not possible to show it and that's why it wasn't proven.

Then, the armed people had to be mentioned and use them to prove they were armed as a result of the defendant's actions. They then speak of weapon deposits, without stating where they were and who established them.

A total lack of statements on material facts resulted in giving a flawed verdict.

Reason IX

Violation of art. 274 C.M.J., combined with art. 328, pt. 7 C.J.M., and 393, pt. 4 C.J.M. Violation of art. 311 C.J.M. combined with art. 304, pt. 10 P.C.; Essential omission; excess of power; violation of the right to a defense.

The publicity of debates is one of the main conditions of repressive ruling. This principle is guaranteed by the C.J.M. through art. 271 and 328 pt. 14 and 15. These dispositions and this principle guarantee the citizen's control on the judicial legality, that's why the defendant and the defense are especially entitled to request and impose the publicity of the debates.

It's true that art. 271, paragraph 2, gives the right to take the disposition of the secret sentence ex officio. But when the parts intervene with such a request, to guarantee the right to a defense, the defendant's team must also be listened to.

In this case, it's visible from the sentence that the Public Ministry asked for a secret hearing during the trial to read a piece of evidence; but the Court stated its decision to declare a secret hearing without asking for the opinion of the Defense, especially since the same Court had decided to hold a secret hearing only when it concerned one part of the interrogation referring to the crime of conspiring against social order.

Romanian Crucible

The Defense was denied its rights by the violation of art. 311 C.M.J., combined with art. 304 pt. 10 P.C.; and the essential omission mentioned for this reason, brings the cessation of the Conviction Sentence, according to the provisions of art. 393 pt. 4 C.M.J.

Reason X

Violation of art. 311 and 312 C.M.J., combined with art. 393, pt. 4 C.M.J. Essential omission. Violation of the right to a defense.

Art. 312 C.M.J. shows that the "President," under the sanction of nullity, asks the defendant if he has anything else to add to his defense, after which he will close the debates and no other act of debate can take place.

In this case, however, these provisions were not respected, expressly under the sanction of nullity.

So, it's clear that as soon as the defendant speaks his last words, the debates are closed and no other act of debate can take place.

The defendant was given the last word, and after that the objection regarding the witnesses was raised again; even though this objection was part of the debate, because, if it had been admitted, the debates would have continued. So, on one hand, even though the debates were closed, an objection regarding the debates was resolved, and on the other hand, the provisions of art. 311 C.M.J. were disregarded, that says: "the defendant and his defense have the last word, under the sanction of nullity."

For these considerations, that show the violation of some dispositions expressly provided under the sanction of nullity, we request the Cessation of the conviction sentence.

Trial Notes

1. Reference to well-known facts: surprised by some of the views expressed by Nicolae Iorga (1871-1940) in the press in relation to some issues with the evolution of commerce (in this case, the place and role of Jews), in a complete contradiction to what he had stated before, Corneliu Zelea Codreanu, even though he imposed on himself and on the Legionary Movement (the All for the Country Party had been dissolved on February 21st 1938), after the dictatorship of King Carol II was established in February 1938, a cautious attitude. He sent a letter to the great historian, qualifying him, among others, as "incorrect" and "dishonest at heart" (see Annex I and Duiliu Sfințescu, ed., *Corneliu Zelea Codreanu. 1899-1938*, ed. III, f.1., Ed Fundației Buna Vestire, 1933, pp. 109-111). Iorga immediately and openly replied, the press being on top of his reaction starting with the 29th of March 1938, these lines grabbing the attention, as they came from a great personality, and above all, from the part of a state minister in the first government of Patriarch Miron Cristea (1868-1939) under the royal dictatorship: "They're sent back, with the most justifiable indication, these witless words from someone who, remembering how much blood has been spilled by him and as a result of his actions, he should descend in his conscience and repent, sparing the country the dangers lurking over it." The interested circles, especially Carol II and the chamberlain, didn't miss the opportunity, intervening and taking approaches that placed the two parties on irreconcilable positions, seeding the sign of a future tragedy. Thus, on the 28th of March, received in an audience with the King, Armand Călinescu (1893-1939) discussed with him the incident and suggested solutions: "I propose a criminal investigation of Codreanu on the subject of the slander of Iorga. Eventually, the arrest of those who'd side with him." After the bad advice from his uninspired chamberlain, N. Iorga notified the Military Prosecution of the slander against a minister in office. The first prosecutor of the Military Court of Army Corps 2, immediately started a public action against Corneliu Zelea Codreanu, the case being taken over by Instruction Cabinet 5 of that courthouse. Summoned for interrogation on the 31st of March 1938, Corneliu Zelea Codreanu was absent. Iorga, who on March 30th, 1938, stopped being a minister in office in order to be appointed a royal counselor, addressed a letter to the Military Court that contained the accusation of "high treason" against the Captain, and he wanted the

Romanian Crucible

letter to be used as testimony, the historian preferring — for reasons of illness and scientific matters –not to come to the trial. The incident aided Carol II and the chamberlain to start the campaign that had already been planned (see A. călinescu's diary entry on March 13th 1938), to quarrel with the Legionary leaders and with the Movement itself. On the night of 16/17th of April 1938 the plan was ignited, debuting with the arrest of Corneliu Zelea Codreanu and the discovery of some "compromising" documents for the Legionary Movement and the Captain, for threats to the security of the Romanian State. We must remember that, on the 16th, 17th, and 18th of April 1938, N. Iorga sent a telegram and two identical letters to Colonel Radu Hotineanu, the Royal Commissary of Army Corps 2, stating that he was withdrawing his slander claims against Corneliu Zelea Codreanu, being convinced that the defendant "doesn't realize what he's doing." Everything was futile. Through the sentence given on April 19th 1938, Corneliu Zelea Codreanu was convicted and sentenced to 6 months in prison, a 2,000 lei fine, and 500 lei in court costs. (For details, see Faust Brădescu, *La Garde de Fer et le terrorisme. A l'occasion du semicentenaire du Mouvement Legionnaire*, Madrid, Edition Carpații/ Traian Popescu, 1979, pp. 144-163). Forced to execute this sentence, Corneliu Zelea Codreanu — through the Ordinance that we reproduced — is sent to this trial staged by Carol's regime, that took place between 23-27th of May 1938. We also know what followed: The Captain was sentenced to 10 years of forced labor, moved from Jilava to Doftana, and finally, to Râmnicu Sărat (for the organization and evolution of the "trial" we sent again to Faust Bradesco, op. Cit., pp. 163-176; *Mișcarea Legionară, Adevărul în procesul Căpitanului*, ediție Traian Golea, Miami Beach, Colecția "Omul Nou", nr. 43, 1980, 250 p.) from where he was taken with other 13 Legionary leaders by a "police commando squad," organized and under the orders of the sovereign and the chamberlain, and all of them were executed under the classic pretext of "attempting to escape from under escort." Such an unfolding of events set a report of cause and effect between N. Iorga's efforts in March-April 1938 and the arrest, conviction, and assassination of Corneliu Zelea Codreanu (see especially the media attacks in September-November 1940, in *Porunca Vremii* from September 8th, 1940; idem. From September 10th, 1940, the resounding article written by I.P. Preundeni, the first editor of the publication called *Disecția unui călău: N. Iorga*; *Buna Vestire* from September 22nd, 1940, etc.), a situation which Horia Sima and his associates exploited in November, 1940, holding power in cooperation with the team of General Ion Antonescu, to plan and fulfill a new political crime, inadmissible, but incredibly and shameful for the Romanian nation, because it was about sacrificing one of the greatest personalities of the national civilization. (For details, see: N. Iorga, *Ultimele*, ed. Stelian Neagoe, Craiova, Scrisul Românesc, 1978, p. LXXIII-LXXXIV; Mircea Mușat, Ion Ardeleanu, *România după Marea Unire*, II/2,

The Trial of Corneliu Zelea Codreanu

1939-1940, Bucureşti, Ed. Ştiinţifică şi Enciclopedică 1988, pp. 812-816; Titus Georgescu, *Nicolae Iorga împotriva hitlerismului*, Bucureşti, Ed. Ştiinţifică şi Enciclopedică, 1991, p. 353-354; Armand Călinescu, *Însemnări politice. 1916-1939*, ed. Al. Gh. Savu, Bucureşti, Ed. Humanitas, 1990, pp. 366-398).

2. Mihail Stelescu (1906-1936), one of the youngest and most appreciated associates of Corneliu Zelea Codreanu in the years when the Iron Guard was active as a political group of the Legionary Movement (April 1930-December 1933), together with Ion Moţa, Vasile Marin, Radu Mironovici, etc. Parliamentarian of the Guard, opposing adversary of I.G. Duca. He resigned from the Legion, establishing, together with other colleagues, the White Eagle (*Vulturul Alb*) group, which in 1934 changed its name to Romanian Crusade (with a newspaper having the same name), and reuniting General N. Rădescu, Panait Istrate, Al. Talex, Gh. Beza, C. Dumitrescu-Zăpadă, etc. The new right-wing political group was decisively anti-communist, hostile to Hitler's fascism, just as the All for the Country Party, which politically represented the Legionary Movement between December 1934 and February 1938. In 1935-1936, M. Stelescu carried out — especially though the Romanian Crusade — a fierce press campaign against the Legionary Movement and Corneliu Zelea Codreanu personally. In a famous letter from April 1935, he impulsively called the Captain a "criminal." The members of his former nest sentenced him to death and savagely assassinated him in a clinic at Spitalul Brâncovenesc. The investigation and the trial that followed didn't manage to find Corneliu Zelea Codreanu guilty of having been involved in the planning and assassination, but the ones who carried it out (Ion Caratănase, Iosif Bozăntan, Ştefan Curcă, I. Atanasiu, Bogdan Gavrilă, Ion State, Ion Pele, Vlad Radu, I. Trandafir, and Ştefan Georgescu) were all sentenced, except for the last two (10 years of forced labor), to labor for life. This group of the ten men rapidly became legends of the Legion called *Decemviri*, just like the assassins of I.G. Duca — *Nicadorii* (Nicolae Constantinescu, I. Caranica, and Doru Belimace), were advanced by Corneliu Zelea Codreanu to the rank of Legionary commanders and awarded with the "White Cross." All of them — Nicadorii, Decemvirii, and Corneliu Zelea Codreanu — were assassinated on the 29-30th of November 1938 (see Ştefan Palaghiţă, *Garda de Fier spre reînvierea României*, ed. A II-a, Bucureşti, Ed. Roza Vânturilor, 1933, p. 52-53; M. Muşat, Ion Ardeleanu, *România după Marea Unire*, II/2, pp. 325-327; Nistor Chioreanu, *Morminte vii*, Iaşi, Ed. Institutului European, 1922, pp. 26-28; *Universul*, nr. 197/19 March 1936; *Adevărul*, nr. 16098/18 July 1936; *Dimineaţa*, nr. 10622/22 July 1936).

Romanian Crucible

3. General Gheorghe (Zizi) Cantacuzino-Grănicerul (1869-1937), a descendant of the Cantacuzino family, and fighter in the campaigns from 1913 and 1916-1918. Regimented after World War I in Grigore Filipescu's Vlad Țepeș League (conservative), deputy in various legislatures, assigned by Corneliu Zelea Codreanu as the head of the new party on the 10th of December 1934 — All for the Country. As he himself stated, Gh. Cantacuzino-Grănicerul accepted to be the leader of the group that politically represented the Legionary Movement (legally recognized on the 25th of March 1935), with the condition that the "spiritual leader" would be Corneliu Zelea Codreanu (see Mircea Mușat, Ion Ardeleanu, *România după Marea Unire*, II/2, pp. 326-329). After the General's death in October 1937, Gh. Clime became the leader of the All for the Country Party (Florea Nedelcu, *De la Restaurație la dictatura regală. Din viața politică a României, 1930-1938*, Cluj-Napoca, Ed. Dacia, 1981, p. 195). Also see the recent memoirs about the General, published by Dr. Haralambie Teodoru (in *Învierea*, nr. 2/ April-June 1993, pp. 23-25).

4. It should be noted that the clarification came in support of, not against Corneliu Zelea Codreanu, as the Ordinance wanted to suggest.

5. The confusion suggested is only intended by the Ordinance, and at that time or later it was often made by the political leaders, historians, adversaries, and even by the members or party members of the Legion. In fact, the Iron Guard and the All for the Country had clearly represented (1930-1933, respectively 1934-1938) the groups that successively had political activity in the name of the Legion of the Archangel Michael (founded in Iași, on the 24th of June 1927, under the leadership of Corneliu Zelea Codreanu). The Legion, frequently called the Legionary Movement at the end of the 1930s, until it was established as such by Royal Decree on 14th of September 1940, a decree that assigned General Ion Antonescu as the Prime Minister, and Horia Sima as the leader of the National-Legionary State and of the Legionary Regime (see *Marshal Ion Antonescu, Un ABC al anticomunismului*, I, ed. Gh. Buzatu, Iași, Ed. Moldova, 1992, p. 83-84; Ștefan Palaghiță, op. cit., p. 140-141). It represented –from the point of view of the leaders — the spiritual side of the action initiated by Corneliu Zelea Codreanu and his friends. While "analyzing" Corneliu Zelea Codreanu, Mircea Eliade observes in *Memorii* that, "for him (for Corneliu Zelea Codreanu), the Legionary Movement didn't represent a political phenomenon, but an ethical and religious essence" (cf. *Memorii. Recoltele solstițiului*, II, 1937-1960, București, Ed. Humanitas, 1991, p. 26). The political groups of the Legionary Movement/Legion were forbidden (as is the case of the Iron Guard, on December 9th 1933, dissolved by the I.G. Duca government, or the case of the All for the Country Party that auto-dissolved at the

The Trial of Corneliu Zelea Codreanu

wishes of Corneliu Zelea Codreanu on February 21st, 1938), but the Legion/Legionary Movement couldn't be dissolved, not even until today, despite all the decrees and measures, that most times meant exterminating its members, taken especially during the communist "era" (see, especially, *Semicentenarul Mișcării Legionare. Legiunea în imagini (1927-1977)*, Madrid, 1977, ed. De Centrul de Studii și Documentare al Mișcării Legionare din Madrid; *Gazeta de Vest — Almanah 1994: Legiunea Arhanghelului Mihail de la trecut la 275umina275*, ed. Ovidiu Guleș, Timișoara, Editura Gordiau, 1994, p. 203). Generally, it is considered that the evolution of the Legionary Movement had two steps: the first was marked by the presence of Corneliu Zelea Codreanu or his direct associates in the leadership of the Legionary Movement (1927-1938/1939), and the second one was determined by the rise and maintenance of Horia Sima (1939-1993) (see especially *Horia Sima și raporturile lui cu Mișcarea Legionară. Documente*, București, 1993). In fact, Horia Sima himself confirmed this reality in some of his memoirs, namely that the Legionary Movement without C.Z. Codreanu meant something else, if not when it came to ideology, but when it came to actions (see especially Horia Sima, *Sfârșitul unei domnii sângeroase. 10 Decembrie 1939- 6 Septembrie 1940*, Madrid, Editura Mișcării Legionare, 1977, passim). During longer or shorter periods of time, the leadership of the Legionary Movement belonged to: Corneliu Zelea Codreanu (1927-1938); Radu Mironovici (1938); Ion Belgea (1938); Constantin Papanace (1938); Horia Sima (1938); C. Papanace (1938); Al. Cantacuzino (1938); Vasile Cristescu-Horia Sima (1938-1939) and Horia Sima (1939-1993) (see Șt. Palaghiță, op. cit., passim; "Cronologie privind istoria Mișcării legionare," in *Istoria Mișcării legionare*, ed. Dan Zamfirescu, București, Ed. Roza Vânturilor, 1993, pp. 15-38). (*Cronologie legionară*... to which further references will be made, first appeared in the newspaper *Cuvântul* on November 9th, 1940. After the war, complete and improved, it was reedited twice by the Legionary Movement in exile, in the collection called "Omul Nou," precisely: *Cronologie legionară*, Salzburg, 1953, nr. 26 and Miami Beach, 1992, nr. 53). The problem with the succession and the successors of C.Z. Codreanu is controversial from a historical point of view. According to Faust Bradesco, on June 16th, 1938, with the Captain's consent, the leadership commandment of the Legionary Movement was established (Ion Belgea, Iordache Nicoară, Ion Antoniu, Gh. Dragomir Jilava, C. Papanace, and Horia Sima), succeeded in October 1938 by a new secret commandment: V. Cristescu, Horia Sima, Priest I. Dumitrescu-Borșa, C. Papanace, N. Pătrașcu, and Al. Cantacuzino (cf. Faust Bradesco, *La Garde De Fer et le terrorisme*, p. 178-179). In May 1939, a new "Commandment of the Legion was founded in Berlin" — I. Dumitrescu-Borșa, C. Papanace, Horia Sima, I. Victor Vojen, Victor Silaghi, and Alexandru Constant (ibidem, p. 189). Regarding the Legionary

276 Romanian Crucible

ranks the Ordinance was referring to, these were: Legionary member, Legionary instructor, assistant commander, Legionary commander, member of the Legionary Senate, and the commander of the Legion. On the other hand, the functions in the Legion were as follows: nest leader, leader of multiple nests, team leader, net leader, county leader, party leader, general secretary, Legionary judge, clerk, etc. (M. Muşat, Ion Ardeleanu, *România după Marea Unire*, II/2, p. 335).

6. Engineer Gheorghe Clime (1889-1939), founder of the Legionary Workers' Corps (1936) and the president of the All for the Country Party (1937-1938). He was arrested and detained in Râmnicu Sărat where he was executed during the carnage that was ordered by Carol's authorities immediately after the Prime Minister Armand Călinescu was shot on the 21st of September 1939, against the Legionaries imprisoned in the Râmnicu Sărat prison, in the Military Hospital in Braşov, and in the concentration camps from Miercurea Ciuc and from Vaslui (cf. Nae Tudorică, *Mărturisiri. În duhul adevărului. Mişcarea Legionară şi Căpitanul aşa cum au fost*, Bacău, Ed. Plumb, 1993, pp. 278-289; *Învierea*, nr. I/ January-March 1993, p. 107; Florea Nedelcu, *De la Restauraţie la dictatura regală. Din viaţa politică a României, 1930-1938*, Cluj-Napoca, Ed. Dacia, 1981, pp. 430-432). As for Gh. Clime, he was tortured and disfigured before being shot on the 21-22nd of September 1939, for the purpose of making him forcefully admit to ordering the assassination of Prime Minister Armand Călinescu. In the assassinations that followed Armand Călinescu's suppression, directed by the new prime minister, General Gh. Argeşanu and the minister of internal affairs, General Gabriel Marinescu, not only the assassins of the former prime minister were executed without a trial, but all of the "old" leadership, the elite of the Legionary Movement, all the former associates of Corneliu Zelea Codreanu (between 250 and 301 Legionaries). According to Ştefan Palaghiţă it was about the "whole Legionary elite" (Ştefan Palaghiţă, op. cit., pp. 1017/1026; Nicholas M. Nagy-Talavera, *The Green Shirts and the Others: A History of Fascism in Hungary and Romania*, Las Vegas: Center for Romanian Studies, 2021, p. 304; Duiliu Sfinţescu, ed., op. Cit., pp. 187-195; Mihai Fătu, Ion Spălăţelu, *Garda de Fier, organizaţie teroristă de tip fascist*, ed. A II-a, Bucureşti, Ed. Politică, 1980, pp. 242-243). The German historian Armin Heinen, the author of one of the most solid monographs dedicated to the history of the Legion, considers the facts under discussion mark the end of the formation founded by Corneliu Zelea Codreanu, as a "socialist movement" (see Armin Heinen, *Die Legion "Erzengel Michael" in Rumanien. Soziale Bewegung und politische Organisation. Ein Beitrag zum Problem des internationalen Faschismus*, Munchen, R. Oldenbourg Verlag, 1986, pp. 364-379).

The Trial of Corneliu Zelea Codreanu

7. *Nicadorii* — the group of the three Legionaries (Nicolae Constantinescu, Ion Caranica, and Doru Belimace) who assassinated Prime Minister I.G. Duca, on December 29th, 1933, in the train station in Sinaia. After the assassination they turned themselves in to the authorities, they were tried, convicted, and sentenced to forced labor for life in 1934. It should be noted that, at the same time, Corneliu Zelea Codreanu, General Gh. Cantacuzino-Grănicerul and 40 other Legionaries considered as "moral authors" were tried as well, but they were all acquitted. Some members of the judge panel, some Generals (Petrovicescu, Dona, and Filip) became members of the All for the Country Party (see N.M. Nagy-Talavera, op. Cit., pp. 285-286; M. Mușat, Ion Ardeleanu, op. Cit., II/2, p. 323-324).

8. Prince Alexandru Cantacuzino (1905-1939), diplomat, advisor to Corneliu Zelea Codreanu, Legionary commander, assassinated while imprisoned in Râmnicu Sărat, on the night of 21/22nd of December 1939 (cf. *Învierea*, nr. 1/ January-March 1993, pp. 157-158). The author of important works that explain the Legionary ideology, published during his life, but also after his death, in the country, and especially abroad, under the care of Romanian editors from abroad: *Între lumea legionară și lumea comunistă*, ed. II, București, 1940; *Românul de mâine*, București, various editions, 1935-1937-1940; *Cum suntem*, ed. II, București, 1940 ș.a.; *Opere complete* (1935-1937), Munchen, 1969 (Col. "Omul Nou" nr. 37) and ed. A II-a, Miami Beach, 1990 (the same collection, nr. 45). In 1936 Alexandru (Alecu) Cantacuzino had an important role in the congress in Târgu Mureș, and in 1936-1937 he became a hero in Spain. As a result, he became the commander of the Moța-Marin Elite Corps. He was arrested and imprisoned, but managed to escape in 1938. He is the author of the Legionary manifesto from the 13th of October 1938, in which they asked for a review of the staged trial of Corneliu Zelea Codreanu, and the end of the anti-Legionary activity that King Carol II and Prime Minister Armand Călinescu were orchestrating. Alecu Cantacuzino became, according to eyewitnesses, a sort of red flag used to taunt the tyrant Carol II (cf. C. Papanace, *Fără Căpitan. Conducerea în a doua prigoană*, Roma, Editura "Armatoli", 1984, pp. 91-98).

9. In October 1923, Corneliu Zelea Codreanu with a group of nationalist students from Iași, Cluj, and Cernăuți (Ion Moța, Corneliu Georgescu, Vernichescu, Ilie Gârneață, Radu Mironovici, Tudor Popescu, and others) planned the so-called "student plot from Dealul Spirii," which aimed at shooting certain "traitorous politicians" (Gh. Mârzescu and others belonging to the group of "Jewish plutocrats," Aristide and Mauriciu Blank). During their meeting in Bucharest (October 8th 1923), they were all arrested. They were tried and acquitted on the 29th of March 1924. A day before, however, Ion Moța, the

Romanian Crucible

president of the Student's Center in Cluj, wanted to punish one of them inside the prison in Vacăreşti, for being found responsible for betraying them –student Vernichescu (from Cluj). Moţa was the only friend of Corneliu Zelea Codreanu that remained in prison, being tried later (September 1924) for his actions, and acquitted (see *Cronologie...*, p. 16-17; Corneliu Zelea Codreanu, *Pentru Legionari*, I, Sibiu, Editura "Totul pentru Ţară," 1936, pp. 168-192; A. Vântu, Ion I. Moţa. "Schiţă biografică," in *Cuvântul Studenţesc*, Bucureşti, year XII, nr. 1-4/ January-February 1937, pp. 2-20).

10. The Ordinance refers to a series of assassinations that marked the evolution of the Legion, and that weighed heavily when looking at the Movement and its political groups as a whole. It is worth remembering that C.Z. Codreanu himself and his comrades, tried later to lessen the impact of those assassinations in the conscience of public opinion: the Captain, for example, referring to the Manciu case, noted it down as a "tragic revenge" (cf. Corneliu Zelea Codreanu, *Pentru Legionari*, I, p. 226), and *Cronologia* from 1940 inserted it among "political moments" (cf. *Istoria Mişcării Legionare*, p. 17). On the other hand, the Communist press and the Marxist history, for reasons easy to understand, found the darkest words to describe the perpetrators — "criminals," followers of a "doctrine of violence," etc. (Mihai Fătu, Ion Spălăţelu, *Garda de Fier...*, pp. 47-50). This happened while the crimes committed by the Communists themselves, before the killing of the Police Prefect of Iaşi, Manciu, and, at the same time, of the Police Inspector Clos, were completely ignored. The peak of ridicule was reached when, to illustrate the "hostility against fascism" of the Romanian nation, they made references to those who were under the "ideological influence" of the Communist Party, so the Communists and the servants of Kremlin- P. Constantinescu-Iaşi, M. Deleanu, Ilie Pintilie, L. Pătrăşcanu, Grigore Preoteasa, Mihail Roller, Walter Roman, Leonte Răutu, Ştefan Voicu, Barbu Zaharescu, etc. (Ibidem, p. 69-70). To not return to the cases quoted in the Ordinance, we ask the reader to check the notes about I.G. Duca's assassination and the one of Mihail Stelescu, and when it comes to the killing of Manciu, which was not ignored in any of the history books about the Legion, details can be found even in Corneliu Zelea Codreanu's book (cf. *Pentru 278umina278s278*, I, pp. 224-249; see *Cazul Manciu*, Orăştie, Tipografia "Libertatea", 1927): the execution, imprisonment, and the trials from Iaşi, Focşani, and Turnu Severin, the acquittal. As far as Dr. C. Angelescu is concerned, Sub-Secretary of State in Iuliu Maniu's government (June-October 1930), he was the victim of an assassination attempt by the Legionary Gh. Beza, who was arrested and defended in Court by Corneliu Zelea Codreanu. The attacker would later show solidarity with Mihai Stelescu.

The Trial of Corneliu Zelea Codreanu

11. The firm conclusion stated in the Ordinance, regarding the "suspicious" origin of the Legionary Movement's funds was not justified, especially when it comes to financial support from Berlin. Not long ago, Armin Heinen (see op. Cit., passim) examined it thoroughly and proved very convincingly that Hitler didn't fund the Legionary Movement and that Corneliu Zelea Codreanu alone was responsible for its destiny. The most recent publication is the partial notes of Radu Lecca, who played an important role in conducting the official and unofficial negotiations, that were often secret, between the political groups in Romania and the Nazi authorities in Berlin, between 1930 and 1940. Lecca claims that the material given to the Communist authorities in Bucharest in 1960, contained details and strong evidence, in the sense that the Legionary Movement and its leaders benefited from the credit of the Nazi Reich. Therefore, he claimed that Friedrich Weber, from the Bucharest office of *Volkischer Beobachter*, had permanent contact with Codreanu's Movement (cf. Radu Lecca, *Eu I-am salvat pe evreii din România*, București, Ed. Roza Vânturilor, 1994, p. 83), that he ensured the transportation of certain Legionaries to Berlin from where they returned with "money and instructions" (ibidem, p. 85), or that "Weber, who came back from Germany (in 1936), told me that the Legionary party, reborn after All for the Country was dissolved, continues to receive aid from Himmler, Goebbels, and Streicher" (Ibidem, p. 100). Goga also confirmed the same situation to Lecca (ibidem, p. 92).

12. The statement in the Ordinance is, however, categorically untrue, devoid of any nuances, which are required in a trial such as a staged one for Corneliu Zelea Codreanu (see the previous note).

13. It will be noticed that after an elementary calculation, the numbers presented are inadequate.

14. Obviously, the lawyer speaks in place of Corneliu Zelea Codreanu.

15. In the debates published in *Universul*, the reproduced text is continued by this statement:...which we published (this is about the Ordinance — our note) in the newspaper on the day of 18th of May (1938)."

16. Among the works attributed to Corneliu Zelea Codreanu (*Scrisori studențești din închisoare, 9 octombrie 1923-30 martie 1924*, Iași, 1925; *Circulări, scrisori, sfaturi, gânduri*, București, 1933 — multiple editions; especially: *Circulările Căpitanului, 1934-1937*, București, 1937; *Circulări și Manifeste, 1927-1928*, București, 1941 and Madrid, 1951; *Cărticica șefului de cuib*, București, 1933, with 12 prior editions: *Cărticica șefului de cuib*, Iași, Tipografia "Presa Bună", 1940, *Carticica șefului de cuib*,

Salzburg, 1952 ("Omul nou" collection, nr. II and Miami Beach, 1991, the same collection, nr. 49); *Însemnări de la Jilava*, Rodstock, 1942, multiple prior editions: *Însemnări de la Jilava*, Salzburg, 1951, "Omul nou" collection, nr. 4 and Munchen, 1968, the same collection, nr. 35, and, recently, *Însemnări de la Jilava*, in Duiliu Sfințescu, ed., *Corneliu Zelea Codreanu, 1899-1938*, ed. A III-a, pp. 141-175; "Însemnări de la Jilava, I-VIII," in *Formula A.S.*, București, an. II, nr. 39-47/1992); *Pentru Legionari*, a whole memorial volume covering the time between March 1919-July 1933, is the most complete, the most quoted, and the most appreciated by biographers. The author expressed himself as categorically and as realistically as possible during the trial: his actions and his beliefs shown in the volume were written "in an honest and correct way. For research on its doctrinal values, *Pentru Legionari* is an indispensable book. The work was designed in two volumes, but only the first one was published after many struggles, in Sibiu. The second one was to talk about the events after 1933, as is stated in the short note on page 476, that succeeds the afterword dated 5th of April 1936 (see Corneliu Zelea Codreanu, *Pentru Legionari*, vol. I, Sibiu, Editura "Totul pentru Țară", Tipografia Vestemean, 1936, p. 482). Corneliu Zelea Codreanu wrote the book *Pentru Legionari* at Carmen Sylva between the 6th of December 1935 and April 1936. The book was published on October 1st, 1936, and immediately became the "main book of the Legionary Movement" (cf. *Cronologie legionară*, p. 25). This book, together with all other works by the Captain and his comrades, were banned during the years of Communist dictatorship, their discovery in the 50s leading to the arrests and convictions of those possessing them. After the first edition, volumes were published that were included in the collection for the exiled Legionaries, "Omul nou" (almost 60 various books between 1951-1993) Salzburg, 1951 (nr. 9); Munchen, 1968 (nr. 36), or Miami Beach, 1990 (nr. 47) considering that representing the 7th edition, and recently, *Pentru Legionari*, came to the attention of specialists and readers in the country, thanks to Ovidiu Guleş and Radu Dan Vlad, who published a xerox edition (Timişoara, Tipografia Gordian, Collection "Documente istorice sechestrate". 1993, 484 p.). The new edition had a preface signed by Horia Sima — "Destinul scrierilor legionare," (pp. 477-482). *Pentru Legionari* benefited from various editions in languages of international use: *Eiserne Garde* (Berlin, 1939 and Munchen, 1976, col. "Omul nou", nr. 38); *Guardia de Hierro* (Madrid, 1940); *For My Legionaries* (*The Iron Guard*), Madrid, 1976; *La Garda de Fer* (*Pour les Legionnaires*), Paris, Editions Promethee, 1938, and Grenoble, 1972 (col. "Omul nou").

The Trial of Corneliu Zelea Codreanu

17. Max Auschnitt was a part of the great group of bankers (together with C. Orghidan, N. Malaxa, I. Bujoiu, I. Gigurtu, E. Wolff, etc.) who during the 1930s became supporters of Carol II. From January 1935, they established the "Union of Metal and Mining Industries in Romania" (President C. Orghidan). In the press of those times (especially the Communist ones — *Scânteia*, nr. 5/ April; idem, nr. 6/1934) it was stated, but not proven, that the members of the "Union," including Max Auschnitt, had supported financially the Legionaries, at a time when Carol II was hopeful about the Iron Guard. Those statements were picked up by Marxist historiography (V. Liveanu, M. Fătu, and I. Spălăţelu). Clear information shows that in January 1941, N. Malaxa supported the Legionaries and the rebellion on 20-24th of January (see Aurică Simion, *Regimul politic din România în perioada Septembrie 1940-Ianuarie 1941*, Cluj-Napoca, Editura Dacia, 1976, pp. 234-235); Mircea Ciobanu, *Regele Mihai şi Exilul românesc*, Iasi, Editura Princeps, 1994, p. 119 and following). For a direct mention of Max Auschnitt, we quote from Constanţa Bogdan ("Baza social-economică a fascismului în România," in *Împotriva fascismului*, Bucureşti, Editura Politică, 1971, p. 35); "To procure" the funds, the Legionary leaders had various "businesses" with the great capitalists, no matter their ethnic origin. Thus, even though they were conducting a strong campaign against the Jews during 1933-1937, they supplied scrap metals to the "Reşiţa" plants, dealing directly with Max Auschnitt. They also took part in the administrative councils of some businesses owned by Jews. Nae Ionescu, for example, starting in 1936 was a member of the administrative council for the Romanian offices of the German company "I.G. Farbenindustrie," where Max Auschnitt participated in its finances." We also must note that Nicolae Ceauşescu himself, in full contradiction with the historical truth, at one point supported the Legionary movement: "...The Legionary Movement, Hitler's agent in Romania, completely serving German imperialism, carried on a profound anti-national campaign, seriously harming the interests of the Romanian nation. Together with the representatives of the monopolistic burghers, it betrayed the interests of the nation, subordinated the country to Hitler's German dominion, putting in danger the existence of Romania as an independent and sovereign state" (cf. *P.C.R. — continuator al luptei revoluţionare şi democratice a poporului 281umin, al traditiilor mişcării comuniste şi socialiste din România*, Bucureşti, Ed. Politică, 1966, p. 39). For a more detailed explanation of the problem, see Larry Watts, *Romanian Cassandra: Ion Antonescu and the Struggle for Reform, 1916-1941*, Boulder-New York, 1993, p. 107 and following (Chapter III — "The King, the "Capitan", and the General, 1933-1937").

18. Victor Iamandi (1891-1940), a minister for various departments in the Liberal governments of I.G. Duca, dr. C. Angelescu, and Gh. Tătărescu, but especially a Head of

Romanian Crucible

Justice in most cabinets during the time of Royal Dictatorship (Miron Cristea, Armand Călinescu, Gh. Argeşanu, and C. Argetoianu, between March 1938 and November 1939). He was assassinated by the Legionaries in Jilava on the night of 26-27th of November 1940 (cf. *Asasinatele de la Jilava..., Snagov şi Strejnicul, 26-27 Noiembrie 1940*, ed. A II-a, Bucureşti, Ed. Scripta, 1992, p. 33).

19. Scarlat Callimachi (1896-1975), a descendant of the royal family of the same name, historian and political man, editor, and sponsor of the left-wing Communist press before and after World War II. He was a close collaborator with the agents of the Communist International in Romania. We found his name in Ana Pauker's phone agenda from Moscow between 1941-1944. He was the first director of the Romanian-Russian Museum in Bucharest (1948-1963) (see Ştefan Ştefanescu, ed., *Enciclopedia istoriografiei româneşti*, Bucureşti, Ed. Ştiinţifică şi Enciclopedică, 1978, p. 78).

20. Vasile Cristescu (Christescu) (1902-1939, professor of ancient history, close associate of Corneliu Zelea Codreanu, remarkable leader of the Legionary Movement, and for a time he was even its commander. After a spectacular escape, he was found and shot by police, on the 26th of January 1936 in his home in Bucharest (see Mircea Nicolau, Vasile Christescu: "Un istoric se seamă şi erou," in *Revista de Vest*, nr. 30 (94), February 1994, p. 29). He is the author of some classic studies about the history of Roman Dacia (see especially *Viaţa economică a Daciei Romane*, Piteşti, 1929; *Istoria Militară a Daciei Romane*, Bucureşti, 1937, etc.), very much appreciated by N. Iorga at the time (cf. N. Iorga, *Istoria Românilor*, I/1, ed. A II-a, Bucureşti, Ed. Ştiinţifică şi Enciclopedică, 1988, passim) (see *Enciclopedia istoriografiei româneşti*, cited edition, p. 96). During a conference held in December 1935, at the Center for Studies of the Legionary Movement, V. Cristescu (who is not related to Eugen Cristescu — the former leader of the S.I.S. in 1940-1944), spoke about a page from the history of the Legion:

"The attack from the 30th of December 1933 in the train station in Sinaia, when Prime Minister I.G. Duca fell, has an explanation and a partial justification. This, however, was not the Captain's decision and it was not an act of his politics, but rather the explosion of a boiler under internal pressure, without any other possibility or solution. From the tragic events that unfolded in the winter of 1933-1934 they didn't gain anything: neither the democratic parties nor the Legionary Movement, and we can also say that democracy was pushed back and the nationalism was in danger, the only ones that gained were the occult forces who instituted the state of siege and the censorship of the

The Trial of Corneliu Zelea Codreanu

press, and that formed a formidable military-police bureaucracy justified by public order and paid for from the state's budget." (*Învierea*, nr. 1/ January-March 1993, p. 22)

21. The work camp at Carmen Sylva (later on Vasile Roaită, today Eforie Nord), which 800 Legionaries attended, led by Corneliu Zelea Codreanu (from the 5th of July to the 10th of September 1935). They built lodges, strengthened the shores, built 1 km of highway, etc. (cf. *Cronologie legionară*, p. 23).

22. *Buna Vestire*, the well-known Legionary magazine (1937-1938 and 1940), which stands next to other newspapers or magazines from those times, with the same orientation, which we examined in the Library of the Romanian Academy in Bucharest, or in the Central University Library "Mihai Eminescu" in Iași: *Pământul Strămoșesc* (starting from 1st of August 1927, the first magazine of the newly established Legion of the Archangel Michael), *Axa* (1932-1933) (during the war, at Rostock, in the Legionary camp led by Horia Sima, 3 more numbers of *Axa* were published by Paul Constantin Deleanu), or *Cuvântul* published by Nae Ionescu. For *Buna Vestire*, inaugurated in September 1940, the head editor was Constantin Noica; *Porunca Vremii* (1934-1937) and *Cuvântul Studențesc* (1934-1937).

23. The deadline for fee payments by the political groups that had submitted lists with candidates for the famous (and controversial) parliamentary elections of December 20th, 1937, which propelled the All for the Country Party into 3rd place (after the National Liberal Party and National Peasants' Party) with 15,58% (478.378 votes and 66 seats in the Chamber) in the preferences of the Romanian electorate (cf. Al. Gh. Savu, *Dictatura regală, 1938-1940*, București, Ed. Politică, 1970, p. 115; Ioan Scurtu, *Din viața politică a României (1926-1947). Studiu critic privind istoria PNȚ*, București, Ed. Științifică și Enciclopedică, 1983, p. 385). They emerged victorious in the circumstances in which, on the 25th of November 1937, a non-aggression electoral pact was signed by Corneliu Zelea Codreanu, Iuliu Maniu, and Gh. Brătianu (cf. Ioan Scurtu, ed. *Istoria României între anii 1918 și 1944. Culegere de documente*, București, Editura Didactică și Pedagogica, 1982, pp. 318-319; Vasile Arimia and collaborators, eds. *Istoria PNȚ. Documente, 1926-1947*, București, Editura ARC 2000, 1994, pp. 173-174) and where other parties joined, such as the Socialist Party of I. Jumanca, the Agrarian Union of C. Argetoianu, and the Jewish Union of Dr. W. Filderman (see *Iuliu Maniu în fața Istoriei*, București, Ed. Gândirea Românească, 1993, p. 47; Corneliu Coposu, *Un moment de răscruce în lupta pentru apărarea libertăților democratice din istoria României: Pactul de neagresiune electorală al opoziției din Noiembrie 1937*) (a manuscript from November 1946, text given to us by the author, whom we thank on this

Romanian Crucible

occasion). Through that pact, the main objective of the opposition was fulfilled: The National Liberal Party and Gh. Tătărescu (see note 58), the Prime Minister in office, and the man of Carol II were defeated in the elections. Mr. Corneliu Coposu rightly observed that the action of solidarity of the opposition from December 1937 was justified: "At that moment, the main adversaries of democracy were King Carol II, with his oligarchic tendencies, and his servile acolytes, with Gh. Tătărescu at their helm, the Gogo-Cuzist Party, the chamberlain, and the obedient political leeches, mockingly called *"carolingieni."* If the recent political history is objectively and critically scrutinized, it is found that, attracted by the nonaggression electoral pact, the Legionaries were disarmed and stopped from fulfilling their terrorist activity, and their dynamism was directed towards an objective goal, aiming to defend the constitutional order" (ibidem).

24. Gh. (Zizi) Cantacuzino-Grănicerul (see note 3).

25. The referrals are made to one of the 20 indictment files.

26. General Ion Bengliu, commander of the Gendarmes during the ministries of Armand Călinescu, and later involved in the repressions of the Legionaries and assassinated by them in Jilava on 26/27th of November (see *Asasinatele...*, p. 33)

27. A reference to the book *Circulările Căpitanului, 1934-1937*, cited edition. For the principles of Legionary ideology shown in *Circulări* and other works, the most convenient ones to look at are: the materials mentioned by Dr. Șerban Milcoveanu in the first two numbers of *Învierea* (nr. 1/January-March 1993 and nr. 2/ April-June 1993) or the texts included by the editor in the previously mentioned *Almanah 1994* (see note 5), published by Gazeta de Vest (cf. *Legiunea Arhanghelului Mihail de la trecut la 284umina284*, ed. Ovidiu Guleș, cited edition, pp. 177-200). To be compared with the older work, well compartmentalized thematically (*Doctrina Legionară: texte alese*, Salzburg, 1952, col. "Omul nou", nr. 18, in three parts: I — The Legionary Movement (what is the Legionary Movement? Legionary spirituality, Legionary faith, the Legion and the country, the Legion and the people, the Legion in relation to history); II — The Legionary (Who are the Legionaries? Legionary life, Legionary virtues, Sins awaiting us); III — Legionary goals (The man of faith, The hero, The Legionary elite, The final goal of the nation, etc.).

28. This is about the well-known national headquarters of the Legionary Movement in the Capital, from Bucharest, Gutenberg street, nr. 3, known as Casa Verde (The Green

The Trial of Corneliu Zelea Codreanu

House), built by the Legionaries between August 1933 and September 1937. Casa Verde was opened on the 25-26th of September 1937 (see *Cronologie legionară*, p. 27).

29. The Peace Treaty from 1/13th of July 1878, signed and ratified by Turkey, Germany, Austro-Hungary, France, Great Britain, Italy, and Russia. As is known, Romania didn't sign this Treaty, even though it applied it (art. 43-57 referred to it in its entirety; among them, art. 43 focused on the conditional recognition of Romania's independence by the Great Powers of the time) (see N. Dașcovici, *Interesele și drepturile României în texte de drept international public*, Iași, Tipografia Al. Țerek, 1936, pp. 316-320; F.C. Nano, *Condica tratatelor și a altor legăminte ale României, 1354-1937*, II, București, 1938, p. 366, no. 1230).

30. Mircea Eliade (1907-1986), writer, diplomat, and historian of religions, student and close collaborator of the brilliant Nae Ionescu (1890-1940). He was distinguished professor of the history of religions at the University of Chicago during the last three decades of his life, and the author of many well-known works in his field of study, which brought him a well-deserved international reputation, surpassing that of his mentor who he never gave up on. Coordinator and principal editor of the monumental *Enciclopedia religiilor* in 16 volumes (the largest work of its kind that has ever been published), a passionate memorialist. His ties to the Legionary Movement during the 1930s (of a doctrinal nature, collaborations with publications, praises of Legionary leaders, especially of Corneliu Zelea Codreanu, etc.) were strictly delimited, which did not exempt him from becoming a target of insidious attacks, especially in the last years of his life, and especially after 1986. According to some opinions, this prevented him from receiving the Nobel Prize, which he rightly deserved. For these aspects, cf., the most recent, Leon Volovici, *Nationalist Ideology and Antisemitism. The Case of Romanian Intellectuals in the 1930s*, Oxford-NY-Seoul-Tokyo, Pergamon Press, 1991, passim, a passionate work against positive nationalism.

31. This is about the foundation of the All for the Country Party (1934-1935).

32. About the Vernichescu case involving Ion Moța (1902-1937), a lawyer, one of the founders of the Legion, first-rank associate of Corneliu Zelea Codreanu, appointed by him, on January 1st 1937, as the deputy of General Cantacuzino-Grănicerul in the All for the Country Party, and the man who left for Spain leading a Legionary delegation to fight on Franco's nationalist side, against the Communists. He was killed on January 13th on the battlefield together with Vasile Marin (1904-1937), a lawyer (see note 9).

286   Romanian Crucible

About Moța and Marin, glorified by the Legionary Movement on a national scale following their tragic destiny, see, first, the special issue of *Cuvântul Studențesc* (a number which became a bibliographic rarity following the Communist searches from 1944-1989), edited by "Uniunea Națională a Studenților Creștini Români" (The National Union of the Christian Romanian Students), year XII, nr. 1-4/January/February 1937 (The studies signed by A. Vântu, Ion I. Moța, already quoted, pp. 2-20 and by Mihail Polihroniade, Vasile Marin, pp. 28-34; Vasile Christescu, *Jertfa lui Ion Moța și Vasile Marin în lumina istoriei*, p. 45; S. Mehedinți, *Urmașii lui Eminescu*, pp. 36-39). From the article titled "Înțelesul plecării noastre în Spania" (în *Cuvântul Argeșului*, nr. 25 from 27th of December 1936) we note: "... If the Cross fell to the ground in Spain, it would shake the foundation in Romania as well, and Communism, if it was victorious from today on, will strike us tomorrow".

33. The reproduced quotes are not exact, so we suggest the reader check Corneliu Zelea Codreanu's book *Pentru Legionari*, I, ediția 1936, or other recent editions.

34. The same idea as the previous note. In the original text, that fragment ends like this: "...they humiliated and exposed to danger the Romanian nation" (cf. Pentru Legionari, I, p. 168).

35. In the original text, such a statement is implicit, not explicit (cf. *Pentru Legionari*, I, p. 212-213).

36. About Gh. Beza's attack on C. Anghelescu (July 1930) (see note 10). More details in Corneliu Zelea Codreanu's book, *Pentru Legionari*, I, p. 385 and following.

37. The "Vlad Țepeș" League — the name of the group led by Gr. Filipescu, which separated in 1929 from the People's Party (Alexandru Averescu) and in March 1932 became the Conservative Party (Mircea Mușat, Ion Ardeleanu, *România după Marea Unire*, II/1, 1918-1933, București, Ed. Științifică și Enciclopedică, 1986, p. 558).

38. About those assassinations, see notes 2 and 10.

39. The Great War of National Unity of all Romanians (1916-1919).

40. The Great Union of all Romanians from 1918.

41. Ion I. Nistor (1876-1962), prestigious Romanian historian, originally from Bucovina, professor at the University of Cernăuți and Bucharest, also a political man. The author of some solid synthesis about the global history of Romanians (in manuscript)

The Trial of Corneliu Zelea Codreanu

or *Istoria Basarabiei* and *Istoria Bucovinei* (cf. *Enciclopedia istoriografiei românești*, ed. Cit..., p. 240-241; Emil I. Emandi, comp., Ion I. Nistor. "Bibliografie selective" in *Europa XXI*, Iași, t. I-II/1992-1993, pp. 155-165).

42. This is about the Nationalist-Democratic Party, led by the unparalleled historian (see Petre Țurlea, op. cit., passim). Even though he was a member of the NDP, Professor Traian Brăileanu did not hesitate, in September 1940, as the Legionary minister of National Education and Arts, to approve the retirement of N. Iorga (ibidem, p. 368-369).

43. "At that time..." — in the post-World War I era.

44. "The mergers that took place..." — an allusion to the political negotiations after 1918, from which N. Iorga's political group couldn't escape either: The permanent divorce with A.C. Cuza, the temporal merger with C. Argetoianu's group (withdrawn from the People's Party in 1923), with Iuliu Maniu's National Party, respectively in 1924 and 1925, contacts with the Liberals in 1926, etc. (see Mircea Mușat, Ion Ardeleanu, *România după Marea Unire*, II/1, pp. 699-706; Stelian Țurlea, op. cit., passim).

45. A.C. Cuza (1857-1947), a renowned politician, a law professor at the University of Iași, and a parliamentary member for decades, poet and publicist, member of the Romanian Academy. He founded, in association with N. Iorga, the National-Democratic Party (1910), but in the circumstances created by World War I, after 1918, their political divorce became permanent. A.C. Cuza with his nationalist political members (not fascist), especially with professor N.C. Paulescu (the one who discovered insulin, but who lost his Nobel Prize to other "authors"), set in Iași the foundation for a National-Christian League (January 1922), which, on the 4th of March 1923 became the League of National-Christian Defense. The founding document of the League of National-Christian Defense, which in 1923-1925 strengthened from the fusion with other right-wing groups, including the National-Romanian Fascists (see Mircea Mușat, Ion Ardeleanu, *România după Marea Unire*, II/1, p. 706 and the next; Gh. T. Pop, *Caracterul 287umina287s287nal și antipopular al activității Partidului Național Creștin*, Cluj-Napoca, Ed. Dacia, 1978, pp. 48-53), was also signed by a young Corneliu Zelea Codreanu. He had managed to gather in Iași the representatives of 42 student groups from the four university centers around the country. And the manifestations that preceded the solemn signing of the founding document of the League of National-Christian Defense, in the auditorium of the University of Iași, reunited over 10,000 people (cf.

288   Romanian Crucible

Pentru Legionari, I, pp. 118-120). A.C. Cuza was the leader of the new group, and Corneliu Zelea Codreanu was charged with handling organizational issues throughout the whole country. In 1927, Corneliu Zelea Codreanu and his group, separated from the League of National-Christian Defense to form the Legion of Archangel Michael. The League of National-Christian Defense survived until the 14th of July 1935, when it merged with the National Agrarian Party led by Octavian Goga, to set the foundation of the National Christian Party, in which A.C. Cuza became an honorific president, and his partner, the executive president (Gh. T. Pop, op. cit., p. 121). As is known, following the results of the elections from the 20th of December 1937 (see note 23), King Carol II entrusted the establishment of a new government to the group Goga-Cuza, that had only received 9.15% of the electoral votes (the 4th place and 39 seats) (cf. Al. Gh. Savu, op. cit., p. 115). With reference to his scientific work concerning the situations of Jews in Romania, A.C. Cuza is qualified by L. Volovici (op. cit., p. 196) as "the most prolific Romanian anti-Semitic author" (see Zvi Hartman, comp., *Antisemitism în România. The image of the Jew in Romanian Society*, Tel Aviv University, 1993, p. 22-23). About Gh. A. Cuza (ibidem, p. 23) and about Nicolae C. Paulescu (ibidem, p. 35-36). However, it should be corroborated with Jean Ancel, Victor Eskenasy, eds., *Bibliography of the Jews in Romania*, Tel Aviv University, 1991, the opinions about the Iron Guard (nr. 45-48, 51, 56, 101, 208, 271, 429-430, 689, 1288, 1351).

46. Mihail Manoilescu (1891-1950), renowned economist and politician, professor at the Bucharest Polytechnic University. Deputy or senator in multiple legislatures (1930-1937), sub-secretary of state and minister in the economic or financial fields in various cabinets (1926-1927, 1930-1931), external minister for the I. Gigurtu cabinet (July-September 1940). Mihail Manoilescu simultaneously carried out a rich scientific activity, very appreciated in the country, as well as abroad. He enjoyed and still enjoys international fame with his works about the theory of protectionism and international trade (editions in Brazil, Italy, England — 1931, Berlin — 1937, Bucharest — 1986) or about corporatism and a single party (multiple editions), as, no less, *Rostul și destinul burgheziei românești* (București, 1942). He had ties with prince, and later King Carol II, but also with the leaders of the Legionary Movements, without being accused — as it happened to the Marxist historians between 1950-1970 — of fascist affiliation and fascist propaganda, recently included in the antisemitic bibliography (cf. Zvi Hartman, *Antisemitism in România*, p. 31-32). It was, in essence, the reason why after 1944 he was imprisoned, meeting his end at Sighet. Mihail Manoilescu is an exceptional memorialist, his works excellently printed in the past few years, having a decisive contribution to clarifying his role and attitude towards the events (some controversial) in

The Trial of Corneliu Zelea Codreanu

which he was involved (see *Dictatul de la Viena. Memorii. Iulie-August 1940*, Bucureşti, Ed. Enciclopedică, 1991; *Tragica predestinare a geniului moldovenesc*, Iaşi, Ed. Moldova, 1993; *Memorii, I-II*, Bucureşti, Ed. Enciclopedică, 1993).

47. Nichifor Crainic (1889-1972), writer, politician, and publicist. Deputy and Minister (1927, 1940, 1941); member of the Romanian Academy and professor at the University of Chişinău and the University of Bucharest, editor (1926-1944) for the magazine *Gândirea* (1921-1944), which gave its name to the current he preached about, distinguished by traditionalism, orthodoxy, and autochthonous (see I. Hangiu, *Dicţionar al presei literare româneşti, 1790-1982*, Bucureşti, Ed Ştiinţifică şi Enciclopedică, 1987, pp. 158-159). His collaboration with the Legionary Movement, which materialized from a doctrinal point of view in the fourth decade, was not smooth and without issues. Even his statements at the "trial" of the Captain were not satisfactory for Legionaries. After 1944, Nichifor Crainic, wrongfully accused of fascist-Legionary propaganda and of collaboration with the Nazis, took refuge in various hiding places. He was "tried" in absentia in 1945 and convicted to life in prison. He was arrested in 1947, and "hosted" for 15 years in Aiud. In his last decade of life, Nichifor Crainic worked hard in "supervised freedom," especially while being a principal collaborator for the magazine *Glasul Patriei*. This is the period when, at the request of officials, he wrote a thorough monograph on the history of the Legionary Movement, which never got to be published, but which served as a source of inspiration for a book that came out in two editions, and whose "authors" didn't have anything better to do than to "overturn" the points of view on this matter (see Nedic Lemnaru, preface by Nichifor Crainic, *Zile Albe- Zile Negre. Memorii*, I, Bucureşti, Casa Editorială Gândirea, 1991, p. XXIV-XXV).

48. Constantin Petrovicescu (1882-1949), a military general. In 1934, he was a member of the Court that judged the Nicadorii, then he openly joined the Legionary Movement. In 1940-1941, he was the head of the Department of Internal Affairs during the short-lived Ion Antonescu-Horia Sima government. He had a special role in the preparation and coordination of the Legionary rebellion (January, 1941), and was considered to be the main culprit after Horia Sima (cf. *Pe marginea prăpastiei, 21-23 of January 1941*, vol. II, ed. A II-a, Bucureşti, Ed. Scripta, 1992, pp. 83-100 and 153-178; Aurică Simion, *Regimul politic din România în perioada septembrie 1940- ianuarie 1941*, passim). As a result, he was tried and convicted to 7 years in prison In 1941 (A. Simion, op. Cit., p. 285), a punishment that he carried out between 1941 and 1944 when Romania was "liberated" by the Soviet troops. C. Petrovicescu remained behind bars, but in May 1946 he was involved in the staged trial of Ion Antonescu and his associates (?!) and

290 Romanian Crucible

sentenced to life in prison (cf. Ioan Dan, *"Procesul" Mareşalului Ion Antonescu*, Bucureşti, Ed. Tempus, 1993, pp. 21-22). He died in prison in Aiud.

49. Ion Antonescu (1882-1946), Romanian Marshal, leader of the Romanian State (1940-1944). He prepared Romania to participate together with the fascist Axis in the war against the U.S.S.R., with two main objectives: restoring the borders of Greater Romania and eliminating the Communist danger (cf. Mareşal Ion Antonescu, *Un ABC al anticomunismului românesc*, I, cited edition, pp. 158-161 — "Ordinul către armată şi Proclamaţia catre Ţară," both from the 2nd of June 1941). After the war, but especially in recent years, numerous volumes appeared in the country as well as abroad (monographs, monographic studies, document collections, memorialist works, articles, etc.) dedicated to the role and place of Ion Antonescu in the era of World War II. We recommend for the reader look at a few different problems: the relationship between Antonescu and Codreanu, with details concerning the "trial" of the Captain (Larry L. Watts, *Romanian Cassandra: Ion Antonescu and the Struggle for Reform, 1916-1941*, ed. Cit., passim); the relations between Antonescu and Hitler, with referrals to the role and the place of the Legionary Movement in this context (Armin Heinen, op. cit., pp. 415-463; Andreas Hillgruber, *Hitler, Konig Carol und Marschall Antonescu. Die290umina290h-rumanishen Beziehungen, 1938-1944*, two editions, Wiesbaden, F. Steiner Verlag, 1954 and 1965); the Ion Antonescu-Horia Sima government (Aurică Simion, *Regimul politic din România în perioada septembrie 1940-ianuarie 1941*, Cluj-Napoca, Ed. Dacia, 1976); The Eastern War, 1941-1944 (Platon Chirnoagă, *Istoria politică şi militară a razboiului României contra Rusiei Sovietice. 22 Iunie 1941-23 August 1944*, Madrid, Ed. "Carpaţi" Traian Popescu, 1955); the overthrow of the government on the 23rd of August 1944 (Ion Suţa, *România la cumpăna istoriei. August'44*, Bucureşti, Ed. Ştiintifică, 1991, Gh. Buzatu, ed. *Actul de la 23 August 1944 în context istoric. Studii şi documente*, Bucureşti, Ed. Ştiinţifică şi Enciclopedică, 1984); "the trial" and the execution (see Ioan Dan, op. cit.; Gh. Buzatu and colab. *Ultimele zile ale Mareşalului Ion Antonescu*, Bucureşti, 1993, Colecţia "caietele Magazin Istoric", nr. 1, with unique illustrations); the Marshall Ion Antonescu from a historical perspective (see. I.C. Drăgan, ed., *Antonescu — Mareşalul României şi răsboaiele de reîntregire, I-IV*, Veneţia, Ed. Nagard, 1986-1990; Gh. Buzatu şi colab., eds., *Mareşalul Antonescu în faţa istoriei*, I-II, Iaşi, Ed. B.A.I., 1990; C. Hlihor, ed., *Mareşalul Ion Antonescu — istoria mă va judeca. Scrieri inedite*, Bucureşti, Ed. Academiei de Înalte Studii Militare, 1993). Among these works, a classic scientific by-product sample and a failed defamation of the Marshal: Eduard Mezincescu, *Mareşalul Antonescu şi catastrofa României*, Bucureşti, Ed. Artemis, 1993, p. 175.

The Trial of Corneliu Zelea Codreanu

50. Corneliu Zelea Codreanu's statements during the "trial" were confirmed, first by Ion Antonescu himself during his testimony (see below the text of the debates). The meeting apparently took place on the [6]th of February 1938 and the General convinced the "Captain" to have a meeting with Octavian Goga, which happened on the [8]th of February 1938, at the residence of I. Gigurtu (see note 61), but not with King Carol II. Regarding this situation, Antonescu finally explained to the Legionary leader: "Mr. Codreanu, don't forget the words of the Holy Scripture: who raises the sword, will die by the sword" (see *Pe marginea prăpastiei, 21-23 Ianuarie 1941*, I, București, Ed. Scripta, 1992, p. 40; Mihail Sturdza, România și sfârșitul Europei. Amintiri din țara pierdută, Madrid-Rio de Janeiro, Ed. Dacia, 1966, p. 160-161; Larry L. Watts, *Romanian Cassandra*, p. 169).

51. Mihail Racoviță (1889-1954), General enrolled, as he himself stated during the "trial," in the Legionary Movement, regarded with suspicion by Marshal Antonescu, who, however, requested his services. The General, however, joined the plot by superior military officers that prepared the blow on the 2^{3r}d of August 1944 (Constantin Sănătescu, C. Vasiliu-Rășcanu, Ilie Crețulescu, etc.) (see *România în anii celui de-al doilea război291umina291l*, vol. I, București, Ed. Militară, 1989, p. 567). In compensation, he was included as Minister of War in the first government formed after the one led by Marshal Ion Antonescu was overthrown, but the divorce with the Communist leaders was not delayed. As "gratitude" for his services in 1944, Mihail Racoviță was imprisoned. He died in Sighet in 1954 (cf. *Din documentele rezistenței*, București, nr. 8/1993, p. 252).

52. This is about the first government led by Iuliu Maniu ([10]th of November 1928-[7]th of June 1930).

53. A reference to the "plot" to coordinate the return of Prince Carol to the country ([6]th of June 1930) and his proclamation as King of Romania ([8]th of June 1930).

54. Iuliu Maniu (1873-1953), an illustrious Romanian politician. Bachelor and Doctor of Law, a deputy in the Budapest Parliament (1906-1910), president of the Ruling Council in Transylvania appointed by the Union Assembly of Romania on the [1]st of December 1918. Leader of the National Party in Transylvania, and — after the merger with the Peasants' Party led by Ion Mihalache (1926) — of National Peasants' Party until 1947 (with a pause between 1933 and 1937). Deputy in the Parliament in Bucharest, president of NPP governments (1928-1930, 1930, 1932-1933). During World War II, the leader of the anti-Antonescu political resistance, and he has special merits for

Romanian Crucible

the turn Romania took in the war — the withdrawal from the fascist Axis and the return to the United Nations (1944-1945). After the war, Maniu became the incontestable leader of the fight against Communism in Romania and against the transformation of a country into a satellite of the U.S.S.R. Involved in a judicial set-up in Bucharest from October-November 1947 (the so-called "trial of the leading clique of the National Peasants' Party"), he was convicted to life in prison. He died in prison in Sighet. In appreciation of the global activity of the illustrious politician, see especially the documents presented at the commemorative symposium organized in February 1993 by the National Christian Democratic Peasants' Party and the Hanns Seidel Foundation (apud *Iuliu Maniu în fața istoriei*, cited edition, pp. 7-121).

55. Alexandru Vaida-Voievod (1872-1950), renowned Romanian politician, leader of the National Transylvanian Party, then of the National Peasants' Party. On several occasions, a minister and even prime-minister (in 1919-1920, 1932, 1933). Especially in the 1930s, he showed interest in the right-wing political groups, and, at one point, he proclaimed himself as the "godfather" of the Iron Guard. Arrested after the war, he died in a communist prison.

56. Sextil Pușcariu (1877-1948), reputable philologist, professor at the Universities of Cluj and Bucharest, a member of the Romanian Academy.

57. About Iuliu Maniu, see note 54. Regarding the testimony of Iuliu Maniu in the "trial" of Corneliu Zelea Codreanu, the reproduced text is not complete. The final version was given in Bucharest in September 1938 and is given out in full in Annex IV of the volume.

58. Gheorghe Tătărescu (1886-1957), Romanian politician. Bachelor of law in Paris, member and one of the political leaders of the National Liberal Party (NLP), repeatedly a state sub-secretary or a minister, the Romanian ambassador in the capital of France (1938-1939), prime-minister (1934-1937 and 1939-1940). Compromised for the ease with which his government accepted, in the summer of 1940, the ceding of Bessarabia and northern Bucovina to the U.S.S.R., Tătărescu was isolated, and he self-isolated during Antonescu's regime, finally forming his own political group separate from the NLP. In the post-war era, his political compromise accentuated at the moment he accepted to be included in Petru Groza's government (March 1945-November 1947), as vice prime-minister and minister of external affairs. The services given to the Communists didn't exempt him, after 1947, from certain hardships, nor from years of detention or house arrest.

The Trial of Corneliu Zelea Codreanu

59. "The new regime" of Carol II (10/1[1]h of February 1938-6th of September 1940).

60. Istrate Micescu (1881-1951), a politician, a law professor at the University of Bucharest, and an illustrious member of the Capital's lawyer's bar. He was the author of the Constitution from 1938. He was a minister of external affairs in the Goga-Cuza government (2[8]h of December 1937-1[0]th of February 1938) and Minister of Justice during Tătărescu's government (see note 58) (2[9]th of November 1939-1[0]th of May 1940). Arrested in 1948, he died in Aiud (see Teodor Rus, "Parchetul general introduce recurs în anulare în 'procesul Istrate-Micescu'," in *"Palatul de Justiţie,"* nr. 12/1993).

61. Ion Gigurtu (1886-1959), Romanian politician, industrialist, and economist. Deputy and minister in various cabinets and finally, prime minister (4th of July-4th of September 1940). He died in prison (see notes 17 and 50).

62. Constantin Argetoianu (1871-1952), a Romanian politician. Deputy and senator, political leader, minister of various cabinets, prime minister (September-November 1939). Author of some rich and colorful memorialist pages, bound in an interesting political journal (pending publication). He was detained and he died in a Communist prison.

63. See note 9. Regarding the facts recorded by Corneliu Zelea Codreanu, cf. *Pentru Legionari*, I, p. 168 and the next.

64. Corneliu Zelea Codreanu's text (*Pentru Legionari*, I, p. 173-174) is much more nuanced than the assumptions of the military senior prosecutor Radu Ionescu.

65. The problem appears controversial, but see below the opinions expressed by Lizetta Gheorghiu during Corneliu Zelea Codreanu's defense.

66. Groundless statement.

67. Groundless statement.

68. Groundless statement.

69. Idem. As counter-evidence, see *Însemnările* by Corneliu Zelea Codreanu, which are his memoirs from Jilava between 1[9]th of April-1[9]th of June 1938, first published only four years after his death (see note 16). The pages from the journal are moving. Here's the following fragment as an example:

Romanian Crucible

Wednesday, 27th of April 1938

Three days from Easter have passed.

None of my family came to me, most likely because they didn't get permission to visit me, or maybe they were arrested and detained somewhere as well.

Time passes slowly when you're alone. Only one man enters this vault three times a day, only for a minute: in the morning at the opening, at 12, when they bring me food cooked in a cauldron, and in the evening.

The sun doesn't shine here, except for a few minutes at 5 in the afternoon, and only through a small corner of the window.

I spend my time crouched on the edge of the bed and writing these thoughts, from time to time, on wrapping paper.

There are no tables or chairs in this place. The short pencil I found in my pocket is coming to an end. I can barely hold it between my fingers. For the rest of the time, I lay under my blanket.

But this dampness passes through the blanket as well as the clothes. For a week since I've been in here, I've never undressed and haven't been taken out in the sun, not even for half an hour to warm up. (see Annex II, Corneliu Zelea Codreanu — Însemnări de la Jilava privind procesul din Mai 1938).

70. That title, which was on page 168 and not on page 163, actually indicates a sub-chapter (*Pentru Legionari*, I, p. 168, upper row, 2-3).

71. Actually, Vernichescu was not assassinated by Moța.

72. See *Pentru Legionari*, I, p. 210, lower rows 14-17.

73. In order to obtain the expected effects, the senior military prosecutor obviously gives a melodramatic discourse.

74. A reference to the Commercial Academy in Bucharest.

75. The statements according to which the doctrine of the Legionary Movement, at least during that respective period, would have been imported or from "foreign" influence

The Trial of Corneliu Zelea Codreanu

are not just in contradiction with reality but proved completely untrue following thorough studies during the last decades, especially Armin Heinen, op. cit., passim; Eugen Weber, *Varieties of Fascism — Doctrines of Revolution in the Twentieth Century*, Princeton-Toronto-London, D. Van. Nostrand Co., Inc., 1964, p. 96 and the next; idem, "Romania," in *The European Right: A Historical Profile*, eds. Hans Rogger and Eugen Weber, Berkeley- Los Angeles, University of California Press, 1965, pp. 501-574; Walter Laquer, ed., *Fascism: A Reader's Guide. Analyses, Interpretations, Bibliography*, Harmondsworth, Penguin Books, 1979, passim; Ernst Nolte, *Three Faces of Fascism*, Paris, Imprimerie Nationale, 1985, p. 321 and the next; Francesco Veiga, *Istoria Gărzii de Fier, 1919-1941. Mistica ultranaționalismului*, București, Ed. Humanitas, 1993, passim; N.M. Nagy-Talavera, op.cit., pp. 246-344). The most relevant seems to be the observation of an international specialist on the problems of European fascism, namely Ernst Nolte who was quoted above, in one of his best-known syntheses (cf. *Der Faschistischen Bewegungen*, Berlin, 1966 and the French edition which we use, *Les mouvements295umina295ss. L' Europe de 1919 à 1945*, Paris, Calmann-Levy, 1969) notes that the Guardist phenomenon appeared to him as the "most original Romanian fascist movement" (p. 240), and generally, "without a doubt, the most interesting and the most complex fascist movement" (p 251). No less significant are the opinions of the late Vlad Georgescu: "Even though the beginning of the Legionary Movement is dated in 1922-1923 when Corneliu Zelea Codreanu first established the Association of Christian Students, then, together with Iași professor A.C. Cuza, the League of National-Christian Defense (LNCD), its final composition took place only in 1927, when the Legion of Archangel Michael was born, known after 1930 as the Iron Guard; nationalist, antisemitic, anti-Western, promoting a messianic spirit, an elitism and a cult for the leader that hasn't existed until then in the Romanian mentality or the political life, the Guard had every feature of contemporary far right-wing movements. Although the origin and the rise of the Legionaries are explained, first, by internal causes, which were not tied to or influenced by Nazism or fascism. It is, however, clear that its ascension was favored by the continuous inclination to the right of the European political life, and by the direct or indirect support it received from abroad." (see *Istoria Românilor de la origini până în zilele noastre*, ed. a III-a, București, Ed. Humanitas, 1992, p. 209).

76. On the contrary, Corneliu Zelea Codreanu consistently rejected any "kinship" between the conceptions of the Legion and other European fascist movements. Opposing opinions only claimed this, as seen: the Captain's judges in 1938, Communist propaganda, and the Romanian or foreign Marxist historians.

296   Romanian Crucible

77. A new rhetorical question.

78. A groundless statement, at least when it comes to Corneliu Zelea Codreanu in 1938.

79. See note 78.

80. See note 78.

81. However, the problem remains to be explained.

82. It has already been mentioned that the most authorized specialist in the field, the German Armin Heinen, proved the opposite, at least when it comes to the situation of the Legionary Movement under Corneliu Zelea Codreanu's leadership (see note 11). It was strange that, at about the same time, in Bucharest, an attempt was made to prove the opposite (see Nicolae Minei, "Corespondență diplomatică București-Bruxelles. Garda de Fier în solda Germaniei naziste," in *Magazin Istoric*, nr. 9/1979, pp. 34-38).

83. See note 23.

84. This was the situation in which Carol II decided to establish his own dictatorship and decapitated the Legionary Movement, realities confirmed by the latest research.

85. Decided following the meeting of Corneliu Zelea Codreanu with Octavian Goga on the [8]th of February 1938, arranged by General Ion Antonescu (see note 50).

86. Ion I. Moța and Vasile Marin, killed on the [13]th of January 1937 in Spain.

87. The situation was real!

88. *Neamul Românesc* (*The Romanian Nation*), a magazine and then a newspaper. The publication appeared uninterrupted for years (1906-1940), exclusively through the material and spiritual efforts of the unsurpassed Nicolae Iorga.

89. "On the occasion of the meetings" — not of Corneliu Zelea Codreanu with Adolf Hitler and Benito Mussolini (which didn't happen), as can be deduced from the text, but during the Captain's interrogations.

90. Allusions to the success achieved in the elections of the [20]th of December 1937.

91. Exact information!

The Trial of Corneliu Zelea Codreanu

92. *Cărticica şefului de cuib*, Iaşi, 1940, cited edition, on note 6, p. 5.

94. Ibidem, p.9.

95. Ibidem, p. 10.

96. Ibidem, p. 10-11 (complete text).

97. Ibidem, p. 19.

98. Ibidem, p. 46-47. See chapter IX with the respective title (pp. 46-50, paragraphs 56-63).

99. Ibidem, p. 47-48.

100. Ibidem, p. 48-49.

101. Radu (Demetrescu) Gyr (1905-1975), poet, professor at the University of Bucharest, awarded prizes from the Society of Romanian Writers and the Romanian Academy for his literary creation materialized in multiple remarkable volumes — *Linişti de schituri* (1924), *Cerbul de297uminaă* (1928), *Poeme de război* (1942) and *Balade* (1943). In recent years, several other volumes have been published, bringing together the poet's creation from his time of imprisonment (almost 20 years): *Poezii — Sângele temniţei* and *Balade* (curated by Mrs. Simona Popa, the daughter of the author, 1992), *Anotimpul umbrelor* (1993), etc. Many of them circulated by the word of mouth, either in Carol's prisons, or then, in the Communist ones, this poem from February 1938 being used by the defense in the "trial" of Corneliu Zelea Codreanu to mark its conclusion: ("... We have so many dead, so many bones"), as well as *Imnul morţilor* (*The Hymn of the Dead*) ("... We don't cry tears of blood/ But we are proud with so many heroes/ No! Our nation is not mourning you/ But it communicates through you") or *Ridica-te Gheorghe, ridica-te Ioane!* a poem for which the author was sentenced to death at the end of the 1950s: "Arise, Gheorghe, on chains, on ropes/Arise, Ioane, on the holy bones, /Upon the last light of the storm/Arise, Gheorghe, arise Ioane!". An exceptional creator, Rady Gyr is part of the elite personalities who have illustrated Romanian spirituality during the twentieth century — Nae Ionescu, Mircea Eliade, Constantin Noica, Emil Cioran, Petre Ţuţea (see Radu Gyr, *Poezii — Sângele temniţei* and *Balade*, Timişoara, Editura Marineasa, 1992, p.6). Recently, the memoirs of Radu Gyr were sent for publication (published as a series in Gazeta de Vest, Timişoara, nr. 24/1993 and following).

ANNEXES

Annex I
The Letter of Corneliu Zelea Codreanu
to Nicolae Iorga

To Professor Nicolae Iorga,

Today, Saturday, the 26 March 1938, at 9 AM, our two restaurants from Obor and Lazăr High School were shut down by the authorities.

The same happened to the colonial store.

To the first one, Chief Commissioner Furduescu came from police station nr. 18, together with three assistant commissioners and a platoon of gendarmes under the command of a sergeant.

To the second one, Chief Commissioner Malamuceanu came, together with two assistant commissioners, and told the staff to get out because they had received an order to evacuate and close the establishment.

Mr. Popescu asked them to show him a warrant. They replied: "We received a verbal command." The staff left without resistance, leaving everything in the hands of the authorities.

I mention as concerns procedure: the lack of sympathy because there should be sympathy even when it comes to the greatest injustices you choose to commit.

It is, in truth, devoid of any sense of sympathy to show up to a commercial business, shut it down immediately, send the staff out into the street, taking from them even the rooms in which they were sleeping.

On top of that, the laughter and the satisfaction of the non-Romanian merchants, who were watching this beginning of Romanian trade collapse under the blows of their dominion.

What would have happened if the authorities said: I inform you that within three days you must get all your affairs in order and shut the establishment down because the Ministry of Internal Affairs made this decision.

The second issue. You refuse to provide a written order under which we can go to court to see who has the moral and legal responsibility for this.

You didn't want to give the order? Well, I'll give it to you as it was received by the local authorities from Mr. Armand Călinescu:

"The Prefecture and the Police Headquarters, the Direction of Security from Bacău, Galați, Piatra-Neamț, Arad

Following the order from the Ministry of Internal Affairs nr. 745/25 and the General Security nr. 1488/25, take measures and deal with the closing of well-known consumption and flow establishments, specified in the annex of order 1821/17/2 ct. Report 25678 00213 86091 22001."

The third remark is that the closing of these two restaurants has caused us bloody material damages and debts that we won't be able to cope with in any way. So great moral damages.

The "Obor" business was opened on the [3r]d of October 1937, with investment expenses valued at 400,000 lei, with a rent of 200,000 lei.

"Lazăr" restaurant was opened in November 1937, with a rent of 280,000 lei yearly and repair investments of 250,000 lei.

In both places, goods, dishes, and cellar wines, the largest part of all these being bought with a credit of two and a half million.

We have gathered all of these things with much work and savings.

When 15 years ago, the youth was noisily protesting against the Jewish occupation (not more noisily than Mr. Iorga in 1906), the leaders of today, the men in the present government, were saying:

The Trial of Corneliu Zelea Codreanu

"This is not the way to solve the Jewish problem. Start trading. Trade like they do."

So, we started. With our souls full of hope. With a passion for work

But when you saw that we started this, that we're fair, that we're able, that our work is blessed by God, you come and destroy this beginning of Romanian trade, maybe the most serious beginning of our time. You come without mercy and smother these attempts, along with all our enthusiasm and so many hopes.

What epithets can I give you? What words from the Romanian language would suit you?

Are you accusing us of making mistakes in the past? Which one of you has not made mistakes? Tell us what we're doing wrong now! You now consider a crime what you yourselves had suggested that we do!

Here comes Professor Iorga, who was shouting four months ago, raising the alarm in the ranks of Christian trade that was defeated by the Jews, even calling for violence; he comes, he pollutes our pure thoughts and takes us, Romanians, down?

No bad words for Professor Iorga, ever. Always with respect and kindness.

It's been raining poison on us for a while.

"Among pots (meaning our restaurants), we plot, we prepare terrible revolutions, and we want to kill people. Souls of assassins, men with revolvers in their hands and pockets."

Well, I can't handle it anymore.

From the depths of my human power, me, the one who has respected you, I say to you:

"You're wrong. You have a dishonest soul."

The basic duty of an honest man is to get information from the man he judges, not just from the lying agents of Armand Călinescu (who yesterday spread a rumor that 16 teams under the leadership of Alexandru Cantacuzino want to kill him).

I can't fight with you. I don't have the genius, nor the age, nor the pen, nor your standing.

I don't have anything. You have everything.

Romanian Crucible

But from the bottom of an injured and wronged soul, I shout and I will shout at you from the depths of my grave: you have a dishonest soul, who has unjustly mocked our innocent souls.

You, who accuse us of violence, after using the worst violence against us, pushing us toward despair and sin, you, who, if anyone would slap you, would have reacted in the same way as I did, but without first going through the physical struggles and the humiliations that we've gone through, to you, those with dishonest souls, we'll prove that we won't react in any way to your provocations.

You didn't seek only to stop our trade and to stifle our spirit, but to beat us, to send us to Snake Island, to stone us, to hang us by our feet, to drive nails into us, and subject us to the most horrible humiliations.

Neither you, Professor Iorga, nor the others, all of you who are responsible for this bloody and unfair oppression, will see any violence or opposition on our part.

From now on, and until I will forever close my eyes, Mr. Iorga, and even after that, I will see you as you deserve to be seen.

CORNELIU ZELEA CODREANU

Bucharest, 26 March 1938.

Annex II
Corneliu Zelea Codreanu — Notes from Jilava regarding the Trial, May 1938

Sunday, 1 May 1938

Yesterday I was taken out of this dungeon for the first time. My legs were unsteady.

Between four soldiers, armed with bayonets, I was taken upstairs to the office. Captain Prosecutor Atanasiu was waiting there for me.

I was terrified. Because I don't trust the justice system at all anymore.

A justice system that judges "on command" and not from its conscience doesn't exist.

He interrogated me for a long time. From 6 PM until 12 at night.

From a neighboring room, I could hear the voices of children and family life.

It seemed to me that I would never get back to those days. And those voices of children reminded me of Cătălina, "mommy's little girl." It seemed to be a farewell the world would send to a man that won't come back to it.

And the captain was constantly questioning me. His questions were referring to the following things:

Is the "All for the Country" Party the dissolved Iron Guard? The Legionary oaths. The meaning of the word "Captain." Wasn't the Legionary judge assuming the role of the State judge?

The secret orders of the Ministry, with the electoral campaign or with the measures against my organization.

What was the purpose of the corps formed by former soldiers? The Moța-Marin Corps?

The apology of the crime, by awarding the White Cross to the imprisoned men.

The secret association. The association "friends of the Legionaries."

Romanian Crucible

And on this line, the Duca case. If I gave a command for his "assassination." So, an attempt to reopen this case, in which I was acquitted with unanimity, as the best proof of our innocence, mine, the General's, and the other comrades.

The Legionary Senate, the rules made by the General, apparently gave the organization a paramilitary character.

But this is not about a trial in which I would be rightfully judged, but a persecution devoid of justice and humanity: in which only God can interfere with his powers.

I returned to my cell at 2 at night, guarded by the same bayonets.

I will miss "mommy's little girl." On my way back, I started thinking again about never getting out of here. I started missing the little girl. And walking among the sentinels, I kept mumbling: and I will miss "mommy's little girl." And I will miss "mommy's little girl."

My heart is painfully pounding.

Today, Monday, the 2nd of May, he came again. And the interrogation ended.

Sunday, 8 May 1938

Last evening, I met the instruction magistrate, Major Dan Pascu, and he informed me that I was going to stand trial for "treason." I was confused for a moment. Then he explained to me that this is related to the possession and publication of secret documents regarding the security of the State, which are classified by article 191 P.C. as "treason."

He interrogated me about the six orders, given by prefects or commanders of Legions of gendarmes to their subordinates, all referring to political-electoral harassment towards my organization. None of these orders concern the security of the Romanian State.

One of the orders is issued by the Prahova prefect, addressed to the factory directors, Jews from Valea Prahovei, asking them to fire Legionary employees. Another issued by General Bengliu, about the gendarmes someone brought from the national-peasant circles from Corso or the Athenée Palace.

I returned to my cell, with my heart pierced by arrows.

I, the leader of the nationalist-Legionary movement, being judged for treason.

The Trial of Corneliu Zelea Codreanu

I didn't eat anything. I went to sleep very late on my wooden bed, and I tossed and turned all night. In the morning, I woke up shouting in my sleep: "Hear that, dear Moța, I'm on trial for treason!"

Monday, 9 May 1938.

Today major Dan Pascu came to see me again. I was escorted by men with bayonets up to the office again.

When I left it, I found the sun, air, and warmth. I felt solace.

The major told me the interrogation was over. I must choose my defense team. Who can defend me? When all our lawyers are arrested, who do I know capable of defending me? I was allowed to think about it until Thursday. He told me the newspapers have published the indictment of Captain Atanasiu. I wonder what my men, all of my people will read? How hard my mother and my poor wife must have cried! Sent to trial for treasoI.

I returned to this cold cell to think. I don't have anyone to counsel with.

These damn gendarme and police orders, how do they impact the idea of State security with their political content? How do they get classified into the terrible articles 190, 191 P.C., that are punishable with 5-25 years of forced labor?

I will ask for some paper and make a request to the commander of the prison to allow my wife to visit me to help me prepare my defense. But how could she come if she's under house arrest? She must be struggling as well. She must be tormenting herself with the poor "mommy's little girl." No hope from anywhere. Only one support: God and the Virgin Mary.

Tuesday 10 May 1938

Since I was imprisoned, I didn't bother anyone with any requests. Today I forwarded the following request to the commander of the prison:

"Mr. Commander,

The undersigned Corneliu Zelea Codreanu, as a prisoner, I respectfully ask you to consider forwarding my request to the legal military authorities for resolution.

306   Romanian Crucible

Because my interrogation is finished and because public action was taken against me based on art. 191 P.C., I request that my wife be allowed to visit me, being urgently necessary to prepare for my trial and hire lawyers, a trial that follows to be judged very soon.

The action opened against me brings up doctrinal discussions and jurisprudence research, which cannot be done in a short time.

This is why I request, for my defense, to urgently allow my wife to come to me.

Also, at the same time, please allow for the attached telegram addressed to my wife to be expedited.

Please receive the assurance of my respect.

Tuesday 10th of May 1938

Corneliu Zelea Codreanu."

Friday 13 May 1938

Yesterday I went to see major Dan Pascu again. A last formality had to be completed to finish the interrogation.

But, to my surprise, two other actions were opened against me for two other offenses:

1. That I armed the citizens of the country, looking to start a civil war.

2. That I was in contact with a foreign state to start a social revolution in Romania.

Obviously, none of these accusations are true.

How terrible it is to struggle underneath such unfair accusations!

God sees it all.

On Monday, they'll handle the last formalities of the interrogation and set a date for my trial.

I'm waiting for Sunday. Maybe some of my family will come to visit me.

I heard that Horia, my brother, was sentenced to one month in prison, and he is detained in a secret location, and has a situation much more dire than mine.

The Trial of Corneliu Zelea Codreanu

I had a guest last evening. When they came to bring me my food, a dog ran between the legs of the sergeant. After he closed the door, the dog came out from under the bed.

It ate with me. I shared my food with it and it got full.

I talked to it for a while and it went to sleep on the concrete floor. I lay down on my mat. I called it to come up, and it did, lay down next to me after licking my hand. It might be a lucky sign.

The dog was well-behaved. I was feeling the breath of another being next to me.

Around midnight, it wanted to get out. I lifted it up through the bars and it left.

Monday 16 May 1938

Major Dan Pascu came to me this morning and the nightmare of this interrogation was over at last.

Every moment, I expect to be presented with forged documents, or to get new charges thrown on my already weak shoulders.

I was told that one of these days my mother and my wife will be allowed to come to me to prepare my defense.

I wonder: what would they say when they'll see me so underweight? Will they cry?

Will they understand the physical and especially the psychological torments that I was subjected to?

They allowed me to spend an hour outside. It's so warm outIe... I walked for a few minutes, but the sun weakened all my limbs and I wasn't able to stand up anymore.

I sat down on a mat and prayed, after which I lay down until my hour passed.

I'm inside again. It feels like an eternity since this morning.

I don't have anyone to talk to.

A sparrow made a nest on my windowsill. It comes here to sleep in the evening. I always give it crumbs.

I wait for them to come bring me the food, but I can't talk to them either.

308 Romanian Crucible

The Lieutenant on duty and the Sergeant are the ones who always come. They're not allowed to speak to me. But they, as well as the commander of the prison are so delicate with me, that it's comforting. The poor soldier, this superior creature who does his duty correctly, strictly executing the orders received, but in whose eyes, you can't see a drop of malice. Elegance of the soul. The school of the Romanian army.

How beautiful it is!

Tuesday, 17 May 1938

Today around 10 am, the Lieutenant came to me and said: "We're going upstairs. Your family is here."

When I arrived upstairs, "mommy's girl" greeted me. I picked her up and kissed her face and eyes, hugging her tight.

My mother and my wife were inside. They both hugged me and started to cry. My poor mother's hands were so cold.

15 minutes passed as if they were a second.

It was difficult for me to ask them about my father.

He was detained in the camp at Miercurea Ciucului. Nobody could see him.

The other brothers are free, aside from Horea, who had a one-month prison sentence.

The 15 minutes passed.

I don't even remember what we talked about. Lizetta Gheorghiu showed me the list of witnesses and lawyers. They told me I would be taken to the Council tomorrow.

I said my farewells with my heart torn.

Their pain hurts me.

Friday, 27 May 1938

A week ago, at 4 in the morning, I was awoken and taken to the War Council in order to study the files and prepare for the trial. There I was in contact with my lawyers every day.

The Trial of Corneliu Zelea Codreanu

Friday, Saturday, and Sunday, we had to look over 20 large files, something extraordinary.

In three days, we had to look for counter-evidence: books, newspapers, parliamentary debates, foreign papers. I had to gather all my materials, orders, circulars, scattered documents, from who knows where. This was even harder because all my people, all who've worked with me, are arrested or detained in camps, or hiding to avoid getting caught. The poor men, young Legionary lawyers, fly away like bees during these three days.

Great lawyers, all refused to defend me: Radu Rosetti, Vasiliu-Cluj, Paul Iliescu, Mora, even Nelu Ionescu, Petrache Pogonat, and Ionel Teodoreanu. They were all afraid of being arrested and taken to the camps. Fear and cowardice!

That's why all my admiration goes to the lawyers: Hențescu, Radovici, Paul Iacobescu, Lizetta Gheorghiu, Caracaș, Horia Cosmovici, Zamfirescu, ColțesI-Cluj...and for all this heroic youth, who didn't back down in face of any threat, who took risks, who faced the storm.

The first hearing took place on Monday morning. The Military Court was formed by the President of Section I, Colonel Dumitru, and four lead officers.

They read the witness lists; all of those in the camps were absent, namely the men I worked with, factual witnesses. The defense asked for the trial to be postponed in order for these witnesses to be brought.

The Court rejected the request of the defense.

The Final ordinance was read.

Full of passions, malice, and untruths. Free, unproven statements, lacking good faith, fairness, and honor.

In the afternoon, from 5 to 12 at night, I was the one who spoke for 7 hours in a row, dispelling the accusations brought against me one after the other.

The next day, *Universul* published, word for word, everything I said, aside from the secret hearing and the matter about the weapons deposits, which censorship shamefully banned.

On Tuesday, I was interrogated by the Prosecutor and I answered every question point by point. In summary, I was sent to trial for treason, articles 190, 191, possession and publication of secret documents concerning the security of the State, based on 6 police and gendarme electoral orders; for art. 209, connections with a

Romanian Crucible

foreign power, in order to receive aid and instructions, for the purpose of starting the social revolution in Romania (based on a false letter that didn't belong to me, which I had never seen in my life), for art. 210, arming the population for the purpose of starting a civil war, based on nothing.

At the last moment, 10 minutes before the Prosecutor had the final word, by true divine intervention, the author of the letter for which I was accused was found. A lawyer, Marinescu from Râmnicu Vâlcea, reading the letter, sees two ideas In it: 1. the idea of "automatic economy" and "mutual enrichment," words, definitions, and thoughts that had never belonged To me; 2. the idea of an "economic alliance."

He remembers reading these things somewhere. He goes to Râmnicu Vâlcea, and indeed he finds the book, given to him by the author with a dedication written by his own hand. On the cover, in the subtitle, he sees the words: "automatic economy," and inside the book, this new economic system is explained in multiple pages.

At the end of the book, he details the other idea in 20 pages or so: "economic alliance," an "international credit," etc., and, as a last piece of luck for us, the handwriting, the dedication, is the same as the one in the letter used against me.

All the lawyers get excited about this miracle and ask the President to call the author as a witness, Mr. Rădulescu-Thanir.

The President rejects the request.

A few of the lawyers goes to see this man. He admits to having written such a letter. He comes to the gate of the Courthouse, but he's stopped from coming in. I bring the matter up again: "Mr. President and Honorary Court, the author of the letter for which I am accused was found. It is Mr. Rădulescu Thanir, a collaborator of the newspaper *Neamul Românesc*; I don't personally know him. I don't know the mysterious means by which his letter was connected to me. He admits that it's his, that he wrote it. Call him in and allow him to explain. Take the measures you deem appropriate."

The President rejects the request.

Finally, my 7 lawyers plead. Impeccable. It Is Thursday night, 12 am, when the Court withdraws for deliberations.

They take me to a room and half an hour later they put me in a van and take me to Jilava.

The Trial of Corneliu Zelea Codreanu

I am calm, with my conscience clear. I know I'm not guilty of anything.

None of the charges against me was left standing.

Here I am, back in my cell. I go to sleep.

Around 4 AM, I am awoken by the sound of footsteps and the latches being pulled. I stand up. The prosecutor, Radu Ionescu, comes in with Registrar Tudor, the commander of the prison, and the other guarding officers.

The registrar reads: "The Military Court answered affirmatively to all the questions. You are sentenced to 10 years of forced labor."

They remain in there for a few more minutes looking at me. The major shrugs wide-eyed.

I'm facing the great injustice that hits me, but I'm calm, with my conscience clear.

I opened the prayer book of St. Antoine to a random page. It opens at 119. I read: "Do it, so I may peacefully receive everything that God sends my way, understanding that is His will."

Notes from the trial:

I was always kept under a very serious and unusual guard. Two gendarmes were always at the door, and a Sergeant was in the room with me. Also, a Sergeant was always around me.

The discussions with the defense, the preparation of the defense, which is always done in secret, were done in front of two police officers.

The lawyers, in order to get to me, had to walk through four rows of body searches, starting from the gate. The halls were full of agents who were spying on the defense, on the witnesses, and on the officers.

Two people couldn't speak without a third one, the spy, moving next to them iIdiately... A heavy atmosphere, suffocating, was pressing on the walls of the Council room and outside it.

Each lawyer or witness was expecting to be taken to a camp at any moment.

Lawyers assigned by magistrates were also picked up from the defense bench.

The lawyers: Colonel Rădulescu and Vlasto.

Others were arrested as well: Corneliu Georgescu, Stănicel, and Popescu Buzău.

The lawyers from the country that registered by telegraph had searches done during the night, and they were told that if they were to leave the city they would be arrested and taken to the camp.

Finally, after many struggles, they managed to get to the trial. When the defense started, they weren't allowed in. The tables were empty this time.

Aside from the seven lawyers that were allowed to speak, the rest were not allowed in.

While the Prosecutor's indictment, that was made by others and only read by him, was immediately published in special editions as a command, under the threat of shutting down the newspapers, and read on the radio, the words of the defense were listened in the Council in an empty hall and didn't get more than 3-4 lines in the press.

The defense was impeccable.

Horia Cosmovici, Hențescu, Lizetta Ghoerghiu, Iacobescu, Ranețescu, Caracaș, you have all my admiration, dear friends. And for all of you who didn't leave my side, you worked, ran, struggled, and shivered waiting for justice to be done.

My last words were:

"Honorary Court, you have in your hands, not just my life, which I'll gladly give, but the honor of the whole Romanian youth. I believe in the Military Justice of my country."

So, the Court had to answer to three charges:

1. Possession and publication of secret documents, classified by art. 190-191.

The evidence proved the 6 orders had a political character. They were simple police search orders targeted at my organization. They didn't concern any aspect of "State security." Similar orders have been read in the Parliament, published in newspapers, politicians also had such orders. Mr. Iuliu Maniu stated he had 16 such orders in a single year, which he had published in a memoir.

Finally, arts. 190-190 regarded the "Crimes against the security of the State" and that the phrase "State security" from art. 190 refers to the external security of the State, meaning they cannot be classified as "treason."

2. The Court had to answer to a second charge:

The Trial of Corneliu Zelea Codreanu

The one saying that I contacted a foreign state in order to receive aid or instructions for starting a social revolution. The statements are based on a false letter that doesn't belong to me.

The author of the letter was found. These accusations are offensive and in bad faith (art. 209).

3. Finally, the Court had to answer to the crime of arming the population, in order to start a civil war to overthrow the government (art. 210).

I proved with principles, deeds, documents, and witnesses that we have never thought about starting a civil war. But not only that: we never thought about causing even the smallest disturbance, the danger from the East watching our every move, our every mistake.

Even like this, the Court, without having even the smallest piece of evidence, was affirmative to every question, sentencing me to 10 years of forced labor.

A great injustice!

May God receive my suffering for the well-being and flourishing of our Nation.

Pain with pain, struggle with struggle, suffering, wound with wound, on bodies and in the soul, grave near grave, that's I we'll ᵂⁱn...

Friday, 3 June 1938

The continuation of the notes from the trial. A campaign of hate.

I don't know if there ever was in the public life of Romania, a man who was attacked with such ferocity, passion, and bad faith by the whole press and by all the Judeo-political clubs as I was from my arrest, during the interrogations, with the purpose of preparing my conviction in front of public opinion.

Nobody in the past of Romanian politics, nobody was the focus of such hate. Nobody was hit as I was without having the possibility to defend myself, without someone to defend me.

Buna Vestire and *Cuvântul* were hit first, being forced to suspend their activity.

Nae Ionescu is in the camp as well.

The others fiercely attack, some as a tactic, some on command.

The attacks were officially ordered by the Ministry of Internal Affairs.

Romanian Crucible

Whoever refused to publish them or dared to discuss them, not even contradict them, was suspended.

There were attacks full of cowardice in *Curentul*, *Neamul Românesc* and in *Capitala*: Șeicaru, Iorga, and Tit^ea nu.

Friday, 10 June 1938

This morning the first sparrow chick from the nest at my Idow flew away... How much emotion anIxcitement for it... The first steps and the first flight in his life. How much care and joy for its mother! The sky is full of its callings, by its advice. Chirping everywhere. Go well, my dear, in holy freedom.

A green locust has been wandering around my cell for a few days. When I go to sleep, it comes near my sheet. Last night it tried to walk on my head. I tried to scare it away. It got scared, jumped, and disappeared. This morning I found it crushed under the mat. I picked it up and took care of it for an hour. I gave it water and sugar and it drank. It got well and flew outside.

Around 1 o'clock, I was called upstairs in the office. An investigation. Captain Tătăreanu from the War Council came to inquire if I had sent a manifest from prison, through which I was urging my men to take "revenge."

It was fabricated, of course.

I gave a statement in this sense. Why do such schemes keep coming my way?

Convicted for a letter that isn't mine. Now there's another.

But I think even the prosecutor is convinced something isn't right.

Last night, I dreamt that I was in a hall full of people. It was so full that I couldn't breathe. The windows were opened. My appeal to I trial was starting... Iacobescu was saying that he was going to speak for two hours. I woke up.

I fell back asleep. I saw myself traveling by train with my mother, my wife, the girl, and Silvia. The train was leaning so much toward the abyss that I thought it would roll over. I then jumped, because it was going slow, and I put my shoulder against itIhe others did the same... It came off the tracks but didn't fal^l into the abyss.

The Trial of Corneliu Zelea Codreanu

Monday, 13 June 1938

I didn't sleep all night. I think my lungs are hurting, in the upper part of my chest, between my shoulder blades. There's a dull pain on both sides and constant heat. I'll call for the doctor.

It will be diffIlt to climb this mountain...

In the afternoon, my lawyers came to see me, because on the 15th, on Wednesday, is my appeal at the Military Cessation Court.

They believe it will be postponed for at least 15 days, because that's the norm.

New reasons for cessation are given and a new term as well.

I studied the reasons with them, and the main ones are:

1. The fact witnesses were not brought, the men from Ciuc, the ones who worked with me. None of them.

2. I was convicted for a letter that didn't belong to me. The author was found, and he gave another letter by which he admitted to being the one responsible for its content and its writing. So the author of the letter is known.

3. Wrong classification. I was charged for a crime against the external security of the State, for treason, and I received a great sentence for it. The orders don't concern the external security of the State, because they do not represent a danger coming from a foreign power that would regard:

A) The integrity of the territory.

B) Independence.

C) Sovereignty.

4. There's absolutely no evidence that I wanted to start a civil war. They talked about weapon deposits, but showed none. Where are they, what do they contain, who found them?

I was convicted for simple statements.

This is something unique in the annals of trials, legal and procedural.

Tuesday, 14 June 1938

Today Lizetta Gheorghiu visited me. The others are still studying.

Romanian Crucible

On this occasion, I gave her a small testament that I wrote today in my cell.

The appeal is tomorrow.

I finished reading "The Epistles of the Holy Apostle Paul." I was profoundly impressed. I admit that until now I have only read some of them and didn't study them sufficiently. I'll write about them later, because this needs to be more detailed.

Last night, I dreamt of Gârneață. He was complaining that it was hard in the camp at Ciuc. I then dreamed of Tell. He was escorted. He ran to Ionică's house. Lastly, I dreamt of Alecu Cantacuzino. I talked to them in a house, but I don't know where.

Wednesday, 15 June 1938

After I finished reading the Gospels, I understood that I'm in prison from God's will; that, even though I am not guilty under the law, He punishes me for my sins and tries my faith. I calmed down. Peace fell over the struggles in my heart as night falls over the torment, turmoil, and tensions of the world. People, birds, animals, trees and weeds, worked and cut earth by the steel plows to take aIst.

Because I was very upset...

The meat on my bones suffered greatly. I don't think I ever had to endure as much as I was enduring now.

I didn't lose "Faith" and "Love," but I felt like I was losing hope.

Physically tormented like a dog (my clothes are full of suffering, there are 60 days since I've been sleeping dressed up on this board covered with a mat. 60 days and 60 nights since my bones suck, like a leech, the dampness that gushes from the walls and from the ground).

For 60 days, I haven't talked to anyone, because nobody here is allowed to talk to me. And at the same time, my morality is charged with treason, declared a foreigner, as I wasn't Romanian, not from my mother's nor my father's side, portrayed as an enemy of the State, overwhelmed by blows and with my hands tied behind my back, unable to defend myself.

My heart is smothered by the suffering, insults, and torments that my men, family, and friends have to endure. I felt as one of the three threads tying a Christian to God snapped: hope. I saw black. I felt as if I was choking.

The Trial of Corneliu Zelea Codreanu

But now that thread is mended, fighting day by day. How? By reading the four Gospels. When I finished them, I felt the three threads again: faith, hope, and love.

And now, having read the letters of St. Paul, I found definite evidence about the Resurrection and the power of Our Savior Jesus Christ. I was impressed by: 1. The honesty and the clean soul of St. Paul; 2. His unblemished Christian life; 3. The dangers and the suffering he endured for the Lord; 4. The serenity and even the joy with which he received those sufferings; 5. His strength to encourage others, so they don't waver in face of suffering and persecution; 6. A shockingly holy love for all his Christian brothers and for his spiritual children; 7. An undefeated zeal, rarely known among the apostles for unceasingly preaching the faith of the Savior Jesus to all the nations; His great knowledge and wisdom.

Almost every letter starts like this:

"I, the prisoner, find myself in chains of faith in Christ, our Lord."

He then writes to Timothy: "Try to come to me soon" (II Timothy, 4, 9). He missed seeing someone as well.

"When you come, please bring me the cloak."

He was cold just like I am.

Finally, as I dove deeper in the letters, I came to the conclusion:

1. We are not Christians. We'reIr from being Christians. So far...

2. We are Christians in form, but we're not Christian in content.

3. Mankind has undergone this process of losing Christianity through the centuries until present tIs, with small twists to the depths... Being a Christian on the surface seems to be the thing that preoccupied people the most.

4. The nature of our time:

We are more concerned about the fight between ourselves and other people, not the fight between the commandments of the Holy Spirit and the lusts of our earthly nature.

We are more concerned, and we prefer victories over people, not victories over the Devil and sin. All great people of today's and yesterday's world: Napoleon, Mussolini, Hitler, etc., are preoccupied more about this victory.

The Legionary Movement is an exception, caring, although insufficiently, about the Christian victory over man for his own salvation.

Romanian Crucible

Insufficiently!

The responsibility of a leader is great.

He must not delight the eyes of his armies with earthly victories, at the same time not preparing them for the decisive battle from which each soldier's soul can be crowned with eternal victory or with eternal defeat.

5. Finally, the lack — at least for us — of a priestly elite that would have kept the sacred fire of the old Christians. The lack of high schooling and great Christian morality.

Friday morning, 17 June 1938

My wife and her mother came to see me on Wednesday, around 5. They told me my appeal wasn't postponed as is normally done, but that it will be judged at 5 in the afternoon and will continue with a night hearing. My wife told me they had summed her to the Băneasa Gendarme Legion, where she had been kept from morning until 1:30 PM, because she's not allowed to get into the house at Casa Verde anymore, that on Friday, she must go and gather her things and on Sunday she must take them by car wherever she wanted.

Her face was visibly upset. Ioving your belongings from your home... Where could you take them? Where would you live? I'm in prison, my defenseless wife is thrown out in the street, with the girl in hand.

What a lack of humanity!... What a lack of kindness!

All three of us kept thinking: Where? Where?

I suggest some locations to I. We don't have enough money to pay rent...

I told her that if my appeal was dismissed, I will be moved from here to Doftana.

She wants to come with the girl and live in the village next to the prison.

I told her that I gave Lizetta Gheorghiu my testament and instructions and I told her a few words about its content.

They were crying, my wife and her mother as well; the girl is only four years old; she doesn't understand anything about the tragedy of these moments when the shadows of death start clouding the thoughts of our family.

After the 15 minutes allowed by the prison, they left.

Now it's Friday morning. I still don't have a reply about my appeal.

The Trial of Corneliu Zelea Codreanu

At our home, at this hour, my wife is packing up and crying about our misfortune.

But this isn't possible. We'll return.

Friday evening, 17 June 1938

Half an hour ago, my lawyers came to see me and told me my appeal at the Military Cassation Court was dismissed.

All of them were upset and gloomy.

I stayed with them for about 15 minutes. I asked them details about the debates. They told me everything in a few words. We said our farewells. I returned to my cell, sat on the edge of my wooden bed, and prayed to God, saying the prayer "Our Father, Lord, be it Your will."

Annex III
Notes from the "Journal" of Carol II
Regarding the Trial of Corneliu Zelea Codreanu

Thursday, 19 May 1938

At 12, Călinescu came to talk about the matter of the Guard. Gănescu says there were errors made in Codreanu's indictment, for example, it was said that hunting weapons have been found during the search, even if they didn't have the required permits. Such things must never be mentioned in documents because they can indite the prosecution. I also received the information that Codreanu's communication with the outside continues through the doctor at Jilava. Călinescu confirmed this, and he reported that measures have been taken and the glty one was moved.

Friday, 20 May 1938

...Today I also met with Comnen who gave me the report on Geneva. Very interesting. It seemed it was the first session in which all, especially the British, were more realistic. There wasn't so much theory but more practice. Unnecessary and embarrassing things happened as well, for example, the participation of the Regent at the meeting in which Lord Halifax buried him mercilessly.

Comnen reports to us that everything went well and that Romania gained a prestige that it has never had before.

The matter of the Guard and my decision to take drastic measures to fix the country had an excellent effect. The issue of the minorities was able to be postponed and it will disappear without us having to take drastic and disagreeable decisions.

What is important in the international field is the union between England and France, maybe even the issue with Czechoslovakia.

Romanian Crucible

Monday, 23 May 1938

In the morning I had a conference with Argeşanu, Călinescu, Comnen, PalTeodorescu, and Glatz to discuss the situation...

The result of the conference is that we must make every effort to remain neutral: and to try to rush the ammunition, especially regarding the anti-aircraft and anti-tank weapons.

I personally onlyIe one way of escape for us, for nothing to happen...

Today, Codreanu's trial started as well. Everything is going as it should. The Court is energetic. Only justified objections have been raised, the one about the missing files.

I received news that the atmosphere in England is very good and it improved since the measures againsIhe Iron Guard were taken.

Tuesday, 24 May 1938

... The trial continues as yesterday. Codreanu is fighting in his usual brave way.

The letters with threats continue to come.

Last night, in the Council of Ministers it was decided to apply for a year the article in the Constitution that provides for the death penalty. This decision was taken because of the many threatening letters sent to the officials regarding Codreanu's trial.

This measure was taken in the Council today, under the presidency of Argeşanu, to avoid putting the Patriarch in a difficult position.

The Patriarch is not against the measure, but because he is the head of the Church, he can't sign this decision. It was the case in the Council, when he didn't oppose the constitutional article, but he refrained from voting.

Wednesday, 25 May 1938

I have certain reservations when it comes to the atmosphere in Codreanu's trial. He has a good defense, even though they deny the evidence. His lawyers are decent. His indictment is weak, with gaps, and it sometimes sounds forced.

Annex IV
The Testimony of Mr. Iuliu Maniu
at the Trial of Mr. Corneliu Zelea Codreanu.
Final text submitted in Bucharest
on 24 September 1938[*]

The question of Corneliu Zelea Codreanu: Why did we agree to the nonaggression pact when our ideologies are so different?

Mr. Maniu's answer: It's true, our ideologies are directly opposed and I don't believe in this country there are two parties that are more categorically opposed than ours.

Our party is a Democratic Party, and I, especially, am a great fanatic of democracy, because I believe that only through it we can evolve as a nation and ensure the durable progressive existence of the State. And for this, I know what democracy in Athens did, which caused science and art to flourish, and made the Greeks shine today like the morning star on the filament of mankind. I know what democracy did in the great empire of Rome, until the corruption of Caesar's dictatorship came. I know what democracy did in England, which began in the twelfth century, its progress based on parliamentary constitutionalism, becoming the most grandiose empire mankind has ever known, which rules a third of the Globe. I know what democracy did in France, which today is the head of civilization, and I know what democracy did in the United States, which today is a sort of referee of our continent.

The Iron Guard, on the other hand, is totalitarian, against democracy, a type of dictatorship. I am a fanatical adversary of any type of dictatorship.

---

[*](From the work *Iuliu Maniu în faţa istoriei* published by Direcţia Departamentelor de Studii, Doctrine, programe a P.N.Ţ.C.D/ Fundaţia Hanns Seidel, Bucureşti: Editura Gândirea Românească, 1993, pp. 227-282).

Romanian Crucible

I favor a foreign policy of collaboration with France, with England, and with the Western democracies. Because this is the only way I see to ensure the integrity of our State, in the terrible turmoil that will soon follow.

Mr. Codreanu is for the foreign policy of Germany, which embodies everything I find dangerous for our State.

Mr. Codreanu's party is an anti-Semitic party, our party, however, is not anti-Semitic. I am especially against any idea of persecution, whatever that might be. The fundamental idea of our party is the national idea and constructive nationalism. And I believe it is the State's duty is to do everything in its power for the Romanian nation to be strengthened and raised up without suppressing and persecuting other nations in the process.

Aside from these things, we are differentiated by our methods of political struggle.

Given these differences in ideology, the following question is natural: how did we end up singing an electoral understanding?

There's a double reason. First, a personal reason: I had not met Mr. Codreanu before signing the nonaggression pact. However, I closely followed his activity and attitude. I was able to find sincerity on his part, consistency and tenacity, qualities which are so rare in our political life and our political leaders.

Aside from this personal reason, I had a political reason as well.

Mr. Codreanu, as well as I, believes that for a healthy national life it is absolutely necessary to respect our national dignity. By naming Tătărescu as Prime Minister, our national dignity was not the only thing affected, but also the spirit of the constitution. That's why we had to shake hands and make the nation reject this attempt to attack our national dignity. We managed to do that.

Mr. Codreanu, as well as I, believes the national idea is the vital factor in the prosperity of a nation. He believes, as I do, that the State, with all its power, must perfect the incomparably beautiful qualities of the Romanian nation that supports the State and give it the possibility by providing it with the material, cultural, and social means to fulfill the mission it has to play in this part of the world.

It's true that Mr. Codreanu, as I said before, has an anti-Semitic conception, one that I don't approve of, but the fundamental idea is identical and I'm sure that the

The Trial of Corneliu Zelea Codreanu

last events will convince him that anti-Semitic politics are not possible in our country.

Aside from this, Mr. Codreanu has the same conviction, as I do, that without respecting the rules of fairness in private and public life, and without keeping account of Christian morality, we will not be able to ensure the survival of our nation; and that abandoning these would mean for our people what it has meant for many other nations in the past: death and destruction. For this, we agree to impose in the private, social, and public life, fairness, honor, and Christian morals, which today — sadly — others disregard.

We also agree that, in a constitutional monarchy, the contact between the Crown and the Nation has to be direct and unperturbed by the interference of improper factors.

Mr. President: I won't allow for this matter to be discussed.

Mr. Maniu: I'll respect your decision, I just wanted to say: I agreed with Mr. Codreanu that the camarilla must be removed.

All these were defining elements that led us to reach an agreement and I'm glad that we did.

Mr. Codreanu's question: If the Liberal Party while governing used the police, security, gendarmes, or the other State authorities to stop the electoral propaganda of the opposing parties?

Mr. President: He opposes this question.

Mr. Codreanu's question: If the practice of our political life, the opposing parties protest in public, in the press, and in the parliament, against electoral interferences, and if they showed copies of the orders issued by the authorities for their subordinates in this matter?

Mr. Maniu's answer: It's true, during all the elections, aside from the ones in 1928 and 1932, which the National Peasants' party organized, the governments have used the executive power, the gendarmes, and the security apparatus for the electoral purposes of the governing party, and they didn't resume only to the activity of State Security. The parties in opposition have always tried to get their hands on the secret orders that were sent to the public forces to stop the opposition in its actions and in its political moves. Therefore, I admit that, in 1927, I had in hand 16 secret orders — confidential, belonging to the public power, through which the executive power was being used by the party in power. More than that, I went to the council president, Ionel Brătianu, and showed them to him in a memoir, as a protest against these interferences. Neither the Prime Minister, nor the authorities charged me with anything because they couldn't, as possession of such secret orders was something every party in opposition did.

Mr. Codreanu's question: If this fact, the one of possessing and obtaining documents by a leader of the opposition could constitute an act of treason, or endanger the State order and public safety?

Mr. Maniu's answer: Never. This is something done all the time.

Mr. Codreanu's question: If Mr. Maniu believes that I was trying to come to power now, from our discussions, did he notice that I was in a rush to come to power?

Mr. Maniu's answer: No. On the contrary, from the conversations we had, I found a great difference in attitude between us: I was insisting that our party must come to power immediately, because it is our natural right, and I considered that it is what the country needed. While Mr. Codreanu was insisting that he was in no rush, that he had time, and that his moment hadn't yet come.

Mr. Codreanu's question: If Mr. Maniu saw me, or the party I led, as a person whose purpose was to overthrow the State order or to start a civil war?

Mr. Maniu's answer: If I ever saw or suspected that I wouldn't have signed the electoral pact with him and I wouldn't have shaken hands over a political campaign, because I always believed, and I still believe, that for our nation and for the Romanian State the worst misfortune would be a rebellion, disorder, or a civil war.

Mr. Codreanu's question: If I discussed with Mr. Maniu foreign policy matters and if during these discussions I showed a personal interest or was exclusively driven by intimate beliefs?

Mr. Maniu's answer: During our discussions, we talked about foreign policy twice. I found we have opposite beliefs in this matter and I tried to convince him the only policy appropriate to the interests of Romania are those of France, England and the great democracies of the West. He contradicted me. This whole discussion took place in a national idea, without observing Mr. Codreanu to have a personal interest.

The Trial of Corneliu Zelea Codreanu

Mr. Codreanu's question: If Mr. Maniu knows of my movement being conspiratorial, occult, or illegal?

Mr. Maniu's answer: During the electoral campaign, I saw the organizations of the Iron Guard that were in the open, with great offense, with outright and energetic manifestations.

The Prosecutor's question: Does Mr. Maniu believe it would have been a good or a bad thing for Mr. Codreanu to have achieved power?

Mr. Maniu's answer: Mr. Codreanu is the leader of a party; I am the president of another party with an opposite ideology. Naturally, I wouldn't have found it good for his party to come to power, because I don't approve of his politics. If I approved of it and found it good for the country, we would have been in the same party.

All the parties want the good of the country, realized through their own means. I believe the only good way to obtain this is through our party. As a result, I don't believe that the governing of any other party, except for the National Peasants' Party, would be beneficial for the country. As I showed, the ideology and the methods of Mr. Codreanu and his party are not something I approve of, so I wouldn't approve of them during governing either.

Finally, for me the will of the nation is decisive and the parties have the right to try to obtain the favor of public opinion, but I don't agree with governments being forced upon the country, against the national will.

Annex V
A letter written by Corneliu Zelea Codreanu,
from the prison at Doftana, to his father,
Professor Ion Zelea Codreanu,
at Miercurea-Ciuc, 30 July 1938[†]

Dear Father,

100 days have passed since we said our farewells, on that night of April 17. I won't tell you here all I've been through. It feels like 100 years have passed. I have suffered a great deal.

But I want to make you happy for once by sending you this letter: the first word you have received from me since then.

I want you to know that I'm healthy. I'm well. I had a weak chest, but I got the right treatment and I'm mended now. I'm at Doftana. Please mail your letters here: Doftana Prison, Prahova county.

Mother has to be encouraged because the unforgiving hammer of pain seems to have struck her chest harder. A lot of pain has befallen our family recently. Me, you, Horea (who's free now), and Ioan.

Therefore, I kindly ask you to write to my mother as well, encouraging her, because I noticed she's been very weak.

Write to Ioan in Constanța county, because he has that glass eye and not a very robust build, and he might be suffering a lot. He has a sentence of 7 months. I have a sentence of 10 years at forced labor.

When you get out of there, please come and visit me, and I'll explain to you everything that has happened.

[†]On the order of Armand Călinescu, this letter was never sent to his father. (From *Învierea*, București, nr. 2/April-June 1993, p. 285-286).

Romanian Crucible

To come here, you must get written permission from the General Direction of Prisons.

I dearly bow to you, and wish you good health and much strength in your suffering. Don't worry about me. I'm well. I'm treated as I should be, humanely and civilized.

I want you to know that even though I've suffered greatly, my faith in God has not left me, but it remains firm, straight as a Romanian sentinel in the middle of a storm.

Corneliu

CENTER FOR Romanian STUDIES

The mission of the Center for Romanian Studies is to promote knowledge of the history, literature, and culture of Romania to an international audience. For more information contact us at info@centerforromanianstudies.com

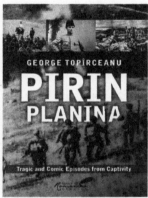
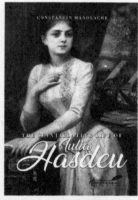

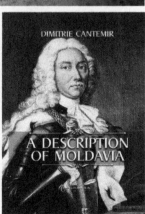

Check out these and other great titles at
CenterforRomanianStudies.com